ON THE CROSS ROAD OF POLITY, POLITICAL ELITES AND MOBILIZATION

RESEARCH IN POLITICAL SOCIOLOGY

Series Editor: Barbara Wejnert

Recent Volumes:

Volumes 1–3:	Richard G. Braungart
Volume 4:	Richard G. Braungart and Margaret M. Braungart
Volumes 5–8:	Philo C. Wasburn
Volume 9:	Betty A. Dobratz, Lisa K. Waldner, and Timothy Buzzell
Volumes 10–11:	Betty A. Dobratz, Timothy Buzzell, and Lisa K. Waldner
Volume 12:	Betty A. Dobratz, Lisa K. Waldner, and Timothy Buzzell
Volume 13:	Lisa K. Waldner, Betty A. Dobratz, and Timothy Buzzell
Volumes 14–17:	Harland Prechel
Volumes 18–21:	Barbara Wejnert
Volume 22:	Dwayne Woods and Barbara Wejnert
Volume 23:	Eunice Rodriguez and Barbara Wejnert

RESEARCH IN POLITICAL SOCIOLOGY   VOLUME 24

ON THE CROSS ROAD OF POLITY, POLITICAL ELITES AND MOBILIZATION

EDITED BY

BARBARA WEJNERT
University at Buffalo, Buffalo, NY, USA

PAOLO PARIGI
Stanford University, Stanford, CA, USA

United Kingdom – North America – Japan
India – Malaysia – China

Emerald Group Publishing Limited
Howard House, Wagon Lane, Bingley BD16 1WA, UK

First edition 2017

Copyright © 2017 Emerald Group Publishing Limited

Reprints and permissions service
Contact: permissions@emeraldinsight.com

No part of this book may be reproduced, stored in a retrieval system, transmitted in any form or by any means electronic, mechanical, photocopying, recording or otherwise without either the prior written permission of the publisher or a licence permitting restricted copying issued in the UK by The Copyright Licensing Agency and in the USA by The Copyright Clearance Center. Any opinions expressed in the chapters are those of the authors. Whilst Emerald makes every effort to ensure the quality and accuracy of its content, Emerald makes no representation implied or otherwise, as to the chapters' suitability and application and disclaims any warranties, express or implied, to their use.

British Library Cataloguing in Publication Data
A catalogue record for this book is available from the British Library

ISBN: 978-1-78635-480-8
ISSN: 0895-9935 (Series)

ISOQAR certified
Management System,
awarded to Emerald
for adherence to
Environmental
standard
ISO 14001:2004.

Certificate Number 1985
ISO 14001

INVESTOR IN PEOPLE

CONTENTS

LIST OF CONTRIBUTORS — vii

EDITORIAL ADVISORY BOARD — ix

PART I
NATIONAL IDENTITY, ETHNICITY, AND PUBLIC POLICY

HOW DID THE IRISH AMERICANS BECOME IRISH? GAELIC SPORTS AND THE ORGANIZATION OF IRISH ETHNICITY IN NEW YORK CITY
Dan Lainer-Vos — 3

SANCTIFIED MOBILIZATION: HOW POLITICAL ACTIVISTS MANAGE INSTITUTIONAL BOUNDARIES IN FAITH-BASED ORGANIZING FOR IMMIGRANT RIGHTS
Marion Coddou — 25

NATIONAL IDENTITY AND GOVERNMENTAL AUTHORITY: THE INTERSECTION OF NATIONAL IDENTITY, IMMIGRATION POLICY, AND THE CHILD WELFARE SYSTEM IN THE UNITED STATES
Joanna Kaftan — 67

REVISITING MOTHERS' PENSIONS: A CRITIQUE OF A SOCIAL SCIENCE CLASSIC AND A NEW ANALYSIS
Sheera Joy Olasky and David F. Greenberg — 93

PART II
POLITICAL ELITES AND POLITICAL CONTENTION

ESSENTIAL CONTESTANTS, ESSENTIAL CONTESTS
John Markoff — *123*

ELITES, POLICY, AND SOCIAL MOVEMENTS
David Pettinicchio — *155*

THE MILITARIZATION THEORY IN POST-SOVIET RUSSIA: DISPELLING THE PATHOLOGICAL LOOK AT POLITICAL AND ADMINISTRATIVE ELITES
Victor Violier — *191*

CHANGING POLITICAL FORTUNES: RACE, CLASS, AND "BLACK POWER" IN THE RISE AND FALL OF A BLACK URBAN REGIME IN OAKLAND
Eric S. Brown — *215*

THE STRENGTH OF CIVIL SOCIETY TIES: EXPLAINING PARTY CHANGE IN AMERICA'S BLUEST STATE
Johnnie Lotesta — *257*

LIST OF CONTRIBUTORS

Eric S. Brown Department of Sociology, University of Missouri, Columbia, MO, USA

Marion Coddou Institutional Research and Decision Support, Stanford University, Stanford, CA, USA

David F. Greenberg Sociology Department, New York University, New York, NY, USA

Joanna Kaftan Department of Social Sciences, University of Houston-Downtown, Houston, TX, USA

Dan Lainer-Vos Department of Sociology, University of California, Irvine, Irvine, CA, USA

Johnnie Lotesta Department of Sociology, Brown University, Providence, RI, USA

John Markoff Department of Sociology, University of Pittsburgh, Pittsburgh, PA, USA

Sheera Joy Olasky

David Pettinicchio Department of Sociology, University of Toronto, Toronto, Canada

Victor Violier Institut des sciences sociales du politique (ISP), Nanterre, France and Political Science Department, Université Paris Ouest Nanterre − La Défense, Nanterre, France

EDITORIAL ADVISORY BOARD

Patrick Akard
Kansas State University

Paul Almeida
University of California Merced

Robert Antonio
University of Kansas

Alessandro Bonanno
Sam Houston State University

Barbara Brents
University of Nevada Las Vegas

David Brown
Cornell University

Kathleen Kost
University at Buffalo

Rhonda Levine
Colgate University

John Markoff
University of Pittsburgh

Scott McNall
California State University, Chico

Susan Olzak
Stanford University

Harland Prechel
Texas A&M University

Adam Przeworski
New York University

William Roy
*University of California
Los Angeles*

David A. Smith
University of California Irvine

Henry Taylor
University at Buffalo

PART I
NATIONAL IDENTITY, ETHNICITY, AND PUBLIC POLICY

HOW DID THE IRISH AMERICANS BECOME IRISH? GAELIC SPORTS AND THE ORGANIZATION OF IRISH ETHNICITY IN NEW YORK CITY

Dan Lainer-Vos

ABSTRACT

This paper examines the construction of ethnic ties between immigrants from different counties in Ireland in New York City. Specifically, it explores an attempt to foster Irish unity and pride through the playing of Gaelic sports in New York City (1904–1916). Rather than treating Gaelic sport as a cultural resource that ethnic entrepreneurs harnessed, the paper treats both Gaelic sports and Irish ethnicity as delicate organizational accomplishment. This paper traces a delicate process of experimentation, spanning more than a decade, at the end of which the organizers of the sport managed to produce gripping, but friendly, rivalries between the different teams. This accomplishment created ethnic institutional scaffolding within which immigrants were more likely to see themselves as Irish Americans rather than merely immigrants from particular counties on the island.

Keywords: Ethnicity; sport; Irish Americans; boundary making; immigrants

This paper examines ethnicity as a practical organizational accomplishment. It focuses on the relationships between ethnic organization and ethnic identity. The paper examines the difficulties involved in organizing ethnic activities, and identifies the mechanisms that organizers introduced in order to enroll potential members and encourage them to cooperate with one another. Specifically, I explore the creation of a Gaelic athletic league in New York City (1904–1916). I trace a delicate process of experimentation, at the end of which, the organizers managed to turn the sometimes violent animosity between teams into friendly rivalries between sports teams representing different counties in Ireland. These friendly rivalries allowed spectators and players to transcend county-level loyalties and imagine themselves as belonging to a larger Irish community.

My focus on the mechanisms that allow potential members to cooperate and develop a sense of shared membership complements recent advances in the study of ethnicity. In an effort to avoid the problem of groupism, e.g., the tendency to treat ethnic groups, nations, and races as discrete, bounded groups (Brubaker, 2004, p. 8), researchers today emphasize the inhomogeneous character of ethnic groups and examine the formation of ethnic categories and boundaries (Barth, 1998; Verdery, 1996). Following Brubaker, this paper takes the inhomogeneous character of ethnic groups as a starting point and focuses on the relationships between the groups that *potentially* make up an ethnic group. It shows how the orchestration of the relationships between different groups — in this case, groups originating from different counties in Ireland — allow members to think of themselves as belonging to the same ethnic category: Irish Americans. My argument is not that Gaelic sport *alone* turned migrants into Irish Americans. A plethora of other processes played a role in this development. Rather, I argue that the orchestration of Gaelic sport provided immigrants (especially those who partook in this activity) with one more institutional setting within which Irishness became attractive and practicable, and hence, a more relevant category. Ethnicity, from this vantage point, is the effect of multiple institutional mechanisms spanning different spheres that render particular ethnic categories salient and attractive to potential members.

Gaelic sports played a central role in the Irish cultural revival of the late 19th century and in Irish nationalism ever since. Following the founders of the Gaelic Athletic Association (GAA) in Ireland, Gaelic sport enthusiasts in New York City believed that playing Gaelic sports would strengthen Irish identity and refute stereotypes regarding the Irish tendency for dissension and violence (Cronin, 1999; De Búrca, 1980; Mandle, 1987; in the United States, see Darby, 2007, 2009). To accomplish this goal, in 1904, Gaelic sports teams in New York established the Irish Counties Athletic Union (ICAU), a governing body that was charged with organizing a championship schedule and regulating the games.

Regulating Gaelic sports, however, proved to be difficult. Gaelic football and hurling were typically played in Celtic Park, which belonged to the Irish American Athletic Club (IAAC) as part of Sunday picnics that were organized by various county-based patriotic and benevolent associations (hereafter, "county associations" or "date holder").[1] Concerned with turnout at their events, the date holders invited the most popular teams week after week and effectively excluded the weaker teams. Furthermore, matches were often marred with delays and disputes that sometimes erupted in violence. Instead of creating a sense of Irish communality, the contests sometimes served to nourish factionalism and fueled anti-Irish stereotypes.

Only in 1916 did a new organization, the Gaelic Athletic Association of New York (GAANY), created a new organizational mechanism – a two-tiered league structure – that managed to regulate the games and unite the different Gaelic teams in the city. The close regulation and the hierarchical structure of the league prevented matches between very unequal teams, reduced the frequency of brawls, and assured that inter-county rivalries remained playful. The GAANY, in effect, created an institutional infrastructure that allowed players and spectators to see themselves as Irish sports enthusiasts over and above their county loyalties.

While the paper focuses on a very specific sphere of activity, it offers insights that are relevant for the study of ethnicity more generally. First, treating ethnicity as a practical organizational accomplishment turns attention to technical and organizational dynamics that has previously remain below the scrutiny of researchers. This attention to detail allows us to take into account the specific predicament of the cultural activity under study. In the case examined here, details relating to the regulation of sport, competition, and regulating the relationships between spectators and players come to play an important role in the analysis.

Second, this paper shows that ethnic group making is not *only* a process through which internal differences are made irrelevant or imagined away. Rather than masking or imagining internal differences away, the organizers of Gaelic sports regulated the relationships between different subgroups so as to allow different subgroups to maintain their difference and yet cooperate with each other (on the role of difference in ethnic and nation building, see Surak, 2012). My focus on the challenge of regulating the tensions between different groups complements approaches that focus on the cultural representation of groups (Anderson, 1991). Successful regulation of the tensions between different subgroups, in this case, between immigrants from different counties in Ireland, makes it easier for people to believe that they belong in the same group. In contrast, failure to regulate the relationships between potential members makes the overarching ethnic categorization less salient.

Third, scholars of immigration have long noticed that ethnic categorization sometime emerge from the process of migration. Migrants from different regions in Italy, for example, discovered their "Italianess" only upon arrival in the United States (Alba, 1985; Conzen, Gerber, Morawska, Pozzetta, & Vecoli, 1992). Typically, scholars attribute this process of ethnicization to exogenous pressures of labeling and stereotyping (Sarna, 1978). While exogenous pressures, no doubt, played an important role in the formation of Irish American identification, this study highlights the importance of endogenous organizational processes for the formation of ethnic bonds among immigrants. Group building and identity formation are not merely a symbolic process of categorization but also a concrete practical organizational process.

This paper is divided into four sections. The section "Ethnicity, Groupism, and Sports" provides theoretical grounds for studying ethnic sports as an organizational accomplishment. The section "Data and Method" briefly introduces the data and method used in this study. Section 3 examines the difficulties encountered by the ICAU. Section 4, "Creating the Gaelic Athletic Association of New York" focuses on the establishment of the new league and identifies the innovations that allowed it to became an obligatory point of passage (Callon, 1999) for hurlers and Gaelic footballers in New York City.

ETHNICITY, GROUPISM, AND SPORTS

Rogers Brubaker notes that despite the triumph of constructivism, many scholars of ethnicity and nationalism still think in "groupist" terms (Brubaker, 2004, 2009). Instead of attending to the heterogeneity of groups, groupist thinking treats ethnic groups as internally homogeneous and externally bounded groups. By treating ethnic groups as stable characteristics of distinct peoples, groupism prevents examination of the processes through which, sometimes, ethnic categories become a tangible social reality (Brubaker, Feischmidt, Fox, & Grancea, 2006).

With a few exceptions (see Fox, 2006; Maguire, 1999), the sociology of sports and ethnicity illustrates the validity of Brubaker's critique. Researchers typically describe sport as a symbolic resource for promoting various goals (Allison, 1986). Allegedly, ethnic or national entrepreneurs advance their goals by harnessing the excitement and camaraderie that sporting events engender (Allison, 2000; Bairner, 2001; Jarvie, 1993). The particular sport played or the style in which teams play substantiate claims of cultural distinctiveness (Hobsbaum, 1992; Maguire, 1999; Tuck, 2003).

The relationship between ethnicity and sports, to be sure, follows no law-like pattern (Allison, 2000; Harris & Parker, 2009). In Ireland, for example, rugby is played on a 32-county basis and serves as a unifying medium (Tuck, 2003). In soccer, however, the island is divided between the north and the south. Finally, hurling and Gaelic football, organized under auspices of the GAA, often serve as a paradigmatic illustration of the use of sports by separatist national movements (Cronin, 1999; De Búrca, 1980; outside Ireland, see Bradley, 1998; Darby, 2009). The diverse circumstances under which sports and politics cross paths seem to support the reading of sports as a kind of symbolic resource that can galvanize diverse identity projects (Allison, 2000; Bairner, 2001; Cronin & Mayall, 1998; MacClancy, 1996).

The theory of sport as a symbolic resource has a tremendous intuitive appeal, but it rests on problematic essentialist assumptions regarding the nature of sport and the groups that engage in it. Treating sport as a symbolic reservoir of excitement and cultural distinction necessarily overlooks the variable expressions of sport. It treats sport as a thing. Sporting events, however, are not always rousing. When the competition between teams is uneven, for instance, sporting events become dull, and spectators leave the stadium well in advance of the conclusion of a game. In other instances, sporting events deteriorate into violent brawls. It takes tremendous efforts to produce sporting events that are exciting and yet controlled and distinct. Likewise, arguing that ethnic entrepreneurs mobilize "their" constituency with sport suggests that the boundaries of the ethnic group are somehow clear and distinct. It implies that members of a putative group and them alone are aroused by a particular sport, as if some predisposition for a sport or a particular style of playing is somehow seated within group members.

As a remedy for groupism, Brubaker suggests treating groupness — the fact that sometimes people experience belonging to a group — as an event and a project (2004, 2009). Treating groupness as an event means examining the bounded nature of particular groups as a dynamic variable (see Okamura, 1981). The salience of particular ethnic categorizations is sometimes overshadowed by other categories (sub- or pan-ethnic, class, gender, place of residence, etc.). At work, for instance, class and occupational distinctions often overshadow ethnic categories. In other situations, ethnic boundaries and belonging may become strongly felt. The task of the researcher is to examine the *changes* in groupness without assuming that ethnic identity somehow exists beneath the surface at all times. In the context of sports, this means paying attention to the entirety of the sporting experience and the categorizations that become salient in given moments, and not only to peak moments when the sense of belonging to a particular group may indeed be high (see Fox, 2006).

Thinking of ethnicity as a project calls attention to the active agents that make ethnic groups. Brubaker cautions that sometimes researchers conflate ethnic groups with the organizations or leaders that claim to speak in their name. To avoid this trap, researchers should begin the investigation at a point when the claims of ethnic leaders find few followers — and describe how such claims, sometimes, become more credible or, on the other hand, fail to gain traction. From this perspective, ethnic entrepreneurs are fundamentally concerned with creating an institutional infrastructure within which the ethnic category becomes more meaningful and attractive. Following Barth (1998), many researchers focus on the creation of ethnic closure (see Wimmer, 2008, 2009), but it would be a mistake to assume that ethnic entrepreneurs limit their efforts to boundary making alone. In addition to demarcating the boundaries between "us" and "them," ethnic entrepreneurs invest efforts in regulating the relationships between the individuals and groups that potentially make up the ethnic group. Successful regulation of the relationships between potential members of an ethnic group increases the likelihood that members would see themselves as belonging to the same group. Failure, in contrast, makes it less likely that participants would see themselves as belonging to that same category (see Lainer-Vos, 2013).

In the field of sports, exploring ethnicity as a project calls attention to how sports enthusiasts go about popularizing particular ethnic sports among those whom they designate as "their" clients. The works of Elias and Dunning (1966, 1986), Dunning (1999), see also Maguire (1992), and Leifer (1998) provide a useful starting points for such an investigation. Elias and Dunning describe modern sport as a delicate organizational accomplishment. Sport, they argue, always hinges between boredom and violence. If sport is too rigidly regulated, it becomes boring. Without proper regulation that restrains impulsive action, it may become too violent. The organizers of modern sport, therefore, must balance the polarity between teams, between attack and defense, between cooperation and competition within teams, between regulators and players, and between elasticity and fixity of rules. Successful sports like soccer developed through a long process of trial and error that shaped the uniquely exciting character of modern sport (1986, pp. 77–78). Leifer's analysis widens the prism beyond the playing field to consider the organizational challenges involved in creating exciting league competitions. In leagues, he explains, more or less the same teams compete against each other with astonishing regularity. Avoiding boredom in this institutional setting demands matching carefully balanced teams, such that the results of games remain uncertain (1998). The multiplicity of the actors involved – players, clubs, owners, commissioners, and so forth, each with their own interests and preferences – renders the establishment of modern leagues an extraordinary organizational accomplishment.

A non-groupist analysis, therefore, should explore the mutual constitution of both sport and ethnicity. Instead of assuming that Gaelic sports have set rules and are exciting for a particular already-existing bounded group (Irish Americans), we start with entrepreneurs who wish to create exciting sport events and mold potential players and spectators into an ethnic group. The starting point of the analysis, in other words, is such that the sport itself is still in the work and the boundaries of the target group are unclear. In following their travails, we identify the difficulties they encounter, and the innovations they introduce in order to produce sport and ethnicity all at once. The analysis, to be sure, does not start with a blank slate. In our case, for example, the term "Irish" was applied to and used by immigrants from Ireland prior to 1904, and Gaelic sports, some version of them, were played in the city since the late 19th century. Yet, as the following sections make clear, both Irishness and Gaelic sports were very much still in the making, and following these entrepreneurs provides a window into how ethnic entrepreneurs organize particular domains of activity such that the category of "Irish" become more attractive and salient in relation to other competing categories.

DATA AND METHOD

This study is based on a thorough investigation of data pertaining to the establishment of Gaelic Athletic league in New York in the American Irish Historical Society (AIHS), the Tamiment Library Special Collection, and the New York Public Library Special Newspaper Collection (NYPL). The AIHS and Tamiment Library hold records of Irish County societies, the organizations that organized games. These materials allow me to understand the place of Gaelic sports within Irish American social life. The Irish weeklies in the NYPL, especially the *Irish American Advocate* (*IAA*), provide close analysis of the games on a weekly basis. In addition to reports of which teams competed, who scored, and so forth, that resemble current detailed sport reporting, the *IAA* published editorial columns, letters from fans, and reports from meetings of various teams and organizing bodies. Unless otherwise noted, dated references are taken from the IAA. Taken together, these sources provide a rich portrait of the Gaelic sport scene in New York City.

While detailed and at times colorful, the data used for this paper, especially the *IAA* coverage of the sport, is not a dispassionate or objective description of events. The *IAA* editors and reporters were themselves Gaelic sport enthusiasts who played an active role in setting the scene of the sport and attempting to stoke Irish pride. This active engagement provides an important advantage because it allows me to trace the difficulties and solutions that these organizers experienced as they experienced it, almost first hand.

To trace the process ethnicity and sport construction, I use a kind of snowballing technique. The investigation begins by identifying an organization who I (and others) believe to play important role in the unfolding events, and following the paper trail, which allows me to identify other actors who collaborate with and sometimes oppose plans (see Latour, 2005). This open-ended inductive approach may leave isolated actors outside of the analysis, but the likelihood that such isolates played an important role in the drama we explore is low. This inductive approach is also uniquely valuable for reconstructing the context within which action took place, and allows me to examine the practices used to influence the formation of Gaelic League with especially high resolution.

The following section explores the problem of organizing Gaelic sport in New York City by focusing on the problems confronting the organizers.

GAELIC SPORT IN NEW YORK CITY

In 1884, Michael Cusack, an enthusiastic athlete and a nationalist, established the GAA in Thurles, Ireland. Cusack sought to replace soccer and rugby, which he described as British impositions, with hurling and Gaelic football. Over the years, Gaelic football and hurling became popular Irish pastimes, and the GAA became strongly associated with the Irish national movement (De Búrca, 1980; Mandle, 1987). Playing hurling and Gaelic football in Ireland is not merely a leisurely pastime; it is also an assertion of national identity and independence.

To the uninitiated, Gaelic football matches look like a combination of rugby and soccer. Teams of 15 athletes play for 60 minutes on a rectangular grass pitch that is a bit larger than a soccer field with H-shaped goalposts at either end. The players advance the soccer-like ball with a combination of carrying, *soloing* (dropping and toe-kicking the ball back into their hands), kicking, or hand passing to other teammates. Two types of scores are possible in the game. Kicking or fisting the ball over the crossbar yields a point. A goal – that is, kicking the ball under the crossbar – yields three points. Hurling uses the same size of teams, field, and scoring system, but the shape of the ball and the technique for advancing it are different. The hurling ball, called *sliotar*, is slightly bigger than a baseball. The players advance the *sliotar* using an axe-shaped wooden stick called a hurley or *camán*. The proper handling of the hurley demands extraordinary skill – hence the game is not easily learned and is less popular than Gaelic football.

Establishing the ICAU

Immigrants from the different counties in Ireland introduced Gaelic football and hurling to New York City in the late 19th century (Darby, 2009). Gaelic games were typically organized by county associations who hired teams to compete as part of their annual Sunday picnics (Tamiment Library, County Societies Collection AIA.003/box 1). In order to regulate the games, in May 1904, representatives of 22 county-based teams established the ICAU. Luke Finn, the first president of the ICAU, explained, "we are here to vindicate our honor from the vile aspersions of those who would proclaim us a disunited people" (February 18, 1905; May 21, 1904;

May 28, 1904; August 6, 1904). The secretary of the new body, Maurice Dawling, further explained that through the play of Gaelic sports:

> Men from the North will meet the South; men from the East will meet the West, and a fact which will be set down in the history ... In fact, the good that this association has before it to do can only be anticipated at present: it is not organized merely for sporting purposes alone, but to bring more closely together the Irish people at this side of the Atlantic in order to defend and uphold that which was too often denied. (July 2, 1904; see also P.J. Purcill, May 28, 1904; July 9, 1904)

While it is tempting to characterize all immigrants from Ireland as "Irish," Dawling's pledge suggests that such categorization is at least in part anachronistic. In some important respects, the "Irish" in New York were divided along lines of county of origin. As John Ridge argues, the particular county from which migrants arrived distinguished several of the so-called "Irish" neighborhoods in the city. "Kerrymen," for instance, populated the old fourth ward, and immigrants from Cork populated the seventh ward. Smaller county-specific pockets existed in other areas and sometimes served as a basis for electoral mobilization (1997). These divisions were also manifested in the predominance of county associations, which dictated the rhythm of Irish communal life in New York in that period (Funchion, 1983). While the category "Irish" was, without doubt, familiar to these immigrants, in certain moments or events, to use Brubaker's terms, it was overshadowed by county loyalties. The leaders of the ICAU saw Gaelic sports as a way to foster Irish unity.

The ICAU modeled itself after the GAA in Ireland both in terms of goals and organizational structure. Like their Irish predecessors, Dawling saw Gaelic sport as a means to revitalize Irish pride and identity. Like in Ireland, only county-based associations were allowed to compete, and an athletic committee scheduled one hurling and two football matches for every weekend. At the beginning of the season, teams were supposed to compete at the provincial level. The winners of the provincial championships would then compete at the inter-provincial level leading to a final (see Finn, June 9, 1906).

While many welcomed the new organization, regulating Gaelic sports in New York City proved to be a daunting challenge. Disagreements over the scheduling of games, matching teams, and disputes over process and scoring emerged almost immediately. First, given the greater popularity of Gaelic football, the ICAU's athletic committee determined that the football matches would take place prior to the hurling match. However, due to frequent delays, the hurling match often ended prematurely due to encroaching darkness (Rechfelt, April 6, 1907; Tullaroan, June 29, 1907).[2] A minority in the ICAU, hurling teams resented their second-class status (see Lennon, May 4, 1907, July 20, 1907; Frank Pilkington, August 31, 1907; July 3, 1909).

Second, teams sometimes refused to play the matches scheduled for them. This problem was related to the monetary interests of the date holders and the radical differences in the quality of the teams. The teams known as the "Big Four" – Kerry, Cork, Kildare, Kilkenny, and Tipperary (the exact composition changed over the years) – operated on a semi-professional basis and enjoyed large fan bases. Other teams were considerably weaker and had few fans. Matches scheduled between uneven teams as well as matches between two weak teams were therefore relatively unattractive, especially for the Big Four teams (see E. J. Condon, December 12, 1908; August 7, 1907). The date holders, who actually arranged and paid for the games, resisted the ICAU's schedule too. Concerned about the turnout for their picnics, these organizations ignored the athletic committee's schedule and hired the Big Four to play against themselves week after week (November 28, 1908).[3] Consequently, not only were weak teams denied the opportunity to practice, but also the repetition robbed matches of the drama associated with infrequent encounters (Leifer, 1998; O'Shea, May 1, 1909; June 6, 1909).

Third, disputes and disorganization frequently disrupted the flow of games. Sometimes the problems were related to the referees who, out of ignorance or error, afforded a goal or a deciding point to the (supposedly) wrong team (see IAA Editor, March 3, 1906; August 18, 1906; October 30, 1908; July 3, 1909). At other times, the spectators and teams accused the referees of intentional bias:

> The gentleman who refereed [last week] ... was partial ... no team can play its best when it knows it is being discriminated against. It feels that it cannot win no matter how it plays, and so plays indifferently .... (*IAA* editor, August 3, 1907)

Selected more or less ad hoc, the referees were often the cause of, rather than those who end disputes.

Fourth, the athletic equipment itself was a source of discord. The goal cage in football and hurling is in the shape of a large "H," as in rugby, but the space under the crossbar is covered with a net, as in soccer. In Celtic

Park, however, the popular venue where games were played, the goal posts were relatively short and the net was absent. As a result, the *IAA*'s editor noted that:

> The first thing that impresses the sportsman, who is a stranger to the games of Gaelic football or hurling ... is the loose scoring feature of either game. When he sees the balls soar high in the game over the goal posts, and the American flag waves a point scored ... and he seems rather surprised that a top cross bar does not connect the point posts .... (August 3, 1907)[4]

This "loose scoring," Liam O'Shea, the lead columnist of the IAA, complained, resulted in frequent arguments (June 12, 1909).

The frequent disputes had a stifling effect on games. Not only did they interrupt the flow of the game, but also sometimes teams that felt themselves wronged simply left the field. Worse, disputes sometimes escalated to violence. Enraged by what they perceived as the dishonest behavior, players or spectators would rush the field and punch the offending party. O'Shea, for example, reported:

> In the second half something else besides football took place. A throw-in was the cause of a little unbilled commotion. The ball was driven out near the north goal, and when the lineman hurled it into the excited players, his action grated on the nerves of a gentleman outside the paling. Before one could say "Jack Robinson," this worthy had entered the field and planted a resounding right-hander in the neighborhood of the lineman's lower lip. (O'Shea, September 10, 1910; see also Martin Sheridan, February 19, 1910; April 13, 1907)

Such incidents would sometimes spiral out of control, involving scores of people (O'Shea, April 7, 1906; April 29, 1907; June 29, 1907; August 24, 1907; November 7, 1908; see also reports in the *New York Times* November 28, 1902; July 9, 1906; February 3, 1907; April 8 1907; August 26, 1907; August 16, 1909; *New York Tribune*, March 14, 1904). In hurling, where each player's hurley stick doubled effectively as a weapon, violence was especially common (McConte, November 29, 1909).

The Crisis of Gaelic Sport

Frustrated by the disorganization of games, in 1908 the football teams of Kerry and Clare counties withdrew from the ICAU and established a competing governing body. Hoping to present itself as the authentic league, the new governing body named itself the United States Provincial Council of the Gaelic Athletic Association (USGAA) (May 23, 1908). Instead of providing a fix, however, the competition for teams between two governing bodies exacerbated the problems discussed previously. Knowing that they can always switch allegiance, players and teams ignored regulations (GAA notes, August 8, 1908; November 14, 1908; "Fair Play" November 28, 1908; February 26, 1910; Pilkington, November 6, 1909; November 9, 1912).

Even worse, the lack of regulation allowed team managers to flexibly assemble dream teams for particular dates. In order to be invited to play, weak teams contracted strong players for specific dates. Born of necessity, this practice had a debilitating effect on participation. Pilkington explained that:

> No matter how bad a player may be, he thinks he is fairly good and should not be culled ... by culling him for an outsider you drive him out of the club, so that in the end you won't have enough [players] to form a team unless you pick. (June 22, 1912; Martin Hurley, May 27, 1911; April 7, 1912; November 21, 1914)

Reflecting on the state of the games, O'Shea noticed "certain disinterestedness [in the game] becomes painfully evident .... Another noticeable feature is the disappearance of several junior football teams, who occupied prominent positions in the Irish athletic calendar some few seasons ago." (November 30, 1912; also May 29, 1909).

The disorganization of the Gaelic sports scene in New York was not a sporting issue alone. Each player who was lost due to the collapse of small teams, O'Shea lamented, "become[s] lost entirely to the G.A.A., if not to Ireland" (May 27, 1911; see also M.J. Murphy, September 24, 1910). A spectator troubled by violent scenes on the field charged:

> How little do those who participate in those scenes realise the death-blow they are striking, and the stigma they are casting, not alone on their country's national pastimes, but on the very heart's core of their country's reputation .... (April 3, 1915; see also Hurly, December 10, 1910)

The *IAA* editor likewise complained: "The reports of our national games in the daily papers have rightly caused many sons of dear old Ireland to blush and hang his head with shame" (January 16, 1915). Instead of fostering unity and pride, during the seasons of 1908–1914, competition between Gaelic teams in New York cultivated clannishness and enmity between counties and actually reinforced anti-Irish stereotypes. Rather than providing institutional scaffolding on which ethnic belonging thrive, the two governing produced discord and reduced participation.

CREATING THE GAELIC ATHLETIC ASSOCIATION OF NEW YORK

Ever since the split in the ICAU, O'Shea advocated for the creation of a unified governing body:

> Assert yourself, boys, and do not let that petty difference prevent you from coming together ... Forget you are Clare men or Cork men and think of yourself as Irishmen; work hand in hand as Irishmen and drop the detestable belief that your own county comes first. (December 17, 1910; see also December 31, 1910; January 21, 1911; January 20, 1912)

Few could oppose O'Shea's suggestions in principle but the date holders and the Big Four teams benefited from the lack of regulation, and therefore creating a unified league proved difficult. Date holders could book the Big Four teams for their events and secure showing and the Big Four teams played practically every week. Therefore, the Big Four and the date holders ignored O'Shea's pleadings. Over time, however, a number of developments undermined the status quo, which made a unified league more likely.

First, the gradual professionalization of the Big Four forced them to charge more for their services. Whereas in 1908, top teams demanded less than a hundred dollars each per match, in 1913 Kilkenny refused to make a show for less than $150. Together with a spike in the rental fee for Celtic Park (from $50 to $100 per weekend), date holders were taking on an increasingly large risk in scheduling matches (Pilkington, April 26, 1913; see also O'Shea, December 2, 1911). Trying to offset the rising costs, the date holders raised the price of admission from 25 to 50 cents a person, but the crowd refused to pay: On July 2, 1911, spectators coming to the Tipperary Men's picnic attacked the gates of Celtic Park with bricks demanding a reduction of the admission fee. The small police force on the premises could not control the riot, and the organizers were eventually forced to slash the entrance fees (O'Shea, July 8, 1911). A few weeks later, angry spectators attempted to burn the fence surrounding Celtic Park (O'Shea, August 19, 1911). Following these incidents, the IAAC instructed date holders to charge no more than 25 cents for admission.

Second, beginning in 1909, a number of soccer teams, some of them predominantly Irish, organized in New York. The problem here was not simply one of competition over spectators. In Ireland, and apparently also in New York, soccer represented English dominance and the decline of Irish culture and distinction. Indeed, in Ireland, the GAA bans "non-Gaelic" games from its stadiums. Alarmed, O'Shea called for a GAA-style ban on soccer teams in order to curb the "drift in the ways of the Saxon" (O'Shea, May 9, 1909; February 10, 1910; March 25, 1911), but a number of date holders decided to hire soccer teams instead of the costly Big Four (July 2, 1910; July 16, 1910; July 23, 1910; August 20, 1910).

In response to these developments, in late 1914 representatives from 24 football and hurling teams formed the GAANY.[5] As with previous attempts, the Big Four ignored the new organization and this presented a serious challenge. To complete a championship series, the GAANY had to persuade at least 22 date holders to invite their teams instead of the Big Four or soccer teams (December 26, 1914; Hurley, March 6, 1915; April 17, 1915). To tempt date holders, the GAANY offered the services of its teams for only $50 per team and promised special consideration in the choice of teams for early booking (O'Shea, June 26, 1915; Hurley, March 6, 1915).

To increase the appeal of its games, the GAANY introduced important reforms. First, the GAANY reduced the number of players from 15 to 13 players in a team (February 6, 1915). This change was designed to increase the speed of the game and help small county organizations form teams. Second, the GAANY encouraged weak teams to recruit strong players in an effort to provide a counter balance to the Big Four (see O'Shea January 2, 1915; February 27, 1915).[6] Third, to limit disputes and delays in the course of games, the GAANY installed nets behind the goal posts. These nets, O'Shea explained, could:

> Save a whole lot of trouble, for fewer arguments would be heard. In either hurling or football the ball, after passing between the posts, rests there, being caught by the screen, consequently saving an amount of trouble. (June 12, 1912; also June 29, 1912; May 1, 1915)

Finally, instead of assigning the current captains of other teams to act as referees, the GAANY recruited retired players who were presumably less likely to harbor a grudge against particular teams (O'Shea, April 24, 1915; July 10, 1915; Touchline, August 7, 1915).

The effect of these changes was not decisive. During the first weeks of the 1915 season, the GAANY managed to secure a showing for its teams in Celtic Park, but the level of play was disappointing. Consequently, many date holders hired the Big Four again, and the GAANY's teams were forced to play in a remote and unpopular location (May 15, 1915).

Toward the end of the 1915 season, O'Shea and his colleagues looked for a way to lure the Big Four to the GAANY. The solution they found was creating a two-tiered league structure:

> What we think would be advisable for the purpose of affiliating all teams would be to form senior and junior football leagues, comprised solely of greater New York teams .... By taking Kerry, Kilkenny, Cork and Kildare with two or four other teams a senior league could be formed easily. (September 18, 1915; see also June 12, 1915)

The division of the football league into senior and junior leagues allowed the GAANY to avoid scheduling games between very unequal teams. The hierarchal structure of the league also provided a justification for unequal compensation for teams. After some negotiation, the representatives of the Big Four and the GAANY agreed to a differential pricing: senior teams would be paid $100 per game, the hurling teams would receive $75 per match, and the teams in the junior league would receive $50 per game (March 18, 1916). In order to increase the number of games played by the Big Four, the GAANY limited the senior league to six teams only – the Big Four along with the two best teams of the GAANY of the 1915 season.

With this new structure, at the opening of the 1916 season, finally, all of the active teams in the New York area were affiliated with the GAANY. The new league structure created a delicate balance between key actors of Gaelic sports in the city. The junior football teams received an opportunity to play regularly and a chance to advance to the senior league. The hurlers were forced to acknowledge their inferior status, but their compensation improved, and they finally played in Celtic Park in front of a large crowd. Finally, the senior football teams looked forward to participating in real championship games without having to compromise their income.

The newly consolidated league created a powerful lock-in mechanism. When, toward the end of the 1916 season, the Kerry football team considered withdrawing, it soon discovered that outside the GAANY, suitable opponents were few and far between. The date holders, too, soon realized that attracting large crowds necessitated working with the GAANY (April 22, 1916). The monopoly over the sport also allowed the GAANY to impose firmer control over the transfers of players and reduce the level of violence on the field (July 10, 1915; February 5, 1916). But the "governing body's greatest achievement [O'Shea argued] ... was in forming a league schedule, which cultivates interest in every league contest." (October 7, 1916). The accumulation of points for winning games created a buildup of momentum leading to the championship match at the end of the season.

The clearest indication of the GAANY's success was its growing popularity and stability. At the end of 1916 season, O'Shea rejoiced:

> Not since the invasion of the Gaels in '88 has hurling and football obtained such a strong hold 'neath Uncle Sammy's starry banner. All that was ever needed of the teams here was to give clean exhibitions, and not until the advent of the Gaelic Athletic Association of America was the game played up to that standard which would make decent Irishmen feel proud of their national pastime. (October 14, 1916; see also December 30, 1916)

During the early 1920s, at the peak of their popularity, the annual picnics in Celtic Park drew crowds of up to 20,000 spectators (Tamiment Library, County Societies Collection AIA.003/box 1; see also Bardy, 2005; Darby, 2007, 2009; Fergus, 1999). Teams from Ireland regularly visited Celtic Park, and Irish American teams traveled to Ireland and participated in the All Ireland championships (New York G.A.A. Board, 1976). While the popularity of Gaelic sports had seen both ups and downs over the decades, the structure of the GAANY remained relatively stable to this day. The successful regulation of games turned Gaelic sports from a potentially cantankerous practice into a pleasurable Irish pastime.

DISCUSSION

Following the development of Gaelic sports in New York allow us to trace the coproduction of both sport and ethnicity. On the one hand, the gradual regulation of Gaelic sports in New York follows the trajectory identified by Elias and Dunning (1986), where loosely regulated and relatively violent practice gradually gives way to more regulated yet still exciting games. But, the success of the GAANY was more than a sportive achievement alone. It was also about the production of Irishness in the city. At the turn of the century, many immigrants from Ireland, no doubt, thought of themselves as "Irish," but on the playing field, and perhaps also in other settings, county loyalties trumped broader sense of Irish belonging. After 1916, the GAANY created an institutional infrastructure wherein immigrants from different counties in Ireland were less likely to exchange blows and more likely to engage each other in a spirit of *friendly competition*. In this sense, successful regulation of the games provided immigrants with one more venue where they could associate with others like them and think of themselves as Irish.

Sunday picnics were obviously but one sphere of activity for immigrants from Ireland in the city. Nevertheless, to the extent that ethnic sense of belonging not only finds expression, but is also manufactured through participation in ethnic activities, the GAANY provided athletes, organizers, and spectators with one additional institutional venue wherein being Irish became more practicable and meaningful in relation to other competing categories of identification.

Focusing on the challenge of regulating sport allows us to perceive both sport and ethnicity as dynamically emerging phenomena. Through much of the period examined here, county-level loyalties overshadowed Irish belonging. On more than one occasion, Gaelic sport was a source of neither excitement nor pride. But a long process of experimentation gradually turned Gaelic sport and Irish ethnicity into mutually reinforcing events.

In addition to bringing the study of ethnicity down to earth, treating ethnicity as a practical organizational accomplishment provides a way to increase the specificity of the field. Attending to difficulties and solution devised by ethnic entrepreneurs turns seemingly technical details that typically remain below the threshold of research into meaningful data. This increased specificity enriches our understanding of what is the stuff that makes ethnicity.

This study points to the importance of understanding the mechanisms that regulate the relationship between the groups that potentially comprise an ethnic group, in this case, between teams representing different counties in Ireland. The problem of regulating relationships is not somehow secondary to a more fundamental question of identification, but complements it. Successful regulation of the relationships between potential members of a putative ethnic group makes it easier for members to imagine that they belong in the same overarching ethnic category. Failure to orchestrate these relationships makes other categorizations (in our case county level affiliation) more credible.

Waters (1990) following Gans (1979), describe white ethnicity as a choice that bears deep affinity to American values. Being ethnic allows one to be special, while at the same time remain rooted in a community (even if a very loose one). The analysis offered here concurs with arguments, but anchors ethnic choices not in the general contradictions of American culture, but in the concrete ethnic organizational scaffolding set in place by ethnic entrepreneurs. Organizational projects like the Gaelic league, operating at the middle range, provide institutional infrastructure that makes ethnic identification meaningful, and attractive, at least to some portion of the potential candidates for an ethnic pedigree. Paying close attention to the organization of ethnic projects, and to the specific dynamics associated with the practical challenges of organizing ethnic activities, can complement studies that focus on the more macro structural dynamics that are involved in the production of ethnicity.

Scholars of immigration have long pointed out that the ethnic categories migrants embrace are not necessarily carried over from the old land but emerge in the place of settlement. For example, in the 19th century, migrants from today's Italy often left Europe as Sicilians, Cambrians, Tuscans, etc. Only upon arriving in the United States, and being treated as Italians, did they discover their national identity and commonalities (Alba, 1985; Conzen et al., 1992; Sarna, 1978). This late embrace of the ethnic or national category is typically interpreted as a reaction to the difficulties of putting down roots in the new land, and especially to negative stereotyping. From this vantage point, immigrant ethnicity is largely reactive and individual response of the many. The Gaelic sport organizers examined in this paper, no doubt, were motivated by a desire to counter negative stereotypes, but my analysis highlights the practical difficulties involved in forming and maintaining ethnic categories, over and above the motivation to do so. It suggests that the process of boundary making is, at last in part, endogenous. In addition, it presents boundary making as an organized activity.

Finally, discussions of boundary making typically focus on the boundaries between insiders and outsiders of particular ethnic categories. Ethnic solidarity or groupness, from this perspective, is premised on the construction of (imagined) internal homogeneity (Barth, 1998). In the case examined here, however, internal boundaries (between immigrants from different counties) were not simply an obstacle (see Surak, 2012). Rather, assuring the relevance of Irishness for the players and spectators entailed perfecting the competition between teams, while framing it as "merely" a sporting competition. County loyalties were in fact conducive to the production of the Irish sense of belonging, as long as these loyalties were treated as a sportive matter. The point is not merely that the ethnic category was nestled within a hierarchy of other categories of belonging (Okamura, 1981; Wimmer, 2009), but that county level attachments, in this case at least, served a productive role in creating a setting within which Irishness became a more meaningful category.

The dynamic of sporting competition that stands at the center of this paper is highly specific, but the organizational framework developed here can enrich studies of ethnicity in other domains. People do ethnicity in a myriad of settings and through diverse organizational mechanisms. Ethnic entrepreneurs who wish to give substance to their imagined belonging by organizing cultural events (Handler, 1988), heritage tours (Kelner, 2010), etc., often discover that their potential compatriots – the individuals and groups that they imagine as part of their ethnic group – are less homogeneous than they initially expected. Different groups, just like the different actors involved in Gaelic sports, have different interests, preferences, and distinct understandings of the significance and scope of the ethnic category, and these differences create obstacles to cooperation. Overcoming these obstacles is rarely just a case of using inspiring rhetoric. More likely, ethnic entrepreneurs have to devise organizational mechanisms that allow diverse groups to cooperate and engage in social practices that endow ethnic categories with meaning and social significance. Identifying the mechanisms that entrepreneurs construct in order to bring various social fragments under the ethnic or national umbrella can yield new insights into the construction of ethnic groups of nation.

NOTES

1. In addition to socializing, county associations offered basic health insurance and a decent burial for their members (Funchion, 1983; Ridge, 1997).
2. The columnists of the *IAA* regularly assumed noms de plume.
3. Sunday picnics were costly, but they were also a lucrative source of income for county associations. During 1905, a successful picnic could yield a profit of $650 ($18,100 in 2015 terms). An unpopular match, however, could lead to a loss (September 9, 1905).
4. In Ireland, the umpire raises a white flag for a point and a green flag for a goal. In Celtic Park, apparently, umpires used the American flag to signal a point and (perhaps, the record is unclear) the Irish flag to signal a goal.
5. The original name was the Gaelic Athletic Association of the United States. Over the years, the association was renamed. I use the current name to avoid confusion with the USGAA.
6. The GAA in Ireland was (still is) committed to amateurism. In New York, however, teams rewarded players with payments or in kind.

REFERENCES

Alba, R. D. (1985). *Italian Americans: Into the twilight of ethnicity.* New York, NY: Prentice-Hall.

Allison, L. (1986). *The politics of sport.* Manchester: Manchester University Press.

Allison, L. (2000). Sport and nationalism. In J. J. Coakley & E. Dunning (Eds.), *Handbook of sports studies* (pp. 345–357). London: Sage.

Anderson, B. (1991). *Imagined communities: Reflections on the origin and spread of nationalism.* New York, NY: Verso.

Bairner, A. (2001). *Sport, nationalism, and globalization: European and North American perspectives.* Albany: SUNY Press.

Bardy, S. (2005). *Irish sport and culture at New York's Celtic Park*. Ph.D. Dissertation, New York University, New York, NY.

Barth, F. (1998). *Ethnic groups and boundaries: The social organization of culture difference*. Prospect Heights, IL: Waveland Press.

Bradley, J. M. (1998). *Sport, culture, politics and Scottish society: Irish immigrants and the Gaelic Athletic association*. Edinburgh: John Donald.

Brubaker, R. (2004). *Ethnicity without groups*. Cambridge: Harvard University Press.

Brubaker, R. (2009). Ethnicity, race, and nationalism. *Annual Review of Sociology*, 35, 21–42.

Brubaker, R., Feischmidt, M., Fox, J., & Grancea, L. (2006). *Nationalist politics and everyday ethnicity in a Transylvanian Town*. Princeton, NJ: Princeton University Press.

Callon, M. (1999). Some elements of a sociology of translation: Domestication of the scallops and the fishermen of St. Brieuc Bay. In M. Biagioli (Ed.), *The science studies reader* (pp. 67–83). London: Routledge.

Conzen, K. N., Gerber, D. A., Morawska, E., Pozzetta, G. E., & Vecoli, R. J. (1992). The invention of ethnicity: A perspective from the U.S.A. *Journal of American Ethnic History*, 12(1), 3–41. doi:10.2307/27501011.

Cronin, M. (1999). *Sport and nationalism in Ireland: Gaelic games, soccer and Irish identity since 1884*. Dublin: Four Courts Press.

Cronin, M., & Mayall, D. (Eds.). (1998). *Sporting nationalisms: Identity, ethnicity, immigration, and assimilation*. London: Frank Cass.

Darby, P. (2007). Gaelic games, ethnic identity and Irish nationalism in New York City C.1880–1917 [1]. *Sport in Society*, 10(3), 347–367.

Darby, P. (2009). *Gaelic games, nationalism and the Irish Diaspora in the United States*. Dublin: University College Dublin Press.

De Búrca, M. (1980). *The GAA: A history*. Dublin: Gill & Macmillan.

Dunning, E. (1999). *Sport matters: Sociological studies of sport, violence and civilisation*. London: Routledge.

Elias, N., & Dunning, E. (1966). Dynamics of group sports with special reference to football. *British Journal of Sociology*, 17(4), 388–402.

Elias, N., & Dunning, E. (1986). *Quest for excitement: Sport and leisure in the civilizing process*. New York, NY: Blackwell.

Fergus, H. (1999). The Gaelic athletic association. In M. Glazier (Ed.), *The Encyclopedia of the Irish in America* (pp. 352–356). Notre Dame: Notre Dame University Press.

Fox, J. E. (2006). Consuming the nation: Holidays, sports, and the production of collective belonging. *Ethnic and Racial Studies*, 29(2), 217–236.

Funchion, M. F. (1983). *Irish American voluntary organizations*. Westport, CT: Greenwood Press.

Gans, H. J. (1979). Symbolic ethnicity: The future of ethnic groups and cultures in America. *Ethnic and Racial Studies*, 2(1), 1–20.

Handler, R. (1988). *Nationalism and the politics of culture in Quebec*. Madison, WI: University of Wisconsin Press.

Harris, J., & Parker, A. (Eds.). (2009). *Sport and social identities*. New York, NY: Palgrave Macmillan.

Hobsbaum, E. (1992). Mass-producing traditions: Europe, 1870–1914. In E. Hobsbawm & T. Ranger (Eds.), In *The invention of tradition* (pp. 263–307). New York, NY: Cambridge University Press.

Jarvie, G. (1993). Sport, nationalism and cultural identity. In *The changing politics of sport* (pp. 58–83). Manchester: Manchester University Press.

Kelner, S. (2010). *Tours that bind*. New York, NY: New York University Press.

Lainer-Vos, D. (2013). *Sinews of the nation: Constructing Irish and Zionist Bonds in the United States*. Cambridge: Polity Press.

Latour, B. (2005). *Reassembling the social: An introduction to actor-network-theory*. New York, NY: Oxford University Press.

Leifer, E. M. (1998). *Making the majors: The transformation of team sports in America*. Cambridge: Harvard University Press.

MacClancy, J. (Ed.). (1996). *Sport, identity and ethnicity*. Oxford: Berg Publishers.

Maguire, J. (1992). Towards a sociological theory of sport and the emotions: A process-sociological perspective. In E. Dunning & C. Rojek (Eds.), *Sport and leisure in the civilizing process: Critique and counter-critique* (pp. 96–120). Toronto: Toronto University Press.

Maguire, J. (1999). *Global sport: Identities, societies, civilizations* (1st ed.). Cambridge: Polity Press.

Mandle, W. F. (1987). *The Gaelic athletic association & Irish nationalist politics, 1884–1924*. Dublin: Helm.

New York G.A.A. Board. (1976). *The New York Irish: Commemorative issue*. Dublin: Gaelic Press.

Okamura, J. Y. (1981). Situational ethnicity. *Ethnic and Racial Studies*, *4*(4), 452–465.

Ridge, J. T. (1997). Irish County societies in New York, 1880–1914. In R. H. Bayor & T. Meagher (Eds.), *The New York Irish* (pp. 275–300). Baltimore, MD: John Hopkins University Press.

Sarna, J. D. (1978). From immigrants to ethnics: Toward a new theory of 'Ethnicization'. *Ethnicity*, *5*(4), 370–378.

Surak, K. (2012). Nation-work: A praxeology of making and maintaining nations. *European Journal of Sociology/Archives Européennes De Sociologie*, *53*(2), 171–204.

Tuck, J. (2003). Making sense of Emerald commotion: Rugby union, national identity and Ireland. *Identities*, *10*(4), 495–515.

Verdery, K. (1996). Whither 'Nation' and 'Nationalism'? In G. Balakrishnan (Ed.), *Mapping the nation* (pp. 235–254). New York, NY: Verso.

Waters, M. C. (1990). *Ethnic options: Choosing identities in America*. Berkeley, CA: University of California Press.

Wimmer, A. (2008). The making and unmaking of ethnic boundaries: A multilevel process theory. *American Journal of Sociology*, *113*(4), 970–1022.

Wimmer, A. (2009). Herder's heritage and the boundary-making approach: Studying ethnicity in immigrant societies. *Sociological Theory*, *27*(3), 244–270.

SANCTIFIED MOBILIZATION: HOW POLITICAL ACTIVISTS MANAGE INSTITUTIONAL BOUNDARIES IN FAITH-BASED ORGANIZING FOR IMMIGRANT RIGHTS

Marion Coddou

ABSTRACT

Scholars have long argued that churches play a critical role in mobilizing communities marginal to the political process, primarily by pooling resources, disseminating information, and providing opportunities for members to develop community networks, leadership, and civic skills. However, recent research suggests that churches only serve as effective mobilizing institutions when they engage in direct political discussion and recruitment. Even so, churches may face economic, legal, and institutional barriers to entering the political sphere, and explicit political speech and action remain rare. Through an analysis of two years of ethnographic fieldwork following faith-based community organizers attempting to recruit Spanish speakers throughout a Catholic Archdiocese into a campaign for immigrant rights, this paper explores the institutional constraints on church political mobilization, and how these are overcome to mobilize one of the most politically marginal groups in the United States today: Hispanic undocumented immigrants and their allies. I argue that scholars of political engagement must look beyond the structural features of organizations to consider the effects of their institutionalized domains and practices. While churches do face institutional barriers to political mobilization, activists who specialize their recruitment strategy to match the institutional practices of the organizations they target can effectively overcome these barriers to mobilize politically alienated populations.

Keywords: Mobilization; organizations; institutional theory; immigrant incorporation; religion; leadership

Scholars of political participation and social movements often characterize churches as organizations uniquely capable of mobilizing the disadvantaged through pooling community resources and developing leadership, civic skills, and networks that can effectively channel community grievances to policymakers (Djupe & Gilbert, 2009; McAdam, 1982; McCarthy & Zald, 1977; Morris, 1984; Ramakrishnan & Bloemraad, 2008; Verba, Schlozman, & Brady, 1995; Wong, 2006). Accordingly, many empirical studies link church attendance or participation in church ministries with increased participation in electoral and non-electoral politics (Beyerlein & Chaves, 2003; Brown & Brown, 2003; Harris, 1999; Jones-Correa & Leal, 2001; Verba et al., 1995). While some scholars suggest that churches encourage the political participation of disadvantaged groups indirectly through the development of civic skills and social capital transferable to the political sphere (Putnam & Campbell, 2010; Verba et al., 1995), others argue that churches only serve as effective mobilizing institutions when they facilitate direct political recruitment (Brown & Brown, 2003; Coddou, 2016; Fitzgerald & Spohn, 2005). Even so, churches face legal, economic, and institutional constraints on their political involvement, and outright political speech and activity remain rare (Beyerlein & Hipp, 2009; Brown & Brown, 2003; Chaves & Anderson, 2008; Jelen, 2001; McDaniel, 2008; Putnam & Campbell, 2010; Wood, 2002). Furthermore, recent research drawing on organizational theories suggests that churches may actually face decreased support from their membership for engaging in activities outside of their traditional domain, such as political advocacy (Coddou, 2015).

In light of these debates, this paper asks how activists overcome church institutional constraints to mobilize politically alienated groups. To answer this question, I focus on the empirical case of Hispanic undocumented immigrant mobilization through Catholic Churches. Hispanic undocumented immigrants are one of the most politically marginal groups in the United States today, due to a lack of legal immigration status, low socioeconomic status, language barriers, and racial profiling in immigration enforcement (Gonzalez, 2011; Portes & Rumbaut, 2006). Yet, they are active and visible participants in the current movement for immigrant rights (Voss & Bloemraad, 2011). Furthermore, while the Catholic Church has a visible and influential presence in the immigrant rights movement, its unique organizational practice of frequently rotating religious leaders among churches raises questions about how such leadership changes might affect local parishioner political mobilization (Heredia, 2011; Mooney, 2009).

Drawing on institutional theories of organizations and two years of ethnographic fieldwork following a faith-based community-organizing group (hereafter FBO)[1] as they attempted to recruit Hispanic immigrants in a Catholic Archdiocese into a campaign for immigrant rights, I argue that the character and level of church political mobilization depends on the strategies used to bridge the institutional boundary between religion and politics. I distinguish between two strategies used by community organizers: model-expanding and model-specializing strategies. The model-expanding strategy sought to stretch church institutional boundaries to include non-routine activities traditionally associated with the political sphere, such as lobbying and protesting, by infusing political action with religious symbols and ideas. In contrast, the model-specializing strategy worked within established institutional boundaries to make routine religious activities, such as religious masses and organized prayer, politically influential by making them issue-focused and public. In short, model-expanding strategies redefine activities outside of traditional organizational models as central to the organization's mission by reinterpreting foundational documents and ideas. Model-specializing strategies instead match and repurpose traditional institutional roles, speech, and activities to new ends, so that the work looks and feels very much like routine action, but is applied to a novel goal. In this context, these differences in approach were most clearly visible in their perceived agent of change, their organizing tactics, and their membership definitions.

The strategies were not equal in their effects, and each produced distinct conflicts and relied on religious leaders in particular ways. I found that the success of the model-expanding strategy in motivating participation in FBO-sponsored events depended heavily on the active support of local religious leaders in legitimating non-routine activities as part of the church's domain. Without the support of religious leaders, this strategy was more likely to provoke confusion and perceptions of domain violation among the more religiously involved lay leaders. On the other hand, the model-specializing strategy facilitated the participation of both religious leaders and members with minimal resistance by offering them a means of supporting the cause through traditional religious roles and activities that fit neatly into their routine church involvement. This made the model-specializing strategy easier to diffuse and sustain.

In the following pages, I first review the empirical context, research design, data, and methods. I then show how churchgoer perceptions of boundaries between religion and politics, community organizer strategies to bridge those boundaries, and religious leader actions interacted to impact the character and level of recruitment and mobilization into FBO-sponsored campaigns and events. I define successful recruitment as taking on core organizing and planning roles within FBO and successful mobilization as attendance at FBO-sponsored events.

This research contributes to the literature on political mobilization and organizations by demonstrating the determinative role of institutionalized organizational models, roles, and practices. It also builds on institutional theory highlighting the risks of boundary blurring and model divergence, by showing how entrepreneurs can bridge established institutional boundaries by pursuing new goals in a way that recognizes and conforms to established organizational models.

RESEARCH SETTING AND KEY THEORETICAL POINTS OF COMPARISON

The Organizational Structure of the Catholic Church

The Catholic Church has a unique hierarchical and bureaucratic organizational structure that offered the opportunity to observe the impact of leadership changes relatively exogenous to church member preferences on church responses to political recruitment. To overview the general structure, local

Archdioceses, which can span multiple counties and are governed by an archbishop and supporting bishops, are organized into geographic parish communities, where residents are expected to attend the church in the parish they reside in, though this does not always happen. A pastor, or head priest, is the highest authority at the parish church. Associate priests may assist pastors, depending on budget and pastor preferences. All of these men are ordained religious leaders and have the credentials to perform the most religious services. Nuns or friars from religious orders may also join the pastor in supporting the parish community. Deacons are another type of religious leader that cannot perform all religious rituals, but can assist the pastor or act as a substitute for certain activities. Given the shortage of Spanish-speaking priests in the Archdiocese, deacons and members of religious orders would sometimes join churches to help pastors who could not speak Spanish minister to the Spanish-speaking community. Lay[2] staff, such as secretaries and religious education coordinators, round out the paid church staff. Members of the parish are called parishioners, and lay leaders are church members who lead or participate in church small groups and ministries. At the Archdiocese level, the Hispanic Pastoral Council (HPC) is a volunteer committee of lay leader representatives from Archdiocese Spanish-speaking churches, which is headed by the Vicar for the Spanish-speaking and coordinates initiatives across churches.

Three features of Catholic organizational structure in particular provide ideal conditions for studying church mobilization into political activity: (1) church pastors are accorded the ultimate power and authority in directing church practice, (2) priests, including pastors, are frequently rotated among Archdiocese churches, and (3) church religious leaders are selected by Archdiocese leaders, not church members. First, the ultimate power that priests, but especially pastors, hold over church institutional practices means that a change in priests can cause significant institutional disruption within a church. Second, the Archdiocese may rotate religious leaders among churches as frequently as every one to two years, and though the pastor usually has a longer tenure (anywhere from 4 to 12 years), pastors also sometimes change very frequently. Third, while previous studies have struggled with the issue of member selection into voluntary organizations, the fact that Archdiocese leaders, not church members, choose church religious leaders make the practices they institute relatively exogenous to member preferences. Together, these three characteristics create a situation in which church members may experience very different institutional environments over the course of their attendance at one church, but have little control over these changes.

The Strategic Restructuring of a Faith-Based Community Organizing Nonprofit

To examine how different churches responded to direct political recruitment, I followed the efforts of a local faith-based community organizing nonprofit targeting Catholic Churches with large Spanish-speaking populations for recruitment in an immigrant rights campaign. At various points in time and place, they were either supported, tolerated, or resisted by church leadership. The faith-based community organization, which I will refer to throughout this paper as FBO to protect confidentiality, was a 501c3 not-for-profit paper of a national interfaith network of congregations organizing for political change on progressive social issues, such as immigration reform, healthcare reform, housing reform, and prison reform. FBO community organizers work with religious congregations to listen to community needs and establish organizing committees of core activists within churches. Through these committees, organizers guide church members through the iterative process of listening to community concerns, researching solutions with issue experts, acting to educate and influence policymakers, and reflecting on their actions and progress. Throughout this process, the organizer usually trains committee members in leadership and organizing skills, such as how to develop a coherent and powerful personal story to share with the media, how to build community networks, how to lobby, and how to identify systemic problems in individual problems. Committee members can also attend FBO state and national conferences and organizing efforts, where they undergo more training and are exposed to more political opportunities.

The particular FBO paper I followed underwent a restructuring that significantly altered the organizing strategy of many of its organizers and provided an opportunity to observe the effects of two unique boundary-management strategies. In the original FBO organizing model, each paid organizer was assigned to a few churches that would pay the local FBO paper for their targeted organizing services. However, the Great Recession had significantly strained their funding streams and reduced the number of organizers they were able to hire. With only about three to four remaining organizers, this paper could no longer dedicate organizers to individual churches.

In a November 2013 meeting about eight months into the fieldwork, local FBO leaders presented their intention to assign some of their organizers to work more directly with particular denominations: one for Catholic Churches, one for Jewish synagogues, and one for Protestant churches, to become "faith specialists" that would revise FBO materials and strategies to better resonate with denominational traditions and worship cultures. This applied organizer talents more effectively by pairing them with denominational structures instead of individual churches, while at the same time addressing difficulties they had applying the one-size-fits-all faith-based approach. One of the organizers, Sandra, who also had a job at the Catholic Archdiocese, became the Catholic faith specialist and partnered with the Archdiocese HPC, headed by the Vicar for the Spanish-speaking, Father Jose, to launch a Catholic organizing effort.[3] Meanwhile, Gabriela, another organizer who was less embedded in religious life and had more experience in secular progressive organizing, continued to follow the FBO interfaith model of organizing. This organizational restructuring had a significant impact on the strategies pursued by the different organizers and their outcomes, and therefore provided an excellent opportunity to compare what I call the model-expanding organizing strategy with the new model-specializing strategy. While the traditional FBO organizing model portrayed FBO as an outside partner supporting social justice organizing efforts in individual churches, the new denominational model blurred distinctions between FBO and Catholic denominational organizations like the HPC, lending it increased legitimacy in the eyes of clergy, lay leaders, and parishioners.

DATA AND METHODS

The data for this paper come from two years of fieldwork in a Catholic Archdiocese covering three counties, including an immigrant gateway city, its suburbs and outlying rural areas. From March 2013 to March 2015, I observed and participated in regular organizational meetings, public events, recruitment attempts, and Catholic masses and small groups. I also attended churches that were not often approached by community organizers due to their geographic distance from FBO headquarters. I focused my observations on the same type of churches that organizers targeted: Catholic Churches with substantial Spanish-speaking populations and masses.

I supplemented participant observation with 41 semi-structured interviews with community organizers, immigrant parishioners and recruits, and church religious and lay leaders to construct organizational profiles and histories, explore church member attitudes about politics, and better understand religious leader positions and church responses to organizing strategies. In the second year of fieldwork, starting in May 2014, I began interviewing key people at the field sites, theoretically selecting interviewees to obtain variation in their level of involvement in the community organizing and their church. Interviews were conducted in Spanish and English and lasted about an hour on average, ranging from 30 minutes to over two hours.

Table 1 outlines interviewee ethnicity, immigrant generation, and their relationship to the churches studied. Thirty of these interviews were with first generation Hispanic immigrants of various national origins, an additional five were with second or later generation Latino church leaders, and the remaining were with non-Hispanic White church leaders. Of the immigrant group, 17 said they were undocumented at the time, and five said they had been undocumented in the past. Interviewees were primarily recruited through fieldwork connections, but I also reached out to religious leaders and other lay leaders at churches of interest using website contact information and snowball sampling. Additionally, a few church members uninvolved in the organizing were recruited for interviews through a needs assessment survey distributed throughout the parishes.

I present data here on the fieldwork observations, member attitudes, and recent organizational histories of eight Catholic Churches. Table 2 lists the churches by their aliases and key features. For more information on data collection and analysis, please see the methodological notes in Appendix.

Table 1. Interviewee Church Affiliation by Ethnicity and Immigrant Generation.

	Hispanic, 1st gen	Hispanic, 2nd gen +	Non-Hispanic, 3rd gen +	Total
FBO professional organizers	2	0	1	3
Religious leaders	5	0	2	7
Lay leaders	12	5	3	20
Parishioners	11	0	0	11
Total	30	5	6	41

Note: In addition to the FBO professional organizers, two of the immigrant parishioners were paid as part time organizers and spoke of their experiences: one before the research period and one toward the end of the research period (who was interviewed twice – before and after she acquired this role).

Table 2. Characteristics of Churches Observed in Fieldwork.

Church Alias	Religious Leader Aliases	Roles of Hispanic Religious Leaders	Pastor Change, 2013–2015	Clergy Campaign Position	Location	Sunday Spanish Masses	Ethnic Diversity	Religious Order
Our Lady of Providence	Father Daniel (former) Father Kevin (current) Father Luis (current) Deacon Enrique (current)	Associate Priest, Deacon	Yes	Indifferent	Suburb	1 out of 4	Mostly White, growing Hispanic	No
St. Frances X. Cabrini Church	Father Luis (former) Father Jose (current)	Pastor	Yes	Varied	City, Hispanic enclave	3 out of 5	Mostly Hispanic	No
St. John Bosco	Father Joe (former) Father Matt (former) Father Albano (former) Father Miguel (current)	Pastor	Yes	Varied	City	1 out of 5	Mostly Filipino and aging White, growing Hispanic	Salesians of Don Bosco
St. Joseph	Father Doherty (former) Father Antonio (current) Father Alberto (current)	Associate Priests, Deacon	Yes	Active	Suburb	2 out of 6	Majority Hispanic, large White, some Filipino, growing Chinese	No

Table 2. (Continued)

Church Alias	Religious Leader Aliases	Roles of Hispanic Religious Leaders	Pastor Change, 2013–2015	Clergy Campaign Position	Location	Sunday Spanish Masses	Ethnic Diversity	Religious Order
St. Lawrence the Martyr	Father Rafael (former) Father Elizondo (former) Father Campos (current)	Pastor	Yes	Varied	City, Hispanic enclave	2 out of 4	Mostly Hispanic	No
St. Martin de Porres	Father Peter Sister Maria	Nun	No	Active	City	1 out of 3	Mostly Black, growing Hispanic	Conventual Franciscan Friars
St. Nicholas	Father Jose (former) Father Lopez (current)	Pastor	Yes	Varied	City, Hispanic enclave	4 out of 5	Mostly Hispanic	No
St. Rose of Lima	Father Cu Father Morrison	Temporary/borrowed priests, Deacon	No	Resistant	City	1 out of 6	Mostly Filipino, aging White, growing Hispanic	No

Note: The religious leader lists only include those referenced in the text or pastors present during the research period.

THEORETICAL FRAMEWORK AND EMPIRICAL EVIDENCE

Institutional Constraints on Organizations

While the standard structural account of organization-based political engagement assumes that networks and skills developed in community organizations (even nonpolitical ones) easily transfer to political action, this ignores the reality of institutional practices and boundaries. Institutional scholars argue that organizational models associated with particular structures, practices, and logics help audiences categorize organizations and provide benchmarks upon which to evaluate them (Hannan, Pólos, & Carroll, 2007; Meyer & Rowan, 1977). To the extent that organizations deviate from established organizational models, they are more likely to provoke confusion and less support from their target audiences, especially when organizational practices appear to conflict with established institutionalized norms in the field (Hannan et al., 2007; Phillips, Turco, & Zuckerman, 2013). In this way, conformity, or at least symbolic conformity, with established organizational models improves organizational survival (Carroll & Swaminathan, 2000; DiMaggio & Powell, 1983; Hannan et al., 2007; Hsu, Hannan, & Koçak, 2009; Meyer & Rowan, 1977; Zuckerman, 1999). Organizations that are difficult to classify, such as generalist organizations spanning multiple market categories, are outperformed when competing with specialist organizations focusing on one market niche (Carroll & Swaminathan, 2000; Hannan & Freeman, 1977; Hannan et al., 2007; Hsu et al., 2009; Zuckerman, 1999; Zuckerman & Kim, 2003; Zuckerman, Kim, Ukanwa, & von Rittman, 2003).

To the extent that churches deviate from their established organizational model and diversify into non-routine activities and programs, they may face penalties in the form of deceased support from their primary membership, especially when they diversify into programs that appear to undermine their primary missions, either through ideological conflict or the reallocation of resources (Coddou, 2015; Phillips et al., 2013). For example, McDaniel (2008) found that the black Protestant church members he interviewed were more open to church political advocacy when the church was not financially struggling to sustain fundamental programs and facilities. In an experimental manipulation of church programs, Coddou (2015) found that as program domain distance increased, support and approval for the church decreased. Specifically, political advocacy incurred significantly higher penalties than social service provision, and political advocacy on "non-moral issues," such as immigration or climate change, invited higher penalties than political advocacy on "moral issues," such as gay marriage. Moreover, these findings are consistent with surveys showing that church participation in political advocacy is relatively low, with church participation in non-electoral activities such as lobbying and demonstrating estimated at less than 10% in 2006–2007, and voter registration at 18% (Chaves & Anderson, 2008). Taken together, these findings suggest that expansion of domain boundaries can be hazardous for religious institutions.

Parishioner Perceptions of the Institutional Boundary between Religion and Politics

The institutional boundary between religion and politics was salient to organizers, religious leaders, and church members, and managing that boundary was a critical part of recruiting church members into political organizing. One of most effective criticisms organizers could receive from church religious leaders was that they were engaged in politics or were "too political." As nonprofits, churches are legally barred from campaigning and contributing to political candidates. While all religious leaders I interacted with agreed that campaigning for political candidates was out of the question, they varied in how they categorized other politically influential activities. Some religious leaders saw speaking out against "structural sin," through protesting, lobbying, educating, and raising awareness around particular social issues, to be central to the church's mission, while others avoided such activities.

Immigrant parishioners expressed very different levels of trust for actors in the religious domain and the political domain. In contrast to almost all other social institutions, where undocumented immigrants feared exposure of their status and deportation, churches were one of the few spaces where immigrants felt safe. No one had ever heard of any raids or detentions at a church, and immigrants generally trusted that their religious leaders would not lead them into any harm or take advantage of them. Carlos, an elderly immigrant parishioner from St. Rose explained to me in mass one day as we were waiting to meet the newest Spanish mass priest:

> The priest is very important. He protects the people of his church and people have a lot of trust in him because they think, a priest isn't going to try to scam me, because a lot of people do try to take advantage of the community, saying they are going to provide a service or do something for someone, and then they take money, and they don't do anything, so the support of the priest is important because they know that the priest won't lead them into anything bad.

Sanctified Mobilization

The trust parishioners placed in the priest put churches in a unique position to support undocumented immigrants that organizers recognized. Erica, a lay leader and immigrant organizer explained:

> The Catholic church I go to, here where I live, the area has a lot of immigrant field workers, so almost all of them go to the Catholic Church [...] so they congregate there and you know that we always have respect for a priest, what the priest says. There's more trust. People feel more welcomed, more trusting in the church. So we try to do all we can in the church so they feel more trusting, more open, because if you invite them to other places, it doesn't give them that trust, not at all.

Organizers and immigrant activists were aware of the special trust immigrants placed in their church leaders and made every effort to acquire the support of religious leaders and host meetings and events within church walls.

On the other hand, almost all immigrant churchgoers interviewed, involved in the immigrant rights campaign or not, either expressed distaste for politics as corrupt and self-serving or simply had no interest in political action. When asked about what politics meant to her, Mercedes, a middle-aged immigrant parishioner at St. Joseph said, "Not credible ... Many times we promise things in order to obtain a position − right? − and we don't follow through. Pure politics." Politicians were untrustworthy and would say anything to be elected, after which they would do only what served them. Teresa, a lay leader very involved in prayer groups at St. Nicholas, explained that politics as she perceived it was never of any interest to her:

> Politics is not something that interests me much, or it was something that I was always indifferent to, something I didn't want to get involved in because politics made me think of liars, or at least the experience in my country is always − more politicians are corrupt or you know that they are robbing and doing things.

In talking with immigrant churchgoers, there appeared to be a clear distinction between the roles played by priests, who put their community's interests first and protected people, and politicians, who put their own interests first and would lie and scam people in pursuit of their own interests.

Furthermore, some immigrant parishioners suggested that engaging in political organizing work had a polluting effect on activists, making them seem more like corrupt, self-serving politicians, and less like good Catholics. Concepción, a middle-aged lay leader who was a political activist in her home country, suggested that political participation made activists seem like politicians themselves, which was contrary to serving the church:

> When you get involved in politics, you want to shine, that your leadership shines, that others see that you are a good person and that others see that you can mobilize people, that you can attract people, that you are a good leader in that sense. No, leadership in

the Church is totally different because Christ is the one that shines. It's Christ that does things, not us.

Participating in politics made people seem self-serving, glorifying their own accomplishments without paying tribute to God. However, Concepción understood the FBO-sponsored immigrant rights campaign as a way of serving God, in that any victories they had would glorify God in His mercy and power. This made organizing through the church different from her activism for women's rights in her home country, which she denounced. Gabi, a lay leader at St. Lawrence who was not involved in the campaign, also suggested a polluting effect:

> I don't know why in all the countries they make the case that when someone gets really involved in a political issue, it's like people see that person as a politician, and it's not true, because I can be involved in a political issue, but from my perspective of being a Christian ... but it's something that people don't manage to understand, so because of that, many times we don't get involved in things like that.

There was no organizing effort happening at Gabi's church at the time that could have provided her with an avenue to participating that was considered appropriate and in line with church teaching, so she thought it better to not engage politically at all. In fact, when I asked her whether anyone had ever invited her to participate in a number of political activities, such as signing a petition or attending a rally, she said, "No, no one has invited me, thank God." For those parishioners who perceived opposing principles in religion and politics, church participation made political engagement less likely.

The Role of Leaders in Defining Organization Domains

The salient institutional boundary between religion and politics presents a puzzle: given the rift, how can we explain church facilitation of member political action? While the emphasis in previous literature is decidedly structural — members' gain access to church networks and their associated resources and information, including political information — a number of studies suggest that religious leaders play an important interpretive role for members, translating political action into mission-consistent terms (Cavendish, 2001; Heredia, 2011; McAdam & Paulsen, 1993). As high status religious authorities, religious leaders can provide legitimacy to new forms of action, increasing their value to members (McAdam & Paulsen, 1993; Rao, Monin, & Durand, 2003). For example, in Heredia's (2011) study of the Catholic Church's involvement in the 2006 immigrant rights demonstrations, the Los Angeles (LA) Catholic Archdiocese channeled traditional religious activities into public, politically influential events, imbuing protest with religious meaning. Religious leaders organized prayer vigils, processions, masses, and collective fasting to pray for politicians to support a just immigration reform (Heredia, 2011). Likewise, Cavendish (2001) found that a priest emphasizing the proselytizing function of church-sponsored anti-drug marches mobilized more participants than priests at the same church who shared information about the marches, but did not make the religious connection clear to congregants. In this way, religious leaders and activists can help members fit political engagement into their routine church participation (Cavendish, 2001; Harris, 1999; McAdam, 1982; McDaniel & McClerking, 2005; McDaniel, 2008; Morris, 1984; Wood, 2002).

Two Strategies: Expanding Church Domains or Working within Them

Aware of the need to make their work relevant to religious communities, community organizers adopted a number of practices to distance themselves from politics and portray their work as not just consistent with, but integral to, religious belief and practice. Generally, this involved incorporating religious rituals, practices, and terminology in meetings and events, referencing religious texts and doctrines, and drawing on spiritual or divine inspiration to motivate organizing. These practices gave parishioners a means of getting involved that was initially familiar to them while steeping the work in an inspiring and hopeful religious message. The incorporation of political activity in the religious realm opened an avenue to political influence for those who had initially expressed little interest in politics.

As mentioned previously, during the two-year fieldwork period, organizers pursued two distinct boundary-management strategies that employed these distancing practices in different ways. Under the strategy FBO employed primarily at the beginning of the fieldwork, which I call the model-expanding strategy, organizers sought to expand church institutional domains to include traditional political activities, such as demonstrating and lobbying, by infusing these activities with religious meaning and symbolism. They distinguished themselves from other political groups by highlighting their moral message and inspiration in faith, and characterized their work as "bringing the Kingdom of Heaven to Earth" by advocating for just laws through routine political engagement. Under the second strategy, which I call the model-specializing strategy, organizers worked within established church institutional boundaries to make routine religious activity, such as religious masses, organized prayer, and charitable services, politically influential making them issue-focused and media-oriented. Each strategy's definition of the agent of change, the appropriate tactics, and the potential recruits reflected their institutional goals (expanding or specializing) and interacted with religious leader response to shape the character and level of recruitment and mobilization into the FBO-sponsored immigrant rights campaign.

Perceived Agent of Change

The conceptualization of the agent of change was the most fundamental difference between the two strategies and motivated the tactics organizers pursued. This was reflected in the way grievances were directed and victories were interpreted. While the model-expanding strategy conceptualized the agents of change as policymakers and government officials, the model-specializing strategy placed God at the center of claims making. In the model-expanding strategy, the work was conceptualized as exercising a "prophetic voice" by demanding that policymakers relieve suffering and make the world a more moral place through the enactment of just laws. The model-specializing strategy conceived of campaign goals as glorifying and praying to God so He would intercede in the world on their behalf. The organizer, Sandra's, interpretation of a common biblical story referenced in the fieldwork, the Exodus story of Moses leading the Israelites out of Egypt, exemplifies the shift. In the model-expanding strategy, the story of Moses represented the ability of a common, unassuming person to answer God's call to liberate his people from slavery. Sandra and other organizers often used it in reflections to inspire and motivate immigrant participants to take on leadership when they did not feel prepared to do so. At one meeting, Sandra described it like this:

> God talked to Moses through the burning bush and told him to lead his people out of slavery, and Moses said, who me? I'm not up to this, I'm no good, I'm a nobody, and God said, just do it! And even though he was an ordinary, common person and didn't believe in himself, God believed in him, and he was able to do it. He was scared, but he did it anyway. We are like Moses. [Other organizations] have their people pouring money into this, donating to political campaigns, and advocating for their own amendments and policies, and we don't have those resources, but we have our suffering and our numbers. We have our core people, but FBO also represents 33 churches in this city, thousands of people, and we can speak for them and with our numbers, put pressure on our legislators and talk about the morality of this. We as Latinos need to

organize and work together and tell our stories because we feel this, our families feel this, and our friends feel this. We don't have money, or education, or documentation, but we have heart, and we have suffering, and we have numbers.

After FBO shifted to the model-specializing strategy, this story took on a new meaning. The focus shifted from Moses' characteristics and actions to God's response to his people's prayers. Sandra later retold the story at an organizing meeting:

> I was talking to Father Charles, and he was telling me about how in Exodus – which talks about the Israelites, and how they were enslaved, and the Pharaoh abused and exploited them – how in Exodus, God is never mentioned once until it says, "and God heard the cries of his people," and then he responds by telling Moses to lead them out of Egypt. That's what we are doing here. We can't rely on politicians or lawyers. Politics is a game, and they are playing a game with each other and with us, but God will hear our prayers and listen. So, when we meet and we do these masses, we are asking God for his help, and God can do anything. Just look at the miracles he has given us. For the first mass, Yéssica was released [from detention]. Then, for the second mass, Victor was released.

Under the model-specializing strategy, instead of using the story to argue that God wanted immigrants to liberate their people by mobilizing parishioners to put political pressure on politicians, Sandra used it to argue that if they prayed in their immigration reform mass, God would intercede on their behalf and facilitate reform through divine intervention. In this strategy, organizers and participants claimed that politicians were just playing political games and could not be trusted – only God could change hearts and minds and bring reform. As these two interpretations of the story also exemplify, the shift in strategy did not just lead to a change in the direction of grievances, but a change in how victories were interpreted.

While using the model-expanding strategy, Sandra often focused on explaining victories in terms of their ability influence politicians, through the political pressure of their numbers or the moral message behind their personal testimonies. However, using the model-specializing strategy, she attributed victories to divine intervention. In one instance under the model-expanding strategy, when a couple of Republican congresspersons signed on to cosponsor a comprehensive immigration reform bill in the House of Representatives, Sandra emphasized that the group had successfully pressured them through a state-wide pilgrimage for immigration reform and church forums that the congresspersons attended. In the same meeting, Sandra explained the impact of daily vigils they had organized outside of a senator's office:

> [The senator] met with some faith leaders last week and mentioned the vigils – she said that she knew the group was standing there every day and admired their persistence and consistency, so the vigils made a difference.

In line with this interpretation, participants who lobbied their public officials expressed amazement and empowerment when legislators responded warmly and sympathetically — they felt that they really had made a difference by telling their story. At one organizing meeting, Rosie, a young member of a small evangelical church, recounted her experience:

> Rosie said she went to a legislator's office to tell her story. The FBO organizers had taught her how to refine her story into a three-minute story or five lines, and she practiced. Then, when she arrived at the office, she didn't expect there to be cameras, but there were reporters there to film her story, and that made her really nervous. She didn't know if it were the cameras, or reliving the story by telling it, but while she told it, she started to cry and couldn't stop crying the whole time. At the end, everyone was really moved. She got the sense that they really did sympathize with her and she had made a difference by telling her story and putting a human face on the issue.

In the model-expanding strategy, while organizers and participants were inspired by their faith, they attributed their accomplishments to their own actions. They were using tactics common in political repertoires to connect with politicians on the basis of a shared faith or sense of morality. Months later, under the model-specializing strategy, when immigrants were released from ICE[4] or Obama introduced a new deferred action program, Sandra instead interpreted it as a miracle. This perspective was echoed by lay leaders. In one meeting in January, we were talking about our personal goals for 2015, and Manuel, a lay leader from St. Nicholas, said:

> My main mission this year is to deepen my faith, because it's only through God that anything happens in this world. For example, this deferred action program — Obama could have done that years before, any time, but he did it in that moment, and he made the announcement on the day of our immigration mass, and it happened because God made it so. I believe it happened that way for a reason, and that if we pray and have faith in God and keep working for God, then eventually, He will give us the reform we need.

While lay leaders under the model-specializing strategy also felt empowered by the work, it was because their policy victories were evidence that God supported them, which filled them with hope, joy, and gratitude. By organizing the masses, they had glorified God in his mercy, and God had answered their prayers. This way of interpreting social justice victories fit neatly into how they discussed and understood life's events in their routine church participation, facilitating their participation in the campaign without the need for a cognitive leap.

Organizing Tactics

While the two strategies shared some tactics in common, such as press conferences, marches/processions, immigration forums, and deportation support services, the model-expanding strategy relied more on routine political activity, such as lobbying and protesting, while the model-specializing strategy drew primarily on routine religious activity, specifically religious masses and organized prayer.

In the model-expanding strategy, organizers trained and guided recruits in grassroots political skills, information, and tactics, but presented them as domain consistent through the use of religious terminology and symbolism. Immigrants organized public "vigils" in support of immigration reform in front of immigrant detention centers and the offices of elected officials, in which they told their stories, sang religious songs, chanted, displayed their demands on posters, gave legislative and deportation case updates, and occasionally did public theater to illustrate the crimes against them in detention centers. About a dozen immigrant activists marched across the state on a "pilgrimage" for a pathway to citizenship, stopping at the offices of elected officials and churches along the way to lobby and raise awareness. At a rally in front of a congressperson's office, immigrants constructed a giant altar, and another rally was organized around an interfaith group of religious leaders washing the feet of undocumented immigrants, a religiously symbolic act of serving those who are stigmatized in recognition of their equality in God's eyes. In this way, grassroots political acts such as lobbying, marching, and rallying were presented as grounded in a living faith. In phone-banking voters or meeting with public officials, immigrants were encouraged to reference their church affiliation to establish themselves as moral citizens in a community of faith. While faith grounded and motivated their entrance into the political sphere, the activities they participated in were fundamentally political. However, organizers avoided the brand of "politics" at all cost due to the perceptions of boundary violation it provoked, instead opting for the term "social justice" to incorporate their activities into church missions.

On the other hand, tactics under the model-specializing strategy primarily revolved around routine religious activity, especially the religious mass and organized prayer. Organizing meetings that had originally involved structured religious reflection, leadership training, and political action planning, now focused almost entirely on planning a monthly religious mass for immigration reform. Immigrant lay leaders took charge in assigning mass roles (lectors, Eucharistic ministers, ushers, etc.), organizing the liturgy, music, and programs, corresponding with religious and lay leaders, announcing the masses in a number of local churches, and coordinating the mass on the day of the event. The mass was usually led by the pastor of St. Frances Cabrini, Father Jose, but was also led by an Archdiocese bishop on two occasions and attended by other local priests serving Hispanic Catholics in their parishes. It was scheduled once a month on Friday evenings and was usually accompanied by another event, such as a press conference with immigrant testimonials, a procession around the neighborhood, or an information forum on an immigrant-relevant issue, such as how undocumented parishioners could register for a driver's license. While the masses were distinct in that they were organized on the topic of immigration, the focus on mass planning and participation allowed church members, especially religious leaders and lay leaders, to support the cause through their routine religious activity and expected roles in the church.

Whereas many events under the model-expanding strategy took place in public spaces and legislator offices, under the model-specializing strategy, almost all activities took place at the church, with one exception – an occasional rosary at deportation and detention hearings. The rosary is a structured meditation and prayer usually taking about 20 minutes and involving the repetition of a number of prayers and a reflection on five "Mysteries," of which there are 20 centered on events in the life of Jesus.[5] As one might imagine, knowledge of how to pray the rosary is a specialized Catholic skill. One rosary prayed before an immigration hearing offers a point of comparison between the two strategies:

> We congregated at the ICE building to attend the hearing of Yéssica. She had crossed the border about a year earlier, fleeing domestic violence and kidnapping in her home country to join her mother in the United States, and had been detained ever since. Outside, Sandra thanked everyone for coming and reminded us of the mass on Friday, then told Yéssi's story. She said we'd start with a prayer, and everyone held hands as Concepción's daughter, Veronica, started with a personal prayer for Yéssi and other immigrants in her situation, then led the rosary as the cameras looked on. We prayed sometimes in call and response, sometimes all together, repeating a number of prayers. Some people remained silent. Sandra joined for the first part, then broke off to talk to the reporters. This went on for some time. When the rosary ended, Sandra said that those who had ID's could go inside while the others could remain outside praying. This marked the end of the demonstration and we went inside to watch the hearing.

Previously, under the model-expanding strategy, ICE vigils to release immigrants from detention were shows for the press, incorporating public theater, loud chanting and singing, testimonials, and speeches. The purpose of this event, however, seemed to be the rosary prayer itself, which was fervent, but solemn in comparison. Those who attended were there to pray for Yéssi and accompany her at her hearing. Others who could not attend prayed and communicated with the group via text message to show their support.

In short, while the model-expanding strategy attempted to mobilize churchgoers into public political activity by incorporating religious terminology and symbols, the model-specializing strategy provided an opportunity for churchgoers to join the cause through routine religious activity, made public through media attention.

Membership Definitions

Finally, the two strategies emphasized different membership definitions in their conceptualization of potential recruits and supporters, again representing a shift toward a more institutionally specialized organizing strategy. While under both strategies, organizers targeted Hispanic immigrant families in Catholic Churches, the first conceptualized potential supporters as immigrant Latinos and allies of all faiths, while the second focused specifically on Hispanic Catholics. Exemplifying the model-expanding strategy, Ana, an elderly long time immigrant activist in the group, emphasized at one meeting: This group is not about religion, it's about faith, and there are no distinctions – we don't try to limit this by religion – we can all work together. In response, immigrant participants did not limit recruitment to their churches, but invited co-workers, family members, college students, and friends from advocacy organizations, support groups, and even their children's dance classes. They stopped the deportation of a Mormon family, and included members who attended small evangelical churches, as well as students from the local community college who said they weren't religious. This broad swath of participants meant that faith was often referenced in general, simple terms so that even those who were not very religious could speak freely about it. Sandra, knowing there were some people attending who were not very religious, introduced one reflection on a prayer written by Archbishop Oscar Romero with the disclaimer: even though FBO is a religious organization, no matter what your beliefs, we can all find inspiration in different stories.

On the other hand, when using the model-specializing strategy, Sandra often emphasized that their focus was now on Hispanic Catholics, saying in one meeting: In the past, we have done a wide information campaign, but I think now we need to focus in on our own people, the Hispanic Catholics.

At first, this shift prompted confusion on the part of long-term members, as this interaction at one of the initial mass planning meetings demonstrates:

> Grecia suggested, what about Honorio for the music? Sandra responded playfully, but my dear, Honorio is a *Mormon*! Grecia looked as if she hadn't expected this response and Sandra offered, it's because he has that great marimba band right? To which Grecia smiled and nodded and Sandra continued, it's a great band and it would be nice to have marimba ... we can ask, but I don't know, since it's a Catholic mass and everything. Grecia's friend, Beatriz, said that she knew people who would be interested in coming, but they go to different churches, and are not Catholic, but this affects us all, regardless of religion, so shouldn't they invite more people? Ana affirmed that it was an interfaith organization based on faith, not religion, and Sandra relented, you're welcome to invite them, of course, everyone is welcome, but this will be a Catholic mass, so it's going to involve Catholic rituals and isn't going to be an ecumenical service, but there will be other opportunities to get the wider community involved, like for the march or for other educational events.

The group's new focus on specialized Catholic tactics required an associated shift in membership. Since most regular participants in the group were Catholics, it did not result in the loss of many participants. Sandra rebranded the group as an official Catholic Archdiocese group, printing shirts and fliers with the new title, the HPC for Social Justice, with FBO portrayed as a partner organization. Their portrayal as a Catholic group then eased their entry into Catholic Churches.

Sources of Conflict and Recruitment Outcomes under each Strategy

Each strategy's management of the institutional boundary between religion and politics led to distinct internal conflicts and recruitment into the core-organizing group. When the model-expanding strategy failed to broker the boundary, it provoked a sense of unease and skepticism among those more deeply embedded in religious life, producing a core organizing team mostly composed of peripheral church members.[6] Conversely, the model-specializing strategy's high valuation of Catholic skills and networks and subsequent rise in lay leader participation led to the exclusion of peripheral church members from core leadership and planning positions.

The model-expanding strategy's attempt to broker the boundary between religion and politics while casting a wide net could unsettle deeply religious church lay leaders. While FBO attempted to attract churchgoers by incorporating religious messages and rituals into traditional political activity, its focus on influencing policymakers made it difficult for lay leaders to make sense of it in the context of their routine church participation. As lay leaders tended to dedicate most of their free time to church ministries, their inability to place FBO within that context disrupted their identity and challenged their involvement. For example, Teresa, a lay leader recruited through an immigration forum at St. Nicholas in Fall 2013, was initially one of the only core activists deeply engaged in religious life through prayer groups and Sunday service. While she initially contributed by directing altar construction for a rally, she often struggled to make sense of her involvement. She reflected in an interview:

> I haven't visualized myself as an organizer. I've been searching: so, Lord, why have you brought me to this group? What is the mission or why do you have me here? Well, finally I've discovered it. I went to a training and I started to do the prayer. We started to pray and Sandra said, "You go." And I said, ok Lord, you wanted me to go to this training because that day, Claudia, who usually did the prayer, didn't come and they chose me to do it [...] So, the way I see it, my mission here at [FBO] is to introduce a little bit of God in the work or deepen a bit the understanding of God.

After this revelation, Teresa used meeting time traditionally reserved for brief religious reflections to give long presentations on Catholic religious teaching lasting from 30 minutes to an hour. While Sandra encouraged her to assume this role, eventually Teresa stopped participating in order to attend job-training classes. Ultimately, because there was no sustained, organizing work happening in her church and the political activities FBO promoted were foreign to her, she perceived her participation in the group as separate from her routine church participation. While Teresa saw that the group had good intentions and the faith-based approach appealed to her, she had difficulty making sense of it within the context of her other religious commitments.

While FBO's boundary stretching confused some lay leaders, it provoked skepticism and resistance in others who believed FBO was instrumentally using religion to gain access to church social and material resources and advance its own political interests (consistent with attitudes toward politicians). When one of the FBO organizers, Gabriela, first started organizing a listening campaign at St. Joseph, she faced opposition from a social outreach group at the church that was seeded by FBO years before. They warned the priests of FBO's ulterior political motives, suggesting it was a political organization in religious clothing. At a meeting between these lay leaders and Father Alberto, a priest supporting the FBO listening campaign, Sara, an elderly Filipina woman, told the priest that

FBO was too confrontational, with marches and rallies attacking officials. Ethel, a middle-aged White immigrant added:

> Social justice is just a term they use to get into the churches, but it masks their true political tactics. It's pure politics, but the way our group does it is to support the community as Jesus would want us to. We walk with Jesus and do it Jesus' way ... We are a cross-section of the church, representing all groups, and we don't agree, but we respect each other – we are not all Democrats or Republicans, but we respect each others' beliefs and we work based on consensus and look for common ground.

After the meeting, Sara told me that two church members with deportation orders who had given their testimony outside a congressperson's office had been taken advantage of, that they were paraded out there by FBO in a way that was beneath their dignity. Even though the event she spoke of included a foot-washing ceremony, religious music, and prayers, the act of holding the event at a congressperson's office as a protest pressure tactic made the event appear too politicized and therefore inappropriate to these lay leaders. They were deeply skeptical of FBO's use of religion under the model-expanding strategy and rejected it as instrumental and calculating. This tension meant that lay leaders usually only joined the organizing effort if their priests actively supported the work, which was relatively rare. As a result, most of FBO's core members under the model-expanding strategy were parishioners peripheral to church networks, who were inspired by the religious message but didn't have strong identity-based connections to the church.

The transition to the model-specializing strategy produced new challenges for FBO, as recruitment and tactics shifted from multi-faith and fundamentally political to firmly Catholic and fundamentally religious. Non-Catholics had very little involvement after this, and peripheral church members found their contribution to the group challenged by lay leaders who had more religious training and greater access to influential church networks. For example, the planning and substantive participation in mass as a lector or Eucharistic minister required formal Catholic training, limiting the contribution of peripheral church members who were usually assigned roles as greeters or ushers and had little say in mass planning meetings. On one occasion, Carlos, an elderly parishioner at St. Rose and dedicated FBO member, was assigned the position of usher at the mass. When he presented himself at his post on the day of the event, Simon, a prominent lay leader, told him they didn't need him. Relating the story to me at lunch one day, he told me he was hurt by his inability to contribute and felt like he couldn't offer anything of value to the group.

Sanctified Mobilization 49

Even when peripheral churchgoers did possess religious skills or connections, they viewed them as painfully insufficient compared to the newly recruited Catholic lay leaders. Even simple acts such as the opening and closing prayers at meetings became intimidating to peripheral church members. Concepción and her family had been volunteering to say the prayers for a few meetings when one day, Sandra asked Carlos to close a meeting with a prayer:

> Carlos smiled uneasily and said, no no no, this lady should do it, gesturing to Concepción. Sandra warmly encouraged him to go ahead and do it, adding that he said such lovely prayers. He continued to humbly refuse as we joined hands, until one of Concepción's daughters volunteered to do it.

Carlos had attended church throughout his life, but the presence of perceived experts made him feel self-conscious. Later, I asked Maricela, another parishioner at St. Rose, about this in an interview, and she reasoned:

> I feel like the new people who arrived feel closer to God, closer to what's correct. I feel like there was an intimidating impact on other people who aren't so religious, and yes, I think that it dispersed our group [...] I feel like people who aren't so involved in church, we feel ashamed of saying something incorrect about religion, or we feel an insecurity that if I say this, and it's not well said, they are going to correct that or they're going to see me in a bad light because I said that, or better to be in the back and quiet than say something that is going to be bad.

The re-conceptualization of the organizing work as fundamentally Catholic suddenly disadvantaged peripheral church members for the same reasons they were marginal members of their church. Lay leaders took charge of publicizing events as well, invoking their close connections with pastors, small group leaders, and religious institutions, and making peripheral members feel as though their contributions in this sphere were pointless and redundant:

> Concepción said that she was attending three different churches that weekend, including Grecia's church, St. Lawrence, and would ask the pastors if she could give an announcement at the pulpit. After most people had volunteered to inform their churches about the mass, Sandra asked Grecia where she would go. Usually very upbeat and optimistic, Grecia shrugged uncomfortably and said that everyone else was already handling it. Sandra said she would give her a spreadsheet of previous mass attendees to call and find her a church to visit.

Even though Grecia attended St. Lawrence on a regular basis, she deferred to Concepción's insider connections as a highly involved lay leader. At another meeting, Concepción was listing the pastors and small groups she had visited to talk about the immigration mass and mentioned

Father Rios, a pastor that Carlos had a good relationship with. At the mention of Father Rios, Carlos opened his mouth as if he wanted to speak, but decided against it. Even the connections peripheral parishioners did have felt redundant and less legitimate compared to lay leaders. While the strategy shift to a specialized Catholic approach successfully attracted those deeply embedded in Catholic religious life, it had the effect of sidelining the peripheral church members who had previously led the group.

Mobilization Outcomes and Reliance on Religious Leaders

Religious leaders played an important mobilizing role under both strategies, but each strategy placed distinct demands on them, which had implications for their participation and criticality to the organizing effort. Under the model-expanding strategy, organizers relied heavily on the active participation of religious leaders to validate and legitimize non-routine activities, such as lobbying and rallying, as within the church's domain. At the same time, the fact that organizing activities were non-routine made it difficult for priests to sustain their active involvement in the face of competing religious duties, especially in the financially struggling churches where immigrants were most likely to congregate. In contrast, the model-specializing strategy's use of routine religious activities, such as the religious mass and organized prayer, not only required less validation from religious leaders, but also gave them the opportunity to support the cause through their established institutionalized roles, facilitating their participation.

Necessary but Fragile Clergy Involvement under the Model-Expanding Strategy

Under the model-expanding strategy, the active involvement of church religious leaders was crucial to the success (or failure) of the organizing effort. Within the same church community over time, participation in FBO campaigns would wax and wane with priest support. Catholic religious leaders, and especially pastors, wield substantial power relative to lay leaders over the direction of the churches they lead, and are treated with a great deal of respect and deference on issues of church practice and policy. Eduardo, a middle-aged lay leader at Our Lady of Providence (OLP), who had recently experienced two pastor changes and two associate priest changes in the past four years, explained:

> It's very important, independent of how the priest comes in and his form of working – and there is a lot of difference – it's important that we as a church are obedient. They are the head and as they want to work, we are going to work.

The power and deference accorded to the pastor in church decision-making meant that parishioners often looked to their pastor to determine valued, expected forms of participation. This was especially true of lay leaders who devoted themselves to the church and looked to the pastor to direct their participation in appropriate and meaningful avenues. Father Peter, the pastor at St. Martin, suggested that lay leader participation in social justice activities relied heavily on his position as pastor:

> I've found that when I was the associate [priest], it did seem like the people who were working for me in these justice issues were people outside the mainstream leadership in the church, but once I became pastor, that got much more crowded. And because – to a large extent, I find that people respond more to Father Peter, and whatever Father Peter wants, rather than what the real valued issue is [...] Once I became pastor, it's, "Whatever the pastor wants, we'll do." [...] I might be speaking out of prejudice, but there's this – a mindset that there are people who are very passionate about church who want to really help out, and the way that you help out in their mind, or also if, unless you have a really well-organized structure, is you ask the pastor, "What do you want me to do, Father? I'll do whatever you want." And so, no matter what the pastor says, they go, "Okay, yes, Father." And so their intent is just to help out the church, which is very good and very noble.

Aside from defining valued church activities for lay leaders, priests also played an important role in motivating church participation in social justice activities and managing any boundary conflicts. While lay leaders from the social outreach ministry at St. Joseph expressed shock and concern over the fact that FBO organizers had held an event at their church, they were very mindful of their priests' support of the event and whether FBO had "gone through the proper channels" in getting approval from their pastor, Father Doherty, or Father Alberto, one of the Spanish-speaking priests. Elena, one of the lay leaders at the meeting told me in our interview:

> I trust Father Doherty, and I trust that when Father Alberto decided to move forward, he'd had a strong conversation with Father Doherty, and that's when I voiced that [...] and so for me, if Father Doherty is ok with it, I am too.

Father Alberto played a critical role in gaining FBO's access to church networks and the trust of its members. He held meetings with FBO organizers and social outreach ministry members to reconcile the two groups, then brought the project to the parish's Hispanic Committee, where the leaders of the Spanish-speaking groups and ministries convened, and asked lay leaders to schedule times with organizers for focus groups about problems facing the community. They complied, and organizers hosted a presentation and listening session in each group. The director of religious education, a paid staff layperson, attended all organizing meetings to help coordinate church actions. One of the most dedicated Hispanic lay leaders at the church opened an organizing meeting with a religious reflection, and other lay leaders attended immigration forums and joined the regular organizing meetings. An event held to report on the results of the listening campaign attracted about 75 parishioners and lay leaders, and was attended by Father Alberto and local officials. However, after the listening campaign report, Father Alberto was asked by the Archdiocese to help with an ecclesiastical tribunal, which took up a great deal of his time and limited his involvement in the organizing work. While the FBO committee formed at his church continued to meet and work together, the number of parishioners they were able to attract to meetings and events dwindled. As the group's activities appeared largely political in nature (attending and speaking at City Council meetings, hosting research meetings with experts on housing policy, and organizing marches), without the priest's active support, lay leaders were largely indifferent to the group, and the core organizing team was largely composed of peripheral church members.

The importance of religious leaders in sanctioning non-routine activities under the model-expanding strategy was especially evident in churches that had experienced many changes in pastors and associate priests. When church leaders were indifferent to social justice work, organizers were allowed to make announcements or use church space for meetings and events, but usually only a small group of peripheral church members got involved, and largely considered it separate from their church involvement. Tony, a long time FBO-affiliate at St. John Bosco told me:

> It's always felt separate because the pastors have never really supported what we've done. Father Joe supported the youth center, but after that there was no real — it always felt like we were tolerated. Then there was one pastor, Father Matt, who really embraced it and turned out a lot of people, especially in the Hispanic community, because he was Hispanic, but basically the stress of being a pastor ... how long was he here? Nine months? ... So we had him for a year and then no support from the pastor, and it really is hard to keep things moving ... [Father Matt] got it from the beginning, he got it. He believed in social justice. When it came time for things to happen, he just, you know, he got up on the pulpit and did not say, "There's a march," he said, "We are going to ..." We put two busses full of people to [the state capitol].

Sanctified Mobilization 53

While Tony could tell me in detail about all of the local organizations and agencies they worked with on health care, housing, and youth campaigns, it always felt like something separate from his church involvement, even though it started in the church and they held regular meetings in the church. Not until the pastor was involved and explicitly made social justice work a central church ministry did it feel like a church effort. During the fieldwork, St. John Bosco had an associate priest supportive of the organizing work, Father Miguel, but he was soon named interim pastor and overwhelmed by other tasks. Father Miguel's actions around an FBO announcement about an upcoming immigration reform rally highlights the interpretive work that priests did to motivate participation in political activities. First, he addressed the issue of immigration reform directly in his homily, using the day's biblical reading about a governor to argue that God wants us to bring the Kingdom of Heaven to earth, asking everyone to repeat this line from the Lord's Prayer together, and said that this was the responsibility of all Catholics. He claimed that the immigration system divided people – papers, no papers – when our goal should be to unify people because we are all God's children. He further argued that Catholics are called to help the poor, the needy, and suffering as Jesus did, and put them first, which is why they needed to work for reform. When it came time for one of the activists, Yennifer, to give the announcement and her testimony about her case, Father Miguel stood up next to her and emphasized how important this work was. Afterwards, many people approached us for more information in the foyer, and Father Miguel gave Yennifer the schedule for a few upcoming church group meetings to present in. A large group of church members from St. John Bosco later attended an October rally. However, his promotion to interim pastor limited his participation, and we saw a subsequent decrease in parishioner involvement in later events.

St. Lawrence also went through pastor changes over the years that significantly impacted the organizing there under the model-expanding strategy. Ana, a long time FBO affiliate who had attended St. Lawrence since she arrived in the United States about 30 years ago, said that the previous pastor, Father Rafael, had been very supportive of their campaign to construct affordable housing in the neighborhood:

> Father Rafael participated with us and he went to the meetings and when there were actions, he was there, and he went to speak with the mayor. When they had already constructed the building at 20th and Florida,[7] through him we communicated with the mayor and through him we had a lot of participation in that, and all the people here, like 25 families, got apartments there, because he was very active.

Ana recounted that at that time, they had organizing meetings as large as 50 people and actions as large as 250 people in the church cafeteria, but currently there were fewer organizers and Father Rafael was replaced by Father Elizondo, who did not support the work, and consequently, there were only two people — Ana and Grecia — who attended FBO meetings from St. Lawrence. Ana reviewed some of the changes:

> I'm sure that with other pastors we always had the cafeteria to do actions, we always did them there in the cafeteria. I'm sure that with Father Elizondo, he would not have allowed it because he doesn't want anything to do with politics.

With a new pastor change happening soon, Ana said they needed a pastor who was "on their side." When I asked her what this meant, she elaborated:

> A father that is with us is one who supports us, who comes to the meetings with us, who accompanies us to speak with politicians, like Father Rafael, who is at actions with us, that is a pastor who is going to be on our side. We need the support of the priest [...] We need priests who accompany us in what we go doing because that way, there is more credibility. The voice of the priest is strong [...] because people believe in him like a person like, bad comparison, but like a God — very faithful people believe that that he is — I think it's also that priests are very important because they convince people, especially if the pastors are good, they convince people.

The idea that the pastor's actions were indicative of God's wishes was echoed by Soledad, a young immigrant and former part time organizer at St. Francis Cabrini, who said, "when the pastor comes [to a meeting or event], it's like God is there." When I asked Ana whether she could organize in her church if there were not any FBO professional organizers, she said, "maybe I could, I believe if the pastor agreed with us, we could meet with him, he could call a meeting, and we could do it." Father Elizondo was the pastor through much of the fieldwork and immigrant activists continually complained about his intransigence to the point of refusing to allow them to make announcements or pass out fliers about events because they were deemed too political.

Immigrant members of St. Rose encountered a similar situation with their pastor, Father Cu, who avoided meeting with them and refused to approve announcements or fliers about upcoming FBO-sponsored events. Because the activists were peripheral to church networks, disapproval from the pastor meant that their access to the church was blocked. However, even those more deeply involved at the church had limited success-attracting volunteers without the active support of a priest. Marjorie, an elderly lay leader and longtime FBO affiliate at St. Rose, talked about how she would invite other lay leaders to an event and no one would show up, but if the priest invited them, like what Father Morrison, an associate priest, did for the Life Walk,[8] it was totally different:

> For [Life Walk], it was the Knights of Columbus and one of the deacons, and the Spanish young adults group ... So it was groups and a couple of individuals ... and for the [neighborhood] walk [against violence], it was kind of sad: there was four of us – they were members of [our FBO committee]. We tried to get some other groups to go, but they didn't.

While Marjorie was able to get a page in the church bulletin about the neighborhood walk against violence and personally spoke to a few lay leaders about the event, including members of the Knights of Columbus, only people form her FBO-affiliated committee showed up. In contrast, when Father Morrison expressed his support for Life Walk at mass and suggested meeting at the church to go together, church groups organized themselves and accompanied him to the event as a large group representing St. Rose.

In short, the respect and reverence accorded to pastors and associate priests over their interpretation of church missions gave them considerable influence over the organizing process under the model-expanding strategy. Even though organizers presented their social justice work as integral to religious participation, as outsiders engaged in traditionally political activity, their efforts to stretch and redefine church institutional boundaries fell flat unless they were validated by the pastor or an associate priest. However, among priests, the extra responsibilities required to actively support the organizing often took a backseat in the face of competing religious duties, limiting priests' ability to support the work.

Familiar, Sustainable Religious Involvement under the Model-Specializing Strategy

In contrast, the model-specializing strategy's use of routine religious activities not only facilitated the involvement of religious leaders, but also rendered their active participation less critical to lay leader involvement and mobilizing outcomes. Priests who were less willing to speak at marches and rallies or attend more politically oriented events could show their support for their immigrant congregants by advertising, attending, or participating in immigration masses. Priests I had never seen at previous FBO events assisted Father Jose at the immigration mass at St. Frances Cabrini, and a bishop led two of the monthly masses over the course of a year. Father Cu, the pastor at

St. Rose who had opposed the distribution of information about FBO events before the strategy shift, allowed activists to pass out fliers about the mass outside the church. Also, Father Rios, a pastor Carlos had consistently described as pro-immigrant but more spiritually oriented, was eager to participate in the masses, and later joined Father Campos, the new pastor at St. Lawrence, to lead a worship service and press conference about the Obama administration's contested deferred action program that was attended by about 50 parishioners. By making prayer and worship a central tactic, organizers provided priests with a way to support the cause within their institutionalized roles as religious leaders, facilitating their participation.

Additionally, the fact that almost all events took place at the church in the form of familiar worship and charitable services facilitated the participation of undocumented members who associated the church with sanctuary. Maria, a middle-aged nun, told me about how she and the pastor at her church presented the immigration reform masses:

> The act of telling you that it's a mass — but a mass in which we are asking God for a just immigration reform for all the people who do not have papers here, or for all the people who have a deportation order or something. Sometimes our people are afraid of going to places where there are a lot of people, or large events, perhaps because of the fear that there will be police, or that immigration will be there, or what will happen? Many people have expressed that they are afraid to go to those places. So, when we announce it in the mass, we tell them, "We are asking God for a just immigration reform. We need you to have a presence as well, so people know that we are serious. We want them to know that it is not only religious leaders that are asking for this, but the people, the community that is asking for this." We are here to support, to push them so that they are motivated.

Acts like this communicated to immigrants that the Church was behind them and would protect them. The idea that participants were making claims to God, not government officials, also motivated immigrants disillusioned with the political process. At one FBO meeting, Concepción related to the group:

> Some people listen to Obama, and he goes back and forth, and they lose faith that anything will happen, and I say, you're losing faith because you're putting your faith in a man, but you need to put your faith in God. I know something will happen — we will resolve this — because I know that it's in God's hands and he is in control, so I am optimistic and I put my faith in God and I believe that we will win this eventually, and in the meantime, we keep praying and informing people [about the mass].

For those who had little confidence in politicians, the idea promoted by the masses that God and the Church were behind them brought renewed hope and faith that change was possible, motivating their attendance and sustained participation. The monthly masses consistently filled St. Frances Cabrini, with about a third to half of parishioners staying after the mass to participate in the forums and information sessions.

While the participation of religious leaders inspired and assured parishioners, the perception that the campaign was a fundamentally Catholic project accorded it a level of credibility and trust that made the active support of local pastors and priests less crucial to lay leader involvement. The result was that the strategy shift gave organizers and activists unprecedented access to Catholic Church networks and lay leader cooperation. At an organizing meeting in January 2015, Sandra and Maricela reviewed the progress over the past few months: they had organized and led immigration forums after Sunday mass in about 10 new churches, with attendance usually over 150 people. Though they still encountered a church or two where lay leaders blocked their entry, and the majority of priests were not interested in getting very involved, in most of the churches they approached, lay leaders helped them organize and advertise the forums. In OLP, a suburban church far from the main organizing effort, lay leaders heard of the immigration forums through their representatives in the Archdiocese Hispanic Pastoral Council. Eduardo, a middle-aged lay leader at OLP shared with me:

> I had the opportunity to attend a meeting two weeks ago where, through the Archdiocese, they are trying to offer help to immigrants, people who do not have legal documents. So, how is the Archdiocese confronting it? It's through finding lawyers and people who are prepared to come here and give information and tell us, "Look, maybe with what [the president's] done recently ... you can fix your papers and you have these requirements and you don't have a criminal record."

Perceiving the project as coming directly from the Archdiocese, Eduardo and another lay leader I interviewed at OLP were eager to help organize the forums and had a few training and organizing meetings planned. However, when I asked OLP's Hispanic associate priest what the role of the church was in helping people overcome the social problems they faced, he responded, "We don't feel very like ... those primarily responsible," but said that the role of church was more to "promote solidarity, support, caring." While the religious leaders at the church were happy to provide church space for the event, they considered it outside of their own primary religious duty to participate directly in the forum. However, in contrast to the trend under the model-expanding strategy, even though priests at this church were not actively involved in the organizing, lay leaders came together to support the project.

Under the model-specializing strategy, even in cases where the pastor disagreed with the immigration masses on their messaging, activists were allowed to promote the mass by making announcements. At St. Nicholas, lay leaders had been organizing the immigration mass when the pastor changed and the new pastor, Father Lopez, said he didn't want to host the immigration mass at his church because he thought the immigration reform message was too political. Still, after the monthly immigration mass moved to St. Frances Cabrini with Father Jose, Father Lopez allowed activists to give announcements about the mass at the pulpit, and lay leaders attending St. Nicholas, such as Concepción and Manuel, continued to dedicate themselves to immigration mass planning and promotion. In short, the use of Catholic religious tactics under the model-specializing strategy provided churchgoers with a means of involvement that was a familiar extension to their routine church participation. The very fact that it was routine made the interpretation and validation of local church priests unnecessary, facilitating the sustained participation of more parishioners and lay leaders from a broader set of churches. In summary, Table 3 outlines differences in strategy characteristics and their impact on recruitment and mobilizing outcomes.

DISCUSSION AND CONCLUSION

Research on immigrant political incorporation and political engagement has found that involvement in community civic organizations, even nonpolitical ones, boosts political participation. The mechanisms behind this relationship most often proposed are largely structural – the development of transferable civic skills and organizational networks that bring access to politically relevant resources and information. However, this characterization of organizational involvement as having mainly a positive influence political engagement ignores the role of institutionalized organizational models in shaping church practice and valued action. In this paper, I document how parishioners' trust in church leaders and perceptions concerning the proper boundaries of church activities can either encourage or limit political activism. I use the case of Catholic churchgoer recruitment into collective action for immigrant rights to determine how political activists manage church institutional constraints on political activity. While previous research on this topic has struggled with member self-selection into particular church institutional contexts, in this research design, I leverage the unique organizational practices of the Catholic Church to observe the impact of frequent leadership changes (and subsequent institutional changes) relatively exogenous to church member political preferences on political mobilization. Drawing on institutional theories of organizations

Table 3. Organizing Strategies and Their Impact on Recruitment and Mobilization through Churches.

Strategy	Model-Expanding	Model-Specializing
Agent of change	Policy-makers — God wants you to liberate your people by pushing for just laws	God — God will hear your prayers and liberate your people
Membership definition	Hispanics (interfaith)	Hispanic Catholics
Tactics	Lobbying, rallies, marches, pilgrimages, vigils, phone-banking, forums, and press conferences	Religious masses, organized prayer, forums, and press conferences
Role of religious leaders	Actively support and legitimize church model expansion by attending political events and meetings, lobbying public officials, directing lay leaders, announcing political events, and providing meeting space at church	Support work through institutionalized role as religious leader by attending or leading mass, overseeing prayer, worship, and press conferences at church, giving or allowing announcements at Sunday mass, and providing meeting space at church
Mobilization and recruitment outcomes	Depended heavily on active role of priest in legitimating tactics; without priest support, core participants are few and primarily peripheral church members with little influence or connection to church networks; with priest support, organizers mobilize a large, diverse cross-section of church members	Greater access to Catholic church networks and greater participation in general, but especially among religious and lay leaders; organizing dominated by lay leaders and lay leaders participate without active encouragement from local priest; larger group of undocumented participants feel safe attending events
Conflict	Domain expansion rejected or confusing: Some lay leaders and religious leaders are skeptical of work because it seems politically instrumental, other leaders are just confused about group's mission and how it squares with their own religious participation	Peripheral church members sidelined from core leadership and planning roles because they do not have valued religious credentials or connections

and two years of ethnographic fieldwork, I argue that mobilizing attempts are more successful and sustainable when organizers effectively manage institutional boundaries around organizational domains.

I highlight two distinct strategies community organizers used to manage the boundary between religion and politics: the model-expanding and model-specializing strategies. While both strategies could successfully mobilize churchgoers, the model-expanding strategy provoked greater resistance and was more difficult to sustain. I found that the model-expanding strategy's attempt to expand church domain boundaries to include non-routine activities, such as political lobbying and protest, depended heavily on the active support and participation of local religious leaders in legitimating this expansion. When religious leaders validated the organizing as within the church's domain and actively supported it, they could mobilize a large, diverse cross-section of the church, lay leaders and parishioners, to participate in FBO-sponsored events. However, the extra responsibilities this entailed often made it difficult for priests to sustain them in the face of competing religious duties, and active priest support was relatively rare. When priests did not actively validate domain expansion, lay leaders and parishioners were largely indifferent to organizers, and organizers were only able to recruit a handful of peripheral church members into their campaign.

In contrast, the model-specializing strategy's reliance on routine Catholic religious activities, such as the religious mass and organized prayer, facilitated the participation of religious and lay leaders because it provided an avenue to supporting the cause through their established church roles. Furthermore, organizers' efforts to match their tactics, framing, and membership with those institutionalized in routine Catholic religious life made the active validation of local church religious leaders less necessary to lay leader and parishioner participation, as boundaries between the organizations blurred. As a result, organizers were able to mobilize more parishioners from a broader set of churches. However, while the model-specializing strategy was more likely to recruit deeply religious lay leaders, the high valuation of specialized Catholic skills, training, and connections also had the side effect of excluding peripheral church members from core leadership roles, as lay leaders took their place.

Contrary to a purely structural account of political mobilization through churches, lay leaders heavily involved in church ministries, small groups, and leadership were the least likely to join the organizing effort when it more clearly involved political tactics and goals and church religious leaders did not actively validate it as within the church's domain. This is because most immigrant churchgoers interviewed perceived strong institutional boundaries between the religious and political sphere, and this decreased the likelihood that the skills and networks they acquired through their religious participation would easily transfer to political action.

These findings contribute to literatures on political mobilization and organizations by showing how organizational domains influence how civic organizations and their members collectively organize and respond to political recruitment. More than providing politically relevant information, resources, and skills, mobilizing organizations build bridges across domains by helping members interpret political opportunities as fitting neatly within their routine organizational participation and roles.

Future research could expand the scope of these arguments by assessing the effectiveness of model-expanding and model-specializing recruitment strategies in other organization types. Researchers should also assess the validity of these claims among the native-born population and politically mainstream groups. These groups may have greater access to a variety of civic organizations and political information and are therefore not so reliant, as undocumented immigrants often are, on the church as a central social institution. As this research shows, all community organizations are not created equal in their effects on political engagement, and research investigating institutional practices across organizations will increase our understanding of political recruitment and mobilization.

NOTES

1. FBO = Faith-Based Organizer.
2. "Lay" people are those without professional religious training.
3. The names of participating individuals and churches have been changed to protect their confidentiality.
4. Immigration and Customs Enforcement.
5. Specialized beads are used to guide the prayer. There are variations on how to pray the rosary but the Common Manner goes like this: 1. Make the sign of the cross. 2. While holding the Crucifix, say "The Apostle's Creed." 3. On the first bead, say the "Our Father." 4. Say three "Hail Marys" on each next bead. 5. Say the "Glory be to the Father." 6. On the first decade bead, announce the First Mystery; then say the "Our Father." 7. Say ten "Hail Marys" while touching each of the following ten beads and meditating on the Mystery. 8. Say the "Glory be to the Father." 9. At the second decade bead, announce the Second Mystery, then say the "Our Father." Repeat steps 7 and 8 and continue with the Third, Fourth, and Fifth Mysteries in the same manner. Finish with the "Hail, Holy Queen" followed by a dialogue and closing rosary prayer. There are four sets of five Mysteries (Joyful, Sorrowful, Glorious, and Luminous). The Mystery set is selected based on the day of the week and the religious calendar.

6. While less relevant to mobilization in churches, the model-expanding strategy also provoked a similar response in non-religious participants and coalition partners. For example, union members invited through the immigrant rights coalition to a rally at a congressperson's office that included religious leader speakers, a giant altar, and an evangelical band complained about the religious nature of the event. Also, students recruited from the local community college by a friend occasionally voiced discomfort or confusion over the use of religious messaging, tactics, or networks, given their own lack of religiosity.

7. Intersection renamed to protect confidentiality.

8. Event name changed to protect confidentiality. The Life Walk is an annual pro-life/anti-abortion march and rally heavily supported and attended by the Archdiocese.

REFERENCES

Beyerlein, K., & Chaves, M. (2003). The political activities of religious congregations in the United States. *Journal for the Scientific Study of Religion, 42*, 229–246.

Beyerlein, K., & Hipp, J. R. (2009). From pews to participation: The effect of congregation activity and context on bridging civic engagement. *Social Problems, 53*, 97–117.

Brown, R. K., & Brown, R. E. (2003). Faith and works: Church-based social capital resources and African American political activism. *Social Forces, 82*, 617–641.

Carroll, G. R., & Swaminathan, A. (2000). Why the microbrewery movement? Organizational dynamics of resource partitioning in the U.S. brewing industry. *American Journal of Sociology, 106*(3), 715–762.

Cavendish, J. C. (2001). To march or not to march: The effect of clergy mobilization strategies on grassroots anti-drug activism. In S. E. S. Crawford & L. R. Olson (Eds.), *Christian Clergy in American politics*. Baltimore, MD: Johns Hopkins University Press.

Chaves, M., & Anderson, S. L. (2008). Continuity and change in American congregations: Introducing the second wave of the national congregations study. *Sociology of Religion, 69*, 415–440.

Coddou, M. (2015). *The impact of organizational domain evaluations on public support of churches: Evidence from a survey experiment*. Doctoral dissertation, Stanford University, Stanford.

Coddou, M. (2016). An institutional approach to collective action: Evidence from faith-based latino mobilization in the 2006 immigrant rights protests. *Social Problems, 63*(1), 127–150.

DiMaggio, P. J., & Powell, W. W. (1983). The iron cage revisited: Institutional isomorphism and collective rationality in organizational fields. *American Sociological Review, 48*(2), 147–160.

Djupe, P. A., & Gilbert, C. P. (2009). *The political influence of churches*. Cambridge: Cambridge University Press.

Fitzgerald, S. T., & Spohn, R. E. (2005). Pulpits and platforms: The role of the church in determining protest among Black Americans. *Social Forces, 84*, 1015–1048.

Gonzalez, R. G. (2011). Learning to be illegal: Undocumented youth and shifting legal contexts in the transition to adulthood. *American Sociological Review, 76*(4), 602–619.

Hannan, M. T., & Freeman, J. (1977). The population ecology of organizations. *American Journal of Sociology, 82*(5), 929–964.
Hannan, M. T., Pólos, L., & Carroll, G. (2007). *Logics of organization theory: Audiences, codes, and ecologies.* Princeton, NJ: Princeton University Press.
Harris, F. C. (1999). *Something within: Religion in African-American political activism.* New York, NY: Oxford University Press.
Heredia, L. (2011). From prayer to protest: The immigrant rights movement and the catholic church. In K. Voss & I. Bloemraad (Eds.), *Rallying for immigrant rights: The fight for inclusion in 21st century America* (pp. 101–122). Berkeley, CA: University of California Press.
Hsu, G., Hannan, M. T., & Koçak, Ö. (2009). Multiple category memberships in markets: An integrative theory and two empirical tests. *American Sociological Review, 74*(1), 150–169.
Jelen, T. G. (2001). Notes for a theory of clergy as political leaders. In S. E. S. Crawford & L. R. Olson (Eds.), *Christian Clergy in American politics* (pp. 28–42). Baltimore, MD: Johns Hopkins University Press.
Jones-Correa, M. A., & Leal, D. L. (2001). Political participation: Does religion matter? *Political Research Quarterly, 54,* 751–770.
McAdam, D. (1982). *Political process and the development of black insurgency, 1930–1970.* Chicago, IL: University of Chicago Press.
McAdam, D., & Paulsen, R. (1993). Specifying the relationship between social ties and activism. *American Journal of Sociology, 99,* 640–667.
McCarthy, J. D., & Zald, M. N. (1977). Resource mobilization and social movements: A partial theory. *American Journal of Sociology, 82,* 1212–1241.
McDaniel, E. L. (2008). *Politics in the pews: The political mobilization of black churches.* Ann Arbor, MI: University of Michigan Press.
McDaniel, E. L., & McClerking, H. K. (2005). Belonging and doing: Political Churches and black political participation. *Political Psychology, 26,* 721–734.
Meyer, J. W., & Rowan, B. (1977). Institutionalized organizations: Formal structure as myth and ceremony. *American Journal of Sociology, 83*(2), 340–363.
Mooney, M. (2009). *Faith makes us live: Surviving and thriving in the Haitian Diaspora.* Berkeley, CA: University of California Press.
Morris, A. D. (1984). *The origins of the civil rights movement: Black communities organizing for change.* New York, NY: Free Press.
Phillips, D. J., Turco, C. J., & Zuckerman, E. W. (2013). Betrayal as market barrier: Identity-based limits to diversification among high-status corporate law firms. *American Journal of Sociology, 118*(4), 1023–1054.
Portes, A., & Rumbaut, R. G. (2006). *Immigrant America: A portrait.* Berkeley, CA: University of California Press.
Putnam, R. D., & Campbell, D. E. (2010). *American grace: How religion divides and unites us.* New York, NY: Simon & Schuster.
Ramakrishnan, S. K., & Bloemraad, I. (Eds.). (2008). *Civic hopes and political realities: Immigrants, community organizations, and political engagement.* New York, NY: Russell Sage Foundation.
Rao, H., Monin, P., & Durand, R. (2003). Institutional change in Toque Ville: Nouvelle Cuisine as an identity movement in french gastronomy. *American Journal of Sociology, 108,* 795–843.

Verba, S., Schlozman, K. L., & Brady, H. (1995). *Voice and equality: Civic voluntarism in American politics*. Cambridge, MA: Harvard University Press.

Voss, K., & Bloemraad, I. (Eds.). (2011). *Rallying for immigrant rights: The fight for inclusion in 21st century America*. Berkeley, CA: University of California Press.

Wong, J. (2006). *Democracy's promise: Immigrants & American civic institutions*. Ann Arbor, MI: University of Michigan Press.

Wood, R. L. (2002). *Faith in action: Religion, race, and democratic organizing in America*. Chicago, IL: University of Chicago Press.

Zuckerman, E. W. (1999). The categorical imperative: Securities analysts and the illegitimacy discount. *American Journal of Sociology, 104*(5), 1398–1438.

Zuckerman, E. W., & Kim, T.-Y. (2003). The critical trade-off: Identity assignment and box-office success in the feature film industry. *Industrial and Corporate Change, 12*, 27–67.

Zuckerman, E. W., Kim, T.-Y., Ukanwa, K., & von Rittman, J. (2003). Robust identities or nonentities? Typecasting in the feature-film labor market. *American Journal of Sociology, 108*, 1018–1074.

APPENDIX: METHODOLOGICAL NOTES

I introduced myself as a researcher to all participants, in meetings, events, and interviews. My position as an outsider was usually apparent by my appearance – I was almost always the only non-Hispanic White person in the room. My status as a non-Catholic White American woman no doubt affected my interactions with people in the field, and certainly constrained my role as an active participant in some ways, especially in Catholic rituals, but also in times of personal sharing on the issue of immigration, which often took the form of concrete concerns for participants and more abstract idealism on my part. However, my outsider status also allowed me to observe the setting with fresh eyes and prompted participants to explain things to me, providing insight into their perspective on particular social contexts and interactions, since my own understanding was not taken for granted.

My ability to understand and speak Spanish was critical, as the majority of meetings, events, and interviews were conducted in Spanish. My position speaking Spanish as a second language in a setting dominated by Spanish often led to situations that drew parallels between myself and immigrant participants regarding their struggles learning a new language and frustration over their ability to communicate as well as they would like with English monolinguals, which built rapport. Because I had usually known them for months and sat through meetings involving a great deal of personal sharing, it was easier to establish the rapport so important to qualitative interviewing with immigrant recruits and community organizers. The interviews I did with others varied in rapport, with some more willing to share than others.

I sometimes took notes while in the field, especially during meetings, and would typically fully record field notes either upon arriving home or within a day or two of the event. Recorded interviews were transcribed and imported along with field notes into qualitative coding software. I then coded these notes and interviews, first through line by line open coding, attaching all possible themes to a line, then through a more focused-coding of key topics and themes. I then wrote memos summarizing these themes and the links between them, some of which became the foundation for sections of this paper. I distinguish between excerpts from field notes and interviews in the text by situating field note excerpts in a particular context. Excerpts from field notes are paraphrased, while interview excerpts are direct quotes, translated from Spanish to English when necessary. Interview excerpts appear in quotation marks unless they are long, in which case they are indented without quotation marks.

NATIONAL IDENTITY AND GOVERNMENTAL AUTHORITY: THE INTERSECTION OF NATIONAL IDENTITY, IMMIGRATION POLICY, AND THE CHILD WELFARE SYSTEM IN THE UNITED STATES

Joanna Kaftan

ABSTRACT

Federal immigration policy embodies national ideas about membership. Nevertheless, attitudes toward immigration within a nation are not invariable. Regional policies vary dramatically in their support or antagonism toward immigrants. In addition, immigration policy profoundly affects other areas of governmental authority. This chapter explores the relationship between state-level immigration policy and family reunification for Hispanic/Latino children in the United States. The quantitative analysis utilizes data from the National Council of State Legislatures

(NCSL) (2008–2014) as well as data gathered from the Child Welfare Outcomes Report published by the Department of Health and Human Services. The results show that while Hispanic/Latino children are not overrepresented in the child welfare systems of the states with the most antagonistic legislation, they are returned to the custody of their parent(s) in smaller percentages compared to whites in the states with the most antagonistic bills compared with the states with the most supportive bills.

Keywords: State immigration legislation; ICE; CPS; reunification

National identity and immigration are clearly linked. The image of the nation helps determine attitudes toward immigration. On the other hand, attitudes toward immigration also help refine how people see itself as a nation. Specifically, immigration policy represents American ideas about national membership and citizenship. It delineates inclusion and exclusion and promotes a particular composition even if it is not fully realized. Shifts in how legal and illegal statuses have been defined reveal how the nation has recreated itself over time. Immigration policy realigns and hardens perceived racial categories into law with tangible consequences.[1] Nevertheless, conceptions of national identity are not uncontested. Regional differences exist and influence ideas about who should be counted as part of the nation. These differences can be observed by examining divergent state-level immigration legislation. What is less evident but nevertheless important, is that nationalism and its connection to immigration legislation impacts other seemingly unrelated social institutions such as the child welfare system in the United States. Regional differences in immigration legislation can result in disparate outcomes for children based on parents' ethnicity and immigration status. Children, even though they are unlikely to directly participate in the construction of national identity or immigration policy, can be the most profoundly affected by them. The costs of the interaction between immigration legislation, immigration enforcement, and child welfare services, for example, are severe. The interaction often leads to the termination of parental rights.

This chapter examines the relationship between state immigration legislation and the formally nonpartisan custody outcomes of the child welfare system. The recent shift in federal immigration policy in the Unites States from the border to the interior has increased the potential for regional policies and attitudes concerning identity to impact enforcement in distinctive ways. State legislatures have been especially active in passing immigration legislation since 2010. Moreover, given that attitudes toward immigration vary across states, an examination of state-level immigration legislation, which mirrors the dominant attitudes toward immigration in a state, along with outcomes for Hispanic/Latino children under the supervision of Child Protective Services in each state is warranted.[2] Specifically, this chapter examines whether the image of the nation as inclusive or exclusive, measured by state-level immigration legislation, varies across the United States and whether differences translate into divergent outcomes in terms of whether Hispanic/Latino children are returned to the custody of their parents — reunified — less often in states with more antagonistic immigration legislation. The following hypotheses guided the analysis.

H1. Mexican border states will have more antagonistic immigration legislation.

H2. States with larger populations will have more antagonistic immigration legislation.

H3. States with larger Hispanic/Latino populations with have more antagonistic immigration legislation.

H4. States with more antagonistic immigration legislation will have higher percentages of Hispanic/Latino children in state care.

H5. States with more antagonistic legislation will have smaller percentages of family reunification for Hispanic/Latino children.

The analysis shows that even though immigration was a salient issue for Mexican border states with California (210), Texas (151), and Arizona (65) introducing large numbers of immigration related bills, Mexican border states did not uniformly present more antagonistic immigration legislation. In the period between 2008 and 2014, out of all of the states, Arizona revealed the most antagonistic climate while California exhibited the most supportive climate toward immigrants. Contrary to the hypotheses, the larger the state population and the larger the Hispanic/Latino population in a state, the less antagonistic the climate. In addition, Hispanic/Latino children are not over-represented within the child welfare systems of the states with the most antagonistic immigration policies. Nevertheless, the states with the most antagonistic legislation have lower percentages of family reunification for

Latino/Hispanic children. In other words, Hispanic/Latino children are not entering the child welfare system at higher percentages than the general population of Hispanic/Latino children in the states with the most antagonistic legislation. Once in the system, however, Hispanic/Latino children are less likely to be returned to the custody of their parents in states with the most antagonistic legislation compared to the states with the most supportive legislation.

NATIONALISM, IMMIGRATION, AND POLICY ENFORCEMENT

It has been argued that established democratic nations such as the United States demonstrate a stable and moderate social and political environment (Billig, 1995, p. 93). In these "settled" nations, national identity is so entrenched that it becomes taken-for-granted and national symbols are not regularly noticed (Billig, 1995, p. 144; cf. Skey, 2009, p. 332). Nevertheless, it is a mistake to assume that modern nation-states do not endure internal conflicts or external challenges (Abell, Condor, & Stevenson, 2006, p. 208). As John Hutchinson (2006, p. 300) points out, "the nation is a process, and a non-linear one, that is reversible." Numerous factors including migration and ideological threat can result in outbursts of nationalist fervor. Debates about migration and multi-culturalism have become increasingly difficult to control (Blokland, 2003; Kundnani, 2001). The contentious presidential primary elections of 2016 clearly illustrate that even in the United States, immigration is a salient and divisive political issue. Differing visions of how inclusive the nation should be have been translated into practice through diverse state-level immigration legislation.

Inherent in the conception of the nation-state is a strong defense of sovereignty (Mayall, 1990; Ngai, 2004). At the federal level, proclamations of an absolute right to define membership are tied to the "right of self-preservation" so much so that the emphasis on sovereignty in immigration policy has produced regulations that would not be tolerated if they were placed on citizens. The emphasis on sovereignty has resulted in the removal of human rights consideration from the development of policy (Ngai, 2004). Immigration enforcement illustrates "the interaction between great material strength and great human vulnerability" (Sassen, 2007, p. 107).

Attitudes toward immigration are not just responses to the challenges of mass immigration. According to Sandovici, Jakobsen, and Strabac (2012) nationalist politicians emphasize national identity. They stress the importance of economic threat and the threat to national identity in their discourse concerning immigrants. The extensive media coverage politicians receive makes these issues seem more important and also spread nationalist attitudes to new groups of citizens while these politicians are in office. Sniderman, Hagendoorn, and Prior (2004) assert that identity threats are more powerful than economic threats in generating anti-immigrant attitudes and that the focus on identity issues leads to more prejudice. The implication is that it is not just the influx of immigrants but the influence of political elites that increases anti-immigrant attitudes (Sandovici et al., 2012, p. 127).

Within the United States, especially since 2010, this influence can be seen at the state level as several states passed "anti-immigration" laws which make immigration offenses criminal at the state level.[3] Whether a state legislature will adopt policies that strengthen immigration enforcement is dependent on party ideology, party control of the legislature and electoral conditions. Conservative Republican state parties controlling the state's legislative institutions are more likely to pass legislation strengthening immigration enforcement. However, they are less likely to do so when Latino's make up a large percentage of the electorate. Legislatures controlled by Democrats are not likely to pass stricter enforcement legislation. In effect, the majority of strengthened enforcement legislation was passed by conservative Republican legislatures in states with small Latino populations. Arizona is the exception (Zingher, 2014).[4]

In addition, after the September 11 attack in 2001, there has been a shift in federal immigration policy focus from the border to the interior. Immigration and Customs Enforcement (ICE) has increasingly relied on local police and law enforcement to detain noncitizens following three programs: 287(g), the Criminal Alien Program (CAP) and Secure Communities. These programs link local law enforcement with immigrant enforcement operations. Even though ICE claims that the focus of these policies is to target dangerous criminals, in practice, these policies have targeted all noncitizens arbitrarily (Wessler, 2011, p. 11). According to Coleman (2007), "the recent criminalization of immigration law, the sequestering of immigration enforcement from court oversight and the enrollment of proxy immigration officers at sub-state scales have been actively pursued so as to make interior enforcement newly central to U.S. immigration geopolitics" (p. 54). These new forms of immigration enforcement, while promoted as an effort to fight terrorism, are actually efforts to stem the migration of unauthorized labor across the United States — Mexico border. In addition, detention — by visibly holding noncitizens — symbolically contains the problem of "illegal immigration" and broadcasts state power as well as the government's ability to secure the border after the September 11attacks (Martin, 2011, p. 481; Mountz, 2004).[5] The shift in a focus to security is evident in the shift of immigration enforcement from the Department of Labor in 1925 to the Department of Justice in 1940 and to the Department of Homeland Security in 2003 (Staudt, 2009, pp. 1–2; Villalobos, 2011, p. 153). Immigration offenses made up about 31.2% of criminal prosecutions in federal court in 2013. Over the past decade, immigration cases have increased by 58.9% (Schmitt & Jones, 2014).

The Intersection of Immigration Enforcement and CPS

Debates about children's rights underscore the practical consequences of immigration law on child welfare services (Martin, 2011). The interaction between Child Protective Services (CPS) and ICE largely determines whether a child is returned to the custody of his/her parent(s). It is estimated that there were 11.3 million unauthorized immigrants in the United States in 2013, a decrease since 2007. About 52% of the unauthorized population is from Mexico. About 60% of unauthorized immigrants live in six states: California, Florida, Texas, New York, New Jersey, and Illinois. About 7% of school-aged children (K-12) have at least one parent who is an unauthorized immigrant (Krogstad & Passel, 2014). The citizen children born in the United States to undocumented parents are casualties of immigration enforcement policies meant to deport large numbers of people. Of the 5.5 million children of undocumented parents, 4.5 million are U.S. citizens (Wessler, 2011). These children have no control over their fate once their parents have been apprehended and their citizenship status cannot be used to keep their families together. The emphasis in controlling undocumented immigration is to deport the undocumented immigrant rather than to prioritize the interests of the citizen-child (Zayas & Bradlee, 2014).

Immigration law provides ICE with discretion in detaining noncitizens (Morton, 2011). As "persons," the rights of undocumented parents are protected under the constitution by the Fourteenth Amendment. Unauthorized immigrants are entitled to due process and equal protection under the Fifth and Fourteenth Amendments. The Supreme Court recognizes the right to parent one's child as "perhaps the oldest of the fundamental liberty interests" (Maddali, 2014, 2000). Nevertheless, discretion is rarely applied in ICE proceedings (Wessler, 2011, pp. 29–31). Federal courts have limited authority to intercede in immigration enforcement practices (Coleman, 2007; Varsanyi, 2008). ICE has well-established authority over territorial sovereignty and security (Martin, 2011).

In cases of parent detention, ICE has emphasized the criminality of the migrant parent and focuses on the parents' agency, autonomy, and intentionality of breaking immigration law.[6] ICE places the responsibility for border security on individual migrants crossing the border illegally and views the United States as the victim of such acts. When viewed solely through the lens of illegal entry, parents hold all of the responsibility but have their parental rights taken away. In such a view, American public interest is prioritized over the claims and needs of specific children (Martin, 2011, p. 489). Current immigration law focuses on the protection of adult citizens' interests but treats the child-citizen not as agent but as object. The negative effects on these children are essentially ignored in the debates about immigration enforcement (Manning, 2011).

Child protective services do not collect information about the immigration status of parents. Estimates are difficult to determine. Nevertheless, the scale of the problem is not insignificant. Looking at available data, within the first six months of 2011, 46,000 parents of United States – citizen children were deported. Conservative estimates from 2011 place 5,100 children of detained or deported parents in foster care and speculate that by 2016, 15,000 children will not be returned to the custody of their parents because of their parents' immigration status. In addition, where the local police are actively involved in immigration enforcement and have signed 287(g) agreements with ICE, children in foster care were about 29% more likely to have a detained or deported parent compared to other counties. The problem is not limited to border states with cases appearing in at least twenty two states (Wessler, 2011). In addition, the Urban Institute estimates that one child is directly affected for every two undocumented immigrants deported as a result of worksite raids (Capps, Castañeda, Chaudry, & Santos, 2007). Within the Pima County Juvenile Court system in Arizona, for example, Rabin (2011) using a sample of voluntary respondents made up of CPS caseworkers, attorneys and judges, found that more than half of the respondents stated that more than 10% of their cases involved at least one undocumented family member. In addition, 83% of the judges in the sample, 70% of the social care providers and 87% of the attorneys encountered one or more cases in the past five years where at least one of the parents were in immigration detention centers. All of the judges, 81% of the social service providers, and 87% of the attorneys had worked with families in which a family member had been deported.

Taking a broader view of the Latino/Hispanic children who come to the attention of the child welfare system in the United States about 92.2% are born in the United States and 7.8% are foreign-born immigrants. These figures suggest that on average, foreign-born Latino/Hispanic children are underrepresented in the child welfare system given that about 9% of Latino/Hispanic children in the United States are foreign born. Nevertheless, representation varies across states and Latino children are overrepresented in some states (Dettlaff & Johnson, 2011).[7] Of the Latino/Hispanic children who come to the attention of child welfare agencies in the United States and who live with a biological parent, 36% have a parent who was foreign born. Overall, children living with a foreign-born parent make up 5.2% of the total population of children who come to attention of child welfare agencies in the United States (Dettlaff, Earner, & Philips, 2009).

NATIONAL IDENTITY, BUREAUCRACY, AND FAMILY LAW

The influence of inclusive versus exclusive ideas of the nation is not limited to immigration legislation. Tensions about identity and ethnicity can infuse family law as well. Maddali (2014) argues that child rearing can be thought of as a way to maintain the dominant Anglo-American identity. Immigrants more closely resembling the values and cultures of Northern Europe have been favored under U.S. immigration law. Language, culture, and values are taught within the family. Beliefs about child raising are bound by ideas concerning race, class, and ethnicity. When members of the dominant cultural group are in a position to make judgments about the parenting practices of subordinate groups, child welfare outcomes can be dramatically affected leading to the termination of parental rights on the basis of parental identities. Three examples from United States history illustrate such outcomes. In the 1880s, "child-saving agencies" transported the poor children of Irish, Polish, and Italian immigrant parents — viewed as nonwhite at the time — from the East coast to the West coast to be raised by families from higher classes. Also, in the 1880s, Native American children were forcibly removed from their parents' homes and placed in boarding schools. In addition from 1958 to 1967, The "Indian Adoption Project" removed Native American children from their homes and placed them for adoption with non-Native American families in the Midwest and East. The rationale for these removals was that raising immigrant children in an English-speaking environment with Anglo-American values and culture is in the child's best interest and also preserves the Anglo-American identity (Maddali, 2014, pp. 652—655). The same argument has been applied as an explanation for the termination of the parental rights of undocumented parents. The argument states that biases against the immigration status, language, race, and culture of undocumented parents along with the view that the United States is a better place for children than poorer countries lead to the termination of parental rights. There is a systemic prejudice against reunifying children with parents in foreign countries (Dettlaff et al., 2009; Maddali, 2014; Rabin, 2011; Thronson, 2008; Wessler, 2011).

Aside from concerns about implicit or overt bias affecting child welfare outcomes, the bureaucracy of state institutions must be considered. Bureaucracy has been argued to be an essential component in the development of nationalism (Breuilly, 1993, p. 21; Gellner, 1983) and bureaucrats have been shown to be essential in the maintenance of nationalisms (Kedourie, 1971). Ideas of the nation must be reinforced in order to remain relevant. Weber (1978) linked bureaucracy to the modern, rationalized state. Weber's six characteristics of modern bureaucracy are particularly salient when considering the procedures of ICE as well as child welfare agencies and how bureaucracy itself impacts child welfare outcomes: (1) the principle of official jurisdictional areas ordered by laws or administrative regulations, (2) clearly established systems of office hierarchy, (3) management based on written documents, (4) specialized training, (5) full commitment, and (6) general rules that govern the functioning of the office with officials having specialized expertise pertaining to these rules. The more specialized modern culture becomes, the more objective, personally detached experts are required. Bureaucracy transforms social action into rationally organized action. Once established it is incredibly hard to destroy and it becomes a tool of the ones controlling it. "Where administration has been completely bureaucratized, the resulting system of domination is practically indestructible" (Weber, 1978, p. 987).

Both ICE and the child welfare system in the United States are clear examples of modern bureaucratic institutions. Jurisdiction is relevant when it comes to child welfare outcomes given that immigration enforcement is centered on federal law and family law at the level of state. Judges in family court have no jurisdiction over ICE facilities and employees.[8] Specialized training is required for both ICE and CPS personnel as well as judges and attorneys working within family court. Nevertheless, while written documentation dictates all action within the child welfare system as well as family court, the lack of explicit policy dealing with parents in detention leaves caseworkers, attorneys, and judges with little guidance — a situation that is antithetical to these institutions' existence.[9] As Weber suggested, the extreme specialization of the child welfare system as well as ICE immigration enforcement also fosters personal detachment.

The structures of ICE and Child Welfare Services as institutionalized bureaucracies, each with established paths, do not interconnect easily. Forceful local level immigration enforcement combined with the obstacles inherent in the ICE detention system and the lack of established child welfare policy concerning reunification with deported parents makes the reunification of children with deported parents unlikely. In particular, immigration enforcement requires local authorities to hold unauthorized immigrants in custody until ICE can transport them to one of more than three hundred and fifty detention centers. On average, detainees are placed more than 370 miles from their homes. Once in ICE custody, parents are exceedingly difficult to track down. According to social workers, attorneys, and judges, the parents "disappear." Immigration detention centers are not public and lists of detainees are not published. Attorneys cannot find their clients and CPS caseworkers are not informed of the parents' whereabouts. ICE does not send notifications when parents are transferred between detention centers. Contacting detainees by phone is challenging since ICE does not have procedures to facilitate such contact. Moreover, the climate of fear in which undocumented immigrants live, makes them less likely to notify child welfare agencies about family members. There is a pervasive fear that such information might lead to the family members' apprehension by ICE as well. As a consequence, the children of detainees are more likely to end up in the foster care system instead of in kinship placements (Rabin, 2011, pp. 17–25).[10]

In order for custody to be returned to parents, CPS requires parental compliance with case plans that generally include parenting classes, drug treatment, and domestic violence prevention courses. Child visitation and contact with CPS are required components of the plan. Nevertheless, there are no services or programs available to parents in detention centers. This is in contrast to many jails and prisons that provide incarcerated parents access to services and programs in order to facilitate the reunification of parents with their children.[11] Juvenile justice judges cannot mandate contact since they have no authority over federal facilities (Rabin, 2011, pp. 11–13).

The choice of whether to fight deportation is especially difficult. Choosing to fight deportation leads to months or years in detention, reducing the chance of reunification. The Adoption and Safe Families Act (1997) (AFSA) mandates that proceedings for parental termination must be initiated if the child has remained in an out of home placement for 15 out of 22 months. This time requirement conflicts with the unpredictable timelines of immigration cases. While some states provide extensions for incarcerated parents, these extensions are not available for detainees (Wessler, 2011). Deportation, on the other hand, reduces the likelihood of reunification because of the difficulty of assessing the adequacy of care provided in another country. Immigration status and the threat of deportation have been used as arguments against custody (Rabin, 2011, pp. 17–25).

In addition, due to the current climate, the length of stay in detention can reinforce the impression that detained parents are criminals and can lead CPS workers to "write off" detained parents (Kerwin & Lin, 2009). The high turnover rates of CPS caseworkers, their limited experience working with social service agencies in other countries, their lack of trust in foreign service agencies, high caseloads, language and cultural barriers as well as bias against immigrant parents all contribute to the reluctance of caseworkers to undertake reunification efforts for parents who have been deported or are facing deportation. Outcomes are highly dependent on the individual caseworkers, attorneys, and judges involved. While the consulate can profoundly impact the outcome of such cases through identifying, evaluating, and communicating with family members from the home country, they are under-utilized (Rabin, 2011, pp. 20–22). Since there are no clear rulings on the relevance of parents' immigration status, parents' undocumented status is informally used to deny custody (Thronson, 2008). Once a parent is deported, unless the consulate is involved, the lack of CPS policy, the lack of caseworker experience dealing with foreign child welfare agencies and bias against placement in foreign countries can "lead almost seamlessly to termination of parental rights" (Wessler, 2011, p. 47).

DATA

Since the main research question of this chapter is whether state-level immigration legislation affects child welfare outcomes for Latino/Hispanic children in state care, the state is the unit of analysis in this study.[12] Data for Puerto Rico and the District of Columbia were included in the analysis resulting in $N=52$. State estimates (2014) for population, number of Hispanic/Latino residents in a state, number of Hispanic/Latino foreign born in the state, percent Latino in the child population of the state and median age of residents were gathered from the U.S. Census Bureau (United States Census Bureau, 2014).[13] These measures are included in the analysis based on the following assumptions. Population size affects access to and the distribution of resources and therefore may affect attitudes toward immigrants. In addition, the size of the Latino/Hispanic population within a state impacts the salience of the immigration debate within a state. The measure for population of Latino foreign born within a state is included given that the attitudes and interests of first generation immigrants differ from other generations (Pew Hispanic Center, 2004). Democratic lean is included to examine whether the dominant political lean of a state affects the number of immigration bills and their tone. The measure for Democratic lean was taken from Gallup polling (Saad, 2012).[14] Lastly, age has been shown to be correlated with political attitudes (Pew Research Center, 2014).

The data on immigration bills (2008–2014) used in this study was gathered from the National Council of State Legislatures (NCSL). The data used in the analysis includes all of the state laws and resolutions that address legal immigration, migrant and seasonal workers as well as undocumented immigration as specified by NCLS: a total of 1885 bills were introduced and 1,130 were enacted between 2008 and 2014 (NCSL, 2014). Utilizing the database of immigration bills, I first developed two separate indexes: Protection Against Undocumented Immigrants and Support for Immigrants. The antagonistic index was based on the combined number (simple count) of bills in a state falling into two categories: bills safeguarding against undocumented immigration and bills outlining specific state penalties. For example, bills listing criminal penalties for unauthorized employment or transporting undocumented immigrants would be classified as antagonistic. The supportive index was based on the combined number (simple count) of bills in a state falling into the following two categories: bills supporting legal immigrants and bills offering relief to undocumented immigrants. For example, bills providing for in-state tuition for unauthorized residents or bills that allow for drivers licenses without the need for immigrant status documentation were categorized as supportive. [15] A third composite index was created subtracting the value of the supportive index from the antagonistic index for each state and is included as a measure of overall state climate. Positive numbers indicate a more antagonistic climate against immigrants while negative values indicate a more supportive climate or less antagonism toward immigrants. The total number of immigration bills by state is also included in the analysis as a measure for the salience of immigration as a political topic within the state. It is important to note that not every bill fit into either the protection against or support indexes. There were a total of 722 resolutions, for example, that could not be coded into one of the two indexes and therefore are not included in the composite climate index. Resolutions tended to be statements of acknowledgment of past immigrant contributions associated with celebrations such as Irish Heritage Day.

Data concerning child welfare outcomes was assembled from the Child Welfare Outcomes Report by the Children's Bureau, U.S. Department of

Health and Human Services (Children's Bureau, 2013). The data for the report comes from the National Child Abuse and Neglect Data System (NCANDS) and the Adoption and Foster Care Analysis and Reporting System (AFCARS). The report is published annually and is mandated by the AFSA of 1997. This study utilizes data for the years 2010−2013 and includes data concerning the percentages of children in the general population of each state by race/ethnicity, the percentage of child victims in each state by race/ethnicity, percentage of reunification − children returned to the custody of parent(s) − by race/ethnicity.[16] An additional variable for representation in the child welfare system was constructed using the percent of Latino/Hispanic children in state care for each state minus the percentage of all Latino/Hispanic children in the state population. Positive values indicate overrepresentation and negative values reflect underrepresentation of Latino/Hispanic children in state care. The two variables − representation and reunification − lend insight into whether cultural threat and/or bureaucracy impact outcomes for Hispanic/Latino children in the temporary managing conservatorship of CPS. For example, if Hispanic/Latino children are overrepresented in the child welfare systems of states with more antagonistic legislation, than it is likely that fear of cultural threat and an exclusive view of United States identity increase the practice of immigration enforcement and potentially increase the reporting of child abuse regarding Hispanic/Latino communities in those states. In contrast, if Hispanic/Latino children are not overrepresented in the welfare systems of states with antagonistic legislation than either the states' more exclusive views of the nation do not impact the procedure of immigration enforcement and abuse reporting; or, the antagonistic climate may make Hispanic/Latino families more likely to hide and avoid social services so that reporting of abuse becomes less likely.

In addition, if percentages of reunification with parent(s) for Hispanic/Latino children are lower in states with more antagonistic legislation, it is not just concerns over cultural threat, through actors' choices in family court decisions, but also bureaucratic procedure and potentially the interaction between CPS and ICE that affect outcomes. If on the other hand, Hispanic/Latino children are not reunified at lower percentages than white children in the states with the most antagonistic immigration legislation, actors' responses to cultural threat and bureaucratic procedure are not biased against Hispanic/Latinos in these states. It is important to note that information about the immigration status of the children in care or their parents is not available since this information is not collected by the Children's Bureau.

ANALYSES AND RESULTS

Means, standard deviations as well as minimum and maximum values are listed in Table 1. The number of bills varied greatly by state with a minimum of two bills in Puerto Rico (three in Wyoming) and a maximum of 210 bills in California. Supporting previous estimates, current census figures combined with child welfare statistics show that in the nation as a whole, Latino/Hispanic children are underrepresented in the child welfare system: 13.36% of children in care are Latino/Hispanic compared to 15.56% of children in the general population. Nevertheless, there were 15 states in which Latino/Hispanic children were overrepresented in the child welfare system. There was also broad variation in overall reunification percentages across states for whites, Hispanic/Latinos as well as total. The combined mean for all groups shows that an average 59.69% of all children in state care were reunified with parent(s) between 2010 and 2013. Delaware had the lowest overall average of reunification, 42.2%, while Puerto Rico had the highest percentage, 80.6%, followed by Wyoming, 75.15%.[17] A one-way analysis of variance (ANOVA) was conducted comparing the rates of reunification for whites, blacks, Hispanics, and Asians. The analysis was

Table 1. Descriptive Statistics.

	Mean	Std. Deviation	Minimum	Maximum
Immigration bills				
Number of bills	36.19	38.276	2	210
Protection against	6.62	7.852	0	46
Support for	7.69	13.922	0	97
Climate: Protective supportive	−1.08	15.699	−87	46
U.S. Latino/Hispanic child population				
Latino children (%)	15.56	13.12	0	59
Latino children in care (%)	13.36	13.73	0	60
Overall reunification				
Total	59.6889	9.14925	42.20	80.60
White	60.0962	9.04728	41.00	77.00
Black	58.1731	11.10153	38.00	83.00
Hispanic	61.4231	9.15091	46.00	80.00
Asian	65.2745	17.23262	0.00	100.00

significant, $F (3, 203) = 3.18$, $p = .025$. Black children ($M = 58.17$, $SD = 11.10$) were reunified with a parent(s) less often than Asian children ($M = 65.27$, $SD = 17.23$). Notably, the overall national reunification average for Hispanic/Latino children does not significantly differ from that of whites.

Bivariate correlations were used to examine the relationship between state population, Hispanic/Latino population, Latino foreign-born population, median age, Democratic lean, number of immigration bills, climate, Hispanic/Latino representation in the child welfare system, and reunification-percentage of Hispanic/Latino children returned to the custody of their parents. Please see Table 2. State population exhibited high bivariate correlations with Hispanic/Latino population and Latino foreign-born population. It was also correlated with the number of immigration bills and climate. Not surprisingly, Hispanic/Latino population was also highly correlated with Latino foreign-born population. Hispanic/Latino population within a state as well as population of Latino foreign born were also correlated with the number of immigration bills and climate. Median age was only correlated with the number of immigration bills in a state while Democratic lean was not correlated with any of the other variables.

Table 2. Bivariate Correlations.

	State Population	Hispanic/Latino Population	Latino Foreign Born	Median Age	Democratic Lean
Hispanic/Latino	.893**				
Latino foreign born	.931**	.954**			
Median age of residents	−.077	−.175	−.101		
Democratic lean	−.086	−.042	−.037	.154	
Number of immigration bills	.777**	.780**	.756**	−.292*	.061
Climate	−.498**	−.579**	−.648**	.050	−.051
Representation[a]	−.093	−.055	−.104	.067	.001
Reunification[b]	−.062	.043	.032	−.024	.107

**$p < .01$, *$p < .05$.
[a]Representation refers to the percentage of children in the child welfare system of the state that are Hispanic/Latino minus the percentage of Hispanic/Latino children in the state based on U.S. census data.
[b]Reunification refers to the percent of Hispanic/Latino children (2010–2013) who were returned to the custody of their parent(s) at the conclusion of their case (trial).

Table 3. Linear Regression Models Predicting Number of Immigration Bills.

	Model 1 – Base Model ($R^2 = .71$)		Model 2 – With Latino Foreign Born ($R^2 = .73$)		Zero-Order Correlations[a]
	B	β	B	β	
(Constant)	129.89		117.76		
State population	.196	.364	.279*	.518*	.777***
Hispanic Latino population	.691*	.454*	1.123*	.738*	.812***
Democratic lean	.078	.142	.081	.148	.060
Median age of residents	−3.084*	−.196*	−2.812*	−.179*	−.273*
Latino foreign born			−1.013	−.442	.756***

***$p < .001$, *$p < .05$.
[a]Correlated with the number of immigration bills.

A sequential multiple regression analysis was used to predict the number of immigration bills introduced. Please note that the total number includes resolutions. Please see Table 3. State population, Hispanic/Latino population within the state, Democratic lean, and median age were entered in the first step. Hispanic/Latino population within the state and median age were significant predictors of the number of bills in a state suggesting that the larger the state's Hispanic/Latino population and the younger the median age, the more state immigration bills ($R^2 = .71$, $F(4,46) = 28.66$, $p < .001$). Latino foreign-born population within the state was entered in the second step. While the zero-order effects suggest that larger Latino foreign born population increases the number of immigration bills in a state, the addition of the variable Latino foreign born did not significantly improve the model ($R^2 = .73$, $F(5,45) = 23.90$, $p < .156$). Nevertheless, the analysis reveals problems of multicollinearity between the variables for Latino/Hispanic population and Latino foreign born. Unfortunately, transformation of the variables did not alleviate the problem.

Another sequential regression was conducted to predict the overall climate toward immigrants – antagonistic index minus the supportive index. Positive values indicate a more antagonistic climate. See Table 4. State population, Hispanic/Latino population, median age, and Democratic lean were entered in the first step. The model was significant ($R^2 = .36$, $F(4,46) = 6.4$, $p < .001$). Hispanic/Latino population was a significant predictor of the climate. The larger the Hispanic/Latino population in a state, the less

Table 4. Linear Regression Models Predicting Climate: Protective Bills-Supportive Bills.

	Model 1 – Base Model ($R^2 = .36$)		Model 2 – With Latino Foreign Born ($R^2 = .51$)		Zero-Order Correlations[a]
	B	β	B	β	
(Constant)	17.39		.244		
State population	.049	.222	.167*	.750*	−.498***
Z-Score: Hispanic Latino population	−.51**	−.801**	.107	.169	−.586***
Democratic lean	−.012	−.055	−.008	−.034	−.050
Median age	−.412	−.063	−.027	−.004	.048
Latino foreign born			−1.43***	−1.51***	−.648***

***$p < .001$, **$p < .01$, *$p < .05$.
[a]Correlated with Climate. Positive values indicate more antagonistic climate.

antagonistic the climate. The addition of Latino foreign born in the second step improved the model ($R^2 = .51$, $F(5,45) = 9.24$, $p < .001$). In the second model, the larger the state population, and the larger the foreign-born population, the less antagonistic the climate. Nevertheless, the same variables, Hispanic/Latino population and Latino foreign-born revealed multicollinearity.

A linear regression testing whether the percent of Latino foreign-born population predicts the percentage of Latino/Hispanic children in the child welfare system was conducted but found no significant result. While the percent of Latino foreign born is only an indirect measure of the unauthorized migrant population within a state, the regression results do not provide evidence that immigration enforcement affects the percentage of Latino children in care.[18] An additional regression analysis was conducted regressing percent Latino foreign born on the representation measure – percent of Latino/Hispanic children in the temporary managing conservatorship of the state minus the percent Latino/Hispanic children in the state's general population based on census figures – but also did not find a significant result.[19]

In order to see if state immigration legislation was reflected in child welfare outcomes for Hispanic/Latino children, a multiple regression analysis was conducted with family reunification – return to parental custody – specifically for Hispanic/Latino children as the dependent variable and included the climate variable along with the variables for state population, Hispanic/Latino population, Latino foreign-born population, median age, and

Democratic lean as independent variables. None of the variables was significant predictors for family reunification for Latino/Hispanic children. When the climate variable was regressed on the representation variable, no significant result was found. These results are not unexpected given that small sample size ($n = 52$) and that the proportion of children with detained parents in care (about 5,100) is small compared with the average total number of children in care (679,000).

The strong variation in total reunification rates along with the variation in the number of bills across states necessitates closer inspection. Please see Table 5 which lists only the states with the most antagonistic and most supportive climates. Only three states had over twenty bills intended to protect against immigration. These were the same three states with the most antagonistic climates (few supportive bills). The same is true for the states with the highest numbers of supportive bills. The same states had the least antagonistic climates. For a clearer comparison, a variable for reunification$_\text{white-Hispanic}$ was created by subtracting the percentage of Hispanic/Latino children returned to the custody of their parents from the percentage of white children returned to the custody of their parents for each state. When the analysis is limited to a comparison between the three states with the most antagonistic and the three states with the most supportive climates — states for which immigration is clearly a salient political issue — climate is correlated with

Table 5. Least and Most Supportive States[a].

State	Number of Protective Bills	Most Protective Climate	Representation ($M_\text{protective} = -3.29$)	Reunification White-Hispanic ($M_\text{protective} = 0.64$)
Arizona	46	46	−4.25	1.65
Tennessee	23	21	−4.75	−1.875
Virginia	23	12	−0.875	2.15

State	Number of Supportive Bills	Most Supportive Climate	Representation ($M_\text{supportive} = 0.27$)	Reunification White-Hispanic ($M_\text{supportive} = -3.69$)
California	97	−87	2.375	−3.9
Illinois	31	−25	−10.925	−3.825
Connecticut	12	−12	9.35	−3.35

[a]Hawaii ranks among the states with the most supportive legislation although the legislation is directed at immigrants from Asia and the Pacific. It is excluded from this list given the small percent of Latino/Hispanic child in state care, 2.7%, between 2010 and 2013.

reunification$_{\text{White-Hispanic}}$, $r(5) = -.861$, $d = 3.46$.[20] These values fall under the threshold of very large effect according to Rosenthal (1996). When compared to white children in state care within the most antagonistic and most supportive states, Latino/Hispanic children were more likely to be returned to the custody of their parents in the states with supportive climates. Latino/Hispanic children were underrepresented in the child welfare system in all of the outliers except for California and Connecticut. Climate and representation are not strongly related given the variation in representation across states, $d = .48$, a small effect. Even so, Hispanic/Latino children are actually underrepresented the child welfare systems of all three of the most antagonistic states. This may reflect Hispanic/Latino's avoidance of social services or hiding behavior as a consequence of a more hostile environment.

While direct measures for the immigration status are not available, Table 6 is included to provide indirect measures for the children in state

Table 6. Comparison of Most Supportive States with States with the Highest Unauthorized Populations and States that Enacted Omnibus Legislation.

	Mean Reunification White-Hispanic/Latino	Mean Difference[a]	Cohen's d[b]
States with most protective/least supportive climate (Arizona, Tennessee, and Virginia)	0.64	4.33	3.46
States with the largest unauthorized populations[c] (California, Texas, Florida, New York, New Jersey, and Illinois)	−2.53	1.16	0.34
States with the highest unauthorized labor force[c] (Nevada, California, Texas, and New Jersey)	−2.69	1.00	0.35
States with the highest K-12 with unauthorized parents[c] (Nevada, California, Texas, and Arizona)	−1.43	2.26	1.18
States that enacted omnibus legislation[c] (Arizona, Alabama, Georgia, Indiana, South Carolina, and Utah)	−1.11	2.58	0.85

[a] $M_{\text{reunification W-H}} = -3.69$ for most supportive states. Since the analysis is based on population data, significance tests are not included.
[b] Standard thresholds for interpreting effect size are .2 small, .5 medium, .8 large, and 1.3 very large.
[c] Krogstad and Passel (2014).

care with detained or deported parents. Table 6 compares the states with the most supportive immigration legislation on the one hand, with groupings of states with the largest unauthorized populations and states enacting omnibus legislation on the other hand. The comparisons provide an indication of whether the size of a state's unauthorized population is related to reunification outcomes. The information in Table 6 illustrates that a state's legislative climate is more important than the size of the state's unauthorized Latino/Hispanic population in terms of family reunification outcomes. While the mean difference between the states with the most protective and most supportive climates was almost three and one half standard deviations, the effect sizes for the mean difference between the most supportive states and the states with the largest unauthorized population, $d = .34$, and highest unauthorized labor force, $d = .35$, were small. The states that enacted omnibus legislation, in contrast, also show lower percentages of reunification than the most supportive states. Importantly, the mean difference between the most supportive states and the states with the highest number of children with unauthorized parents is also large, $d = 1.18$. These are the states where children of an undocumented parent(s) are more likely to enter the child welfare system. Even though this comparison includes all Hispanic/Latino children in care and is not limited to children of undocumented parents, this result nevertheless, suggests that once within the child welfare system, children of undocumented parents are less likely to be reunified with their parent(s).

CONCLUSION

Differing conceptions of national inclusion and exclusion are visible in state immigration legislation. Not all state-level immigration legislation is antagonistic toward immigrants. Notably, proximity to the Mexican border does not necessarily lead to more antagonistic legislation even though Mexican border states introduced a large number of immigration bills during the period between 2008 and 2014. Arizona revealed the most antagonistic climate while California exhibited the most supportive climate toward immigrants. Additionally, the larger the Hispanic/Latino population in a state, the less antagonistic the climate.

Moreover, state immigration legislation is correlated with child welfare outcomes for Hispanic/Latino children in the states where immigration is a salient political issue. This suggests a relationship between inclusive or exclusive conceptions of the nation and outcomes for Hispanic/Latino children in the child welfare system. States with the most antagonistic legislation have lower family reunification percentages for Hispanic/Latino children compared with percentages of reunification for white children than the states with the most supportive immigration bills. In other words, Hispanic/Latino children are less likely to be returned to the custody of their parents in the states with the most antagonistic immigration legislation compared with the states with the most supportive immigration legislation. Significantly, Hispanic/Latino children are not overrepresented in the states with the most antagonistic legislation. This suggests that it is not at the point of immigration enforcement that the discrepancy in outcomes comes about. Instead, the difference arises during the period of the CPS review process. Concern over cultural threats and the biases of individual actors cannot be discounted. In addition, the effects of institutionalized bureaucracy should not be underestimated. Additional research concerning the interaction between CPS and ICE is warranted.

LIMITATIONS

Data on the immigration status of the parents of children within the child welfare system is not available. Given that tracking the immigration status of the parents of children within the child welfare system would have detrimental consequences for the children in care, this information may never be obtainable. Without such measures, it is impossible to directly see if immigration policy affects reunification expressly for the children of detained or deported parents. It is impossible to precisely determine whether the disparities in reunification percentages for Hispanic/Latino children compared with those for white children are solely a consequence of the number of children with detained or deported parents in a state or whether it is a result of a hostile atmosphere toward the Hispanic/Latino population in general in those states.

NOTES

1. The national quota system, stemming from the 1920s, classified all Northern European nationalities as part of the white race and capable of assimilation. Mexicans, in contrast, even with formal USA citizenship, were viewed as alien (Ngai 7–8).

2. The analysis focuses on children in the temporary managing conservatorship of the state/Child Protective Services, 2010–2013. It does not include children in Immigration and Customs Enforcement (ICE) detention centers.

3. These laws foster a view of unauthorized immigrants as "unworthy and illegal." A common assertion is that if a person comes across the border illegally, everything they do inside the United States is then illegal. Since Latinos make up the largest percentage of unauthorized immigrants, these conceptions of illegality are transferred to the larger Latino community (Maddali, 2014, pp. 652–655). It is important to note that perceptions of Hispanic immigrants as criminals persist even though data show that first generation Hispanic immigrants are less likely than natives to engage in criminal activity (Gonzales, Knight, Morgan-Lopez, Saenz, & Sirolli, 2002; Hagan & Palloni, 1999; Martinez & Valenzuela, 2006).

4. Interestingly, higher rates of enforcement have been linked to increasing the undocumented population. The increased costs of undocumented migration result in increased length of stay. While documented Latino residents may leave because of the hostile environment, undocumented immigrants are less economically mobile and settle for undesirable positions that have been left vacant. Estimates show that undocumented immigrants stay in the Unites States for seven months longer, on average, than their documented equivalents (Rocha, Hawes, Fryar, & Wrinkle, 2014).

5. It is estimated that nearly half of undocumented immigrants in the United States entered the country legally but overstayed their visas or violated visa terms (Pew Hispanic Center, 2006). Overstaying one's visa is subject to civil removal proceedings but not to criminal prosecution. Nevertheless, little distinction is made between drug dealers, immigrants and terrorists in terms of the control solutions used (Villalobos, 2011, p. 153). Approximately 50% of detainees are housed in facilities with criminal detainees (Human Rights First, 2011).

6. See *Emptage et al. v. Torres et al.* Transcript of the Injunction for equitable Relief, 23.

7. Studies have shown that the core values and beliefs rooted in Latino culture offer protective factors for the family (De LA Rosa, 2002; Dettlaff & Johnson, 2011; Holleran & Waller, 2003). It is also possible that Latino/Hispanic residents are more likely to fear authorities and avoid social service in states with more antagonistic immigration legislation.

8. There is a long legal history detailing family law as a state issue. The unwillingness for federal courts to consider family law cases stems from federal court tradition and jurisprudence. Nevertheless, there have been heated clashes over the role of federal courts in domestic relations and the Supreme Court has decided many constitutional questions related to the family (Cahn, 1994; Harbach, 2009).

9. The U.S. Department of Health and Human Services released an information memorandum on February 20, 2015 offering new guidance on best practices to safeguard children in cases where the parent is detained or deported (Chiamulera, 2015). Included in the list of recommendations is the need to educate courts, providers, and caseworkers about the unique needs of immigrant families.

10. In Texas, for example, first (8%) and second (20%) generation Latino children are less likely to be placed with relatives than the general population of out of home placements (25%) (Vericker, Kuehn, & Capps, 2007).

11. It is important to note that CPS has policies about working with incarcerated parents. Enhanced visiting programs exist to facilitate reunification (Block & Potthast, 1998). Programs differ by state. In Texas, for example, policy informs

CPS workers that "Parents who are incarcerated must continue to be involved in service planning and relationship-building activities with the child that may include: visitation between the parent and child; letter writing; phone contact; or other activities deemed appropriate" (Child Protective Services, 2011).

12. Children in state care refer to children in the temporary managing conservatorship of the state, under the supervision of CPS. These were not children in ICE detention centers. These children were removed from the custody of their parent(s) and were in either foster care, in kinship placements or in residential treatment facilities until the trial determined custody.

13. Population values for state, Hispanic/Latino residents and Latino Foreign born are per 100,000 in this analysis.

14. Gallop decides the political orientation of states by subtracting the total percentage of adults in a state identifying or leaning Republican from the percentage of adults in the state identifying or leaning Democratic. Positive values suggest that a state is more Democratic while negative values suggest that a state is more Republican. The measure is based on interviews with more than 321,000 U.S. adults. Data is weighted to match the demographic parameters of the U.S. Census.

15. Bills emphasizing support of legal immigrants are included as measures of support for immigrant populations within states.

16. Reunification is one of four possible outcomes in CPS cases. The other outcomes include permanent managing conservatorship (PMC) to relatives or family friends; the termination of parental rights where the child is available for adoption; and, the last outcome possibility is PMC to the state. In the last case the child become a ward of the state indefinitely.

17. Factors that contribute to the variation in reunification rates across states include demographics and family structure. African American children are less likely to be reunified with parents than whites and Latino/Hispanics. Race interacts with family structure. Children from single parent families are reunified more slowly than children from two-parent families (Harris & Courtney, 2003).

18. It is important to note the small sample size, $n = 52$, and the large variation across states.

19. Defining the representation variable as a ratio resulted in non-significant findings as well.

20. Pooled standard deviation was calculated assuming population values ($r^2 = .74$).

REFERENCES

Abell, J., Condor, S., & Stevenson, C. (2006). 'We are an island': Geographical imagery in accounts of citizenship, civil society and national identity in Scotland and in England. *Political Psychology, 27*, 207–226.

Adoption and Safe Families Act. (1997). Retrieved from https://www.gpo.gov/fdsys/pkg/PLAW-105publ89/html/PLAW-105publ89.htm

Billig, M. (1995). *Banal nationalism*. London: Sage.

Block, K. J., & Potthast, M. J. (1998). Girl scouts beyond bars: Facilitating parent-child contact in correctional settings. *Child Welfare, 77*, 561–578.

Blokland, T. (2003). Ethnic complexity: Routes to discriminatory repertoires in an inner-city neighborhood. *Ethnic and Racial Studies, 26*, 1–24.

Breuilly, J. (1993). *Nationalism and the state.* Chicago, IL: University of Chicago Press.

Cahn, N. R. (1994). Family law, federalism and the federal courts. *Iowa Law Review, 79*, 1073–1126.

Capps, R., Castañeda, R. M., Chaudry, A., & Santos, R. (2007). *Paying the price: The impact of immigration raids on America's children.* Retrieved from http://www.urban.org/publications/411566.html

Chiamulera, C. (2015). When an immigrant parent is detained or deported: Child welfare best practices. *Child Law Practice, 34*, 60.

Child Protective Services. (2011). *6414.2 Parental participation DFPS handbook.* Retrieved from http://www.dfps.state.tx.us/handbooks/cps/files/CPS_pg_6400.asp.

Children's Bureau, U.S. Department of Health and Human Services. (2013). *Child welfare outcomes report data.* (Data Set) Retrieved from http://cwoutcomes.acf.hhs.gov/data/overview

Coleman, M. (2007). Immigration geopolitics beyond the Mexico–U.S. border. *Antipode, 39*, 54–76.

De La Rosa, M. (2002). Acculturation and Latino adolescents' substance use: A research agenda for the future. *Substance Use and Misuse, 37*, 429–456.

Dettlaff, A. J., Earner, I., & Philips, S. D. (2009). Latino children of immigrants in the child welfare system: Prevalence, characteristics, and risk. *Children and Youth Services Review, 31*, 775–783.

Dettlaff, A. J., & Johnson, M. A. (2011). Child maltreatment dynamics among migrant and U.S. born Latino children: Findings from the National Survey of Child and Adolescent Well-being (NSCAW). *Children and Youth Services Review, 33*, 936–944.

Gellner, E. (1983). *Nations and nationalism.* Ithaca, NY: Cornell University Press.

Gonzales, N. A., Knight, G. P., Morgan-Lopez, A. A., Saenz, D., & Sirolli, A. (2002). Acculturation and the mental health of Latino youths: An integration and critique of the literature. In J. M. Contreras, K. A. Kerns, & A. M. Neal Barnett (Eds.), *Latino children and families in the United States: Current research and future directions* (pp. 45–74). Westport, CT: Praeger.

Hagan, J., & Palloni, A. (1999). Sociological criminology and the mythology of Hispanic immigration and crime. *Social Problems, 46*, 617–632.

Harbach, M. J. (2009). Is the family a federal question? *Washington & Lee Law Review, 66*, 131–202.

Harris, M. S., & Courtney, M. E. (2003). The interaction of race, ethnicity, and family structure with respect to the timing of family reunification. *Children and Youth Services Review, 25*, 409–429.

Holleran, L. K., & Waller, M. A. (2003). Sources of resilience among Chicano/a youth: Forging identities in the borderlands. *Child and Adolescent Social Work Journal, 20*, 335–350.

Human Rights First. (2011). Jails and jumpsuits Transforming the U.S. Immigration detention system – A two-year review. Retrieved from http://www.humanrightsfirst.org/wp-content/uploads/pdf/HRF-Jails-and-Jumpsuits-report.pdf

Hutchinson, J. (2006). Hot and banal nationalism: The nationalization of the masses. In G. Delanty & K. Kumar (Eds.), *The SAGE handbook of nations and nationalism* (pp. 295–306). London: Sage.

Kedourie, E. (1971). *Nationalism in Asia and Africa.* London: Weidenfeld and Nicolson.

Kerwin, D., & Lin, S. Y. (2009). *Immigration detention: Can ICE meet Its legal imperatives and case management responsibilities?'* Retrieved from http://www.migrationpolicy.org/research/immigrant-detention-can-ice-meet-its-legal-imperatives-and-case-management-responsibilities

Krogstad, J. M., & Passel, J. S. (2014). *5 facts about illegal immigration in the USA. PEW research center.* Retrieved from http://www.pewresearch.org/fact-tank/2014/11/18/5-facts-about-illegal-immigration-in-the-u-s/

Kundnani, A. (2001). In a foreign land: The new popular racism. *Race and Class, 43*, 41–60.

Maddali, A. (2014). The immigrant "other": Racialized identity and the devaluation of immigrant family relations. *Indiana Law Journal, 89*, 643–702.

Manning, R. (2011). Punishing the innocent: Children of incarcerated and detained parents. *Criminal Justice Ethics, 30*, 267–287.

Martin, L. (2011). The geopolitics of vulnerability: Children's legal subjectivity, immigrant family detention and U.S. Immigration law and enforcement policy. *Gender, Place and Culture: A Journal of Feminist Geography, 18*, 477–498.

Martinez, R., & Valenzuela, A. (2006). *Immigration and crime: Race, ethnicity and violence.* New York, NY: New York University Press.

Mayall, J. (1990). *Nationalism and international society.* Cambridge: Cambridge University Press.

Morton, J. (2011). *Exercising prosecutorial discretion consistent with the civil immigration priorities of the agency for the apprehension, detention and removal of aliens.* U.S. Department of Homeland Security, U.S. Immigration and Custom Enforcement. Retrieved from https://www.ice.gov/doclib/secure-communities/pdf/prosecutorial-discretion-memo.pdf

Mountz, A. (2004). Embodying the nation-state: Canada's response to human smuggling. *Political Geography, 23*, 323–345.

National Council of State Legislatures [NCSL]. (2014). *Immigration enactments database.* (Data File) Retrieved from http://www.ncsl.org/research/immigration/immigration-laws-database.aspx

Ngai, M. M. (2004). *Impossible subjects* Princeton, NJ: Princeton University Press.

Pew Hispanic Center. (2004). Generational difference fact sheet. *Hispanic Trends,* March 19. Retrieved from http://www.pewhispanic.org/2004/03/19/generational-differences/

Pew Hispanic Center. (2006). Modes of entry for the unauthorized migrant population. *Hispanic Trends,* May 22. Retrieved from http://www.pewhispanic.org/2006/05/22/modes-of-entry-for-the-unauthorized-migrant-population/

Pew Research Center. (2014). The politics of American Generations: How age affects attitudes and voting behavior. *FactTank News in Numbers,* July 9. Retrieved from http://www.pewresearch.org/fact-tank/2014/07/09/the-politics-of-american-generations-how-age-affects-attitudes-and-voting-behavior/

Rabin, N. (2011). *Disappearing parents: A report on immigration enforcement and the child welfare system.* Retrieved from http://www.law.arizona.edu/depts/bacon_program/disappearing_parents_report.cfm

Rocha, R. R., Hawes, D. P., Fryar, A. H., & Wrinkle, R. D. (2014). Policy climates, enforcement rates, and migrant behavior: Is self-deportation a viable immigration policy? *Policy Studies Journal, 42*, 79–100.

Rosenthal, J. A. (1996). Qualitative descriptors of strength of association and effect size. *Journal of Social Service Research, 21,* 37–59.
Saad, L. (2012). *In the U.S., blue states outnumber red states, 20 to 12.* Retrieved from http://www.gallup.com/poll/160175/blue-states-outnumber-red-states.aspx
Sandovici, M. E., Jakobsen, T. G., & Strabac, Z. (2012). Political nationalism and attitudes towards immigration: The interaction of knowledge and policy. *International Journal on Minority and Group Rights, 19,* 115–127.
Sassen, S. (2007). The limits of power and the complexity of powerlessness: The case of immigration. *Harvard Unbound, 3,* 105–115.
Schmitt, G. R., & Jones, E. (2014). *Overview of federal criminal cases fiscal year 2013.* Retrieved from http://www.ussc.gov/sites/default/files/pdf/research-and-publications/research-publications/2014/FY13_Overview_Federal_Criminal_Cases.pdf
Skey, M. (2009). The national in everyday life: A critical engagement with Michael Billig's thesis of Banal Nationalism. *The Sociological Review, 57,* 331–346.
Sniderman, P., Hagendoorn, L., & Prior, M. (2004). Predisposing factors and situational triggers: Exclusionary reactions to immigrant minorities. *American Political Science Review, 98,* 35–50.
Staudt, K. (2009). Violence at the border: Broadening the discourse to include feminism, human security, and deeper democracy. In K. Staudt, T. Payan, & Z. A. Kruszewski (Eds.), *Human rights along the US-Mexico border: Gendered violence and insecurity* (pp. 1–27). Tucson, AZ: University of Arizona Press.
Thronson, D. (2008). Custody and contradictions: Exploring immigration law as federal family law in the context of child custody. *Hastings Law Journal, 59,* 453–514.
Troxel v. Granvill. (2000). 530 USA 57, 65.
United States Census Bureau. (2014). *Population estimates.* (Data Set) Retrieved from http://www.census.gov/popest/data/state/totals/2014/index.html
Varsanyi, M. (2008). Rescaling the 'alien', rescaling personhood: Neoliberalism, immigration, and the state. *Annals of the Association of American Geographers, 98,* 877–896.
Vericker, T., Kuehn, D., & Capps, R. (2007). Latino children of immigrants in the Texas child welfare system. *Protecting Children, 22,* 20–35.
Villalobos, J. (2011). Promises and human rights: The Obama administration on immigrant detention policy reform. *Race, Gender & Class, 18,* 151–170.
Weber, M. (1978). *Economy and society.* Los Angeles, CA: University of California Press.
Wessler, S. (2011). *Shattered families: The perilous intersection of immigration enforcement and the child welfare system.* Applied Research Center. Retrieved from https://www.raceforward.org/research/reports/shattered-families
Zayas, L. H., & Bradlee, M. H. (2014). Exiling children creating orphans: When immigration policies hurt citizens. *Social Work, 59,* 167–175.
Zingher, J. (2014). The ideological and electoral determinants of laws targeting undocumented migrants in the U.S. States. *State Politics & Policy Quarterly, 14,* 90–117.

REVISITING MOTHERS' PENSIONS: A CRITIQUE OF A SOCIAL SCIENCE CLASSIC AND A NEW ANALYSIS

Sheera Joy Olasky and David F. Greenberg

ABSTRACT

We identify methodological weaknesses in a paper by Skocpol, Abend-Wein, Howard, and Lehmann (1993) on the origins of mothers' pensions in the American states in the early twentieth century. These include a sub-optimal and potentially biased strategy for assessing the impact of state characteristics on the time to adoption of pensions, as well as the use of a backward stepwise regression procedure for selecting independent variables. To determine whether Skocpol et al.'s conclusions remain valid, we recreated most of their dataset and used methods that are more appropriate for the analysis of duration data, including the Cox and complementary cloglog event history procedures. While we find support for several of their claims, our findings allow for a more straightforward interpretation of the role of explanatory variables, and the temporal dependence of the adoption process.

Keywords: Skocpol; mothers' pensions; women's associations; welfare state; event history analysis; stepwise regression

INTRODUCTION

More than 20 years ago, Theda Skocpol and her collaborators (Skocpol, Abend-Wein, Howard, & Lehmann, 1993) published a path-breaking study of the enactment of mothers' pensions (i.e., welfare payments) in the United States. The paper, part of a larger study published the previous year (Skocpol, 1992), challenged widely prevalent understandings of the United States as a laggard in the adoption of welfare policies (Garfinkel, Rainwater, & Smeeding, 2010; Orloff, 1988). Skocpol et al. [hereafter SAWHGL], demonstrating that most American states adopted welfare state policies before the federal government did, showed that earlier explanations of policy innovation failed to provide satisfactory explanations for the spread of mothers' pensions, and they provided evidence for the importance of women's political interventions on behalf of this policy. This demonstration helped to motivate a theoretical shift from the state-centered theorizing of Skocpol's earlier work to a polity-based analysis in which social movements and other non-state actors figured prominently.

The paper was also important methodologically as one of the first sociological investigations into the amount of time it took governments to adopt a new policy.[1] As such, it has been a highly influential work, with a Social Science Citation count of 84 as of this writing. Although the study has drawn both conceptual and methodological criticism (see Baker, 1993; Domhoff, 1995; Sparks & Walniuk, 1995; but see Skocpol, 1995 for a reply), it is rightly praised for these contributions. Nevertheless, the authors employ several statistical procedures that are poorly suited for their purposes, and they fail to use or mention established alternative approaches. The weaknesses of the procedures the authors did adopt are potentially serious enough to warrant a re-analysis to determine to what extent SAWGHL's findings hold up when better procedures are used. This paper takes up that challenge. It introduces no new theories; it restricts itself to testing those of SAWHGL using better statistical methods.

SKOCPOL ET AL.'S APPROACH

In the original article, SAWHGL set out to explain the temporal pattern of mothers' pension legislation enactment across the American states in the decades prior to the adoption of the federal Social Security Act in 1935. They argued that previous explanations for the diffusion of other state policies, such as a state's "innovation score," do not explain the pattern of adoption in the mothers' pension case. Rather, mothers' pensions spread more quickly across the states than would be expected, with many states adopting before their score predicts they should have. Instead they argued that women's voluntary associations allowed women an avenue through which they could advocate for pensions, so that the timing of pension endorsements by local women's groups should account for the pattern of pension enactment by state governments.

To assess the impact of these endorsements and other theoretically relevant independent variables on the speed of adoption of mothers' pensions by the American states, SAWHGL divided the adoption dates into seven intervals: 1911–1913, 1914–1915, 1916–1917, 1918–1920, 1923–1928, 1931–1934, and post-1935, while two periods in which no events occurred, 1921–1922 and 1929–1930, were excluded. They coded these time periods by their ranks, so that the earliest period was coded as six, and the last period as zero. They then estimated an ordinary least squares (OLS) regression using this ordinal coding as the dependent variable.

SAWHGL began with a large set of predictors presumed to be theoretically relevant. To identify those to be included in their final model, they used two separate but related two-stage approaches to select independent variables for their regressions. In both approaches, they began with the selection of 24 predictors. Seven were dropped because they were strongly correlated with one another or were logically overlapping, leaving 17 potential explanatory variables for further analysis. They then estimated backward stepwise regressions of the outcome variable, beginning with all 17 regressors. Variables whose regression coefficients were not significant were dropped one at a time until just three variables were left, all of them making significant contributions based on their t statistics.[2]

CRITIQUE

The first of the questionable procedures in SAWGHL's work is their use of OLS regression to assess the impact of independent variables on times to adoption. It has been known for several decades that OLS regression is not ideal for studying the impact of predictors on the time to the occurrence of an event. Event history analyses are considered preferable because they avoid certain biases associated with the use of OLS regression to study durations (Box-Steffensmeier & Jones, 2004; Cleves, Gutierrez, Gould, & Marchenko, 2008, p. 2; Hosmer, Lemeshow, & May, 2008; Klein & Moeschberger, 2003). Software that can carry out event history analyses has been available for more than three decades (Tuma, 1982), and is now incorporated in widely used commercial statistical packages.

One of the reasons event history analysis is preferred to OLS regression in studying times to events is its ability to handle right censoring (cases that did not experience the event of interest in the time span of the study). The relevance of this issue can be seen by considering SAWHGL's treatment of the two right-censored cases in the dataset, Georgia and South Carolina, both of which failed to adopt mothers' pensions during the time under analysis, 1910–1935. In their regressions, SAWHGL treated these states just like the adopting states, and assigned them a value of zero when operationalizing the timing of adoptions. They did this both in their ordinal scale and in their alternative constructions of the adoption variable, which include a continuous variable representing the number of years prior to 1935 that a state adopted pension legislation (as explained in their Endnote 2). While they consider a value of zero on their ordinal scale to represent adoption "after 1935," this value really means that the state had not adopted legislation by the study's end in 1935. On a scale designed to capture when a state experienced this event, assigning a value to states that did not experience the event is problematic.

By assigning a value of zero to Georgia and South Carolina, SAWHGL are coding these two states as though they had passed legislation in 1935. Through additional research we found that these two states did in fact adopt pension legislation in 1937, but in 1935 there was no way to know whether these states would later adopt mothers' pensions or whether they would fail to do so. Assigning them the value of zero, which implies a 1935 adoption, leads to an under-estimation of the mean time to adoption.

While SAWHGL could have extended their period of analysis to 1937 in order to observe the final two cases of pension legislation adoption, thereby avoiding the issue of censored cases, this choice would have required the strong assumption that the political atmosphere was no different after the adoption of federal legislation than it was before. Dropping these cases would have been equally problematic, as the necessary assumption that these later- or never-adopters did not differ in meaningful ways from the states that adopted earlier is untenable. In contrast, event history approaches are designed to handle such right-censored cases (Box-Steffensmeier & Jones, 2004; Cleves et al., 2008; Hosmer et al., 2008; Klein & Moeschberger, 2003).

SAWGHL's operationalization of the adoption and endorsement variables also raises questions. The 26 years under observation are not broken up equally over the adoption scale values, but instead are partitioned according to what appears to be an arbitrary coding scheme: while the three years in the 1911–1913 period are coded six, the six-year period from 1923 to 1928 is assigned the value two. Some years in which no adoptions occurred, such as 1921, 1922, 1929, and 1930 are not represented by a value at all, while the years 1924–1927 saw no adoptions, yet are included in the 1923–1928 adoption category. As we will soon discuss, these decisions have an impact on our ability to interpret changes in the time to adoption.

SAWHGL rationalize their coding scheme by arguing, "a single chronological year of time simply does not have the same meaning throughout the 1911–1935 period" (at 687). This assertion could mean that for some unknown, ineffable reason unrelated to the variables selected on the basis of theoretical considerations, the chances of adoption were higher in some periods and lower in others. It could also mean that the variables included in the model as regressors had impacts that varied with time, although the results that they present offer no evidence that this is the case, and the statistical methods they used would be incapable of revealing this.

In fact, the assumptions that they make about the relationship between time and adoptions are possibilities to be tested, not assumed. If, for example, there had been a "pro-reform" sentiment in some years but not in others, this would be a potential explanation for the timing of adoptions, and could be treated as such. However, they did not even determine that, given a constant rate of adoption realized stochastically, there could have been a few years in which, completely by chance, no adoptions took place.

Table 1, which displays the number of enactments in each year from 1911 to 1935, and Fig. 1, which graphs these counts, demonstrate how these concerns are relevant. The figure shows a burst of legislation beginning shortly after Illinois became the first state to adopt, followed by a period of declining adoption rates, which stabilize at a very low level for a period of years in which stragglers adopted. As such, we see no basis for cutting up the time span after 1917 into discrete intervals, or for the rest of the choices regarding cutting points that SAWGHL have made. Indeed, all of the SAWHGL choices regarding cutting points seem arbitrary.

Why, for example, is 1914 joined with 1915, rather than with the 1911–1913 interval? Why is 1916 chosen to begin another time interval, rather than being grouped with the 1914–1915 interval? Why were the years 1921, 1922, and 1935 dropped for lack of observations, while the years 1932–1934, during which there were also no observations, were retained and lumped together with 1931? The choices seem lacking in rationale, and could have been made differently. Consequently, while SAWGHL's assumption that social time does not flow at a constant pace could perhaps be justified, the manner in which they implemented their construction of

Table 1. Enactments of Pension Legislation by *Year* and SAWHGL Category.

Year	Enactments	SAWGHL's Time Coding
1911	1	
1912	0	
1913	18	6
1914	1	
1915	8	5
1916	1	
1917	6	4
1918	1	
1919	3	
1920	1	3
1921	0	Omitted
1922	0	Omitted
1923	2	
1924	0	
1925	0	
1926	0	
1927	0	
1928	2	2
1929	0	Omitted
1930	0	Omitted
1931	2	
1932	0	
1933	0	
1934	0	1
1935	0	0

time appears whimsical. Moreover, the creation of seven ordinal values that are then treated as values of a continuous outcome variable in a regression equation would have been completely irrelevant for the purpose of assessing the time dependence of the predictors even if the cutting points chosen for time had been better justified.

To assess the meaningfulness of the SAWHGL periodization, we estimated a Poisson regression of enactments against *Year*, treating *Year* as a continuous variable, and the number of states at risk as an exposure. This procedure postulates a long-term rate whose natural logarithm depends linearly on *Year*, with the number of events in a given year occurring randomly about the expected value. As expected, the coefficient for *Year* was negative and highly significant. A goodness of fit test for this model based on the Pearson chi-square statistic was highly significant, indicating that the

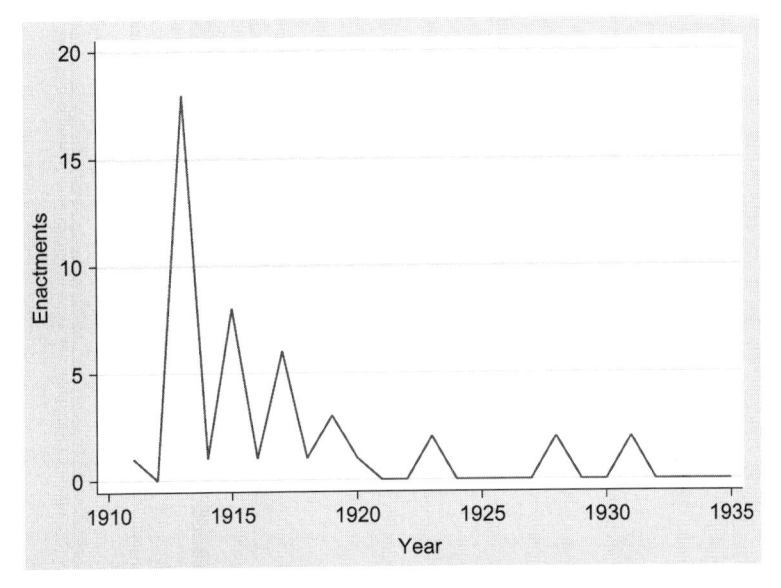

Fig. 1. Enactments of Pension Legislation, 1911–1935.

assumption of a uniform process for the entire time span is not valid. However, when the estimation was restricted to the post-1915 years, the coefficient for *Year* was not statistically significant, and the goodness of fit test failed to achieve statistical significance at the 0.05 level ($p = 0.06$). This test result indicates a satisfactory fit, consistent with a constant adoption rate for this period. When the estimation was repeated with a negative binomial regression (a procedure appropriate when unmeasured heterogeneity is present, even this minimal periodization proved to be unnecessary). Any periodization of the years following the initial burst of activity is unnecessary.

This procedure just described does not test for the possibility that the three predictors in the SAWHGL model have different effects at different points in time. A non-parametric test of that possibility could, in principle, be carried out by introducing six dummy variables for the periods after the first, along with interaction terms for the products of each of these dummies with the three predictors of the theoretical model. Doing so would entail the introduction of 24 additional free parameters. Given the small number of states and time points in our study, this is not a viable option, and it is understandable that SAWHGL did not adopt it. We do, however, test the proposition that endorsements made at different times had different impacts.

Two additional concerns stem from SAWHGL's treatment of the ordinal duration variable as though it were interval-level. As they have coded it, the adoption variable can take on only a small set of integral values. However, OLS imposes no limitations on the value of the outcome, and predicts values that fall between the seven integral values of the adoption scale, which represent "adoption waves" of varying duration. These predictions may be difficult to interpret.

Additionally, the results based on the assumption of an interval-level outcome to make sense, the differences between values must be meaningful, so that a change of one unit anywhere along the scale is understood to have the same consequences. That this is not the case is evident in a comparison of the difference between the values zero and one on the adoption scale with the difference between one and two. An increase from zero to one means moving from not passing pension legislation before the Social Security Act to passing it in the final four-year interval; increasing from one to two, however, represents a move from an adoption in the final interval to an adoption during the preceding six-year interval. This implies that the difference between no adoption and adoption is of the same magnitude as that of moving the adoption forward by six years. There is no reason to assume that this is true. Likewise, their procedure assumes that the difference between two consecutive intervals, such as 1911–1913 and 1914–1915, is the same as the difference between intervals separated by a stretch of years in which no adoptions took place, as in the case of 1918–1920 and 1923–1928 or 1923–1928 and 1931–1934.

Similar problems are associated with SAWHGL's construction of their women's voluntary association endorsement variable. As their Appendix shows, pension endorsements were made between 1912 and 1919. SAWHGL broke this time period into four categories each lasting two years, so that an endorsement in 1912–1913 is coded four, while states are coded zero if there is no evidence of women's groups' endorsements at all. Thus, for values one through four, increasing the endorsement variable by one unit corresponds to an endorsement having been made during the preceding two-year interval, while increasing from zero to one represents a move from no endorsement to an endorsement in 1918–1919, or the last time period during which endorsements were made. We question the assumption that the difference between no endorsement and an endorsement is comparable in its effect on adoption timing to the difference between moving from an endorsement in the years 1918–1919 to one in the 1916–1917 period. We also remain unconvinced that their endorsement categories should be treated as interval-level.[3]

The difficulties created by these variable constructions may explain why SAWHGL's results seem so incongruous and their treatment of time is inconsistent. Nothing in their analysis supports their contention that endorsements had differential effects on adoption over time, yet they write, "Moving from no evidence of endorsement to the earliest endorsement(s) in 1912–1913 advances the timing of enactment of mothers' pension legislation by about four years during the 1910's (and by about 10 years afterward)" (at 694). Despite their earlier argument that a single chronological year of time is a poor metric for measuring adoption time, and the efforts that they undertook to periodize their adoption variable, they present their conclusions in terms of single years, and speak of time as a continuous variable with a uniform meaning throughout the time span under study.

We also find cause for concern in the two stepwise approaches SAWHGL use to settle on their final model. While each approach begins with a different configuration of variables, both involve estimating a series of regressions in which independent variables are dropped one at a time based on significance tests for each variable, until only endorsements, school expenditures and percent of the workforce that is female are statistically significant and are retained in the model. Given the small number of observations in their regression, it is understandable that SAWHGL did not want to work with a full set of 24 variables in their model; including a large number of explanatory variables uses up degrees of freedom, risks over-fitting the data, and raises the possibility of encountering problems with high multi-collinearity.[4] However, the manner in which they chose to deal with these problems is not ideal.

The procedure of dropping non-significant variables sequentially until all the variables that remain show statistical significance is widely used, but it is flawed. The first issue arises in all multivariate analyses with multiple independent variables. When more than one coefficient is being tested for significance, the probability of obtaining a significant coefficient by chance is magnified. A test in which the researcher sets a nominal level of 0.05 or 0.01 as the cutoff for each coefficient implies a much higher probability of finding at least one coefficient to be statistically significant in a population by chance. Indeed, assuming independence of tests, when 17 correlations are subjected to significance testing at a nominal level of 0.05, the chances of finding three that are "significant" in a population where all of the correlations are zero is just marginally higher than 0.05. To avoid the elevated chances of a Type I error, researchers commonly use a Bonferroni correction to adjust the probability associated with each estimate.

Because SAWGHL include all of their independent variables in the initial regression, their computation of degrees of freedom based only on the retained predictors understates the relevant degrees of freedom. In so doing it also under-estimates their standard errors and confidence limits, inflates their t statistics, and leads to p values that are unrealistically small, misleading the researcher as to the significance of estimates. Consequently, the estimates of parameters for variables retained in the model will not be as precise as they appear to be (VanSteelandt, Bekaert, & Claeskens, 2010). This, in turn, increases the likelihood that a variable will be wrongly retained as a predictor (Babyak, 2004; Carver, 1978; Cohen, 1990, 1994; Copas, 1983; Derksen & Keselman, 1992; Harrell, 2001; Leigh, 1988; Meehl, 1990; Shaver, 1993; Thompson, 1993, 1995, 2001; Whittingham, Stephens, Bradbury, & Freckleton, 2006). For these reasons, Moody and Marvell (2010) observe that in a backward stepwise regression "it can be difficult to determine which variables are truly irrelevant and should be dropped from the analysis, and which are truly relevant, but apparently insignificant owing to the presence of irrelevant variables" (at 698).

Second, the order in which variables are dropped in a stepwise procedure can be sensitive to slight changes in the correlations among the variables. As a result, sampling error alone can affect the choice of variables for inclusion (Snyder, 1991; Thompson, 1995). Moreover, the exclusion of variables because they fail to achieve statistical significance is tantamount to accepting the null hypothesis when it may be false (Greenland, 2008). To guard against such issues arising, if multi-collinearity is present, some variant of factor analysis or scale construction would provide a less problematic way to reduce the number of variables, and degrees of freedom used in significance tests can be corrected by the researcher as well (Whitaker, 1997).

SAWHGL justify their choice of Model 13 as their final model based in no small part on the significance testing they have done and the fact that all its variables are significant. For the reasons we have just outlined, their p values cannot be taken at face value, raising questions as to whether Model 13 is, in fact, the proper model from which to draw substantive conclusions.

The final problem with their analysis concerns the variables *School expenditures per capita* and *Percent workforce female*. Although these were the two variables for which SAWHGL made data available in their Appendix, we chose to locate the data ourselves for an additional analysis not reported here. Surprisingly, we were unable to find the data as presented in the appendix, at least as the variables are described in the body of

Table 2. Descriptive Statistics.

Variable	Mean	SD	Minimum	Maximum
Enactment year	1913.52	1.05	1911	1915
Year of endorsement	1912.52	0.90	1912	1914
School expenditures (SWHGL)	18.73	5.16	5.56	26.71
School expenditures (Authors')	6.18	1.79	2.31	9.28
Female workforce (SAWHGL)	20.84	5.05	15.00	35.20
Female workforce (Author's)	0.16	0.05	0.08	0.29
Proportion Literate	0.95	0.04	0.79	0.98
Child labor exemption	0.12	0.33	0.00	1.00
Party competition	68.56	12.93	52.78	98.78
Women's clubs ($\times 10-3$)	0.10	0.05	0.03	0.20
Age of AFL	13.20	11.51	0.00	45.00
Reform vote	11.62	3.20	4.31	18.07

the article. Although our data and the SAWHGL data for these variables are highly correlated, we decided to explore whether the models' implications differed depending upon whether we used the data presented in SAWHGL's Appendix or those we collected. Detailed information about our data sources and variable construction appear in our appendix. Descriptive statistics for the variables we used in our analysis appear in Table 2.

METHODS AND FINDINGS

We had initially hoped to test the effects of all of SAWHGL's 24 independent variables on the time to adoption of mothers' pensions using their data set with improved methods for the analysis. To this end, we sought to obtain a copy of the original data set from the authors. Unfortunately, Professor Skocpol informed us that she was unable to provide us with a copy of the data set. We then tried to locate her co-authors, and succeeded in finding just one. Professor Howard told us that he no longer had a copy of the data either.

Having failed to obtain the data from the original researchers, we set out to reconstruct it ourselves. At times this proved to be a challenging task. The paper is vague about the location of some of the sources of the data, and Skocpol herself was unable to direct us further about any of the variables used in their article. Ultimately, we were unable to locate some of the sources, and in some instances where we could find sources, the numbers we found did not correspond to those in the paper. In addition, the paper is sometimes unclear about how variables were constructed from the raw data. We reconstructed the data as best we could, using the variable descriptions presented in the article. In an appendix, we discuss each of the SAWHGL variables in detail and outline how we handled the problems we encountered.

To carry out our analysis of the timing of the adoption of mothers' pensions, we first used the semi-parametric Cox regression, followed by the complementary loglog (cloglog) regression model. The former has been used for many years to study the timing of political events and would have been available to SAWHGL at the time of the publication of their original work; the latter has emerged more recently as an attractive alternative to the Cox model for handling data that are measured at discrete intervals, though generated by an underlying continuous time process with proportional hazards.[5] We carried out both estimations in version 11 of Stata.

We chose the semi-parametric Cox regression, as opposed to a parametric event history analysis model, as the former does not require the researcher to make assumptions about the exact functional dependence of the base hazard rate on time. This is often an advantage, particularly when there is no theoretical basis on which to choose a distribution, as improperly specifying the distribution can have serious implications and may result in misleading conclusions (Box-Steffensmeier & Jones, 2004, p. 47). Further, if, as SAWHGL suggest, there are intangible differences between groups of years, the Cox regression will handle them automatically in its baseline hazard. To handle ties, which are instances in which more than one state adopted mothers' pensions in the same time period, we used the Efron procedure.

The cloglog regression is easily applied to survival analysis data and offers a complement to the continuous time Cox model in that it is well suited to handle data that, though generated by the same continuous time process, are observed only at discrete times. Like the Cox model, the cloglog approach allows the baseline hazard to be fully non-parametric by introducing a set of dummy variables into the model, one corresponding to each year in the dataset.

We also estimated versions of these models that take into account unobserved heterogeneity by including a frailty term with a gamma distribution in the Cox model and a normal distribution in the random effects cloglog model. Although it may be reasonable to speculate that there could be omitted or unmeasurable differences among states that would influence their likelihood of pension adoption, in both approaches the likelihood ratio test did not provide evidence that unobserved heterogeneity is present.

In both the Cox and cloglog analyses we used cluster robust standard errors to account for the presence of repeated observations within states. Formal testing confirmed the validity of the proportional hazards assumption in all cases, rendering a time-varying covariate model unnecessary.

We proceeded to carry out such estimations in two stages. First, we used only the three independent variables that SAWHGL found to be significant in their restricted model, namely *Year of endorsement*, *School expenditures per capita*, and *Female workforce* (percent of the workforce composed of women). We call this their "final model," and it corresponds to Model 13 in their Table 2. We then replicated what we call their "full model" by including six[6] of the seven non-significant additional variables found in their Model 10. We provide details for the seven variables that the full model includes above and beyond the final model in our appendix.

Defining the time at risk is crucial in event history analysis, as the method discards any information on events that occur before the onset of risk or after the study has ended. We define the time at risk as the period between the data of the first adoption (1911) and the passing of the Social Security Act of 1935, as SAWHGL did, so that our dependent variable was the number of years after 1911 that a state adopted a pension. By defining the onset of risk as the first instance of adoption, we avoid the question of how to determine when a state seriously began to consider passing mothers' pensions legislation; the first state's adoption signals the beginning of the potential spread of the legislation among states (Berry & Berry, 1990, p. 398). However, by starting the risk period in 1911, we lose the first case (Illinois), and this case may provide valuable information about early adopters. To ensure that our results are not being unduly influenced by our decision regarding the time of entry into the risk set, we estimated the models again, this time defining the onset of risk as either 1910 or 1909, with no meaningful differences in our conclusions.

In estimating these models, we employed two primary approaches to operationalizing the endorsement variable: (1) SAWHGL's five categories of endorsement year as described earlier; and (2) a set of four time period dummy variables, each one corresponding to a value of SAWHGL's categories, so that period 1 represents 1912–1913 and period 4 represents 1918–1919. A state that did not receive an endorsement was coded as zero for all time periods, as were Illinois and New Jersey, the two states in which an endorsement occurred post-adoption.[7] Using the set of time period dummy variables allows us to avoid the problem of interpretation prompted by SAWHGL's endorsement categories, while still allowing the impact of an endorsement to vary depending on when it occurred. An increase in one unit can be interpreted meaningfully, comparing the hazard rate of adoption in states that saw an endorsement in that time period to the hazard rate in states that did not.

The results of the endorsement period dummy variable approach, which suggested that allowing for the effect of an endorsement to vary with time was not necessary in all cases, prompted us to explore the use of a simple binary indicator for the presence or absence of an endorsement. In this coding, if a state received an endorsement in 1912–1913, it would have a value of one on the binary variable from 1912 through its final observation, while a state that endorsed in 1918–1919 would have a value of zero until 1918, when its value would become one and it would then remain so until the state's exit from the analysis.

In Tables 3 and 4, we present the findings from our Cox and cloglog analyses, respectively, including comparisons across SAWHGL's final model and full models, both the ordinal scale and time period dummy endorsement variables, and the data provided by SAWGHL and the data that we located. Table 5 presents findings for the three models in which the null hypothesis for the equality of the time dummy variables could not be rejected, Cox Model 5 and cloglog Models 5 and 7.

To assess which sets of estimates to take seriously, we employ several statistics to aid model selection, presented at the bottom of the regression tables. These include the Akaike Information Criterion (AIC), Bayesian Information Criterion (BIC), and a sample-size adjusted BIC (aBIC); for each of these statistics a smaller value implies a preferable model[8] (Ando, 2010; Claeskens & Hort, 2008; Konishi & Kitagawa, 2008) taking into account both goodness of fit and parsimony. There are, however, no significance tests for these information statistics, so it is not possible to tell whether the differences in information criteria among models are statistically significant. Thus, while these measures serve as a guide, they cannot be treated as dispositive, and substantive and methodological concerns must play a strong role in determining which model is preferred.

That being said, these statistics do point to Models 5, 6, and 1 as being preferred. Both the Cox and cloglog models provide strong support for Models 5 and 6, which are the restricted final model with our set of endorsement dummy variables. In Tables 2 and 3, we see that in the Cox and cloglog approaches Model 5 has the lowest aBIC, while cloglog Model 6 beats Model 5 by just a hair in terms of AIC values. The BIC offers a slightly different view, as in both the Cox and cloglog approaches it favors Model 1, which is the restricted model with the SAWHGL school and female workforce data and their endorsement category variable. For all

Table 3. Cox Proportional Hazard Regression Results, Final, and Full Models.

	Cox 1[a] Final	Cox 2 Final	Cox 3 Full	Cox 4 Full	Cox 5 Final	Cox 6 Final	Cox 7 Full	Cox 8 Full
Endorsement								
SAWHGL	2.26**	2.32**	2.28**	2.20**				
Period 1					15.73**	17.83**	16.97**	17.26**
Period 2					8.32**	7.49**	7.16**	6.31**
Period 3					9.09**	8.57**	6.93**	6.35**
Period 4					3.50*	3.12*	2.44**	1.94
SAWHGL school exp	1.13**		1.14**		1.10**		1.10*	
SAWHGL % work fem	0.97*		0.98		0.97*		0.99	
Author's school exp		1.45**		1.42*		1.35**		1.31
Author's % work fem		0.98		1.02		0.96		1.01
Proportion literate			0.28	16.77			8.82	155.85
Child labor exemption			0.57	0.48			0.61	0.52
Party competition			1.16	0.68			0.62	0.47
Women's clubs			1.29	1.20			1.15	1.11
Age of AFL			0.99	0.99			0.99	0.99
Reform vote			1.03	1.05			1.02	1.02
AIC	220.6	223.4	230.3	232.7	215.9	218.0	226.4	227.1
BIC	232.1	235.0	264.9	267.3	238.9	241.1	272.6	273.3
aBIC	222.6	225.5	236.3	238.8	219.9	222.0	234.5	235.2
Wald test ¢					0.07	0.02	0.03	0.01
LR Test (final vs. full)			0.89	0.84			0.96	0.82

[a]Exponentiated coefficients.
Wald test and likelihood ratio test p values. *$p < 0.05$, **$p < 0.01$.

Table 4. Complementary Log-Log Regression Results, Final and Full Models.

	Clog 1[a] Final	Clog 2 Final	Clog 3 Full	Clog 4 Full	Clog 5 Final	Clog 6 Final	Clog 7 Full	Clog 8 Full
Endorsement								
SAWHGL	2.67**	2.71**	2.91**	2.59**				
Period 1					25.04**	32.88**	50.72**	55.84**
Period 2					9.90**	9.51**	9.37**	7.99**
Period 3					12.87**	12.84**	8.81**	9.06**
Period 4					4.59**	3.61*	3.13*	2.30
SAWHGL school exp	1.17**		1.22**		1.14**		1.14*	
SAWHGL % work fem	0.97*		0.98		0.96**		0.99	
Author's school exp		1.69**		1.59*		1.68**		1.62*
Author's % work fem		0.98		1.03		0.95		1.01
Proportion literate			0.02	5.03			12.08	362.20
Child labor exemption			0.55	0.47			0.59	0.49
Party competition			1.34	0.61			0.65	0.60
Women's clubs			1.18	1.00			0.89	0.70
Age of AFL			0.97	0.97			0.95	0.95
Reform vote			1.11	1.16			1.14	1.12
AIC	151.0	153.5	158.0	161.5	144.5	144.4	151.4	151.8
BIC	203.4	205.9	231.4	234.9	207.3	207.2	235.3	235.6
aBIC	155.9	163.0	164.8	170.3	150.3	153.6	159.2	160.7
Wald test ⊄					0.22	0.04	0.10	0.03
LR Test (final vs. full)			0.55	0.68			0.54	0.60

[a]Exponentiated coefficients.
Wald test and likelihood ratio test *p* values. *$p < 0.05$, **$p < 0.01$.

Table 5. Regression Results Using Binary Endorsement Variable.

	Cox 5B[a]	Clog 5B Final	Clog 7B Full
Endorsement	8.71**	12.32**	12.87**
SAWHGL school exp	1.11**	1.14**	1.13*
SAWHGL % work fem	0.96**	0.95**	0.97
Proportion literate			0.05
Child labor exemption			0.97
Party competition			0.34
Women's clubs			0.98
Age of AFL			0.98
Reform vote			1.16
AIC	212.5	141.1	150.1
BIC	224.0	193.5	223.5
aBIC	214.5	146.0	156.6

[a]Exponentiated coefficients; cloglog time variables omitted due to space constraints.
*$p < 0.05$, **$p < 0.01$.

models, the likelihood ratio test shows that the full model does not improve the fit over the restricted model significantly, as shown by the probabilities presented in each table.

The AIC and aBIC statistics show that for each of the four general models (restricted and full, each with the original SAWHGL data and our alternative data), the model with our endorsement dummy variables is superior to its counterpart with the SAWHGL endorsement category variable. While this alone may not be sufficient rationale for preferring our endorsement time period dummy variables to the SAWHGL endorsement category variable, it complements the argument in favor of the dummy variables on theoretical and methodological grounds.

To present the substantive findings of our analyses, we turn first to the results from the cloglog regression found in Table 4, which, as we noted above, is currently the preferred approach when the data are available measured at discrete intervals. Models 1 and 3, which include the SAWHGL school expenditures and female workforce data and the original endorsement category variable, do support the claim that an endorsement is associated with pension adoption: in both models the endorsement variable has a significant and sizeable effect, with hazard ratios of 2.7 and 2.9 respectively, so that an increase of one unit on the endorsement scale nearly triples the risk of pension adoption. Unfortunately, as discussed at length earlier, this interpretation is problematic, given that an increase of one unit in the endorsement variable has no consistent meaning across its values.

Models 5 and 7, which also use the SAWHGL school and female workforce data but include our set of time dummy endorsement variables rather than the endorsement category variable, also show endorsements to be significantly associated with the adoption of mothers' pension legislation in each of the endorsement time periods, yet in a manner that allows for a clear understanding of the meaning of this impact. In Model 5, for example, one sees that each of the endorsement dummies is significant, with effects that are quite sizeable: the hazard ratio for the first endorsement dummy shows that an endorsement in 1912–1913 increased the risk of adopting mothers' pensions by a factor of 25 over states that did not receive an endorsement in this time period; in Model 7 the same variable increases the risk of pension adoption by 50 times for those states that did receive an endorsement over those states that did not receive one during this time.

However, this finding must be viewed with caution, as formal significance testing does not allow us to reject the null hypothesis of the equality of the coefficients of the endorsement dummy variables. Thus, in contrast to the claims articulated in SAWHGL, these models offer no compelling evidence that the effect of an endorsement differed depending upon when it was proffered.[9] In Table 4, we present the results of Cox Model 5B and cloglog Models 5B and 7B, which are analogous to Models 5 and 7 found in Tables 2 and 3, using the binary endorsement variable in the place of the set of endorsement period dummies. These models also support the claim that endorsements significantly shortened the time to pension adoption, as the cloglog regression finds that the risk of adoption for states that did receive an endorsement was more than 12 times higher than that of a state that did not receive one, with the implication that the effect was the same no matter when the endorsement was made.

Models 1, 3, 5, and 7 support SAWHGL's claims regarding the positive effect of school expenditures on pension adoption, while only Models 1 and 5 confirm the negative impact of the percentage of the workforce composed of women, which is also in keeping with the conclusions in SAWHGL. We also replicate their finding that none of the additional predictors has a significant impact on pension adoption.

Models 2, 4, 6, and 8, all of which use the school expenditures and female workforce data that we located, offer a slightly different picture. In trying to locate the school expenditures per capita data, we came across several potential measures, any of which seemed that it could be the variable that SAWHGL had intended to measure. As explained in more detail in the appendix, ultimately we chose the measure "spending per capita of the total population for 1909–1910," which had the highest correlation with the data provided in SAWHGL and appeared to best match their variable description; this variable had the added benefit of offering the best information criteria statistics.

Results from the cloglog models show that while the inclusion of these alternative data does not alter the conclusions about the impact of school expenditures, except perhaps to increase the magnitude of their impact on the rate of pension adoption, a difference is seen in that the female workforce variable fails to achieve significance in Models 3 and 6, which are the final versions of the model and should show a significant effect. Interestingly, this was the variable that, although not significant in their full model, was included by SAWHGL in their final model.

The effect of endorsements on pension adoption also differs in the models using these alternative data. While the results of these models using the endorsement category variable are unchanged, using our data affects the impact of the endorsement period dummies in two ways. In Model 8, the dummy for the final 1918–1919 time period no longer has a significant impact on pension adoption; and formal testing of the endorsement period dummies shows that the impacts of endorsements on pension adoption differ significantly among the time period dummy variables. In particular, an endorsement had a much greater impact on pension adoption if it occurred in the earliest time period.

Turning to Table 3, we see that for the most part, the results using the Cox method support the same conclusions as the cloglog models, finding that endorsements significantly shortened the time to adoption of pension legislation with very large effect sizes, and both school expenditures and female workforce measures had significant impacts in the hypothesized directions. The Cox model diverges from the cloglog model in two ways: in the Cox Model 7, formal testing of the endorsement dummy variables reveals that the coefficients are statistically different from each other, while the cloglog version cannot reject the null hypothesis; and in the Cox Model 8, our school expenditures' data variable fails to reach significance, leaving adoption explained solely by the first three endorsement dummy variables.

CONCLUSION

In our re-analysis of SAWHGL, we find that, broadly speaking, many of their claims hold up, despite problems inherent in their methods. Our findings support their conclusions that the endorsement of mothers' pensions by women's voluntary associations, school expenditures per capita, and percentage of the workforce composed of women all had a significant impact on the timing of mothers' pension adoption, although our conclusions differ slightly when using the data that we located for the last two measures. In contrast to SAWHGL's claims, our findings are equivocal as to whether the effect of endorsements differed depending upon when they were proffered.

Our analysis improves upon SAWHGL's, in that their efforts to relate the timing of endorsements to pension adoptions were carried out via variables that are troublesome to interpret and their conclusions about the specific nature of this influence, particularly those pertaining to the varying influence of regressors over time, are ultimately unpersuasive. Through the use of a set of dummy variables to represent the endorsement time periods, our findings are easily understood as the period-specific impact of endorsements on the risk of pension adoption. In the models where the effect of endorsements was found to be consistent with constancy over time, our findings are also straightforward, revealing that the rate of pension adoption was 8–13 times higher for those states that did receive an endorsement over those that received no such endorsement.

NOTES

1. Previous social science studies of time to events had been focused on events happening to individuals, such as deaths and births.
2. We replicated SAWHGL's regression analysis and also found that all three predictors are significant when OLS is used. However, like Sparks and Walniuk (1995), we were unable to replicate the coefficients as presented in SAWHGL; our results are the same as those of Sparks and Walniuk as found in their Table 1.
3. See Welch, Schwartz, and Woloshin (2005) for the implications of assuming a continuous relationship without testing the validity of this assumption. They advocate for the use of categorical variables, which we implement in our analysis (Moehling, 2002).
4. How important this would have been in their data we do not know, as SAWHGL do not tell us how strongly correlated the pairs of variables were when one of them was deleted on grounds of multi-collinearity.
5. See, for example, the course notes from Stephen Jenkins Essex Summer School Course on survival analysis, particularly chapters 2 and 6, for a helpful discussion. Available at https://www.iser.essex.ac.uk/resources/survival-analysis-with-stata. (Last accessed October 26, 2012.)
6. We were unable to locate the circulation figures for the *Delineator*. We did locate circulation data for the *Woman's Home Companion*, but ultimately were unsure as to how similar the two magazines were, and chose to exclude the variable. We discuss this further in the appendix.
7. In their article, SAWGHL coded these two states for the year in which the endorsement was made, even though it occurred post-adoption.

8. The AIC, BIC and ABIC statistics penalize the log-likelihood for the number of parameters estimated, but do so using different formulas (Bollen & Long, 1993).

9. At the same time, obviously, we cannot exclude the possibility that there is some time dependence that is too small to achieve significance in our sample.

REFERENCES

Ando, T. (2010). *Bayesian model selection and statistical modeling*. New York, NY: CRC.

Babyak, M. A. (2004). What you see may not be what you get: A brief, nontechnical introduction to overfitting in regression-type models. *Psychosomatic Medicine, 66*, 411–421.

Baker, P. (1993). Featured review. *American Historical Review, 98*, 458–460.

Berry, F. S., & Berry, W. D. (1990). State lottery adoption as policy innovations: An event history analysis. *American Political Science Review, 84*, 395–414.

Bollen, K., & Long, J. S. (1993). *Testing structural equation models*. Newbury Park, CA: Sage.

Box-Steffensmeier, J. M., & Jones, B. S. (2004). *Event history modeling: A guide for social scientists*. New York, NY: Cambridge University Press.

Burnham, W. D., & Flanigan, W. (1984). *State-level presidential election data for the United States, 1824–1972 [Computer file]*. ICPSR00019-v1. Ann Arbor, MI: Inter-university Consortium for Political and Social Research [distributor]. 197? doi:10.3886/ICPSR00019

Burnham, W. D., Clubb, J. M., & Flanigan, W. (1991). In ICPSR (Ed.), *State-level congressional, Gubernatorial and senatorial election data for the United States, 1824–1972 [Computer file]*. Ann Arbor, MI: Inter-university Consortium for Political and Social Research [producer and distributor]. doi:10.3886/ICPSR00075

Burnham, W. D. (1984). Partisan division of American State governments, 1834–1985 [Computer file]. In ICPSR (Ed.), *Conducted by Massachusetts institute of technology*. Ann Arbor, MI: Inter-university Consortium for Political and Social Research [producer and distributor]. 198? doi:10.3886/ICPSR00016

Carruth, H. WHC circulation by states. *Hayden Carruth Papers, Box 9*.

Carver, R. P. (1978). The case against statistical testing. *Harvard Educational Review, 48*, 378–399.

Claeskens, G., & Hort, N. L. (2008). *Model selection and model averaging*. New York, NY: Cambridge University Press.

Cleves, M., Gutierrez, R., Gould, W., & Marchenko, Y. (2008). *An introduction to survival analysis using stata* (2nd ed.). College Station, TX: Stata Press.

Cohen, J. (1990). Things I have learned (so far). *American Psychologist, 45*, 1304–1312.

Cohen, J. (1994). The earth Is round ($p < .05$). *American Psychologist, 49*, 997–1003.

Copas, J. B. (1983). Regression, prediction and shrinkage (with discussion). *Journal of the Royal Society B, 45*, 3311–3354.

Derksen, S., & Keselman, H. J. (1992). Backward, forward and stepwise automated subset selection algorithms: Frequencies of obtaining and noise variables. *British Journal of Mathematical and Statistical Psychology, 45*, 265–282.

Domhoff, G. W. (1995). The death of state autonomy theory: A critique of Skocpol's. "*Protecting Soldiers And Mothers.*" Retrieved from http://sociology.ucsc.edu/whorulesamerica/theory/skocpol.html. Accessed on August 9, 2011.

Fink, G. M. (1975). *State labor proceedings: A bibliography of the AFL, CIO, and AFL-CIO proceedings, 1884–1974.* Westport, CT: Greenwood Press.

Garfinkel, I., Rainwater, L., & Smeeding, T. (2010). *Wealth and Welfare States: Is America a Laggard or Leader?* New York, NY: Oxford University Press.

General Federation of Women's Clubs. (1909). Directory. [Microform].

Greenland, S. (2008). Variable selection versus shrinkage in the control of multiple confounders. *American Journal of Epidemiology, 167*, 523–529.

Harrell, F. E., Jr. (2001). *Regression modeling strategies: With applications to linear models, logistic regression and survival analysis.* New York, NY: Springer.

Hosmer, D. W., Jr, Lemeshow, S., & May, S. (2008). *Applied survival analysis: Regression modeling of time to event data* (2nd ed). New York, NY: Wiley.

Inter-university Consortium for Political and Social Research. (1994). *Candidate and constituency statistics of elections in the United States, 1788–1990 [Computer file].* ICPSR 07757-v5. Ann Arbor, MI: Inter-university Consortium for Political and Social Research [distributor]. doi:10.3886/ICPSR07757

Klein, J. P., & Moeschberger, M. L. (2003). *Survival analysis: Techniques for censored and truncated data* (2nd. ed.). New York, NY: Springer.

Konishi, S., & Kitagawa, G. (2008). *Information criteria and statistical modeling.* New York, NY: Springer.

Leigh, J. P. (1988). Assessing the importance of an independent variable in multiple-regression – Is stepwise unwise? *Journal of Clinical Epidemiology, 41*, 669–677.

Meehl, P. E. (1990). Why summaries of research on psychological theories are often Uninterpretable. *Psychological Reports, 66*, 195–244.

Moehling, C. M. (2002). *Mothers' pensions and female headship.* Retrieved from http://www.econ.yale.edu/seminars/labor/lap02/Moehling-021004.pdf

Moody, C. E., & Marvell, T. B. (2010). On the choice of control variables in the crime equation. *Oxford Bulletin of Economics and Statistics, 72*, 696–715.

Ogburn, W. F. (1912). *Progress and uniformity in child-labor legislation: A study in statistical measurement.* New York, NY: Columbia University. Retrieved from https://archive.org/details/progressuniformi00ogburich.

Orloff, A. S. (1988). The political origins of America's belated welfare state. In M. Weir, A. S. Orloff, & T. Skocpol (Eds.), *The politics of social policy in the United States* (pp. 38–80). Princeton, NJ: Princeton University Press.

Rusk, J. G. (2001). *A statistical history of the American Electorate.* Washington, DC: CQ Press.

Shaver, J. P. (1993). What statistical significance is, and what it is not. *Journal of Experimental Education, 61*, 293–316.

Skocpol, T. (1992). *Protecting soldiers and mothers: The political origins of social policy in the United States.* Cambridge, MA: Harvard University Press.

Skocpol, T. (1995). The enactment of mothers' pensions: Civic Mobilization and agenda setting or benefits of the Ballot? Response. *American Political Science Review, 89*(3), 720–730.

Skocpol, T., Abend-Wein, M., Howard, C., & Lehmann, S. G. (1993). Women's associations and the enactment of mothers' pensions in the United States. *American Political Science Review, 87*, 686–701.

Snyder, P. (1991). Three reasons why stepwise regression methods should not be used by researchers. In B. Thompson (Ed.), *Advances in educational research: Substantive findings, methodological developments* (Vol. 1, pp. 99–105). Greenwich, CT: JAI Press.

Sparks, C. L., & Walniuk, P. R. (1995). The enactment of mothers' pensions: Civic mobilization and agenda setting or benefits of the ballot? Comment. *American Political Science Review, 89*(3), 710–720.

Thompson, B. (1993). The use of statistical significance tests in research: Bootstrap and other alternatives. *Journal of Experimental Research, 61*, 361–377.

Thompson, B. (1995). The importance of structure coefficients in regression research. *Educational and Psychological Measurement, 45*, 203–209.

Thompson, B. (2001). Significance, effect sizes, stepwise methods, and other issues: Strong arguments move the field. *Journal of Experimental Education, 70*, 1182–1189.

Tuma, N. B. (1982). *Invoking RATE*. Menlo Park, CA: SRI International.

U.S. Bureau of Education. (1911). *Report of the commissioner of education, 1912: Volume 2*. Washington, DC: GPO.

U.S. Bureau of the Census. (1913). Illiteracy. In *Thirteenth Census of the United States Taken in the Year 1910: Population* (pp. 1185–1291). Washington, DC: GPO.

U.S. Bureau of the Census. (1933). Sex and occupation of gainful workers. In *Fifteenth Census of the United States, 1930: Populations* (pp. 35–69). Washington, DC: GPO.

Vansteelandt, S., Bekaert, M., & Claeskens, G. (2010). On model selection and model misspecification in causal inference. *Statistical Methods in Medical Research, 21*(1), 7–30.

Waller-Zuckerman, M. E. (1989). Old homes, in a city of perpetual change-women's magazines, 1890–1916. *Business History Review, 63*(4), 715–756.

Welch, H. G., Schwartz, L. M., & Woloshin, S. (2005). The exaggerated relations between diet, body weight, and mortality: The case for a categorical data approach. *Canadian Medical Association Journal, 172*(7), 891–895.

Whitaker, J. S. (1997). Use of stepwise methodology in discriminant analysis. Paper presented to the Southwest Educational Research Association, Austin. Retrieved from http://ericae.net/ft/tamu/STEPWISE.htm. Accessed on December 24, 2010.

Whittingham, M., Stephens, P. A., Bradbury, R. B., & Freckleton, R. P. (2006). Why do we still use Stepwise modeling in ecology and behaviour? *Journal of Animal Ecology, 75*, 1182–1189.

APPENDIX

Adoption of Mothers' Pensions

SAWHGL operationalize pension adoption using a seven-part ordinal scale ranging from a value of six in instances in which a state adopted during the 1911–1913 period, to zero for those states that had not adopted by 1935.

We use a dataset containing one observation per state per year in which it was at risk of pension adoption, beginning risk in 1911. States received a value of zero for all years in which they did not adopt, and a value of one for the year in which they did adopt legislation. Those states that passed legislation exited the dataset after adopting; the two states that did not adopt received a value of zero for all years between 1911 and 1935. These data are available in the appendix of SAWHGL (see Table 1).

Women's Group Endorsements

Endorsements occurred between 1912–13 and 1918–1919. SAWHGL break this time period into five categories, where a value of four equals an endorsement in 1912–13 and zero when there is no evidence of women's group endorsements. In two cases, Illinois and New Jersey, endorsements occurred after pensions were adopted, although SAWHGL still assign them the value of the year in which the endorsement occurred. We retained this coding when using their endorsement category variable, but we assigned these two states a value of zero for each of our endorsement time period dummies, with the idea that the endorsement could not have influenced adoption if it came post-adoption.

We operationalized endorsements in two ways: (1) we replicated *SAWHGL categories,* as described above; and (2) to handle the interpretation problem outlined in the paper, we included four time period dummy variables, one for each of the time periods of endorsement identified by SAWHGL. In instances in which testing did not support the need for periodization of endorsement effects, we used a binary variable for whether a state experienced an endorsement. These data are available in the appendix in the original article.

Percent Workforce Female

SAWHGL describe this as the 1910 percent of the total gainful workforce 10 years or older consisting of females. In our research, we were unable to find the data that they provided in their Appendix. We located the *Author's percent female workforce* in the 1930 Census, Chapter 2 "Sex and Occupation of Gainful Workers" Tables 5 and 7 (U.S. Bureau of the Census, 1933). Their variable has a mean of 25.8% and a range of 15−59.4%. Our variable has a mean of 18.15% with a range of 8.17−36.76%. The correlation between both sets of values is 0.94.

Per Capita State Expenditures on Public Schools

We were unable to replicate the data as presented by SAWHGL in their Appendix, even after considering several interpretations: for either the 1909−1910 or 1910−1911 years, either the school expenditures per capita total population or expenditures per capita average school attendance, all of which are found in the Commissioner of Education's annual reports.

While the choice did affect some levels of significance for the school expenditures and female workforce variables, none changed the conclusions about the effect of endorsements. We ultimately chose to present the 1909−1910 expenditures per capita total population, with the idea that when SAWHGL wrote "per capita," they meant "per capita total population," and the 1909−1910 year had by far the highest correlation of all four measures with the data in SAWHGL.

Our data, *Author's school expenditures* came from the Commissioner of Education's 1911 Annual Report, Table 15 (U.S Bureau of Education, 1911). SAWHGL's data have a mean of $15.17 and a range of $4.17−27.73. Our data's mean is $4.9 with a range of $1.29−9.21. The correlation between the two sets of values is 0.97.

State-by-State Per Capita Magazine Circulation

SAWHGL use 1920 state-by-state circulation figures for the women's magazine the *Delineator*, a magazine that advocated for mothers' pensions during the 1912−1913 period.

We were unable to find these data; instead we located 1908−1909 state-by-state circulation figures for the *Women's Home Companion* (see Carruth Papers, Box 9). While there is no indication that *WHC* endorsed pensions, its national circulation figures put it close to the *Delineator* in terms of readership during the decade (Waller-Zuckerman, 1989, p. 737). That being said, the variable had no substantive effect on the results, so given the questions about its relationship to endorsements, we chose to omit it in the final model configurations.

Literacy

We use the same variable as described in SAWHGL, defined as the proportion of each state's population over age 10 that could read and write in 1910. The source for *Proportion literate* data is the 1910 Census, Chapter 8, Table 19 (U.S. Bureau of the Census, 1913).

Age of State Federation

Age of AFL replicates SAWHGL's variable, defined as the number of years that each state's Federation of Labor had been in existence at the end of 1912 (Fink, 1975).

Party Competition

SAWHGL computed a party competition score for each state in 1910, 1912, 1914, and 1916 by averaging the percentage of seats held by the majority party in the state Senate, the percentage in the House of Representatives, and the percentage of the vote earned by the Governor's party. The scores for each year were averaged, resulting in one value representing party competition over the decade.

We replicated this score using data available from ICPSR study nos. 16 and 75 in creating *Party competition score* (Burnham, 1984; Burnham, Clubb and Flanigan, 1991). In cases where 1910 data were missing because an election was not held, we used the results from 1908. In the event an election was held in an odd year, the results were applied to the following year. Additional data were found in *A Statistical History of the American Electorate*, Tables 7–39, 7–40, and 7–41 (Rusk, 2001).

Average Reform Vote

SAWHGL define this as the average percentage of presidential votes cast for the Progressive Party in 1912, the Socialist Party in 1912, 1916, and 1920 the Prohibition Party in 1916, all of which we located in ICPSR study no. 19 (Burnham & Flanigan, 1984). They also include votes for the

Farmer-Labor Party in 1920, and we included in the total tally votes in all of the states in which the Farmer-Labor candidate, Parley Christensen, appeared on the ballot, as found in ICPSR study no. 7757 (ICPSR, 1994).

We found SAWHGL's explanation to be open to several interpretations, but ultimately chose to construct our variable *Reform vote* by tallying by state both the total number of votes received by these parties over all of the above elections and the total number of votes cast in all of these elections, dividing the first by the second to create each state's average over the decade.

Density of Women's Clubs

Our variable *Women's clubs* is the same as in SAWHGL (although rescaled), defined as the number of local General Federation of Women's Clubs per 100,000 residents in 1908. We found this in the 1907 General Federation of Women's Clubs Directory (1909).

Exemptions

Child labor exemption is a dichotomous variable indicating whether or not a state exempted children from labor laws if they were orphans, children of widows, or children of disabled parents. We assigned a state a value of one if it had any of the three exemptions, which is what we believe SAWHGL did. We located these data in Ogburn (1912), Table 19.

PART II
POLITICAL ELITES AND POLITICAL CONTENTION

ESSENTIAL CONTESTANTS, ESSENTIAL CONTESTS

John Markoff

ABSTRACT

Social scientists continue to invest a great deal of effort in constructing superior measures of democracy without arriving at any consensus. Reflections on this state of affairs frequently refer to an essay of more than a half-century ago in which the philosopher W. B. Gallie analyzed the characteristics of what he called "essentially contested concepts." Gallie's account of the properties of these concepts, however, is inadequate. It looks more promising to explore the contestants and the contests and especially the dynamic roles played by social movements in the history of democracy. Gallie's focus on a debate among philosophers needs to be incorporated within a larger a larger field of social conflict.

Keywords: Democracy; social movements; contested concepts; antislavery

INTRODUCTION

Debates about the meaning of democracy are commonplace. In fact, such debates have been part of the entire history of modern democracy since the late eighteenth century. It is tempting to attribute the ever-unresolved character of such discussions to some property or problem in the concept itself. Students of political philosophy have been active participants in such reflections and historians of ideas have traced their analyses. But the developing field of social movements and contentious politics suggests another approach to the conceptual debates. Democracy has been a term invoked in great political struggles from the 1780s on. Since that revolutionary moment, it has been a term used by actors, not just dispassionate analysts, and its meanings have changed in the course of social contention. The sorts of political systems that came to be called democracies, in fact, have been fertile soil for the specific kinds of contention we associate with social movements; these social movements have been among the important shapers of change in the meanings of democracy. In studying the changing meanings of democracy, therefore, we will learn much from the history of the contentious processes in which democracy has been under debate and especially from the study of the social movements that have made so much of those debates happen.

In the early sections of this chapter, I will closely examine a major philosophical contribution, W. B. Gallie's idea of "essentially contested concepts," which has stood for more than half a century as a touchstone in scholarly reflection on why consensus on what democracy is has proven so elusive. Gallie's effort to show that these properties explain why philosophers have been unable to agree will be shown to be inadequate. I will argue that it is the embeddedness of debates about democracy within social conflict that has repeatedly shifted the meanings of democracy. Indeed, intimations of such conflict keep creeping into Gallie's own account, despite his effort to isolate philosophers and philosophy. This leads to the suggestion that the way to approach the meanings of democracy is through the study of the actors that deploy this term and the conflicts in which they are engaged. In particular, drawing on the work of recent scholars of social movements, I argue that the entire history of modern democracy is linked to the history of social movement activism. I illustrate this with a brief discussion of the movement for the abolition of slavery, whose actions redefined democratic practice as incompatible with the ownership of one human being by another.

CONTESTED CONCEPTS

One of the few constants in social scientists' discussions of democracy is their continual rediscovery that their peers do not use this two and a half millennia-old word in a consistent manner and that no amount of brainpower expended on improving its definition and no expenditure of energy poring through sources in order to measure what are taken to be its components seem terribly likely to generate a consensus. Trying to make sense of this recurrent experience by scouring the footnotes invoked in previous efforts will before very long lead to the striking title "Essentially Contested Concepts" that at least gave the problem a name. In presenting his paper on this theme to the Aristotelian Society in 1956, Gallie (1956) launched a phrase that half a century later still seemed useful to students of democracy. A hunt for citations with "Google Scholar" in May 2016 finds 2879 references, and at an increasing rate.[1] Every 10-year interval since 1956–1965 shows more citations than the previous one, up through 2006–2015. In 2015 alone this paper was cited 245 times. An Ngram analysis of the phrase "essentially contested concept[s]" shows a modest occurrence in the 1960s, a rise from the early 1970s until 1990 and a high level since then. As an additional illustration of its continuing currency, we may note that when Collier and Levitsky (1997, pp. 430–433) heroically grappled with bringing order to the "hundreds of subtypes" of democracy that by their count have been generated by scholarly efforts at precision they quickly found their way to Gallie's "famous analysis."

This chapter adds a small but crucial element to that analysis. Gallie (p. 168)[2] himself took "democracy" as a concept that approximated his formulations and used it, along with "Art," "Social Justice," and "adherence to, or participation in, a particular religion" as "live examples" (p. 180). Gallie contended that concepts of this sort have the following seven properties, to which I will attach brief labels based on Gallie's rubrics for ready reference.

Evaluation

They refer to something that is valued (p. 171). Although Gallie's examples suggest that he tended to be thinking about things that were positively evaluated, the critical element for his argument only requires that there is an act of evaluation, that the concept is, as he puts it, "appraisive." Negative judgments, as I will develop below, turn out to be quite important.

Complexity

Such concepts refer to something internally complex in the sense that they are made up of distinguishable components (p. 171).

Weighting

In taking these first two properties together so as to evaluate some particular instance of such a concept, its "component parts or features" might be assigned different weights by different evaluators (p. 172).

Openness

Such concepts are "open" in the sense that evaluations carried out according to the three properties above might be modified at some later time (p. 172). Gallie does not offer much guidance on how this might come about, but we may easily suggest that different efforts at evaluation (by the same or different evaluators) might either identify the components of this complex concept differently, evaluate the components differently or weight them differently in arriving at an overall evaluation.

Recognition of Debate

Those engaged in evaluation are aware that others are doing their own evaluations by their own criteria and therefore "to use an essentially contested concept means to use it against other uses and to recognize that one's own use of it has to be maintained against these other uses. Still more simply, to use an essentially contested concept means to use it both aggressively and defensively" (p. 172).

Authoritative Exemplar

Such concepts are connected to some original "exemplar whose authority is acknowledged by all the contestant users of the concept" (p. 180). In other words, there is some foundational instance that contestants would agree constitutes an instance, although they may well disagree about why it is an instance and about the degree to which more recent experiences constitute later instances.

Progressive Character

Finally, the very competition among those who use these concepts differently "enables the original exemplar's achievement to be sustained and/or developed in optimum fashion" (p. 180).

Gallie sees the first five of these as "the formally defining conditions of essential contestedness" (p. 180). These five conditions also cover concepts that are merely and much less interestingly "radically confused" (p. 180) and which therefore might be clarified, made more precise, divided into separate concepts to avoid confusion, or just abandoned. So why continue to use such troublesome terms? It is the last two conditions that "justify the continued use" (p. 180) of the concept despite the problems inherent in the first five conditions. If only those first five conditions were present, debate would be irresolvable but pointless, and debaters would be well advised to find something else to do. Add those final two conditions and things get more interesting: debate is still irresolvable but there is some point to keeping the debate going because debate advances the values that the foundational exemplar exemplifies.

It is evident that "democracy" meets the first five of these conditions, less obvious that it altogether meets the final two. Let us consider each condition in turn.

Evaluation

Democracy is frequently a term of evaluation and in the early twenty-first century almost always refers to something highly prized. At earlier moments it commonly carried a strongly negative charge, as when the Prussian government announced in 1793 that its army had entered Poland to combat the "the spirit of French democratism" and "to subdue the malevolent who are stirring up troubles and insurrection, to restore and maintain order and public confidence, and to insure that the well-intentioned inhabitants are effectively protected" (Lutostański, 1918, pp. 139–140). Eighteenth century Europeans would have known something about how ancient authors evaluated political arrangements as good to the extent that the rulers governed in the broad public interest and bad when they governed only in their own. They would have found some differences among the ancient authors they knew in whether democracy was taken to be the good or bad version of rule by the many.[3] But democracy was commonly taken to be something well worth avoiding so that it was fortunate that it did not seem at all practicable on the large territorial scale of a modern state.

There is much more to learn about the changing valuation of democracy[4], but by the early twentieth century an American president could claim the defense of democracy as a good reason to take his country into a war that by 1917 had already killed millions. A century later still, another US president would reverse that Prussian evaluation, when he claimed his armies were occupying another country to encourage democracy, and were subduing the malevolent while restoring security to the well-intentioned inhabitants (Sanger, 2004, p. A1).

Complexity

Even before the European and western hemispheric revolutions of the late eighteenth and early nineteenth centuries, notions of democracy abstracted from the institutions of ancient city-states were multifaceted, including as they did: (a) mechanisms for choosing incumbents of office (mostly by lot); (b) sharp limitation on the length of incumbency; (c) intensive participation by citizens in popular assemblies with decision-making authority; (d) broad equality of political rights among a numerous subset of inhabitants; and (e) restriction of full political rights to certain categories of inhabitants (citizens not foreigners, men not women, adults not children, the free not the slaves) (Hansen, 1991). Most notions of democracy involved a "people" governing itself on a demarcated territory (although the territorial boundaries might be uncertain and subject to change). The subsequent history of "democracy" as applied to national states has only complicated things further, a great deal further, by posing a great range of criteria, leading some to propose the extraordinary variety that Collier and Levitsky (1997) call "democracy with adjectives."

Weighting

Even before the European and western hemispheric revolutions of the late eighteenth and early nineteenth centuries, the weighting of the various elements could vary from one author to another. Rousseau, for example, is much noted as "the theorist *par excellence* of participation," as Pateman (1970, p. 22) puts it. But citizen participation has often been seen as less important, or as severely limited, or even undesirable. Rousseau's contemporary d'Argenson (1764, p. 7) held that "[i]n a true democracy one acts through deputies and those deputies get their authority by election." The subsequent history of "democracy" as applied to national states since the late eighteenth century has suggested many different weightings. The relative weight to be given to liberty and equality, for example, has itself been a discussion without end, as exemplified by the endless invocations of Tocqueville's thoughts on the potential conflict of these two important principles.[5] The geographically vast alternations of democratic advances and reversals of the second half of the twentieth century have suggested to comparativists that there would be considerable payoff to developing standardized indicators of democratization in order to develop and test hypotheses about democracy's causes and (less commonly) consequences. But with no consensus on weighting democracy's components, researchers, symptomatically, were inspired to construct not one universally used data set, but several quite different ones that stress different elements (see e.g., Mainwaring, Brinks, & Pérez-Liñan, 2001). Even before the great global wave of democratization that began in the early 1970s, a survey of such measures of democracy noted their wondrous variety (May, 1973).

Openness

Social arrangements that might strike an observer as highly democratic at one moment might be very differently evaluated later on. When Tocqueville visited the United States in 1831–1832 he marveled at the advanced character of the democracy he found there. Among many elements that impressed him, was what he called America's "universal suffrage" (Tocqueville, 1994 [1835, 1840], v.1, pp. 57, 197, 199, 200) and he pontificated that "[a]t the present day the principle of the sovereignty of the people has acquired in the United States all the practical development that the imagination can conceive" (1994 [1835], v.1, p. 57). But in the early twenty-first century few would regard as terribly democratic any country, like Tocqueville's America, in which women could not vote, in which millions were enslaved, and in which ethnically distinctive minorities were denied political rights. To take another example, the Boer Republics formed by nineteenth century white Dutch speakers moving north away from the British-controlled areas of southern Africa impressed one comparative student of democracy, Bryce (1901, v.1, p. 380) at the turn of the twentieth century as "highly democratic"; the Orange Free State seemed to him "an ideal commonwealth" (Bryce, 1899, p. 314). A century later, in a democratized South Africa still confronting the legacy of racial exclusion such a summary judgment would be a lot less likely.

Recognition of Debate

The frequency with which the academic literature on democracy includes definitions of it is clear enough evidence of widespread awareness of other possible meanings than one's own. Definition-mongering is so common because we know our own scholarly use of "democracy" is not consensual among scholars. Our own definition stakes out a claim in conflict with other definitions. For a scholar to discuss democracy is to enter a debate about what democracy is. That's how it is "essentially" contested.

As an example consider the influential and exclusive stress on incumbency of office through contested elections of Schumpeter (1943, p. 269), who defined democracy as "that institutional arrangement for arriving at political decisions in which individuals acquire the power to decide by means of a competitive struggle for the people's vote." Schumpeter embeds his own favored definition within an extensive critique of the flaws of earlier ones (1943, pp. 243–273). In the long tradition of developing quantitative measures of democracy, it is common to encounter the claim to have developed a new measure that avoids the defects of one's predecessors. (See Mainwaring et al. (2001) for a good example of this genre, good both in the quality of its arguments and in the sense that it exemplifies the genre well.)

Authoritative Exemplar

According to Gallie, this sixth condition is part of what keeps the debate worthwhile. Participants agree on some splendid instance of the concept, though they do not agree on what that concept is. But – and here I'm fleshing out what is pretty sketchy in Gallie – that common focus on the splendid instance helps keep the conversation going. Discussions of democracy down to about the early nineteenth century approximated this condition fairly well, since most agreed that there were splendid ancient examples.[6] As one late 17th dictionary commented: "democracy only flourished in the republics of Rome and Athens" (Furetière, 1970[1690]), summing up a commonplace of his day. Occasionally the term was used to cover a few contemporary arrangements such as the United Provinces of the Netherlands, Swiss cantons, or the new Rhode Island settlements of the 1640s.[7] In the 1780s, however, the word began to acquire new layers as the form "democrat" began to be widely used (Brunner, Conze, & Kosseleck, 1972, v. 4, p. 854; Palmer, 1953; Rosanvallon, 1995), indicating a determination to make democracy in the present rather than simply draw lessons, often cautionary ones, from its existence in a distant past.

The problem about Gallie's sixth condition is not that there was and has remained a great deal less agreement on what are the modern instances. The French Revolution, to take an example from the turbulent late eighteenth century, is today mined both for examples of democracy and anti-democracy. The Venezuela of Hugo Chávez, to take an example from the turbulent early twenty-first century, for a time occasioned enormous debates among my students. Such disagreements are evidently part and parcel of the very notion of essentially contested concepts and Gallie only insists on agreement about some foundational instance. The problem, rather, is that the very openness to reevaluation embodied in his fourth criterion has meant that the classical instances are likely to be radically revaluated when modern students think about them. Some important attributes of ancient democracy are valued very negatively by twenty-first century democrats – restrictions of citizenship rights to men and the role of slavery, for example. In addition, multiparty competition for office plays a critical role in many (not all, to be sure) definitions that are in play two and a half millennia later. So for some moderns those ancient exemplars would turn out not to be exemplars at all. Schumpeter, for example, as quoted above, put electoral competition at the center of his influential definition, which would probably have ruled out Athens, where elections were far less important than in modern democracy[8] and where analogues for party competition for the few elective offices were altogether lacking. In a recent survey, Tilly (2007, pp. 26–27) finds the case against identifying Athens as the inventor of democracy stronger than the case for doing so. So in actual fact the debate about democracy goes on, even though the ancient exemplar is a lot less often taken as an exemplar.

One can track "democracy" and related words using the searchable database of more than 2600 French books of the Project for American and French Research on the Treasury of the French Language, organized by the Centre National de la Recherche Scientifique and the University of Chicago. From the beginning of the seventeenth century down to the close of the revolutionary upheavals of Europe and the New World (which I will operationally call "before 1820"), 21% of all books discussing "democracy" (or closely related terms) have some passage in them referring to Athens in the same paragraph as democracy. After that point, as discussions of democracy were more likely to be about current issues or social struggles, that figure falls to 10%. Beyond 1950, the number of instances in the rather small sample of included materials (as of 2009) is actually zero (ARTFL Project). As an additional complication, the ancient models themselves underwent revision, not only because discussion of them was embedded in contemporary conflict over democracy, but because of the autonomous deepening of scholarship in significant degree driven by the discovery and utilization of previously unknown or unused sources. Aristotle's uniquely detailed *Constitution of Athens*, for example, was rediscovered "in the 1880s in the sands of Egypt" (Hansen, 1991, p. 9), but the corresponding empirical materials he and his students put together on 157 other city-states have never turned up.

This suggests that the mechanisms sustaining debate were not correctly specified by Gallie when he attributes critical significance to a consensual exemplar.[9]

Progressive Character

Gallie's seventh criterion suggests that the very competition among definitions is progressive in the sense that the competition itself sustains or advances what the consensual exemplar embodies[10]. If the sixth criterion helps sustain the debate, this last criterion makes the game worth the candle. The debate itself advances the values the debate is about.

Now it is certainly a readily defensible proposition that many places are more democratic today than they were in even the recent past. It is even a defensible proposition that places that were held to be quite democratic in the past are even more democratic today, as judged by evolving standards of democracy. The early twenty-first century United States, for example, was a great deal more democratic by many of the prevailing standards of its own era than was the early nineteenth century United States whose democratic character was so celebrated and analyzed by Tocqueville.

One may ask whether Gallie's notion of progressive competition allows an adequate place for those moments when by evolving democratic criteria things are running in the anti-progressive direction. Or when, depending on one's criteria, things were headed in both directions at once. But more fundamentally, can changes in ideas be understood without considering how those ideas are intertwined among other processes? Something very important is missing from Gallie's account.

PHILOSOPHER CONTESTANTS

From his very title, Gallie claims to be discussing "concepts." But if they are contested, who is doing the contesting? And is the contestation a consequence of certain characteristics of the concepts, the contestants, or perhaps both? Or is it perhaps a cause? Let us see what Gallie's treatment suggests, again examining each of Gallie's seven points. It will turn out that it is late in Gallie's own progression through them that he tells us who the contestants are and it will further turn out that he mostly defines them very narrowly, a narrowness to which he cannot consistently adhere, something that will be very instructive.

Evaluation

The very first of Gallie's attributes involves judgments about valued achievements. If we think of individuals as the makers of such judgments, we are soon considering cognitive or affective processes because we will be exploring how it is that some institutional arrangements are understood to be democratic and other not and we will be exploring the feelings those arrangements evoke. If we are methodological individualists, we will think that processes internal to those individuals are critical to an account of judgments. If we favor relational accounts of social life, when we want to know how it is that things come to be differently valued, and how it is that judgments are arrived at, we will be thinking about social processes, not simply individual cognitions or feelings. In a relational account, we will, for example, be interested in the ways in which information flows through social networks or collectivities elicit emotions. But in either the individualistic or the relational version we are led to reflect on the actors who think and not just their thoughts.

Complexity

The second point at first glance refers to the concept in itself — how complex is it? But let's take a second glance. A current level of complexity may come out of a history that has added and subtracted meanings as actors deploy contentious language (Tarrow, 2013).

Weighting

The third item on the checklist considers "rival descriptions of its total worth" and some may be wondering about how the rivals are constituted and through what means they manifest their rival descriptions. Are the rivals professors whose rivalry is displayed through mutually derisive footnotes? Crowds shouting in the streets? Lobbyists hiring public relations firms? Political parties buying TV airtime? Government agencies spreading disinformation? Two people on a street corner cursing a tyrant? We may well want to know more about the rivals and the conflict between them and not just about the rivals' rival descriptions.

Openness

Is openness is an attribute of a concept or of an ongoing conflict? Students of long-term conflicts are likely to pay attention to actors with shifting resources and constraints – including shifting alliances and enemies and opportunities to act – who are at different moments more or less creative in using those resources and seizing those opportunities, and more or less plain lucky in terms of the outcomes produced by the joint decisions of themselves and other participants in conflict. Such actors redefine the concepts deployed in their quarrels, sometimes including their concepts of themselves. Actor constitution, to borrow a term from McAdam, Tarrow, and Tilly (2001, pp. 315–321) is an important part of many (most? all?) conflicts. In this light, it is noteworthy that the widespread label "democrat" dates from the 1780s, the moment that debates about democracy escaped the confines of the philosopher's study and became a practical category, not just a category of technical analysis, to borrow some useful terminology from Cooper (2005, p. 62).

Recognition of Debate, Authoritative Exemplar, Progressive Character

When Gallie gets to his fifth through seventh conditions, he explicitly discusses the contestants: "each party recognizes the fact that its own use of it is contested by those of other parties ...." Although he tells us nothing about how such recognition is achieved, he directs our attention at this point precisely to those "parties." And his seventh attribute, the progressive sustenance or development of the values embedded in the concept, implies human actors, too, since there is presumably some judge somewhere making the judgments as to the progress of the debate. Perhaps the contestants, or some of them, are the judges.

Gallie's own account of the actors he has in mind is incomplete. The contestants he claims to be interested in are identified as "philosophers" and he has an implicit theory of their motives from which certain social processes seem to follow. Philosophers are seekers of conceptual clarity. If only the first five conditions were met the philosophers' quest might lead to simply separating the contested and irresolvable meanings into distinct terms by creating neologisms, deploying adjectival descriptors, numbering distinct meanings (as in democracy$_1$ means this while democracy$_2$ means that). They might even be interested in the muddle itself. But they do not stop there because of conditions 6 and 7: the common exemplar of the multiple meanings and the sense that philosophical discussion is in fact advanced by continuing the endless conversation.

In the essay's second sentence he directs us toward the kind of contestation that is a "ground for philosophical enquiry" (p. 167). In the second paragraph he gives us a picture of actors, and as we shift from the passive verbs of the opening paragraph ("concept ... liable to be contested," "assumption cannot be made," "picture painted in oils") to humans acting, the protagonists turn out to be identified through formulations like "a philosopher might in some way discover ... " or "a philosopher might propose a meaning" (p. 167). He soon connects certain concepts to "a number of organized or semi-organized human activities: in academic terms they belong to aesthetics, to political philosophy, the philosophy of history and the philosophy of religion" (p. 168).

Let's consider the last of these, his religion rubric. Gallie does not state any intention to consider how most of us use concepts as we pray, blaspheme, attend religious services, wrestle with tough choices in light of ethical teachings, experience solidarity with fellow adherents, are disgusted by the wickedness of governments, seek comfort in grief and reassurance in the dead of night, loath those whose practices differ from our own, experience compassion for those whose practices differ from our own, find purpose in the apparent senselessness of the world, try to recall something our parents said a long time ago, and most of the other very many ways many humans are religious. He restricts his concern to the use of concepts by the learned as they carry on the philosophy of religion. Distinguishing "practical life" from "philosophy," he makes clear that it is ongoing unresolved disputes in the latter realm that are of interest (p. 169). His preview of the paper's conclusion is in the same vein as he promises to lead up to "what seem to me the most important implications of my new grouping of concepts for general philosophy" (p. 170).

When we get to democracy, however, Gallie does not hew with any consistency to philosopher contestants. Here's who he says actually makes claims about what democracy is: "We of the western tradition" (p. 185), "certain churches" (p. 185), "those governments which insist on their democratic character" (p. 186), "many and various political movements [that] claim to draw their inspiration from the French Revolution" (p. 186), and "groups of men and nations" (p. 186). Maybe the philosophers are lumped in among some of these categories, but every one of them is a lot broader than a particular profession or academic department. Despite his stated intention other contestants claim his attention. At the beginning of his most extended discussion, he explains that he is not going to discuss "questions of actual practice" (183) in which what is debated is whether "actual political conditions" are appropriately characterized by one or another meaning of democracy. But we have seen that when he identifies actors debating democracy, he is not able to avoid people very much involved in ongoing struggles.

TURBULENT DEMOCRACY

Let me suggest a different approach. Rather than just some vague references to the world beyond the philosopher's office, the question of the contestants might well be placed at the center of inquiry. I believe a few quick observations about democracy's turbulent history are adequate to demonstrate that the essentially contested character of democracy is accounted for by the characteristics of the *contestants* and of the *contests*. Let us situate ourselves at one important moment in the history of democracy – the revolutionary upheavals of the late eighteenth and early nineteenth centuries – and look downstream toward the future. In newly independent states on the western side of the Atlantic and in the war- and revolution-ravaged states of Europe the very old word democracy entered many a discussion of the cause for or against which people fought. Nonetheless, it was only to a very limited degree that the new institutions that fleetingly or durably emerged from Warsaw to Rio de la Plata were modeled on the institutions and practices of the ancient exemplars.

It would have seemed a familiar enough notion to devotees of the Athenian exemplar to confine full citizenship rights to adults not children, men not women, the free not the slaves, Athenians not foreigners. But when we get to the organization of government and the procedures for acceding to office, there is practically no resemblance to ancient practice at all. In fact, the vast procedural differences between ancient practices and the new institutions made some leery of using the term democracy at all to describe the new order while others were inconsistent in their usages (Rosanvallon, 1995). But the rejection of ancient practices despite the retention of the word did not mean that those first democrats were aiming at the sorts of institutions that are implied by the everyday understandings of democracy of the twenty-first century. The new constitutions of the era did not promote election-contesting political parties, or great bureaucratic machines, or influence-seeking lobbies, or challenging social movements. Yet every one of these central institutions of all modern democratic states was created and along with them the innumerable conflicts such institutions sustain.

These institutions were either hardly imagined at all by the founding generation of modern democracy or outright loathed. In revolutionary France to say someone was a member of a party was just a tad short of an accusation of treason against the unitary People. In post-revolutionary America, it was the style to situate state capitals away from the big towns to get the government away, even physically, from popular movements. And eighteenth century and early nineteenth century constitution-writers took little notice of growing central bureaucracies. No matter: all modern states, democratic or otherwise, have vast, powerful bureaucracies and all democratic states see people organize to win elections, to influence the elected and appointed officials, and to challenge the very rules of the game. That modern democracies have inherent conflicts between expert bureaucracies and elected legislatures has been a commonplace of sociology since at least Max Weber. By the late-nineteenth and early twentieth centuries a great deal of political science research was uncovering the unanticipated practices that developed around the constitutionally prescribed institutions of modern democracies. The study of party organization and tactics, of interest groups and lobbies, and of the behavior of electorates were launched and were already well-developed by the early twentieth century (e.g., Bryce, 1901; Ostrogorski, 1974 [1910]; Siegfried, 1913). Since social scientists have been writing for more than a century of how democracy in practice fosters parties, bureaucracies and lobbies, and about how voters choose, I will confine myself briefly to sketching why democracy also fosters social movements.

SOCIAL MOVEMENT CHALLENGERS AND POWERHOLDERS DEBATE DEMOCRACY

Social movements have long drawn much attention, too, but only recently, it seems to me, have they been explicitly approached by scholars as a constituent element of democracy. Nonetheless the relevant scholarship is vast. Historians have discussed the emergence and impacts of a great variety of movements in many countries. When social movement scholars deploy such central concepts as "opportunities" and "frames," they repeatedly show us how democratic practices constitute opportunities for movements and how movements with some frequency pitch appeals to the public values of democracy (e.g., McAdam, McCarthy, & Zald, 1996; Tarrow, 2011). They have also shown us multiple instances of movement action effectively enlarging or diminishing democratic practice and even the definition of democracy and I will briefly develop several examples below. Movement scholars are now recently trying to spell out the nature of what appear to be a wide range of linkages that have made the history of modern democracy and the history of social movements intertwined. The current best account is Tilly's (2006, pp. 179−208; 2008, pp. 71−87; Tilly, & Wood, 2009, pp. 123−143). Let me summarize the argument in the form of nine brief points.

1. The claims by powerholders to rule on behalf of, in the interests of, and by the will of the people encourage people to press their claims in public.
2. The claims by powerholders to rule on behalf of, in the interest of, and by the will of the people suggests to powerholders themselves that their struggles with other powerholders may be advanced by selectively encouraging popular mobilization.
3. Electoral processes are decided by numbers and thereby make the demonstration of numbers of adherents a potent tool for getting one's way. Not surprisingly, the "demonstration" has become the most commonly identifiable form of social movement activism (see e.g., Favre, 1990).
4. The freedoms of speech, publishing, and organization without which meaningful electoral contests are not possible and without which meaningful legislative debates are not probable radically reduce the risks in challenging powerholders so long as contestants adhere to acceptable bounds. Democratic procedures reduce the costs of much social movement activism.
5. An important subset of movements generates demands for a more democratic order. Participants in such conflicts find themselves likely not merely to be debating which changes would more correctly embody a democracy that all understand the same way but also to be debating what democracy *really* means − more freedom? More equality? More scope for majority rule? More protection for minority rights? Et cetera. And, for that matter, debating what freedom really means, what equality really means, also et cetera.
6. An important subset of movements generates demands for a less democratic order. Antidemocratic movements, like democratic movements, can flourish when powerholders claim to rule by virtue of popular will, when freedoms of speech, publication, and organization are protected, when elections become occasions for mobilizations. Such movements, too, alter the rules, and summon forth anti-antidemocratic movements

in turn, which shift them further. The result is generally something other than stasis and in defining themselves against each other; democratic and antidemocratic movements are continually engaged in redefining democracy as well.

7. The parties, lobbies, and bureaucracies that all democracies nurture constitute a rich environment that also sustains movements. The excluded frequently find in the parties, lobbies, and bureaucracies infuriatingly antidemocratic targets that have excluded them from effective decision-making and whose antidemocratic practices are readily denounced. But parties and lobbies can spin off movements, and movements can spin off parties and lobbies.[11] In nineteenth century Europe socialist parties competing at the ballot box and socialist movements engaging in popular mobilization were intimately intertwined, as were fascist parties and movements after the First World War.

8. The parties, lobbies, and bureaucracies that all democracies nurture encourage the development of a variety of skills that are then available to movements, too: fundraising, spin-doctoring, publicity, seeking the patronage of the powerful, flattering publics, framing issues.

9. Last, but certainly not least, there is no end point at which democratic political structures will have already fostered all the movements they will ever foster. Democratic movements spin off newer democratic movements. Some are inspired by a movement organization, but favor other tactics, or goals, or alliances, or reach out to other constituencies. Some of those active in organizations struggling for a truer democracy will discover the inadequacy of the democracy their own organization embodies and attempt to reform it, or to set up some new, more satisfactory organization (for compelling examples from the US civil rights movement, see Polletta, 2002). One might take as paradigmatic the ways in which the United States' struggle for women's rights was galvanized in the 1840s by women active in the transnational antislavery movement of the first half of the nineteenth century who were dismayed at their marginalization as women within that movement itself. Its leaders later dated the origins of the suffrage movement to women being forbidden to speak at a London antislavery conference in 1840[12] (Dubois, 1999, pp. 53–78; Evans, 1977, p. 46; Stanton, Anthony, & Gage, 1881, pp. 50–62).

It is not only challenging movements that debate what democracy is. So do powerholders. After British colonists in North America with the considerable aid of European allies had defeated the greatest naval power of the age, Haitian self-liberated ex-slaves with no allies fought off the armies of three empires, and French forces for a brief moment dominated Europe from Madrid to Moscow, powerholders came to embrace new formulas for rulership. The writing of constitutions, for example, spread quickly, even in conservative European states, not to mention throughout the western hemisphere. The French defeat sparked a wave of constitution-writing in the German states (Nipperdey, 1996, pp. 237–243; Sheehan, 1989, pp. 411–425). Even the restored French monarchy itself issued a constitution in 1814, granted, so its royal preamble tells us, in recognition "of the wishes of our subjects" (Duverger, 1960, p. 80). Claiming democratic legitimation became important even for those who hoped to limit or even halt democratic movements, a propensity still notable two centuries later (Markoff, 2015).

FROM THE AGE OF DEMOCRATIC REVOLUTION FORWARD: TRANSNATIONAL STRUGGLES OVER SLAVERY

Let me provide an instructive example of conflict, including social movement activism, shifting the meanings of democracy.[13] At the beginning of the twenty-first century, few could imagine democracy without election-contesting political parties, secret ballots, or women's suffrage, or could imagine democracy with slavery. Personal freedom, broad equality of political rights, protections for citizens against arbitrary retaliation from governments, and collective organization for contesting political power are elements of most current democratic definitions. All were debated. There is little reason to think the future of democratic practice will involve less innovation than in the past and if the arguments presented here are correct there is little reason to think that the future of democracy will be any less contentious, too. By way of illustration, I will briefly examine the contentious processes that, beginning with the onset of modern democracy in the social upheavals of the late eighteenth and early nineteenth centuries, radically challenged a common social practice and in so doing altered the meanings of democracy.

We may identify an important turning-point in the global history of democracy in the 1780s, when the term "democrat" was first widely used, often negatively, in lively political and social struggles, first in the Low Countries, then in revolutionary France, and then in conflicts from Poland to the Americas (Markoff, 1999). This was a moment when the term democracy stopped being mainly a concept deployed in interesting debates about hypothetical political systems and became part of the language with which some challenged the powerful and others tried to retain their power. At the time, the expanding colonial enterprises of Europeans were profoundly tied to colonial slavery. Not only did Britain, France, the Netherlands, Spain, Portugal, and Denmark all support this practice in their overseas possessions, but at the moment of its independence a democratizing United States was on its way to outstripping all the rest in the eventual size of its slave population. It was hardly obvious at the outset that the Age of Democratic Revolution, as its historians have often dubbed that transnational moment, was going to lead to the end of human beings owning other human beings.

The democracy launched at that moment became incompatible with slavery through insurrection, warfare, and the social movement activism nurtured by democratization itself. To begin with movements among the enslaved: Slave resistance, including sabotage, flight, and rebellion had long troubled colonial slavery but had nowhere crippled it. Resistance began on the slave ship (Rediker, 2007) and continued on land. In some places, escaped slaves set up counter societies, but at first lacked the intention and almost always lacked the capacity to end slavery itself. But the revolutionary era was an exceptionally propitious moment for one French colony.

Among the many abuses of the Old Regime challenged in the famous grievance lists of 1789, slavery was close to being totally ignored (Drescher, 1987, p. 54). When the structure of hierarchical distinction that elevated some over others was challenged in the celebrated "abolition of feudalism" (Markoff, 1996), slavery was conspicuously absent. Some French revolutionaries were of the view that the cause of human rights in which they had enlisted was incompatible with Caribbean slavery and their Society of the Friends of Black People pressed their case with the new, revolutionary National Assembly. But the planters, slavers, and merchants of the Atlantic port cities also quickly mastered the skills of lobbying. Armed with the simple but powerful argument that should the legislature declare abolition, the colonies would simply break with France, they more than counterbalanced the antislavery movement. To the disappointment and disgust of those for whom "the rights of man," just proclaimed, were incompatible with slavery, the great majority in the new legislature were not prepared to act.

But the example of turbulence in the metropolis, the appropriation of ideas of human freedom, dignity, and equality, and the opportunity presented by a France in military and political turmoil were conditions under which colonial nonwhites, like metropolitan whites, demanded their rights and colonial slaves revolted. At the same time, the revolutionary government was becoming more radicalized in many domains. At a particularly radical moment in Paris, the French, faced with the likelihood of mobilized rebel ex-slaves in charge in the Caribbean in any event, formally abolished slavery in 1794. When Napoleon's coming to power brought the metropolitan turmoil to an end, France rescinded that abolition in 1802 (Hunt, 2007, pp. 160–167).

Haiti's rebels, in ultimately establishing the first of the new republics to have abolished slavery, had to fight off the large French force bent on re-enslaving them, as well as British and Spanish forces who each tried to take Haiti away from a locally weakened France. But while war and revolution ended Haitian slavery, the French had managed to reinstall it elsewhere. While the increasing centrality of parliamentary politics to Britain enabled social movements as part and parcel of British democratization (on which more below), the very different French political order only enabled effective antislavery agitation at moments of revolutionary crisis. In 1848, the suddenly (and briefly) redemocratized French state found its enduring colonial slavery an embarrassment and complied with the abolitionist demands of its relatively small movement, this time for good.

The story in Spain's American mainland colonies went differently in detail, but resembled Haiti's in the opportunities created by war, revolution, and national independence. In the early nineteenth century, with most of the country overrun by French forces, in the holdout zone of southern Spain, a meeting of the Cortes – the parliament – was convened to mobilize unoccupied Spain, including Spain's overseas territories. (This body ultimately adopted a liberal constitution in Cádiz in 1812). The convening of the Cortes opened up a debate in the Americas about just who ought to be represented and how, and the elections became an important point of mobilization for what turned into a long, complex series of independence struggles that drove the Spanish army off the continent. In the same year the Cortes set about its work, 1810, revolutionary Creoles overthrew Spanish officials in Santiago, Buenos Aires, Bogotá, Cartagena, and Cali, launching an extended period of multisided warfare, and inaugurating democratic processes at some times and places, destroying those processes at others. Weakening of local authorities meant increased opportunities for slave resistance, flight, and mobilization; the Spanish and rebel military recruitment allowed individual slaves to bargain for freedom in return for service; and the struggle for black allegiance led to commitments to end slavery collectively, something that happened in one new country after another, in several legislated stages, beginning with Chile in 1811. At the same time an astonishing array of democratic, semi-democratic and authoritarian practices were invented as Spanish rule ended across the continent, sometimes following one another in rapid succession[14] (Andrews, 2004; Rodríguez, 1998).

A different pattern of contention unfolded in Britain, where popular mobilization intersected with parliamentary politics and the mass media of the day. Parliament had become the place where major decisions were made and people could keep abreast of pending legislation in the already well-developed press. In the 1790s, social movement organizers used the newspapers to publicize a vast petition campaign condemning slavery (Drescher, 1987). Ending at least the slave trade (if not slavery itself), was more readily imaginable because one of the least of the slaveholding colonizers, Denmark, had ended it as of 1803 (Green-Pedersen, 1979). In 1807, Parliament acceded, giving further encouragement to what was by now a broad, transnationally connected movement for the complete elimination of slavery.

Colonial slave insurrection remained part of the contentious mix. The ongoing British parliamentary debates were triggers for major slave revolts. Literate slaves could read the press and the illiterate could overhear their masters' complaints about the progress of parliamentary abolitionism. Large-scale rebellions in Barbados, Demarara, and Jamaica deepened abolitionist conviction in Britain but they encouraged the slaveholders of the US South to further dig in their heels (Davis, 2006, pp. 211–223). Following a period of widespread contentious mobilization, a notable component of which was over slavery, Parliament opted for a limited extension of the right to vote that weakened the parliamentary strength of the planter interests. The British movement eventually triumphed in a series of parliamentary enactments between 1834 and 1838 that ended British colonial slavery. But this hardly meant that Britain dropped out of the transnational story, because the British now attempted to organize international action against the slave trade and deployed their own Navy to help curtail it, hoping to relieve any competitive disadvantage of their own now slaveless colonies (Bethell, 1970; Daget, 1979; Howell, 1987; LeVeen, 1977; Lloyd, 1949; Ward, 1970).

In both Britain and the United States, the interplay of parliamentary politics, judicial action, electoral campaigns, and social movement mobilizations preceded apace with powerfully active abolitionist movements a vital, continuing part of the mix. In Britain, the intensity of antislavery mobilization and parliamentary discussion made the antislavery movement one of the important issues around which the politics of the streets and the politics of legislation began, in the early nineteenth century, to move in a mutually supportive rhythm. Participation in the movement was on a vast scale. In its 1792 campaign, 519 antislavery petitions gathered 390,000 signatures. In 1814, some 800 petitions had 750,000. The year after the expansion of British suffrage, in 1833, 5000 petitions displayed 1,500,000 signatures. One was a half-mile long statement sewn and pasted together and signed by 350,000 women, who had not been given a vote the year before but were determined to make their voices count. That same year Parliament freed the 800,000 colonial slaves (Davis 238). Activists also organized boycotts of slave-grown sugar (with possibly some 300,000 families joining in during the early 1790s); mobilized Quaker and Evangelical congregations (including the expulsion of Quaker slaveholders); and held meetings beyond count (Drescher, 1987). British antislavery activism was a formative experience for democratic citizenship and subsequent social movement activism not only because of the numbers of participants but because of the forms of action developed in antislavery causes, as shown in rich detail by Tilly's (2008) statistical analyses of changing patterns of contention.

In the United States, as in Haiti and Latin America, war and revolution galvanized antislavery actions. As New England's rebellious colonists mobilized to throw off British rule, wartime formation of black units kicked off emancipatory processes. In the South, the British were more inclined to bid for slave support than the planters who led the revolutionary movement. Wartime conditions and British inducements led to the enormous loss of 80–100,000 slaves, many leaving with the defeated forces, something that strengthened Southern intransigence at the beginning of the new republic (Davis, 2006, pp. 147–152). In the new republic, the growing US antislavery movement was deeply connected to the British one, and like the British, found in democratic processes a vital series of opportunities, in which petitioning, demonstrating, pamphleteering, the judicial arena, electoral campaigns, and congressional debates all came to intersect. But the US movement grew far larger. By the 1830s there were 1300 local antislavery groups, with 100,000 members. In 1840, their presses put out three million pieces of literature. As in Britain, women activists strongly outnumbered men (Davis, 2006, p. 260). And as in Britain as well, the struggles around slavery became an important part of reforging democracy as citizens developed new modes of participation in public life. Indeed, the cause of freedom for the slaves became conflated with the cause of democratic liberties for all. In 1836 proslavery forces prevailed in Congress to bar the receipt of antislavery petitions, one of the abolitionists' potent mobilizing devices. Antislavery activists now saw themselves as advancing the rights of democratic citizens to advocate their views and produced a further flood of defiant petitions. By 1856, Republican Party campaign slogans commonly yoked together "Free Soil, Free Speech, Free Labor, Free Press" (Fischer, 2005, p. 295).

But social movement activism on slavery had a distinctive US component: the mobilization by its champions of a proslavery movement as well, equally capable of availing themselves of the opportunities for public activism of democratic politics, and even equally capable of framing their own cause as "freedom" (Fischer, 2005, pp. 274–354). On the one side, personal freedom became a part of a more inclusive notion of democratic equality. On the other, freedom came to be associated with unconstrained domination of some over others. Some in the South recalled that Athenian slavery was a foundation for Athenian wealth and Athenian democracy.[15] The mutually reinforcing spiral of threat and response, one form of the "movement-countermovement mobilization" described by Meyer and Staggenborg (1996), made Unites States antislavery not only even larger than the British movement but injected a much greater radical component into the antagonistic camps and ultimately led to the bloodiest war in United States history. To take one instance of this dynamic: Proslavery won a great victory with the passage of the Fugitive Slave Law of 1850, which not only required the federal government to seize escaped slaves wherever they might be, thereby removing the protection of free soil legislation in northern states, but also allowed it to deputize even unwilling local citizens to assist them. In one spectacular incident, it took 15,000 soldiers to drag away one fugitive slave in Boston in the face of 50,000 citizens who tried to prevent this (Davis, 2006, p. 265).

The upshot of all this turmoil for the present argument is simple. It was not by conceptual debate alone, or even primarily, that slavery became incompatible with democracy, but through a series of partially autonomous and partially linked struggles of the most intense kinds, carried on in many countries. The forms of contention include revolution, war, and insurrection. In countries where governments claimed that their legitimate power derived from popular consent and that electoral processes were essential to select and validate powerholders, this contention included social movement activism. Indeed, antislavery activism was even a seedbed for other social movements. To take one very concrete example, it was in abolitionism that militant women, with no voting rights, honed skills of organizing, public speaking, petitioning, badgering elected officials, and pamphleteering, all of which served them in good stead when their marginalization within abolitionism itself led some to form new organizations to work for women's rights, a cause to which they brought abolitionism's themes of liberation and fundamental human equality. And on a transnational scale it was the intersection and accumulation of all these forms of contentious action (and much more, since my brief sketch omits the Dutch, Brazilian, and Spanish abolitions) that redefined democracy, not just particular instances of democracy, as incompatible with enslavement. There is simply no way to understand this without paying attention to the various antislavery organizations, the acquiescent or resistant powerholders, the candidates for elective office, the planners of insurrections, the commanders of armies and navies, the proslavery mobilizations, and the resources available to such contenders, their possible allies and audiences.

Of course conceptual questions were part of this story, from notions of "the rights of man" that were put forward in the revolutionary era (Hunt, 2007), to ideas of liberty fully compatible with enslavement (Fischer, 2005, pp. 284–293, 308–321), to Lincoln's redefinition of the meaning of "all men are created equal" (Wills, 2009, pp. 54–55). But there is simply no way to tell this story without embedding it in the insurrections, wars, and revolutions of the time as well as the social movements ubiquitous in democratic states. While conceptions of democracy were invoked at critical points in some of these struggles, conceptual analysis of possible meanings of democracy can illuminate but a small part of a very large transformation in human affairs. In much-quoted words, Frederick Douglass observed: "Those who profess to favor freedom, yet deprecate agitation, are men who want crops without plowing up the ground, they want rain without thunder and lightning" (Fischer, 2005, p. 274).

SOCIAL CONFLICT PRODUCES CONCEPTUAL COMPLEXITY

The upshot of all this is quite simple. Democratic practices guarantee debate without end about what democratic practices are, could be, and should be. Now it may be the case that the conceptual complexity of democracy — an intertwined bundle of rules for how government works, how officeholders come to power, how citizens are linked to states and what their rights are, how the divide between citizens and noncitizens is drawn, and more besides — plays a part (Markoff, 2011). As a historical contention, I would suggest that already at that moment in the revolutionary 1780s and 1790s when "democrats" announced their presence, the "democracy" they had learned about was already a complex, multifaceted thing and the ancient exemplars of their imaginations had all sorts of rules and procedures that lent themselves to different emphases. But as a thought experiment, even if we imagine that somehow those first democrats actually had some consensus among themselves on some simple, unambiguous concept, the processes I have just sketched would have in and of themselves guaranteed something like the essential contestation we have had ever since. This contestation would generate conceptual complexity even if that were not an initial condition. In other words, Gallie's second and third characteristics need not be present initially since they will be produced by conflict itself. My counterfactual proposition is that even if modern "democracy" had not been born conceptually complex and essentially contested at the end of the eighteenth century, it would rapidly have assumed that status because of the conflictual actors it inevitably summons forth.

Rousseau's excoriation of the disappointing character of citizen participation through parliamentary election is well known[16], but to his contemporary D'Argenson it was obvious that "[i]n a true democracy one acts through deputies and these deputies have their authority by virtue of election" (d'Argenson, 1764, p. 7). In the new United States, antifederalists based their disapproval of the newly written constitution on their understanding of ancient models stressing the virtue of citizens, something achievable only in small communities whose governors not only shared in local traditions but were known to and under the scrutiny of those they governed. However, the trio who authored *The Federalist* argued that a properly designed governing machine in combination with a large and diverse society would more effectively protect the public interest through the play of countervailing powers (Sunstein, 2009). Beyond a rather widely shared sense that democracy had hitherto denoted something more negative than positive, the generation that founded modern democracy agreed little on how a modern democracy could work or should work.

It is surely empirically accurate that at least the educated, or most of them[17], in that first democratic generation would have agreed on the ancient exemplars, but this is clearly no longer the case, and Gallie's sixth condition is no longer particularly apt. Why does that matter? The sixth condition is a big part of what he claims makes the game worth the candle for the philosophers who constitute the contestants he says he is considering. If there weren't that kind of agreement, why not just create new labels with distinct definitions?

If one were to imagine a philosophy seminar cut off from the world and populated by beings motivated only by a thirst for conceptual clarity, perhaps that sixth condition would indeed be essential to make sense of their continuing to debate since at least the 1780s such a murky, confusing, complex, and contradictory concept. It seems a great deal simpler, however, to recognize that the walls of the seminar are not very thick, that its participants participate in many other things as well, and that their debates are part of larger ones. And, as I've noted, Gallie implicitly recognizes this. What makes democracy essentially contested is the contestants – powerholders claiming democratic authority for their actions, party politicians whose path to office passes through elections, and especially the activists of challenging movements that intermittently demand that democracy be understood differently as an inseparable component of their struggles to change it.

The movements have been among the most important causes of ongoing democratization in a wide variety of ways. Their goals have often involved new procedural rules and redefinitions of the boundaries of citizenship. Even when engaged in highly particularistic campaigns they have often advanced the interests of previously marginalized groups and have often shifted the rhetoric of democracy in support of their own goals. The give-and-take of movement recruitment, planning, fund-raising, and coalition-formation has often buttressed habits of transregional and transclass connection that undergird or reinforce elements of democratic practice. (For the importance of such processes to US democracy, see Skocpol, 2003).

Finally, movements have been the most important gadflies, swarming around dubious claims of powerholders to democratic practice and pushing things, sometimes in small steps, toward the less dubious. One of the most important characteristics of democratic legitimacy claims has been the ways in which their fanciful character, though no less fanciful than claims that monarchs are God's stand-ins on earth, have virtually invited movements to try to make things more real (Markoff, 2011). Negative evaluations of the actual state of things in light of democratic pretensions have been a recurrent powerful weapon in movement arsenals. Just consider as one much-quoted instance of the genre Frederick Douglass's: "What, to the American slave, is your Fourth of July?" This is why I highlighted the importance of negative judgments when I outlined Gallie's argument: not because of some logical property of negation, but because of the role of sorrow and anger and disgust in energizing social activism, as students of movements are exploring of late (e.g., Goodwin & Jasper, 2004; Goodwin, Jasper, & Polletta, 2001; Gould, 2009).

IN CONCLUSION

There surely are concepts whose scholarly use is advanced by debates in which the only protagonists are scholars. But it is characteristic of the sort of concepts that Gallie is talking about, according to his own analysis of them, that debates in the world beyond the studio are not merely the subject matter for contemplation but a part of where the contemplating happens. The debates go on in the village, the street, the workshop, the palace, and the battlefield, as well as in the seminars. Many social scientists have made impressive and unpersuasive efforts to convince their colleagues of the superiority of some favored definition of democracy. But it has not been possible to seal off the scholar's study and develop a fixed, dispassionate language of analysis unaffected by the usages of the streets, fields, factories and palaces, and the fortunes of battle.

Quite a number of important concepts debated by social scientists, in fact, are used by actors engaged in conflict as well as analysts claiming to advance knowledge, as Cooper (2005, pp. 62–63) points out. The ways in which their usages by various actors, including the learned, jostle each other is something that analysts need to address.

The argument presented here would shift the focus from the concept to the contest, to suggest that we focus more on the actors, their actions, and the consequences. We need to understand how the actors are constituted, how they respond to opportunities and constraints, how they form and respond to rivals, opponents, allies and audiences. We need to examine the ways in which powerholders claiming democratic authority have advanced particular understandings of democracy and how those aiming to influence those powerholders — or to replace them — have done so as well. We certainly need to understand those actors' concepts but we need to understand them *as* actors' concepts, including understanding who the actors are, and the circumstances in which they act and in which those concepts are used. Among these circumstances, moments — or epochs — of contention are likely to be especially fruitful for observing how meanings change. With regard to the study of democracy, this will take us not only into the study of parties and lobbies but into the study of the social movements whose history is inextricably, essentially intertwined with that of democracy itself.

NOTES

1. This includes references to several republications (Gallie, 1962, 1964, 1968).
2. All page numbers without other attribution are drawn from the original publication (Gallie, 1956).
3. Aristotle's *Politics* makes democracy the bad version and Polybius makes it the good version (Hansen, 1991, p. 66).
4. An important contribution for Western Europe and North America in the Age of Revolution is Innes and Philp (2013). We need to learn more about other places and later times.

5. Central concepts like liberty and freedom have complex histories of their own (Fischer, 2005; Foner, 1998; Patterson, 1991; Przeworski, 2003).

6. Before the nineteenth century, however, references to ancient democracy were likely to be either to abstract conceptualizations of a type of political system or to features of the Roman republic. And when Athens was discussed, it was often not in connection with its distinctive fifth century institutions. It was in the nineteenth century that Athens specifically became the key exemplar of ancient democracy, an image that it has retained (Hansen, 1992). Since Gallie's argument seems as well served by a generic notion of exemplar (like "ancient democracy") as by something quite particular (like "5th century Athens"), I don't see this as a major problem for his argument. In Gallie's own "artificial example" of sports competition (176), the exemplar "might have the form either of one prototype team of players, or of a succession (or tradition) of teams."

7. For the Netherlands and Switzerland, see d'Argenson (1764, p. 8, 11). As for Rhode Island: "It is ordered and unanimously agreed upon, that the Government which this Bodie Politick doth attend unto in this Island, and the Jurisdiction thereof, in favour of our Prince is a DEMOCRACIE, or Popular Government; that is to say, It is in the Powre of the Body of Freemen orderly assembled, or the major part of them, to make or constitute Just Lawes, by which they will be regulated, and to depute from among themselves such Ministers as shall see them faithfully executed between Man and Man" ("Government of Rhode Island", 1641).

8. Fifth century Athens had about 1100 formal positions whose incumbents were chosen by lot and about 100 who were elected, often for short terms, but in a few cases for several years (Hansen, 1991, pp. 232–237). Manin's (1997) splendid study shows the profound significance of the rejection of lot in the institutional design of the new political systems that emerged out of the social upheavals of the late eighteenth and early nineteenth centuries and the establishment of representation through elections. Since lot had been so strongly associated with democracy, emphasizing decision-making by elected representatives was at first widely understood as rejecting democracy and only later as redefining it.

9. Gallie in practice turns out to allow an exemplar to mean not a single instance but "a long tradition" (p. 186) that is taken as authoritative by proponents of particular notions of democracy, so he might be untroubled by the Athenian problem. He realizes, however, that there is perhaps more than one tradition that might be invoked, acknowledging parenthetically that there are "perhaps a number of historically independent but sufficiently similar traditions" (p. 186). He offers no reasons, however, to convince a skeptic that democrats have drawn on either a single or on significantly similar traditions.

10. In fact, Gallie advances the rather stronger requirement that things not merely advance but do so "in optimum fashion" (p. 180). I am unable to see that this stronger condition plays any role in his argument, and I will ignore it here, sticking to the weaker condition of progress whether or not optimal.

11. Clemens (1997) provides an instructive study of late-nineteenth and early-twentieth century US movements for "reform." The political parties of the day were widely experienced as unresponsive to the concerns of many citizens who, as "workers", "farmers", or "women" created new organizational forms and deployed new tactics to advance their goals.

12. "The movement for woman's suffrage, both in England and America, may be dated from this World's Anti-Slavery Convention" (Stanton & Cady, 1881, p. 62).
13. This section draws from Berlin (2003), Blackburn (1988), Davis (1975, 2006), and Drescher (1987, 1999, 2009).
14. These early nineteenth-century democratic and semi-democratic practices are at last receiving the attention they deserve for their role in the world history of democracy. (See e.g. Posada Carbó, 2008; Valenzuela, 2006).
15. For the argument that black slavery fostered solidarity and an egalitarian political culture among colonial whites that encouraged the downwards extension of political rights among them, see Morgan (1975).
16. "The people of England regard itself as free, but it is strongly mistaken. It is free only during the election of members of Parliament. As soon as they are elected, slavery overtakes it, and it is nothing. The use it makes of the short moments of liberty it enjoys merits losing them." (Rousseau, 1943 [1762], p. 340).
17. Rousseau (2002 [1755], p. 10), dissenting as often, doubted the democratic credentials of Athens, which "was not, in fact, a democracy but a quite tyrannical aristocracy, ruled by the learned and by orators."

ACKNOWLEDGMENT

I thank Amy White for her research assistance.

REFERENCES

ARTFL Project. http://humanities.uchicago.edu/orgs/ARTFL.
Andrews, G. R. (2004). *Afro-Latin America, 1800–2000*. Oxford: Oxford University Press.
Berlin, I. (2003). *Generations of captivity: A history of African-American slaves*. Cambridge, MA.: Belknap Press of Harvard University Press.
Bethell, L. (1970). *The abolition of the Brazilian slave trade: Brazil, Britain and the slave trade question, 1807–1869*. Cambridge: Cambridge University Press.
Blackburn, R. (1988). *The overthrow of colonial slavery, 1776–1848*. London: Verso.
Brunner, O., Conze, W., & Kosseleck, R. (1972). *Geschichtliche grundbegriffe: Historisches Lexikon zur politisch-sozialen Sprache in Deutschland*. Stuttgart: Klett Verlag.
Bryce, J. (1899). *Impressions of South Africa*. London: Macmillan.
Bryce, J. (1901). *Studies in history and jurisprudence*. New York, NY: Oxford University Press.
Clemens, E. S. (1997). *The people's lobby. Organizational innovation and the rise of interest group politics in the United States, 1890–1925*. London: University of Chicago Press.
Collier, D., & Levitsky, S. (1997). Democracy with adjectives: Conceptual innovation in comparative research. *World Politics, 49*(3), 430–451.
Cooper, F. (2005). *Colonialism in question: Theory, knowledge, history*. Berkeley, CA: University of California Press.
d'Argenson, R. L. (1764). *Considérations sur le gouvernement des anciennes provinces*. Amsterdam: Rey. As found on the website of ARTFL (American and French Research on the Treasury of the French Language).

Daget, S. (1979). British repression of the illegal french slave trade. In H. A. Gemery & J. S. Hogendorn (Eds.), *The uncommon market: Essays in the economic history of the Atlantic slave trade* (pp. 419–442). New York, NY: Academic Press.

Davis, D. B. (1975). *The problem of slavery in the age of revolution.* Ithaca, NY: Cornell University Press.

Davis, D. B. (2006). *Inhuman bondage: The rise and fall of slavery in the new world.* Oxford: Oxford University Press.

de Tocqueville, A. (1994 [1835, 1840]). *Democracy in America.* New York, NY: Knopf.

Drescher, S. (1987). *Capitalism and antislavery: British mobilization in comparative perspective.* New York, NY: Oxford University Press.

Drescher, S. (1999). *From slavery to freedom: Comparative studies in the rise and fall of Atlantic slavery.* New York, NY: New York University Press.

Drescher, S. (2009). *Abolition. A history of slavery and antislavery.* New York, NY: Cambridge University Press.

Dubois, E. C. (1999). *Feminism and suffrage. The emergence of an independent women's movement in America, 1848–1869.* London: Cornell University Press.

Duverger, M. (1960). *Constitutions et chartes politiques.* Paris: Presses Universitaires de France.

Evans, R. J. (1977). *The feminists. women's emancipation movements in Europe, America and Australasia, 1840–1920.* New York, NY: Barnes & Noble Books.

Favre, P. (Ed.). (1990). *La manifestation.* Paris: Presses de la Fondation Nationale des Sciences Politiques.

Fischer, D. H. (2005). *Liberty and freedom. A visual history of America's founding ideas.* Oxford: Oxford University Press.

Foner, E. (1998). *Story of American freedom.* New York, NY: Norton.

Furetière, A. (1970 [1690]). *Dictionnaire Universel, Contenant Généralement Tous les Mots Français, Tant Vieux Que Modernes, et les Termes de Toutes les Sciences et des Arts.* Geneva: Slatkine Reprints.

Gallie, W. B. (1956). Essentially contested concepts. *Proceedings of the Aristotelian Society* 105 (new series), (pp. 167–198).

Gallie, W. B. (1962). Essentially contested concepts. In M. Black (Ed.), *The importance of language* (pp. 121–146). Englewood Cliffs, NJ: Prentice Hall.

Gallie, W. B. (1964). *Philosophy and the historical understanding.* New York, NY: Schocken Books.

Gallie, W. B. (1968). *Philosophy and the historical understanding* (2nd ed.). New York, NY: Schocken Books.

"Government of Rhode Island". (1641). *Avalon law project.* Retrieved from http://avalon.law.yale.edu/17th_century/ri02.asp).

Goodwin, J., & Jasper, J. M. (Eds.). (2004). *Rethinking social movements. Structure, meaning and emotion.* Lanham, MD: Rowman and Littlefield.

Goodwin, J., Jasper, J. M., & Polletta, F. (Eds.). (2001). *Passionate politics. Emotions and social movements.* Chicago, IL: University of Chicago Press.

Gould, D. (2009). *Moving activism: Emotion and ACT UP's fight against AIDS.* Chicago, IL: University of Chicago Press.

Green-Pedersen, S. (1979). The economic considerations behind the Danish Abolition of the negro slave trade. In H. A. Gemery & J. Hogendorn (Eds.), *The uncommon market:*

Essays in the economic history of the Atlantic slave trade (pp. 399–418). New York, NY: Academic Press.

Hansen, M. H. (1991). *The Athenian democracy in the age of Demosthenes: Structure, principles and ideology*. Oxford: Blackwell.

Hansen, M. H. (1992). The tradition of the Athenian democracy, AD 1750–1990. *Greece and Rome*, *39*(1), 14–30.

Howell, R. (1987). *The royal navy and the slave trade*. London: Croom Helm.

Hunt, L. (2007). *Inventing human rights*. New York, NY: Norton.

Innes, J., & Philp, M. (Eds.). (2013). *Re-Imagining democracy in the age of revolutions*. Oxford: Oxford University Press.

LeVeen, E. (1977). *British slave trade suppression policies, 1821–1865: Impact and implication*. New York, NY: Arno Press.

Lloyd, C.. (1949). *The navy and the slave trade: The suppression of the African slave trade in the nineteenth century*. London: Longmans, Green.

Lutostański, K. (1918). *Les Partages de la Pologne et la lutte pour l'indépendance*. Lausanne and Paris: Payot.

Mainwaring, S., Brinks, D., & Pérez-Liñan, A. (2001). Classifying political regimes in Latin America, 1945–1999. *Studies in Comparative International Development*, *36*, 37–65.

Manin, B. (1997). *The principles of representative government*. Cambridge: Cambridge University Press.

Markoff, J. (1996). *The abolition of feudalism. Peasants, lords and legislators in the french revolution*. University Park, PA: Penn State University Press.

Markoff, J. (1999). Where and when was democracy invented? *Comparative Studies in Society and History*, *41*, 660–690.

Markoff, J. (2011). A moving target: Democracy. *Archives Européennes de Sociologie/European Journal of Sociology*, *52*(2), 239–276.

Markoff, J. (2015). *Waves of democracy. Social movements and political change* (2nd ed.). London: Paradigm Publishing.

May, J. D. (1973). *Of the conditions and measures of democracy*. Morristown, NJ: General Learning Press.

McAdam, D., McCarthy, J. D., & Zald, M. N. (Eds.). (1996). *Comparative perspectives on social movements: Political opportunities, mobilizing structures and cultural framings*. Cambridge: Cambridge University Press.

McAdam, D., Tarrow, S., & Tilly, C. (2001). *Dynamics of contention*. Cambridge: Cambridge University Press.

Meyer, D. S., & Staggenborg, S. (1996). Movements countermovements, and the structure of political opportunity. *American Journal of Sociology*, *101*(6), 1628–1660.

Morgan, E. S. (1975). *American slavery, American freedom: The ordeal of colonial Virginia*. New York, NY: Norton.

Nipperdey, T. (1996). *Germany from Napoleon to Bismarck, 1800–1866*. Princeton, NJ: Princeton University Press.

Ostrogorski, M. (1974 [1910]). *Democracy and the party system in the United States*. New York, NY: Arno Press.

Palmer, R. (1953). Notes on the use of the word 'democracy', 1789–1799. *Political Science Quarterly*, *68*, 203–226.

Pateman, C. (1970). *Participation and democratic theory*. Cambridge: Cambridge University Press.

Patterson, O. (1991). *Freedom in the making of western culture.* New York, NY: Basic Books.
Polletta, F. (2002). *Freedom is an endless meeting. Democracy in American social movements.* Chicago, IL: University of Chicago Press.
Posada Carbó, E. (2008). 'Sorpresas de la historia'. Independencia y democratización en Hispanoamérica. *Revista de Occidente, 326–327,* 109–125.
Przeworski, A. (2003). Freedom to choose and democracy. *Economics and Philosophy, 19,* 265–279.
Rediker, M. (2007). *The slave ship. A human history.* New York, NY: Viking.
Rodríguez, O., J. E. (1998). *The independence of Spanish America.* Cambridge: Cambridge University Press.
Rosanvallon, P. (1995). The history of the word 'Democracy' in France. *Journal of Democracy, 6,* 140–154.
Rousseau, J. J. (1943). *Du contrat social.* Paris: Aubier Montaigne.
Rousseau, J. J. (2002). *Discours sur l'économie politique.* Retrieved from http://classiques.uqac.ca/classiques/Rousseau_jj/discours_economie_politique/discours_eco_pol.pdf.
Sanger, D.. (2004). The 2004 campaign: On the trail – Political memo; at all bush rallies, message is 'freedom is on the march'. *New York Times,* October 21.
Schumpeter, J. (1943). *Capitalism, socialism and democracy.* London: Allen and Unwin.
Sheehan, J. J. (1989). *German history, 1770–1866.* Oxford: Clarendon Press.
Siegfried, A. (1913). *Tableau politique de la France de l'Ouest sous la Troisième République.* Paris: B. Grasset.
Skocpol, T. (2003). *Diminished democracy. From membership to management in American civic life.* Norman, OK: University of Oklahoma Press.
Stanton, E. C., Anthony, S. B., & Gage, M. J. (1881). *History of woman suffrage, vol. 1: 1848–1861.* New York, NY: Fowler and Wells Publishers.
Sunstein, C. (2009). The enlarged republic – Then and now. *New York Review of Books, 56*(5). Retrieved from https://www.nybooks.com/articles/2009/03/26/the-enlarged-republicthen-and-now/
Tarrow, S. (2011). *Power in movement* (3rd ed.). Cambridge: Cambridge University Press.
Tarrow, S. (2013). *The language of contention. Revolutions in words, 1688–2012.* New York, NY: Cambridge University Press.
Tilly, C. (2006). *Regimes and repertoires.* London: University of Chicago Press.
Tilly, C. (2007). *Democracy.* Cambridge: Cambridge University Press.
Tilly, C. (2008). *Contentious performances.* Cambridge: Cambridge University Press.
Tilly, C., & Wood, L. J. (2009). *Social movements, 1768–2008* (2nd ed.). London: Paradigm.
Valenzuela, J. S. (2006). Caudillismo, democracia y la excepcionalidad chilena en América Hispana. *Revista de Occidente, 305,* 11–28.
Ward, W. E. F. (1970). *The royal navy and the slavers: The suppression of the Atlantic slave trade.* London: Pantheon Books.
Wills, G. (2009). Lincoln's black history. *New York Review of Books,* 52–55.

ELITES, POLICY, AND SOCIAL MOVEMENTS

David Pettinicchio

ABSTRACT

Given the growing interest in social movements as policy agenda setters, this paper investigates the contexts within which movement groups and actors work with political elites to promote their common goals for policy change. In asking how and why so-called outsiders gain access to elites and to the policymaking process, I address several contemporary theoretical and empirical concerns associated with policy change as a social movement goal. I examine the claim that movements use a multi-pronged, long-term strategy by working with and targeting policymakers and political institutions on the one hand, while shaping public preferences — hearts and minds — on the other; that these efforts are not mutually exclusive. In addition, I look at how social movement organizations and actors are critical in expanding issue conflict outside narrow policy networks, often encouraged to do so by political elites with similar policy objectives. And, I discuss actors' mobility in transitioning from institutional activists to movement and organizational leaders, and even to protesters, and vice versa. The interchangeability of roles among actors promoting social change in strategic action fields points to the porous and fluid boundaries between state and nonstate actors and organizations.

Keywords: Social movements; policy; institutional activists; political entrepreneurs; policy communities; strategic action fields

In a recent exchange with *BlackLivesMatter* activists, Democratic presidential frontrunner, Hillary Clinton, explained her beliefs about social and political change to activist Julius Jones:

> I don't believe you change hearts. I believe you change laws, you change allocation of resources, you change the way systems operate. You're not going to change every heart. You're not. But at the end of the day, we can do a whole lot to change some hearts, and change some systems, and create more opportunities for people who deserve to have them. (http://www.nbcnews.com/news/nbcblk/blacklivesmatter-activists-confront-clinton-incarceration-n411536)

In addition to reflecting a cautious response about social change and activism, as Haberman of the *New York Times* (August 19, 2015) writes, it also alludes to a particular view of social movements, "that movement politics gets you only so far, and that activists must pave the way for those in office to act." Indeed, Clinton's statement points to several key debates in political sociology including the extent to which social movements matter in shaping policy, the distinction between "insiders" and "outsiders" in promoting political change, whether *real* policy change occurs incrementally or in punctuated bursts, and whether efforts at changing "hearts and minds" and "changing laws" are distinct (if not opposing) projects.

Social movement scholars have become increasingly interested in the relationship between social movement mobilization and policymaking. Resource mobilization theory provided a framework for understanding social movements as an "extension of institutionalized action" (see Jenkins, 1983; see also McCarthy & Zald, 1977). Social movement scholars also emphasized the role of political process and political opportunity structures either as control variables (often using some measure of the presence of sympathetic elites, see Meyer & Minkoff, 2004; Tarrow, 1998) and/or as a mediating variable (e.g., Amenta, 2006; Amenta, Caren, & Olasky, 2006 on political mediation theory) between mobilization and policy outcomes.

But, with a growing focus on the direct role of movements in the policy-making process, scholars have had to refine their theoretical and empirical understandings of political institutions and policy elites vis-à-vis social movements in shaping policy. Asking whether social movements matter in shaping policy has led to important advances in situating the work of social movements in the agenda-setting phase of policymaking — that is, where issues are debated and framed (see Amenta, Carens, Chiarello, & Su, 2010). Social movements are thought to have the most influence in shaping issue discourse in this prepolicy phase and in doing so, indirectly shape policy outcomes.

A second important development involves rethinking the boundaries between state and nonstate, whereby political elites and social movement actors work inside a network or field that transcends institutional boundaries. The growing recognition of the role of institutional activism and political entrepreneurship in promoting movement causes has blurred the distinction between an insider and outsider particularly since actors can easily transition from roles as policymakers to movement activists and vice versa (Banaszak, 2005, 2010; Pettinicchio, 2012, 2013). Specifying the ways in which political elites, social movement organizations (SMOs), and activists routinely interact contributes to our understanding of the networks of incumbents and challengers who coordinate their efforts to shape policy.

Finally, scholars have drawn from the work of institutional and welfare state scholars pointing out that while movements do shape policy outcomes, movements are also shaped by policy (Meyer, 2005). Policies provide both resources and opportunities for SMOs, advocacy groups, and regular citizens to mobilize the law, often targeting (and sometimes solicited by) the very institutions and actors who enacted them (Pettinicchio, 2013).

This paper outlines these and other developments drawing from numerous examples including, among others, the black civil rights movement, the women's movement, the environmental movement, and the disability rights movement. First, I outline a broad framework for situating social movements in the policymaking process. I discuss the conditions under which movements matter in shaping public preferences and/or the policy agenda, as well as how to make sense of short-term and long-term objectives given the protracted interaction between movement groups and policymakers. I then specifically discuss the ways in which so-called outsiders are able to shape the agenda-setting phase of policymaking, especially the kinds of opportunities institutional arrangements and political entrepreneurship create for social movements to have access to the policymaking process. Third, I expand on how policy-domain approaches in agenda setting help specify the concept of political opportunities for movements to influence policy. This is followed by a discussion of how strategic action fields shed light on the ways in which social movement actors and political elites work together to affect change through the use of both institutional and extrainstitutional strategies. I point to how distinctions between an "insider" and an "outsider" have consequently become blurred and how movement actors and policymakers move quite fluidly in their roles within this strategic action field. I conclude the paper by addressing the so-called "chicken-and-egg" problem (see Meyer, 2005) regarding how movements are hypothesized to influence policy while policies can also create or undermine opportunities for social movements.

SITUATING SOCIAL MOVEMENTS WITHIN THE POLITICS OF POLICYMAKING

While social movement scholars on the one hand traditionally viewed challengers working too closely with policymakers and within political institutions as counterproductive to mobilization (Burstein, 1991; Piven & Cloward, 1977; Tarrow, 1998), policy scholars on the other hand ignored exogenous factors, like the role of social movements, in influencing policy (see Wilson, 2000 on policy regime models).

Social movements are about changing "hearts and minds" as well as policy (Tilly, 1984). Importantly, these should not be seen as two distinct or competing endeavors. In the case of the black civil rights movement, activists sought to raise awareness and shape public attitudes outside the U.S. South hoping that this would pressure political elites to take action, while simultaneously targeting economic and political institutions in the South (McAdam, 1982; Morris, 1984). In the case of gender equality, feminists quickly realized that targeting policy would not necessarily undermine deeply rooted cultural and normative beliefs about gender and gender roles (Taylor & Whittier, 1995; Van Dyke, Soule, & Taylor, 2004). Activists therefore targeted political institutions as well as encouraged public questioning of gender norms and gendered structural inequalities. This means that movement targets and objectives range from proximate and short-term to distant and long-term. Thus, social movements have, to use Cockburn's (2007) terminology, a short and long agenda.

Social movements may focus more of their time on shaping hearts and minds than they may on altering structural arrangements. Social movements can target public preferences rather than seeking to change the preferences of political elites. This might be because issues are politically closed or simply not on the policy agenda. Other times, when public preferences evolve to coincide with those of a movement, movement activists and organizations may have more leverage in influencing policy change by channeling public preferences towards policymakers. Sometimes, movements may seek to change public opinion and target policy elites concurrently, whereby sympathetic policymakers and social movement activists join forces to mobilize public preferences hoping to affect policy outcomes in their favor.

When the public is divided, or a given issue is not especially salient among constituents, political elites may be more likely to pursue their own policy preferences and/or work with interest and social movement groups aligned with their preferences to shape policy outcomes (Burstein, 2003; Pettinicchio, 2010). In this case, both policymakers and movement representatives benefit. Political elites, interest groups, and SMOs may find it easier to "craft" or frame an issue in the absence of public debate (see Jacobs & Shapiro, 2000) which in turn, can both direct and intensify issue salience among the public (for instance, see Beckett, 1994 on claimsmaking activity in the "War on Drugs and Crime").

When public issue salience is low, SMOs and interest groups have more control over the message. That is not to say that all groups necessarily have equal access to policymakers. Rather, as Brinton and Francisco (1983) argued in their work on subsystem politics and American policy corporatism, formal organizations are part of an expanding professional advocacy network that is more likely to coordinate with policy elites. They can amplify certain frames while diverting attention away from less favorable ones (Burstein, 2003; Cobb & Elder, 1983). Pettinicchio (2010) outlined the relationship between elite and public policy preferences in legalizing same-sex marriage in Canada. The fact that the Canadian public remained split but uninterested in gay marriage allowed more liberally minded political elites in the Liberal minority government to work with key LGBT and other sympathetic organizations in framing and pursuing marriage equality.

However, public and elite policy preferences may also present a challenge for social movements and interest organizations. Policymakers may be influenced by their own or their party's ideology which may not align with activist and social movement ideology. In a similar vein, public interest and high issue salience can complicate rather than amplify a movement's message especially if public preferences do not coincide with those of a movement or interest group (Burstein, 2003).

The effects of SMOs, interest groups, public preferences and political elites on policy change are therefore contingent on numerous institutional, organizational and cultural factors. And, theories about the effects of political organizations on policy outcomes are abound yet, as Burstein and Linton (2002) noted, scholars have either treated the effects of SMO's on policy as taken-for-granted and/or have not adequately outlined how social movements specifically influence policymakers and policies. In his recent volume on advocacy and the U.S. Congress, Burstein (2014) criticized studies that lumped all forms of movement activity into "protest" − especially since some of these activities include lobbying efforts − commonly regarded as an institutional tactic. Additionally, not all SMO tactics have the same effect in shaping elites' policy preferences (see also Gamson, 1975 on organizational success and failure).

Earlier work by Burstein (1985, 1998, 1999) questioned the direct role of social movement protest in shaping policy outcomes, especially in that protests may have diminishing returns or outright negative effects on policymaking (see also Olzak & Soule, 2009). Additionally, scholars studying interest and lobby groups pointed out that certain kinds of information − information about the size of the constituency and technical policy information − are especially important in influencing policymaking. Yet, others like Agnone (2007) in his work on the environmental movement, showed that protests do matter in changing elite policy preferences. Agnone hypothesized that protests amplify the effects of public preferences on policy by making those preferences more salient to political elites. Importantly, Agnone concluded that specifying the role of social movements in the policymaking process requires situating social movements in the broader institutional and policy context which fluctuates over time.

Thus, the role of social movements in the policymaking process raises questions about short-term and long-term social change processes. Piven and Cloward's (1971, 1977) analysis of the poor people's movement and American welfare policy in the 1960s suggested that institutions are inherently stable over long periods of time but for certain points where change comes in bursts. It is here where movements are able to meaningfully affect change. As Costain's (1981, p. 101) work on the women's movement showcased, the ability of movements to shape policy is no small feat given that policymaking tends to proceed incrementally while movements tend to respond in a punctuated manner thus making it difficult for movements to be included in the political process. Tarrow (1993) also described so-called "extraordinary policymaking" pointing to a seemingly rare occurrence when changes in institutions arise as a result of collective action by "outside" challengers.

But, Tarrow went on to claim that sympathetic elites are necessary in translating protest into actual political outcomes − that protest is a necessary but insufficient condition for extraordinary policymaking. Indeed, the rise of resource mobilization and political process theories provided the theoretical basis for understanding the routinization of movements. In the "movement society" (Meyer & Tarrow, 1998), social movements have become increasingly flexible, able to engage in both institutional and extrainstitutional activities. Life cycle perspectives suggest that movements engage in various activities and shift their targets over their life course often as the result of policy and other institutional change (Blumer, 1951; Shultziner, 2013; Tilly, 1978).

As scholars' focus grew to include the ways in which movements influence politics over protracted periods of time, it became increasingly necessary to think about how movements are transformed by political victories and defeats (see for instance, Taylor's, 1989 work on abeyance processes in the women's movement and Haines' (1984) work on radical flank in the civil rights movement). In addition to entering periods of abeyance where movements are more inward focused, movements also endure in large part because they become more "institutionalized." SMOs become increasingly formal and professional (see Staggenborg, 1988). As incumbent groups (Gamson's, 1975), they use more institutional forms of action like lobbying, legal mobilization, and testifying before government hearings.

Professionalization and formalization often occur following policy outcomes that encourage and facilitate the ability of movement actors to work with insiders. But, this does not necessarily mean that institutional tactics come at the expense of extrainstitutional ones. Haines found that in the 1960s, institutionalization of the black civil rights movement led to fractionalization whereby white groups (in the government, private business and philanthropic sectors) increased funding for moderate rights groups as a response to the efforts of radical black organizations — what Haines called a "radical flank effect." Similarly, following *Roe v. Wade*, informal prochoice groups professionalized, increasingly working with federal policymakers and state legislatures (Staggenborg, 1994). Yet, these SMOs were also quite flexible engaging in both institutional and extrainstitutional activities (see Staggenborg, 1989). And, environmental organizations emerged alongside state institutions like environmental regulatory agencies and bureaus (Johnson, 2008). Nevertheless, the environmental movement's success relied on the efforts of both professionalized and volunteer groups using both institutional and extrainstitutional tactics (Andrews & Edwards, 2005; see also Andrews & Edwards, 2004).

Therefore, movements may work with, and benefit from access to, sympathetic elites in an incremental fashion over long periods to shape policy outcomes. Working to affect (and subsequently implement and enforce) policy requires continued organizational access to the political process as well as recurring interaction with sympathetic elites. For example, legal mobilization and lobbying efforts by the NAACP in the 1940s and 1950s shaped rights discourse and eventually allowed for activists to pressure the government to act on civil rights legislation (McAdam, 1982). In the case of disability rights, movement activists formed close ties with disability rights political entrepreneurs throughout the 1970s and 1980s especially given that key movement figures had at some point, occupied positions in the government where they learned about, and participated in, the creation of rights-based legislation (see Pettinicchio, 2013; Scotch, 2001).

Numerous other examples highlight the importance of movement interaction with elites over time in influencing policy, as well as how policy influences movement mobilization. Gupta's (2009) analysis of the anti-death penalty movement pointed to incremental policy outcomes not only as ends, but also as important factors shaping future movement trajectories. Incremental changes in European sexual harassment policies allowed for political innovations as well as space for outsiders to participate in the policymaking process (Zippel, 2006). Peng and Wong's (2008) discussion of the development of the welfare state in Asia highlighted the ways in which social movements played a critical role in the evolution of political institutions and policy over a sustained period of time.

In addressing how movements matter in the policymaking process, it is crucial to outline the ways in which movements gain access to political elites and the political process, as well as describe how prolonged interaction with political elites takes shape and the consequences this has on social change. There is growing consensus in the social movements and public policy literatures that SMOs and social movement activists have the most influence on policymaking when they participate in the hearings phase of the process − that is, where information about proposed policies and issues are presented, and where actors seek to frame problems and solutions in particular ways to advance a certain policy agenda.

"PRE-POLICY": SETTING THE AGENDA

One need only turn to the recent Benghazi controversy as an especially salient example of how political elites − political entrepreneurs seeking to change the course of politics[1] − use congressional committees and the hearing process in their claimsmaking activity. The Benghazi hearings played an important role in shaping both elite and public perceptions about key political actors in the current administration as well as the 2016 Democratic presidential nominee, Hillary Clinton. As Democratic strategist, Donna Brazile, told Anderson Cooper on CNN (October 21, 2015), members of the committee are just "there to make a point."

Thus, committees and hearings matter. Committees are the "nerve ends, and the workshops and laboratories of Congress" (Smith & Deering, 1990, p. 1), they are about "property rights over public policies" (King, 1997, p. 11). Congressional hearings are where political elites seek to stake claims on and influence policy outcomes. As Burstein and Hirsh (2007, p. 179) described, hearings are "an efficient way to gather information and exert influence" and that "simply holding a hearing on an issue communicates a committee's belief that an issue is important."

Movement scholars studying a range of causes have recently pointed out that social movements tend to matter most in the agenda setting or "pre-policy"[2] phase of policymaking. At this early stage, frame contestation manifests itself in committee hearings where social problems, issues, and policy solutions are defined (Burstein & Hirsh, 2007; Costain, 1992; Gamson & Modigliani, 1989; Johnson, 2008; King, Bentele, & Soule, 2007). Depending on how one defines protest,[3] social movement scholars see movements as indirectly shaping policy outcomes by creating or expanding policy areas, shaping the network of actors involved in a policy domain, and in turn, shaping political discourse around issues (Sawyers & Meyer, 1999, p. 190). Scholars claim that movements have a much more difficult time shaping policy at the final stages of the policymaking process (Johnson, Agnone, & McCarthy, 2010; Olzak & Soule, 2009) where institutional rules and norms make it largely impossible for outsiders to have a say in the content of legislation.

The hearings phase then provides an important opportunity for outsiders to have input on the framing of problems and policies. As Costain (1981, p. 112) claimed, "the ability of government to design policy responsive to new interests, as well as old, hinges critically on the ease with which new interests seeking change in existing policies gain an initial hearing from government decision-makers." Hearings not only provide spaces for outsiders to have a place at the table given that they are often brought in by elites to testify about an aspect of a proposed policy or issue problem, but hearings also signal that political elites have prioritized and increasingly legitimized an issue, allocating institutional resources to that policy area. This means that an increasing number or intensity of hearings is associated with political opportunities for outsiders to interact with policymakers.

Based on this premise, Sheingate (2006) used the example of biotechnology issue attention to highlight what he called the "congressional opportunity structure." Akin to the broad concept of political opportunity structure well-known to movement scholars, Sheingate posited that the ways in which actors can introduce new ideas, challenge the status quo, and pressure other actors to pursue a given policy course, is dependent on whether there are opportunities to do so. By opportunity, he meant the informal jurisdictions of government committees — that is, what congressional committees hold hearings on rather than what the congressional rules state is their actual jurisdiction. He found that committees with broad, less concentrated jurisdictions spanning many topics, offers "would-be entrepreneurs [with] greater resources and opportunities to introduce new issues that further stretch the boundaries of committee authority" (Sheingate, 2006, p. 856).

As jurisdictions broaden and issue attention increases, there is mounting conflict around issues driven in part by the fact that political entrepreneurs are engaged in jurisdictional claimsmaking. Scholars suggest that social movement groups and leaders are more likely to be brought into this broadening policy network to help bolster elite claims, or as Schattschneider (1960) argued, to help mobilize bias — to create an impression that community stakeholders have a say in a policy issue when in fact it is largely driven by elite policy preferences. Elites use outsiders to advance policies they prefer (McCarthy & Zald, 2002).

No doubt, movements can also benefit from this increasing access to the agenda-setting process. But, it is not always clear, given the specific issue or policy domain, whether movements have a role in expanding issue attention — whether hearings are held as a result of outside pressure — or whether political elites hold hearings intending to invite movement actors who they see as allies in helping convince other political elites to pursue certain policy directions (see Walker's, 2014 recent discussion of elites and top-down participation). It may be the case that both occur, where initial access provides movements the ability to beget more attention through positive feedback processes. This seems to largely depend on both the institutional and movement contexts at a given time, and on existing policy in that issue area. For instance, drawing from Taylor's (1989) work on abeyance structures in the women's movement, Sawyers and Meyers (1999) argued that the failure of the women's movement to shape two relevant policy domains — fetal protection and family leave — is in part explained by the movement's exclusion from those policy areas. In other words, the movement failed to influence policy because movement groups and leaders were left out of the agenda-setting process. However, Pettinicchio (2013) and Scotch (2001) showed that the evolution of disability rights-based discourse in Congress had little to do with outside social movement mobilization. Rather, many who worked closely on rights-based policy in the government would later create disability movement organizations and coordinate protest demonstrations — mobilization around those very laws that established disability rights as a policy area. In many ways, elites created opportunities for social movement groups to participate in subsequent policymaking. It is important to note that groups do not have equal access to elites, and elites will likely seek to coordinate with social movement and interest groups that are ideologically and tactically congruent.

These processes point to a dynamic interplay between elites and social movements in shaping the policy agenda — about why issues sometimes seem ignored, and at other times, seem highly salient. In their two seminal volumes on agenda setting in U.S. Congress, Baumgartner and Jones (1993) and Jones and Baumgartner (2005) claimed that cognitive and institutional limitations on the ability to process information and prioritize issues leads to issues "bursting" onto the policy agenda in a punctuated fashion. Punctuated equilibrium theory — the theory that issues experience periods of stability but occasionally are punctuated with bursts of creative ferment and dramatic expansion — is quite compatible with the notion of cycles of protest or contention whereby movement activity seems to peak at some points, and then declines and remains stable at other points (Tarrow, 1998). Not surprisingly, scholars including Baumgartner and Jones attributed issue attention to social movement activity and changes in public preferences — two so-called "exogenous" and demand-side forces acting on political institutions. Within this framework, social movements have a critical role in expanding conflict around issues. Movement organizations and activists can do so directly by disrupting existing relations within government around certain policy domains. They can also expand conflict indirectly by changing public preferences about issues which in turn signals to policymakers that their voters' preferences about an issue or policy requires action on their part. Under these circumstances, political elites seeking policy change can more easily mobilize conflict and challenge the status quo, especially when structural opportunities, such as venues with broad jurisdictions and interests, present themselves. Sawyers and Meyer (1999) referred to this approach, which emphasizes how networks around particular policy domains change and issues evolve, as an "issue-specific model of political opportunity."

Outside pressure exerted by social movements does not always play a role in reshaping political discourse or expanding conflict around issues. Take for instance the changing image of nuclear energy. In the 1940s and 1950s, a tight-knit policy network arose around nuclear energy. This meant that a limited number of venues such as the Joint Congressional Committee on Atomic Energy and the Atomic Energy Commission created a small, closed field — a policy monopoly — encompassing government officials, scientists, and public utilities (Baumgartner & Jones, 1993; Campbell, 1988; Duffy, 1997).

With low issue salience and holding few public hearings, this policy monopoly crafted and controlled the positive image of nuclear energy. But by the end of the 1960s, the nuclear image turned increasingly negative. Although often attributed to the rise of outside pressures from labor unions, antinuclear, environmental, and anti-war activists, Baumgartner and Jones pointed to pre-existing dissent from within the policy monopoly itself which ultimately signaled its demise. When scientists in the field began to oppose the nuclear industry, it ate away at the legitimacy of the "experts" controlling the nuclear policy monopoly. They sought to move the debate around nuclear energy outside the existing policy subsystem in order to create spaces and opportunities to reframe the issue. New proenvironmental policy initiatives at the end of the 1960s allowed for numerous congressional venues to emerge, as well as new spaces within the executive branch, such as the Environmental Protection Agency (EPA). These endogenous changes to the policy monopoly were eventually bolstered by exogenous changes as a growing focus on environmental regulation and increasing congressional oversight placed much more attention on the issue. Thus, the story of how nuclear energy went from having a tremendously positive image to one that is considerably negative, involved the interplay between both endogenous and exogenous institutional changes as well as challenges from state and local governments, and movement activists who became an increasingly relevant part of the nuclear strategic action field.

One of the shortcomings of theories overemphasizing the role of exogenous and demand-side explanations for how issues and policies evolve is that they ignore the routine access many SMOs enjoy and use to influence change when issues are not seemingly in periods of heightened attention (or "punctuated" to use Baumgartner and Jones' terminology). This is in fact one of the major criticisms put forth by path-dependent scholars regarding models of policy change (Hogan, 2006; Howlett & Cashore, 2009;

Pierson, 2003; Streek & Thelen, 2005). These scholars argued that even though exogenous shocks may lead to bursts of attention, the content of that attention and subsequently, how that content is translated into policy change, reflects the incremental work that preceded punctuation (Deeg, 2001; Rixen & Viola, 2014). As Streek and Thelen (2005, p. 22) succinctly put it, "for external shocks to bring about fundamental transformations, it helps if endogenous change has prepared the ground."

The movement towards disability rights highlights the importance of incremental changes to existing disability policy which later was able to expand more dramatically in the early-1970s. Throughout the 1950s and 1960s, political elites incrementally proposed changes to an existing policy image of disability couched in service provision – namely, vocational rehabilitation. The evolution of disability policy from economic integration, to removing physical barriers, and guaranteeing equal access to public transit gave rise to a language of rights that was not able to fully materialize until the end of the 1960s. The 1960s reflected an institutional environment undergoing important change – like for instance, the rise of more liberally minded politicians to positions of power (Polsby, 2004). This had important consequences for the broader social welfare policy field that in the past had been blocked from policy innovation. Not surprisingly, the late-1960s and early-1970s saw new political opportunities for disability rights entrepreneurs like Rep. Charles Vanik and Sen. Hubert Humphrey who proposed an amendment to the 1964 Civil Rights Act to include disability as grounds for discrimination. And, although this failed, the language of rights and nondiscrimination survived and became enshrined in the 1973 Rehabilitation Act due to the efforts of disability rights entrepreneurs.

Situating social movements within the policymaking process requires assessing the extent to which changes come about endogenously, how conflict expands outside an existing policy network, how outsiders work to promote conflict and change, and how they do so by working with political elites. The evolution of disability policy came to include civil rights. This took shape inside an existing policy network and when external institutional changes eventually rippled through the disability policy area, it created new opportunities for conflict around the disability policy image to expand, allowing disability policymakers to pursue alternative policy trajectories (such as civil rights). In addition, it showcases the kinds of institutional environments under which state and nonstate actors work closely together to either maintain the status quo or challenge it.

POLICY COMMUNITIES AND POLITICAL OPPORTUNITIES

Movement scholars have pointed to the political opportunity structure as one of, if not *the*, key institutional or set of institutional factors shaping mobilization — from timing, to targets, to tactics. Identifying political opportunities is seen as necessary for understanding the rise of contentious politics. Traditionally, the perspective emphasized conflict between resource-poor outsiders and influential elites (Costain, 1992; Piven & Cloward, 1977; Tilly, 1978) through the use of "non-institutionalized means" (McAdam, 1982).

Yet, given that the relationship between social movements and the political opportunity structure is inherently "process-oriented" (see Meyer, 2004; Olzak, 1989) — that is, that it takes shape over an extended period of a movement's life course — political process models have in turn provided scholars with a framework for shedding light on routine interactions between challengers and elites, as well as the ways in which elites can facilitate the role of social movement actors in shaping policy outcomes (Carens, 2007; McAdam, McCarthy, & Zald, 1996; Meyer & Imig, 1993). Updated versions of the theory then, combined with the rise of resource mobilization theory, came to focus much more on the institutionalized relationship between movements and political elites (see Amenta et al., 2006; Johnson et al., 2010) where cooperation between the two may be just as likely as conflict.

However, the theory has also been heavily critiqued as too broad and as poorly operationalized (Meyer & Minkoff, 2004; Opp, 2009) leaving many unanswered questions: how are political opportunities identified by activists? Who benefits from these opportunities? And importantly, *how* do activists benefit from political opportunities? Increasing efforts to link social movements to policymaking through specific mechanisms at both the micro and macro levels have drawn more attention to the shortcomings of political process models and the political opportunity structure. There is a renewed call for a more specific set of institutional and actor-centered factors that facilitate or constrain social movement efforts. The research on agenda setting — particularly policy-domains and policy network approaches (see Dowding, 1995; Knoke, 1993; Knoke & Laumann, 1982; Marsh & Rhodes, 1992; Moore, 1979) — offers a useful analytical framework for clarifying the nature of political opportunities for specific social movements, activists, organizations, as well as opportunities associated with specific outcomes, like policy change.

Although the agenda-setting literature has pointed to institutional arrangements that shape the policy agenda space in general ways, work has also shown that agenda-setting processes vary considerably by issue domain. Factors accounting for variation include: the extent to which policy monopolies or communities exist, the kinds of actors (institutional and movement) involved in the policy area, the extent to which a policy network is embedded in other policy networks, and whether there is elevated public and media issue salience. Baumgartner and Jones, who championed these broad agenda-setting processes, organized their volume around specific cases of agenda setting that fit different patterns of issue attention. For example, in the cases of nuclear power, tobacco, and pesticides, policy monopolies gave way to looser policy networks or policy communities as conflict around these issues emerged. This was not the case, however, for urban disorder, which had no policy monopoly around it. Urban disorder reflected a broad jurisdiction — from public transportation to racial urban unrest — making it difficult to establish distinct issue boundaries around this policy field. Each time this policy area experienced punctuation, citizens and the media were paying a great deal of attention to urban social problems.

In the case of disability, issue expansion was the result of political entrepreneurship. There were no discernable changes in public preferences and issue salience preceding issue expansion. Although disability was governed by a policy monopoly that focused on rehabilitation and other service provision, it had developed extensive ties to social welfare — a burgeoning policy area in the 1960s — that in part created important institutional opportunities to transform disability policy (Pettinicchio, 2013). Disability issue expansion points to the ways in which policy networks overlap and intersect with other related networks and how changes in the broader field can disorganize existing policy domains.

These cases also reveal that distinct policy networks offer different degrees of access depending on how tightly knit these networks are. Virtually all policy networks extend beyond the government to include nonstate actors from business and industry, the nonprofit sector, and interest and social movement groups. However, policy monopolies, often referred to as "iron triangles," are usually quite closed making it difficult for outsiders and challengers to gain access (Cobb & Elder, 1983; Kriesi, 2004; Schattschneider, 1960). Policy communities, on the other hand, are a much looser network of actors reflecting a heterogeneous, if not conflicting, set of policy ideas (Baumgartner & Jones, 1993). Sometimes, newer issues, particularly issues that touch on a myriad of related topics (like urban social problems), emerge with no policy subsystem governing them. Alternatively, and often as a result of institutional disruption, existing monopolies too can fall apart allowing for a looser network of actors to form new policy communities around issues. This is important for understanding social movements' access to the policymaking process because the more disorganized an issue area, the more likely challengers can help shape its reorganization (DiMaggio, 1991; McAdam, Tarrow, & Tilly, 2001). For instance, McCarthy's (2005) study of antidrug issue coalitions demonstrated how coalitions mobilized both elite and public support to challenge existing public health policy. Unlike iron triangles, membership in the coalitions was loosely defined, allowing members including movement organizations, community groups, professionals, and political elites, to come in and out of mobilizing efforts. McCarthy referred to these coalitions as "Velcro triangles" precisely because actors and organizations entered and exited this advocacy coalition with relative ease.

STRATEGIC ACTION FIELDS: HOW SMOs AND POLITICAL ENTREPRENEURS CHANGE POLICY TOGETHER

Policy fields or networks form as a result of the coordination, cooperation (sometimes reluctantly), and coalition building by strategic actors seeking to shape the policy agenda (Henry, 2011; Knoke, 1993). Policy communities persist when incumbents institutionalize a field by creating norms and assign values to the efforts of its actors. This means that elites confer legitimacy to certain kinds of organizations, structures and policy frames, and delegitimize others. Outsiders also confer a policy network's legitimacy as they acknowledge the expertise of elites (see Brym, 1980 on elite theory, experts and political change). Challenges to the policy community in turn become less likely.

Policy networks and communities are, in Fligstein and McAdam's (2012) terms, strategic action fields where socially skilled actors seek to affect change. Their field theory provides a useful framework for shedding light on the relationship between social movements and policymakers given its emphasis on how policy networks transcend institutional or state boundaries to promote particular policies.

In the United States, policy networks within which political entrepreneurs shape the policy agenda are no doubt grounded in the congressional committees that have some legitimate claim over an issue area (Baughman, 2006; King, 1997; Smith & Deering, 1990). However, scholars, including Fligstein and McAdam, conceived of a broader space within which entrepreneurs and activists work to promote change. These actors — from social movement activists to congressional committee chairs — are "policy actors pursuing a matter of public policy important to them for instrumental reasons" (see Miller & Demir, 2007, p. 137). Consequently, this understanding helps specify why and how social movement actors and other nonstate actors form ties with political elites because they have similar policy objectives and goals. Policy communities therefore consist of intersecting networks of actors embedded in various organizations and institutions creating a strategic action field where social change takes place.

Members of policy communities influence how issues are defined and in turn, determine policy trajectories. However, as networks that transcend organizational and institutional boundaries (which include nonstate actors), power is not evenly distributed among actors in the community. Power arises from a combination of various sources — from material resources, to status (e.g., the "expert"), to personality and social skill. Additionally, positions within a network also matter. For instance, government actors may have more direct control over policy decisions than nonprofit or interest groups even though all are integral parts of a policy network. Yet, as Dowding (1995) notes, power imbalances within a network cannot be too great if a policy community is to endure given that large power imbalances lead to zero-sum gains. Thus, while power can emanate from sources outside a specific policy domain (Knoke & Laumann, 1982), power is also contextualized in terms of the norms and culture of a policy network of actors with different interests who come together seeking broadly similar objectives.

Political elites bring their expertise (real or perceived) to a specific policy area. To be sure, the influence of elites can be confined to their respective policy domains (see Dahl, 1961; Polsby, 1963). However, they are also embedded in a broader field of elites that transcend area boundaries (for instance, elected officials may sit on multiple related and unrelated congressional committees). Indeed, being situated within different policy networks increases access to information and in turn actors' clout (Knoke, 1993; Moore, 1979; Sabatier & Jenkins-Smith, 1999). Field theory explicitly acknowledges that subfields draw from broader fields within which political elites are embedded. That is, civil rights, disability, education, national security, and agriculture do not, as subgovernments, exist in a vacuum. Policy communities therefore reflect aspects of the broader field including norms and values, as well as long-standing social cleavages and conflicts. Nonetheless, individual policy communities also consist of their own emergent norms particular to their network and, as Knoke (1993) highlighted, extant political conflicts and divisions may be set aside by actors working to achieve similar goals in a policy area.

For instance, the field of racial politics in the South which transcended economic, cultural, and political lines, was left largely unchallenged by outside actors including the federal government. It enabled the institutionalization of segregation in the South even though relevant actors and groups were themselves embedded in a national American racial field outside the South. Eventually, as Fligstein and McAdam argued, this existing field of racial politics dominated by Jim Crow, Dixiecrats, and other white Southern elites, was disrupted by exogenous shocks; the depression, presidential support for civil rights (i.e., Truman in 1946), and the Supreme Court case, *Brown v. Board of Education*. These changes in the field of racial politics created an opportunity for contentious politics with the rise of the civil rights movement in the 1950s. As a result of important policy and legislative victories after 1964, as well as broader changes outside the civil rights field (including changes in Cold War era politics, the "revenge" of the Dixiecrats, and the rise of Americas rights revolution in the late-1960s and early-1970s, see Skrentny, 2002), the civil rights field recrystallized around the policy goal of ending overt and covert forms of segregation and discrimination with key incumbents in the executive branch and the courts interpreting and enforcing new legislative victories.

Both Fligstein and McAdam and Baumgartner and Jones agree that exogenous shocks reshape the network of actors — the field — involved in a policy issue. In periods of field disorganization, political entrepreneurs seek to reshape policy images by using their skill to convince others that their policy solutions are the most obvious and suitable. Entrepreneurs can you use their positions of power, resources, personality, "expertise," and scientific evidence and personal narratives to make an issue that was once seen as contentious as taken-for-granted (Birkland, 2007; Carmines & Stimson, 1989; Cobb & Elder, 1983; Riker, 1982; Roa, Morrill, & Zald, 2000; Schattschneider, 1935). This also means that individuals have varying levels of influence on policy given their backgrounds and status within policy networks.

In seeking to redefine issues and policies following disruptions to strategic action fields, hearings again become an important site of frame contestation that bring together political elites, social movement actors, and other relevant parties. Hearings act as important filters where policy initiatives are directly shaped. Hearings played a critical role in reshaping the positive image around nuclear power into a negative one, and hearings helped set the environmental agenda when it came to the shift from conservationism to pollution, clean air, and the destruction of the ozone layer. Committees and hearings, as well as the interests of political entrepreneurs, provide social movement groups with opportunities for "input and review" and as a result, "grievances are channeled into institutionalized means of participation" (Rochon & Mazmanian, 1993, p. 78).

The evolution of disability as a policy issue provides a particularly cogent example of the ways in which the reconfiguration of policy networks created opportunities for issue expansion as well as new access points for SMOs and interest organizations. Disability always had a place on the policy agenda. Policymakers mostly drew from their experience in existing social policy (especially health and education) and expanding interests in veterans' health and social issues to establish a new field of rehabilitation. This came to dominate and indeed, shape disability as a policy area in a path-dependent way by defining a set of policy solutions around integrating people with disabilities into the mainstream of life (i.e., this often meant achieving economic self-sufficiency among people with disabilities).

Throughout the 1940s until the early-1960s, government officials, leaders of incumbent disability groups like the Easter Seals and March of Dimes, and professional health and welfare groups like the Council of State Administrators of Vocational Rehabilitation, formed a close-knit disability policy monopoly revolving around vocational rehabilitation. Not surprisingly, it was here that rehabilitation reached its pinnacle as a policy framework and as an industry, reflecting the professional, ideological, and personal backgrounds of those in this policy monopoly. Many of these policymakers had ties to the health and philanthropic sectors, and many drew from related policy areas adding disability to their policy portfolios.

By the mid-1960s, many working within this area had begun addressing architectural barriers and equal access to public transportation because these were framed as immediately related to vocational rehabilitation. What good is vocational rehabilitation when people with disabilities cannot access places of work? Using strong supporting ideas such as increasing employment opportunities so that people with disabilities can be "tax payers rather than tax burdens," and unquestioned scientific evidence about rehabilitation and special education, policy "experts" (see Altman & Barnartt, 1993; see also Berkowitz, 1987) were largely uncontested and elites and the public outside this monopoly deferred to their expertise.

The basis for much of rights-based policy began to emerge through incremental changes in the 1960s by this policy network. However, it was not allowed to flourish because disability rights entrepreneurs faced institutional barriers – chief among them, that conservative Southern Democrats blocked most of their efforts deemed too costly. But when Congress liberalized, new opportunities, like the creation of new venues in Congress (for instance, the Subcommittee on the Handicapped among others), became available for an expanding set of actors to pursue various policy areas, including disability rights. This reflected a broader change in the political opportunity structure where an activist government politicized a variety of social issues and existing vocational rehabilitation policies became subsumed in Johnson era Great Society initiatives. It was during this time, as Baumgartner and Jones illustrated with their extensive longitudinal hearings data, that social welfare issues burst onto the policy agenda. In the case of disability, the number of committees holding disability-related hearings expanded and as a result, so did the disability-related agenda space (Pettinicchio, 2013).

The erosion of the client-service policy monopoly created new spaces for political entrepreneurs in both Congress and the executive branch seeking to alter the course of disability policy. It was in this context that Sen. Bob Bartlett proposed the Architectural Barriers Act in 1967, Rep. Mario Biaggi in 1969 proposed an amendment to the Mass Transportation Act such that people with disabilities "have the same right as other persons to utilize mass transportation," and Vanik and Humphrey in 1971 proposed amending the Civil Rights Act to include disability. At the time, the Health, Education and Welfare Department (HEW) had greatly expanded its portfolio dealing with an increasing number of constituencies that it, in turn, championed. HEW's Office of Civil Rights played a particularly critical role in generously interpreting and expanding congressional intent on civil rights for people with disabilities, often to the chagrin of top members in the administration. Importantly, these structural changes helped to lift the cognitive barrier among policymakers that disability policy was, as a matter of fact, based exclusively on a client-service model.

Both the movement for black civil rights and disability rights were situated within a broader network of actors in intersecting fields who routinely interacted with each other to produce consensus about the ways in which issues were defined and how policies developed. Both cases also highlight the extent to which "outsiders," including social movement actors, are included in policy networks, highly dependent on the environment within which policy networks themselves are embedded. When a policy monopoly controls a policy domain as was the case with rehabilitation in disability, only incumbent groups might have access to the network and venues in government to shape policy. When a policy community emerges around a policy domain — a broader, looser field of actors working in a policy area (see Dowding, 1995; Heclo, 1978) — social movements are more likely to be involved in generating conflict and challenging the policy status quo especially when they side with sympathetic policymakers in those policy domains seeking to undermine it.

The evolution of disability rights showcases how slow and incremental, and faster and more punctuated change, shaped the expansion and the content of the disability policy agenda. It also points to the overlapping policy networks between disability and other social policy issue areas, and how disability policymakers pursued rights legislation in the absence of issue salience among the public or with the media. This alludes to key supply-side variables, like the availability of venues and the entrepreneurial efforts among political elites in shaping policy. But, it also points to the kinds of relationships political elites forge with nascent advocacy organizations and movement leaders forming a strategic action field whose members sought to expand conflict when institutional activism was not enough to overcome political hurdles.

INSIDERS, OUTSIDERS, AND INSTITUTIONAL ACTIVISM

The expansion of the agenda space and the broader and looser network of political actors who stake claims on issues, facilitates the ability of so-called outsiders, like SMOs, to influence policymaking. As Stearns and Almeida (2004) suggested, movements often form strong ties with political elites which helps the movement gain legitimacy while movements can help promote the interests of government actors and agencies from the outside. Indeed, policy entrepreneurs often rely on interest groups and SMOs to participate in agenda setting to help expand their claimsmaking activity. As Pettinicchio (2013, p. 83) claimed, strategic action on the part of entrepreneurs "involves the ability of actors to create consensus around an issue through frame alignment as well as the mobilization of inside and outside actors into a coalition that assists in that effort." This means that entrepreneurial efforts inside institutions can generate opportunities for social movement actors to have a place at the policymaking table. Thus, both movement activists and political elites can be institutional activists when they have the ability to work within, and have access to, institutional resources.

An institutional activist in the broadest sense is an actor who can affect social change from within institutions – an elite with disproportionate access to political resources (see Khan, 2012 on the "Sociology of Elites"). However, the concept has been used to characterize a variety of different types of elites pursuing social change. Institutional activist has been used synonymously with concepts like sympathetic elites (Tarrow, 1998), political entrepreneur (Reichman & Canan, 2003; Roa et al., 2000; Skrentny, 2002), elite mobilization (McCarthy, 2005), and inside agitator (Eisenstein, 1996). Because social movements and issue areas reflect varying degrees of outsider status, it in part explains why the term institutional activist has been used so broadly: it reflects dimensions of exclusion vis-à-vis institutions. As Banaszak (2005) claimed, individuals can be legally excluded from the polity as was the case with African Americans in the United States. But, in the case of people with disabilities, they were normatively excluded because it was generally believed that people with disabilities could not advocate on their own behalf. Thus, the role institutional activists play is highly dependent on how much exclusion a movement or constituency experiences.

One important distinction that has emerged is in regards to the overlap between the issues institutional activists promote and social movement causes. Traditionally, institutional activists were thought of as working on *pre-existing* social movement causes (Pierson, 1994; Santoro & McGuire, 1997; Tilly, 1978). This might be a result of the legacy of theories like political process that tend to treat political elites as reactionary rather than as proactive. Elites are thought to either accommodate challengers' demands or they increase repression which ultimately signals declining mobilization (Koopmans, 1993; McAdam, 1982; Tarrow, 1998, 1989). Santoro and McGuire (1997) argued that black and feminist policymakers took on the cause of affirmative action inside institutions following heightened periods of movement mobilization and policy change while Staggenborg (1991) pointed to the important role of prochoice policymakers working within legislatures to expand abortion rights.

However, institutional activists can be much more entrepreneurial in working on issues prior to movement mobilization than originally conceived (see Pettinicchio, 2012, 2013). For instance, rights and antidiscrimination legislation for people with disabilities was largely the result of a "movement in the government" (Scotch, 2001). In this case, institutional activists *were* disability rights entrepreneurs; their actions were not motivated by outside pressures from movements or constituents. At the same time, the actions of these policymakers had a profound impact not only in politicizing people with disabilities – that is, in helping make people with disabilities citizens entitled to rights – but also provided policy tools to mobilize against the government when it began to back-stepping on implementing disability rights legislation. In fact, when the government stalled in writing and publishing disability rights regulations, many in the Office of Civil Rights, dismayed by the delay, encouraged disability activists to protest against Joseph Califano, the HEW secretary.

In addition, many disability rights movement leaders and key actors had important ties to the government. For example, Judy Heumann, who interned in Sen. Harrison Williams' office, also created one of the first disability advocacy and protest groups, Disabled in Action. Jill Robinson, a Community Services Administration (CSA) staff member and intern in the National Center for Law and the Handicapped participated in the HEW protests. Other leaders would go on to become political elites themselves. Lex Frieden, who served as executive director of the National Committee on the Handicapped and who helped draft the Americans with Disabilities Act (ADA) in the late 1980s, was the secretary of the advocacy group American Coalition of Citizens with Disabilities in the mid-1970s. Ed Roberts, considered the father of the Independent Living Movement in the early-1970s became Director of the California Department of Vocational Rehabilitation in 1976. And, Justin Dart, the leader of the Texas Independent Living Movement in the 1970s became member of the Texas Governor's Committee for Persons with Disabilities in the early-80s and was later appointed by President Reagan to the National Committee on the Handicapped. As co-chair of the Congressional Task Force on the Rights and Empowerment of People with Disabilities, Dart also played a critical role in helping draft the ADA.

Political elites and social movement activists formed a strategic action field. Together, they pressured the government to act on disability rights. This showcases the kind of alliances formed between so-called insiders and outsiders in affecting change drawing from both institutional and extrainstitutional resources. Importantly, it also points to the ways in which activists inside and outside the government use both institutional and extrainstitutional tactics and strategies depending on the nature of their challenge, political opportunities, and threats. It is a salient example of the porous boundaries between state and nonstate actors and organizations and the interchangeable role of citizen activist and elite or institutional activist within the field.

Social movement scholars struggle to define the role of movement activists when they work closely with political elites. For instance, Jenkins and Eckert (1986) showed how professionalization and elite patronage in the black civil rights movement in part weakened movement challenge. In the women's movement, formal organizations that engaged in lobbying activity were thought to not fit the feminist idea of nonhierarchical organizations; that using institutional tactics legitimizes existing institutional arrangements (Costain, 1981). And, Meyer's (1993) work on the nuclear free movement suggested that institutionalization served to coopt or depoliticize the movement.

However, scholars have increasingly recognized the back-and-forth between the work of institutional activism and grassroots activism. Costain and Majstrovic's (1994) work on the women's movement showed that relationships between outside challenges and insider actions are reciprocating. Similarly, Coy and Hedeen's (2005) work on the mediation movement identified the importance of oscillating between institutional work and work challenging institutions as a way to avoid potential cooptation. Ultimately, what these various cases point to is the important joint role of both insiders and outsiders in affecting policy.

HOW POLICIES MOBILIZE CONSTITUENCIES

The dominance of political process models in the study of social movements has focused mainly on the extrainstitutional basis of state—movement interaction (Goldstone, 2003; Jenkins & Klandermans, 1995). However, as the discussion so far illustrates, movements often have prolonged, routinized and indeed, institutionalized interactions with policymakers. In addition to the important role of entrepreneurship and institutional activism in creating opportunities for social movements in policymaking, an often-overlooked process is how policies create social movements. Referring back to Meyer's (2005) discussion of social movements and policy, there is a "chicken-and-egg" relationship between the work of policy insiders and the efforts of challengers. In earlier work, Sawyers and Meyer (1999) posited that policies are not always an outcome of social movements but rather, policies reflect a dimension of the political opportunity structure. That is, policies can generate mobilization.

Costain's (1992) *Inviting Women's Rebellion* explained how Congress acted as an initiator on women's issues. The amount of attention Congress paid to women's issues increased following President Kennedy's creation of the President's Commission on the Status of Women (Rupp & Taylor, 1987). As Costain (1992, pp. 20–21) noted, "The shift from a friendly but somewhat ambiguous relationship between government and women in the fifties to unalloyed support at the federal level in the sixties seems promising as an explanation for the timing of the women's movement." The 1970s saw both a proliferation of women's advocacy groups as well as an increase in both insider and outsider activity (Costain, 1992; Minkoff, 1995; Soule, McAdam, McCarthy, & Su, 1999) which coincided with increasing government attention to women's rights (such as the Equal Rights Amendments, the right to choose, etc.). Congressional interest peaked in the early-to-mid-1970s surrounding the ERA amendments (Soule et al., 1999). Although interest eventually declined, women's issues continued to have a place on the policy agenda.

Similarly, following the Clean Air Act Amendments and the establishment of the EPA, congressional issue attention on the environment increased. It also coincided with the rise of large professional environmental advocacy groups and a spike in protest activity (Olzak & Soule, 2009). As Johnson (2008, p. 3) noted, "The year 1970 marked the beginning of an environmental era in American public policy."

Policies can mobilize activists to protest because they provide a framework, like new entitlements, on which constituencies can mobilize (Ingram & Smith, 1993; Reese & Newcombe, 2003). In the case of disability, few protests took place before the introduction of disability rights and antidiscrimination legislation in 1971. Not only did the early-1970s see the proliferation of disability advocacy organizations, it also saw the emergence of a sustained protest wave that mobilized around the rights enshrined in legislation which was largely the result of political entrepreneurship. By lunging forward on disability rights only to back step when costs of accommodation became a driving force behind growing opposition, the federal government through its policy innovations, "invited a disability rebellion."

These cases reveal that social movements and grassroots activism become important forces in protecting and expanding existing policies. On November 2, 1972, young disability activists organized by the group Disabled in Action, tied up traffic in New York twice that day protesting against President Nixon's vetoing of the Rehabilitation Act. Judy Heumann, Disabled in Action's founder, told reporters that a main goal of the protest, which was a response to threats to an existing policy proposal, was to make "the public aware of the plight of the handicapped." Policy breakthroughs indeed mobilize constituents (Campbell, 2005; Pierson & Skocpol, 2007; Pratt, 1976; Skocpol, 2007; Walker, 1991). They change the relationship between the government, citizens, and issues where the growth of advocacy organizations, lobbying, protests, and public awareness campaigns in turn reify policy and protect it from retrenchment efforts. Importantly, efforts by elites and movement activists alike target political institutions while also seeking to affect public preferences and attitudes about those policies.

DISCUSSION AND CONCLUSION

Social movements seek to change existing understandings about how to address issues, social problems, and collective grievances. They do so by targeting political elites and institutions, as well as public attitudes. Movements "seek to realize their objectives not only by influencing public policy but also by changing private behaviors, challenging accepted cultural understandings, and transforming the lives of their adherents" (Schlozman, Page, Verba, & Fiorina, 2005, p. 65). To return to Clinton's comments discussed in the paper's introduction, when movements seek to shape politics and public preferences, they are not necessarily engaged in two countervailing efforts. Rather, as combined efforts in a multipronged and often long-term strategy, working with policy elites can aid in further entrenching policies, and can also work to shape public attitudes which in turn bolsters the legitimacy of movements and policies alike.

Two trends have raised questions about how we know whether social movements matter — in Giugni's (1998) words, whether it was worth the effort. The first is the growing interest in social movements as policy agenda setters. The second is that social movements are increasingly thought of as part of "everyday politics" (Goldstone, 2003; Meyer & Minkoff, 2004; Pettinicchio, 2012). These shifts in how we view social movements in relation to political institutions, policymakers, and policy outcomes, have important empirical and theoretical consequences. They require thinking more about the ongoing relationship between activists and political elites specifying how so-called outsiders gain access to the policymaking process. Sometimes, movements can pressure elites to be included in the policy process but more often than not, opportunities become available to movements as a result of institutional changes, such as the expansion of venues for claimsmaking, and because political elites seek to form ties with activists to advance their position. Policy-domain approaches provide a useful framework for specifying political opportunities for social movements associated with short-term and long-term outcomes.

There are two main ways in which movements matter for policymaking. The first involves the role of movements in shaping how policies are framed in the prepolicy phase. But, politics often continue following the enactment of legislation. Therefore, the second way social movements matter for policy involves protecting policy from potential threats and retrenchment efforts by opponents. This too involves a long-term strategy of policy monitoring to ensure that policies are properly and appropriately implemented and enforced. This in part is what scholars mean when they claim that policies create constituents; that movements mobilize these constituents following policy innovations that further their entrenchment.

If indeed, as Tarrow argued, political elites are necessary for translating protest into policy outcomes, the numerous examples provided in this paper of the kinds of routine access outsiders have to the political process suggest that the influence of movements on setting the agenda may not be as "rare" or "extraordinary" as is generally assumed.

Drawing from current theoretical debates in the study of institutional change and social movement mobilization, I outlined the ways in which consequential policy change can result from the interplay between incremental, endogenous efforts, and punctuated bursts brought on by exogenous shocks. I claimed that social movements are transformed by institutional changes including the collapse of policy monopolies and the rise of looser policy communities that provide movements with certain advantages, including access to the policy process. This sheds some light on how so-called outsiders challenge the status quo and achieve routine access to policymakers: they are often invited to participate in the agenda-setting phase of policymaking and sometimes, encouraged by political entrepreneurs to use extrainstitutional tactics when institutional activism is not enough to overcome political hurdles. As part of a strategic action field, SMOs and actors are critical in expanding the debate outside narrow policy networks. They generate conflict by disrupting existing "cozy" relationships between policymakers, and by raising awareness among the public about alternative policy frames and policy solutions.

When it comes to policymaking, political elites and social movement activists – socially skilled actors – enter into a symbiotic relationship. Political elites rely on challengers to expand the conflict outside of political institutions. At the same time, if the goal of a movement is to influence the policy agenda and policy itself, then there are certain benefits when policymakers confer legitimacy upon movement efforts.

I also pointed to the porous boundaries between state and nonstate actors and organizations. Combined with strategic action fields, the concept of institutional activism highlights actors' mobility in transitioning from a position inside institutions to positions as movement leaders and even protesters, and vice versa. Relatedly, these concepts and theories shed light on the flexibility among social change actors who can use both institutional and extrainstitutional resources and strategies together to shape policy outcomes. What the various examples discussed in this paper suggest is that having ties to political elites does not preclude movements from protesting against political institutions.

As social movement scholars and political sociologists increasingly look to synthesizing existing theories to provide a framework for understanding how social movements influence policymaking, we must overcome certain conceptual hurdles and assumptions about insiders and outsiders. The first challenge involves endogeneity. That is, social movements cannot be both part of political institutions and also be affected by these very same political institutions because this would mean that the variables expected to affect an outcome are also a part of that outcome (Pettinicchio, 2012). Blurring the lines between insider and outsider makes these distinctions messy. However, part of the solution to this problem involves clarifying and specifying concepts like political opportunity structure as well as the goals and objectives of social movements. Second, in examining the prolonged interaction between elites and activists, it becomes important to confront the possibility of cooptation — a process whereby authorities manage outsider threats by superficially institutionalizing challengers so that they can maintain the status quo (see Michels, [1911] 1962; Selznick, 1949). Although this can occur, as theories of agenda setting, strategic action fields, and political entrepreneurship suggest, elites can also challenge the status quo, and in doing so, often rely on the efforts of outsiders, like social movements. Finally, we must overcome the negative connotation that has surrounded "institutions" and "institutionalization" including the contrast that is often made between so-called elite theories of democratic policymaking (often associated with terms like "overhead democracy" or "juridical democracy") and pluralism. In seeking to specify the role of social movements in shaping the policy agenda, we must reconcile the idea that elite and movement preferences often coincide, with the more sinister view that when outsiders work too closely with institutions and insiders, they become "imbued with their logic and values" (Tarrow, 1989, 1998).

The paper's broader contribution lies in its goal of helping to "put social movements in their place"; the title of McAdam and Boudet's (2012) recent volume. They referred to two trends that have narrowed the field of social movement inquiry. The first is that the focus of scholars on movement actors and organizations has ignored how other actors, including policymakers and other political elites, also shape social change. Second, the study of social movements has tended to focus on mobilizing efforts or episodes of contention associated with immediate outcomes (usually deemed successful in some way). This has led to an overall neglect of the more protracted back-and-forth between movements and elites where outcomes are not immediate. Thus, to borrow from McAdam and Boudet, thinking more about the link between social movements, elites, and policymaking supports a more "Copernican" view of social change efforts, where social movements are not always at the center of the political universe.

NOTES

1. This is the definition of political entrepreneur provided by Schneider and Teske (1992, p. 737).
2. Edwards, Barrett, and Peake (1997, p. 547) and Smith (2000, p. 80) referred to agenda setting as "pre-policy."
3. Some think of it as strictly disruptive, others count lobbying activities as a form of protest (see Meyer & Tarrow, 1998; Norris, 2002; Rucht, 2007).

REFERENCES

Agnone, J. (2007). Amplifying public opinion: The policy impact of the US environmental movement. *Social Forces, 85*, 1593–1620.

Altman, B., & Barnartt, S. N. (1993). Moral entrepreneurship and the passage of the ADA. *Journal of Disability Policy Studies, 4*, 21–40.

Amenta, E. (2006). *When movements matter: The Townsend plan and the rise of social security.* Princeton, NJ: Princeton University Press.

Amenta, E., Caren, N., Chiarello, E., & Su, Y. (2010). The political consequences of social movements. *Annual Review of Sociology, 36*, 287–307.

Amenta, E., Caren, N., & Olasky, S. (2006). Age for leisure? Political mediation and the impact of the pension movement on U.S. old-age policy. *American Sociological Review, 70*, 516–538.

Andrews, K. T., & Edwards, B. (2004). Advocacy organizations in the U.S. political process. *Annual Review of Sociology, 30*, 479–506.

Andrews, K. T., & Edwards, B. (2005). The organizational structure of local environmentalism. *Mobilization, 10*, 213–234.

Banaszak, L. A. (2005). Inside and outside the state: Movement insider status, tactics, and public policy achievements. In D. S. Meyer, V. Jenness, & H. Ingram (Eds.), *Routing the opposition: Social movements, public policy and democracy.* Minneapolis, MN: University of Minnesota Press.

Banaszak, L. A. (2010). *The women's movement inside and outside the state.* New York, NY: Cambridge University Press.

Baughman, J. (2006). *Common ground.* Stanford, CA: Stanford University Press.

Baumgartner, F. R., & Jones, B. D. (1993). *Agenda and instability in American politics.* Chicago, IL: University of Chicago Press.

Beckett, K. (1994). Setting the public agenda: 'Street Crime' and drug use in American politics. *Social Problems, 41*, 425–447.
Berkowitz, E. D. (1987). *Disabled policy: America's programs for the handicapped.* New York, NY: Cambridge University Press.
Blumer, H. (1951). Collective behavior. In A. M. Lee (Ed.), *Principles of sociology* (pp. 67–121). New York, NY: Barnes & Noble.
Birkland, T. A. (2007). Agenda setting in public policy. In F. Fischer, G. J. Miller, & M. S. Sidney (Eds.), *Handbook of public policy analysis: Theory, politics and methods* (pp. 63–78). New York, NY: Taylor and Francis.
Brinton, M. H., & Francisco, R. A. (1983). Subsystem politics and corporatism in the United States. *Policy and Politics, 11*, 273–293.
Brym, R. (1980). *Intellectuals and politics.* London: George Allen & Unwin.
Burstein, P. (1985). *Discrimination, jobs, and politics: The struggle for equal employment opportunity in the United States since the new deal.* Chicago, IL: Univ. Chicago Press.
Burstein, P. (1991). Policy domains. *Annual Review of Sociology, 17*, 327–350.
Burstein, P. (1998). Bringing the public back in: Should sociologists consider the impact of public opinion on public policy? *Social Forces, 77*, 27–62.
Burstein, P. (1999). Social movements and public policy. In M. Giugni, D. McAdam, & C. Tilly (Eds.), *How social movements matter* (pp. 3–21). Minneapolis, MN: University of Minnesota Press.
Burstein, P. (2003). The impact of public opinion on public policy: A review and an agenda. *Political Research Quarterly, 56*, 29–40.
Burstein, P. (2014). *American public opinion, advocacy and policy in congress: What the public wants and what it gets.* New York, NY: Cambridge University Press.
Burstein, P., & Hirsh, C. E. (2007). Interest organizations, information, and policy innovation in the U.S. congress. *Sociological Forum, 22*, 174–199.
Burstein, P., & Linton, A. (2002). The impact of political parties, interest groups, and social movement organizations on public policy: Some recent evidence and theoretical concerns. *Social Forces, 81*, 381–408.
Campbell, A. L. (2005). *How policies make citizens: Senior political activism and the American welfare state.* Princeton, NJ: Princeton University Press.
Campbell, J. L. (1988). *Collapse of an industry: Nuclear power and the contradictions of U.S. policy.* Ithaca, NY: Cornell University Press.
Carens, N. (2007). Political process theory. In G. Ritzer (Ed.), *Blackwell encyclopedia of sociology.* New York, NY: Blackwell.
Carmines, E. G., & Stimson, J. A. (1989). *Issue evolution: Race and the transformation of American politics.* Princeton, NJ: Princeton University Press.
Cobb, R. W., & Elder, C. D. (1983). *Participation in American politics: The dynamics of agenda building* (2nd ed.). Baltimore, MD: Johns Hopkins University Press.
Cockburn, C. (2007). *From where we stand: War, women's activism and feminist analysis.* London: Zed Books.
Costain, A. (1981). Representing women: The transition from social movement to interest group. *Western Political Quarterly, 34*, 100–115.
Costain, A. N. (1992). *Inviting women's rebellion.* Baltimore, MD: Johns Hopkins University Press.
Costain, A. N., & Majstrovic, S. (1994). Congress, social movements and public opinion: Multiple origins of women's rights legislation. *Political Research Quarterly, 47*, 111–135.

Coy, P. G., & Hedeen, T. (2005). A stage model of social movement co-optation: Community mediation in the United States. *Sociological Quarterly, 46*, 405–435.

Dahl, R. A. (1961). *Who governs? Democracy and power in an American city*. New Haven, CT: Yale University Press.

Deeg, R. (2001). *Institutional change and the uses and limits of path dependency: The case of German finance*. MPIfG Discussion Paper 01/6 Max Plank Institute for the Study of Societies.

DiMaggio, P. (1991). Constructing an organizational field as a professional project: U.S. art museums, 1920–1940. In W. W. Powell & P. J. DiMaggio (Eds.), *The new institutionalism in organizational analysis* (pp. 267–292). Chicago, IL: University of Chicago Press.

Dowding, K. (1995). Model or metaphor? A critical review of the policy networks approach. *Political Studies, 43*, 136–158.

Duffy, R. (1997). *Nuclear politics in America: A history and theory of government regulation*. Lawrence, KS: University Press of Kansas.

Edwards, G. C., III, Barrett, A., & Peake, J. (1997). The legislative impact of divided government. *American Journal of Political Science, 41*, 545–563.

Eisenstein, H. (1996). *Inside agitators*. Philadelphia, PA: Temple University Press.

Fligstein, N., & McAdam, D. (2012). *A theory of fields*. New York, NY: Oxford University Press.

Gamson, W. (1975). *The strategy of social protest*. Homewood, IL: Dorsey Press.

Gamson, W., & Modigliani, A. (1989). Media discourse and public opinion on nuclear power: A constructionist approach. *American Journal of Sociology, 95*, 1–37.

Giugni, M. (1998). Was it worth the effort? The outcomes and consequences of social movements. *Annual Review of Sociology, 98*, 371–393.

Goldstone, J. (2003). *States, parties and social movements*. Cambridge: Cambridge University Press.

Gupta, D. (2009). The power of incremental outcomes: How small victories and defeats affect social movement organizations. *Mobilization: An International Quarterly, 14*, 417–432.

Haines, H. (1984). Black radicalization and the funding of civil rights: 1957–1970. *Social Problems, 32*, 31–43.

Heclo, H. (1978). Issue networks and the executive establishment: Government growth in an age of improvement. In A. King (Ed.), *The new American political system*. Washington, DC: American Enterprise Institute.

Henry, A. D. (2011). Ideology, power, and the structure of policy networks. *Policy Studies Journal, 39*, 361–383.

Hogan, J. (2006). Remoulding the critical junctures approach. *Canadian Journal of Political Science, 39*, 657–679.

Howlett, M., & Cashore, B. (2009). The dependent variable problem in the study of policy change: Understanding policy change as a methodological problem. *Journal of Comparative Policy Analysis, 11*(1), 33–46.

Ingram, H., & Smith, S. R. (1993). *Public policy for democracy*. Washington, DC: Brookings Institution.

Jacobs, L. R., & Shapiro, R. Y. (2000). *Politicians don't pander: Political manipulation and the loss of democratic responsiveness*. Chicago, IL: The University of Chicago Press.

Jenkins, C. (1983). Resource mobilization theory and the study of social movements. *Annual Review of Sociology, 9*, 527–553.

Jenkins, C., & Klandermans, B. (1995). *The politics of social protest*. Minneapolis, MN: University of Minnesota Press.

Jenkins, J. C., & Eckert, C. M. (1986). Channelling black insurgency: Elite patronage and professional social movement organizations in the development of black movement. *American Sociological Review, 51*, 812–829.

Johnson, E. (2008). Social movement size, organizational density and the making of federal law. *Social Forces, 86*, 1–28.

Johnson, E., Agnone, J., & McCarthy, J. D. (2010). Movement organizations, synergistic tactics, and environmental public policy. *Social Forces, 88*, 2267–2292.

Jones, B. D., & Baumgartner, F. R. (2005). *The politics of attention*. Chicago, IL: University of Chicago Press.

Khan, S. R. (2012). The sociology of elites. *Annual Review of Sociology, 38*, 361–377.

King, B. G., Bentele, K. G., & Soule, S. (2007). Protest and policymaking: Explaining fluctuation in congressional attention to rights issues, 1960–1986. *Social Forces, 86*, 137–163.

King, D. (1997). *Turf wars*. Chicago, IL: University of Chicago Press.

Knoke, D. (1993). Networks of elite structure and decision making. *Sociological Methods & Research, 22*, 23–45.

Knoke, D., & Laumann, E. O. (1982). The social organization of national policy domains: An exploration of some structural hypotheses. In P. Marsden & N. Lin (Eds.), *Social structure and network analysis* (pp. 255–270). Beverly Hills, CA: Sage.

Koopmans, R. (1993). The dynamics of protest waves: West Germany, 1965–1989. *American Sociological Review, 58*(5), 637–658.

Kriesi, H. (2004). Strategic political communication: mobilizing public opinion in, audience democracies. In F. Esser & B. Pfetsch (Eds.), *Comparing political communication. Theories, cases, and challenges* (pp. 184–212). Cambridge: Cambridge University Press.

Marsh, D., & Rhodes, R. A. W. (Eds.) (1992). *Policy networks in British government*. Oxford: Clarendon Press.

McAdam, D. (1982). *Political process and the development of black insurgency, 1930–1970*. Chicago, IL: University of Chicago Press.

McAdam, D., & Boudet, H. (2012). *Putting social movements in their place: Explaining opposition to energy projects in the United States, 2000–2005*. Cambridge: Cambridge University Press.

McAdam, D., McCarthy, J. D., & Zald, M. N. (1996). Introduction: Opportunities, mobilizing structures, and framing processes – toward a synthetic, comparative perspective on social movements. In D. McAdam, J. D. McCarthy, & M. N. Zald (Eds.), *Comparative perspectives on social movements: Political opportunities, mobilizing structures, and cultural framings* (pp. 1–20). Cambridge: Cambridge University Press.

McAdam, D., Tarrow, S., & Tilly, C. (2001). *Dynamics of contention*. Cambridge: Cambridge University Press.

McCarthy, J., & Zald, M. N. (2002). The enduring vitality of the resource mobilization theory of social movements. In J. H. Turner (Ed.), *Handbook of sociological theory* (pp. 533–565). New York, NY: Kluwer Academic/Plenum.

McCarthy, J. D. (2005). Velcro triangles: Elite mobilization of local antidrug issue coalitions. In D. Meyer, V. Jenness, & H. Ingram (Eds.), *Routing the opposition: Social movements, public policy, and democracy* (pp. 87–115). Minneapolis, MN: University of Minnesota Press.

McCarthy, J. D., & Zald, M. N. (1977). Resource mobilization and social movements: A partial theory. *American Journal of Sociology, 82*, 1212–1241.

Meyer, D., & Minkoff, D. (2004). Conceptualizing political opportunities. *Social Forces, 82*, 1457–1492.

Meyer, D. S. (1993). Institutionalizing dissent: The United States structure of political opportunity and the end of the nuclear freeze movement. *Sociological Forum, 8*, 157–179.

Meyer, D. S. (2004). Protest and political opportunities. *Annual Review of Sociology, 30*, 125–145.

Meyer, D. S. (2005). Social movements and public policy: Eggs, chicken and theory. In D. S. Meyer, V. Jenness, & H. Ingram (Eds.), *Routing the opposition*. Minneapolis, MN: University of Minnesota Press.

Meyer, D. S., & Imig, D. R. (1993). Political opportunity and the rise and decline of interest group sectors. *Social Science Journal, 30*, 253–270.

Meyer, D. S., & Tarrow, S. (Eds.) (1998). *The social movement society: Contentious politics for a new century*. Lanham, MD: Rowman & Littlefield.

Michels, R. ([1911] 1962). *Political parties: A sociological study of the oligarchical tendencies of modern democracy*. New York, NY: Collier Books.

Miller, H. T., & Demir, T. (2007). Policy communities. In F. Fischer, G. J. Miller, & M. S. Sidney (Eds.), *Handbook of public policy analysis: Theory, politics and methods* (pp. 137–147). New York, NY: Taylor and Francis.

Minkoff, D. (1995). *Organizing for equality*. New Brunswick, NJ: Rutgers University Press.

Moore, G. (1979). The structure of a national elite network. *American Sociological Review, 44*, 673–692.

Morris, A. (1984). *The origins of the civil rights movement*. New York, NY: Free Press.

Norris, P. (2002). *Democratic phoenix: Reinventing political activism*. New York: Cambridge University Press.

Olzak, S. (1989). Analysis of events in the study of collective action. *Annual Review of Sociology, 15*, 119–141.

Olzak, S., & Soule, S. A. (2009). Cross-cutting influences of environmental protest and legislation. *Social Forces, 88*, 201–225.

Opp, K.-D. (2009). *Theories of political protest and social movements*. New York, NY: Routledge.

Peng, I., & Wong, J. (2008). Institutions and institutional purpose: Continuity and change in East Asian social policy. *Politics and Society, 36*, 61–88.

Pettinicchio, D. (2010). Public and elite policy preferences: Gay marriage in Canada. *International Journal of Canadian Studies, 42*, 125–153.

Pettinicchio, D. (2012). Institutional activism: Reconsidering the insider/outsider dichotomy. *Sociology Compass, 6*, 499–510.

Pettinicchio, D. (2013). Strategic action fields and the context of political entrepreneurship: How disability rights became part of the policy agenda. *Research in Social Movements, Conflict and Change, 36*, 79–106.

Pierson, P. (1994). *Dismantling the welfare state? Reagan, thatcher, and the politics of retrenchment*. Cambridge: Cambridge University Press.

Pierson, P. (2003). *Politics in time: History, institutions, and social analysis*. Princeton, NJ: Princeton University Press.

Pierson, P., & Skocpol, T. (2007). The rise and reconfiguration of activist government. In P. Pierson & T. Skocpol (Eds.), *The transformation of American politics* (pp. 19–38). Princeton, NJ: Princeton University Press.

Piven, F. F., & Cloward, R. (1977). *Poor people's movement*. New York, NY: Pantheon.

Piven, F. F., & Cloward, R. A. (1971). *Regulating the poor: The functions of public welfare*. New York, NY: Vintage, Random House.

Polsby, N. W. (1963). *Community power and political theory*. New Haven, CT: Yale University Press.

Polsby, N. W. (2004). *How congress evolves: Social bases of institutional change*. New York, NY: Oxford University Press.

Pratt, H. J. (1976). *The gray lobby*. Chicago, IL: University of Chicago Press.

Reese, E., & Newcombe, G. (2003). Income rights, mothers' rights, or workers' rights? Collective action frames, organizational ideologies, and the American welfare movement. *Social Problems*, *50*, 294–318.

Reichman, N., & Canan, P. (2003). Ozone entrepreneurs and the building of global coalitions. In C. Humphrey (Ed.), *Environment, energy, and society: Exemplary works*. Belmont, CA: Wadsworth Publishing.

Riker, W. H. (1982). *Liberalism against populism: A confrontation between the theory of democracy and the theory of social choice*. Prospect Heights, IL: Waveland Press.

Rixen, T., & Viola, L. A. (2014). Putting path dependence in its place: Toward a taxonomy of institutional change. *Journal of Theoretical Politics*, *27*, 301–323.

Roa, H., Morrill, C., & Zald, M. N. (2000). Power plays: How social movements and collective action create new organizational forms. *Research in Organizational Behavior*, *22*, 239–282.

Rochon, T. R., & Mazmanian, D. A. (1993). Social movements and the policy process. *Annals of the American Academy of Political and Social Science*, *528*, 75–87.

Rucht, D. (2007). The spread of protest politics. In R. J. Dalton & H.-D. Klingemann (Eds.), *The Oxford handbook of political behavior* (pp. 708–723). Oxford: Oxford University Press.

Rupp, L. J., & Taylor, V. (1987). *Survival in the doldrums*. New York, NY: Oxford University Press.

Sabatier, P. A., & Jenkins-Smith, H. C. (1999). The advocacy coalition framework: An assessment. In P. A. Sabatier (Ed.), *Theories of the policy process* (pp. 117–168). Boulder, CO: Westview Press.

Santoro, W. A., & McGuire, G. M. (1997). Social movement insiders: The impact of institutional activists on affirmative action and comparable worth policies. *Social Problems*, *44*, 503–519.

Sawyers, T. M., & Meyer, D. S. (1999). Missed opportunities: Social movement abeyance and public policy. *Social Problems*, *46*, 187–206.

Schattschneider, E. E. (1935). *Politics, pressures and the tariff: A study of free private enterprise in pressure politics, as shown in the 1929–1930 revision of the tariff*. New York, NY: Prentice-Hall.

Schattschneider, E. E. (1960). *The semisovereign people: A realist's view of democracy in America*. New York, NY: Holt, Rinehart, and Winston.

Schlozman, K. L., Page, B. I., Verba, S., & Fiorina, M. P. (2005). Inequalities of political voice. In T. Skocpol & L. R. Jacobs (Eds.), *Inequality and American democracy: What*

we know and what we need to learn (pp. 19–87). New York, NY: Russell Sage Foundation.
Schneider, M., & Teske, P. (1992). Toward a theory of the political entrepreneur: Evidence from local government. *American Political Science Review, 86,* 737–747.
Scotch, R. (2001). *From good will to civil rights.* Philadelphia, PA: Temple University Press.
Selznick, P. (1949). *TVA and the grassroots.* Berkeley, CA: University of California Press.
Sheingate, A. D. (2006). Structure and opportunity: Committee jurisdiction and issue attention in congress. *American Journal of Political Science, 50,* 844–859.
Shultziner, D. (2013). The socio-psychological origins of the Montgomery bus boycott: Social interaction and humiliation in the emergence of social movements. *Mobilization, 18,* 117–142.
Skocpol, T. (2007). Government activism and the reorganization of American civic democracy. In P. Pierson & T. Skocpol (Eds.), *The transformation of American politics* (pp. 39–67). Princeton, NJ: Princeton University Press.
Skrentny, J. (2002). *The minority rights revolution.* Cambridge: Harvard University Press.
Smith, M. A. (2000). *American business and political power.* Chicago, IL: University of Chicago Press.
Smith, S., & C. Deering. (1990). *Committees in Congress.* Congressional Quarterly.
Soule, S. A., McAdam, D., McCarthy, J. D., & Su, Y. (1999). Protest events: Cause or consequence of state action? The U.S. women's movement and federal congressional activities, 1956–1979. *Mobilization, 4,* 239–255.
Staggenborg, S. (1988). Consequences of professionalization and formalization in the pro-choice movement. *American Sociological Review, 53,* 585–606.
Staggenborg, S. (1989). Stability and innovation in the women's movement. *Social Problems, 36,* 75–92.
Staggenborg, S. (1991). *The pro-choice movement.* New York, NY: Oxford University Press.
Stearns, L. B., & Almeida, P. D. (2004). The formation of state actor-social movement coalitions and favorable policy outcomes. *Social Problems, 51,* 478–504.
Streek, W., & Thelen, K. (Eds.) (2005). *Beyond continuity: Institutional change in advanced political economies.* New York, NY: Oxford University Press.
Tarrow, S. (1989). *Democracy and disorder. Protest and politics in Italy 1965–1975.* Oxford: Clarendon Press.
Tarrow, S. (1993). Social protest and policy reform may 1968 and the Loi d'orientation in France. *Comparative Political Studies, 25,* 579–607.
Tarrow, S. (1998). *Power in movement.* Cambridge: Cambridge University Press.
Taylor, V. (1989). Social movement continuity: The women's movement in abeyance. *American Sociological Review, 54,* 761–775.
Taylor, V., & Whittier, N. (1995). Analytical approaches to social movement culture: The culture of the women's movement. In H. Johnston & B. Klandermans (Eds.), *Social movements and culture.* London: UCL Press.
Tilly, C. (1978). *From mobilization to revolution.* New York, NY: Random House.
Tilly, C. (1984). *Big structures, large processes, huge comparisons.* New York, NY: Russell Sage.
Van Dyke, N., Soule, S. A., & Taylor, V. A. (2004). The targets of social movements: Beyond a focus on the state. In D. J. Myers & D. M. Cress (Eds.), *Authority in contention* (Vol. 25, pp. 27–51). Research in Social Movements, Conflicts and Change. Bingley, UK: Emerald Group Publishing Limited.

Walker, J. L., Jr. (1991). *Mobilizing interest groups in America: Patrons, professions and social movements*. Ann Arbor, MI: Michigan University Press.

Walker, E. T. (2014). *Grassroots for hire: Public affairs consultants in American democracy*. New York, NY: Cambridge University Press.

Wilson, C. A. (2000). Policy regimes and policy change. *Journal of Public Policy, 20*, 247–274.

Zippel, K. (2006). *The politics of sexual harassment: A comparative study of the United States, the European Union and Germany*. Cambridge: Cambridge University Press. #BlackLivesMatter Activists Confront Hillary Clinton on Incarceration. NBC News. Retrieved from http://www.nbcnews.com/news/nbcblk/blacklivesmatter-activists-confront-clinton-incarceration-n411536. Accessed on August 18, 2015.

THE MILITARIZATION THEORY IN POST-SOVIET RUSSIA: DISPELLING THE PATHOLOGICAL LOOK AT POLITICAL AND ADMINISTRATIVE ELITES

Victor Violier

ABSTRACT

This paper aims, through the specific example of the plenipotentiary envoys — a.k.a. the polpredy, *at questioning Law as a legitimate knowledge of the political elite in post-Soviet Russia. The term legitimate has to be understood as both a legitimated and a legitimating knowledge.*

A new level of administration was set by Vladimir Putin right after his election in May 2000 and has become a symbol of the militarization of political elites in Russia, concretized by a massive recruitment of people from the so-called power ministries. Beyond this, in the context of a closed institutional game and the power's will to neutralize a whole bunch of the political game's rules, law also becomes a ground on which to build a control of the political and administrative elites' recruitment. Our approach blends a critical overview of the literature and a prosopographical study of more than 20 members of Russian top political elites between 2000 and 2012, corresponding to Putin's three first mandates as the head of the Russian state — two as President and a third one as Prime Minister under Dmitri Medvedev's Presidency.

Our study led us to the conclusion that, not only should we regard Law as esteemed but also, and above all, as invested with an instrumental function by the power in place, but also those who long to be in power.

Keywords: Militarization; law; legitimacy; state building; political and administrative elites; political culture

THE OSCILLATIONS OF RUSSIAN FEDERALISM

The evolution of Russian federalism since the end of the USSR may be compared to that of a pendulum (Gel'man, 2006, p. 104). During the 1990s and the Presidency of Boris Yeltsin — from December 25, 1991 to December 31, 1999 — the power of the different "subjects of the Federation," as the various entities of the Federation are called, continually expanded while the Central power became weaker and weaker. To maintain his power, Yeltsin concluded agreements with the local barons and thus delegated large elements of the state sovereignty to the provinces. This process was particularly accurate concerning the Republics within the Russian Federation. The central power even started to sign bilateral treaties with more and more subjects of the Federation. It started, for instance, with The Republic of Tatarstan on February 15, 1994 (Gazier, 2002, pp. 194–195; Lallemand, 2010, p. 130). In this context, a large number of subjects felt free to adopt local laws, rules, regulations, and policies that were not in line with national laws. Some of those laws were even unconstitutional, regarding the Constitution of the Russian Federation adopted on the December 25, 1993. Therefore, a "transactional federalism" (Gel'man, op. cit., p. 107) or "Federalism on a-case-by-case basis" was born. This led to the conclusion that "During the 1990's, Russia had as many regional political regimes as provinces" (Lallemand, op. cit., p. 131). This asymmetry (Daucé, 2008, p. 46; Lallemand, 2010, p. 130) reached its peak with the financial and economic crisis that occurred in August 1998. The regional executives had become extremely powerful and the obvious inability of the central power to deal with the multifaceted crisis — that was symbolized by the collapse of the rouble which resulted in the Russian government and Central Bank devaluing the rouble and defaulting on the debt − raised the question of the federal power's future (Mendras, 2007, pp. 127−132). The nomination of Yevgeny Primakov as Prime Minister in September 1998 was one of the last attempts to restore central power over the provinces. Less than a year later, Yeltsin and his entourage chose Vladimir Putin as the new Prime Minister and, even more, the designated successor to become the second President of the Russian Federation (Gazier, 2002, p. 181; Sakwa, 2008, pp. 121, 123−124).

The Putin Presidency has consisted from the beginning in an authoritative recentralization of power. After being chosen to act as interim President on the evening of the January 31, 1999, Vladimir Putin's position was then confirmed by the presidential election held in March 2000. In fact, after competing as an independent, he was elected in the first round with more than 53% of the vote out of a total of 11 candidates. Since he came to power, Vladimir Putin has shown his intention to stop the movement of decentralization initiated under Yeltsin's Presidency (Gazier, 2002, p. 203). It was even illustrated while he was still Prime Minister by the invasion of the secessionist Republic of Chechnya that took place on August 26, 1999 and started the second Chechen war in response to the invasion of Dagestan by the Islamic International Brigade (Le Huérou, 2010; Merlin, 2007).

THE ESTABLISHMENT OF THE POLPREDY, HOW THE ROT HAS SET IN ...

As a newly elected President, Vladimir Putin then put forward two main concepts to symbolize the re-ordering of the State order, and, consequently, of Russian federalism. The first concept is the so-called "power vertical." It consists of implementing a straight hierarchy between all levels of administration, each one obeying to the upper one (Gazier, 2002, 2008; Kossolov, 2007). The second concept is the "dictatorship of law," which comprises two lines. On the one hand, it means that all local and regional laws, rules, and policies now have to match the Constitution of the Russian Federation. On the other hand, it also means that every administration, every company or individual is submitted to the law. This second part has been almost theoretical but has constituted a convenient political weapon for President Putin. A relevant illustration of this was the so-called "Khodorkovsky case" that started after Mikhail Khodorkovsky was arrested on October 25, 2003 in Novosibirsk (Siberia) and his company forced into administration by the State. Indeed, the trial of the wealthiest man in Russia at that time — according to Forbes magazine — was a clear demonstration of the State power over individuals and local or national lobbies (Daucé, op. cit.; Favarel-Garrigues, Sapir, & Rousselet, 2004).

As for policies, Vladimir Putin has introduced several State reforms since he took office. The creation and appointment of the so-called polpredy on the May 13, 2000 is one of them. In fact, he used the presidential decrees (Ukaz) N° 849 to 855 "*O polnomočnom predstavitele prezidenta rossijskoj federacii v federal'nom okruge*" to create this new level of the state administration. The polpredy are part of the presidential administration, regularly considered the most powerful corps within the State. There were seven delegates for the entire territory at the very beginning. An eighth one was appointed to the North Caucasian Federal District which resulted from the division of the Southern District decided in 2010 by Dmitri Medvedev after he succeeded Vladimir Putin. The polpredy are supposed to control the actions of the governors and the presidents of the Republics and to ensure that local legislation complies with the State Constitution. We can add that the creation of the polpredy was complemented by additional measures tending to a recentralization of the State power, such as the suppression of direct universal suffrage for the election of the Governors and Presidents of Republics.

In a nutshell, presidential plenipotentiary envoys became the champions of the new centralism (Gel'man, 2006) and the vertical of power since they were nominated to tame the regional entities emancipated during the Yeltsin years. They also serve as an example of the reshaping of the Russian political and administrative elite, from which we can observe both the configuration and evolution of Russian elites since the fall of the Soviet Union.

THE SHORT-SIGHTEDNESS OF THE MILITARIZATION THEORY

An Attractive Paradigm ...

What we see as the "militarization theory" consists in a widespread paradigm dominating a large amount of issues about Russian elites and revolving around the issue of a "militarization of power" (Raviot, 2008, p. 48). Russia is considered a hybrid political regime (Diamond, 2002). Its "degree of democracy" is regularly debated, The Russian political regime being thus usually classified between the western liberal "consolidated democracy" (Linz & Stepan, 1996) and the politically "closed regimes" (Levitsky & Way, 2002; Schedler, 2002). It is also considered as a "democracy with adjective" (Collier & Levitsky, 1997): administrated, directed, Potemkin etc. Thus, one of the key aspects that has been widely portrayed by both scientific and media analysts during the last fifteen years would be a so-called militarization of Russian elites. A few months after Vladimir Putin came to power, what we decided to call "The militocratic paradigm" was developed. Indeed, according to most analysts, the arrival of Putin to power has entailed the appointment of an increasing number of people from military structures to positions of power. Thus, according to this analysis, the entire political regime of contemporary Russia has been affected by the massive penetration of military people.

The term 'militocracy' was used for the first time – to our knowledge – by Olga Krychtanovskaya and Stephen White. In an article published in 2003 in *Post-Soviet Affairs* and entitled "Putin's Militocracy," they clearly insist on what they consider a major transformation in Russia since the 2000s. Their statement is doubly linked to the incoming of numerous military personnel. Firstly, they consider that Vladimir Putin has played a major role in the recruitment of his previous colleagues at every level of administration. Therefore, this penetration would be the result of a *well-planned policy* from the newly elected President to secure his position by reshuffling the administration main body. Secondly, this reshuffling would affect even the form of the state and the political regime of Putin's Russia. It would put an end to Russia's transition to democracy and create a military regime. As an example of this decisive conceptual shift in meaning, we can quote the title of an article from *The Economist* magazine published in 2007: "The Making of a New KGB State." At the core of the article the author asserts *"Men from the FSB and its sister organisations control the Kremlin, the government, the media and large parts of the economy – as well as the military and security forces. (...) The KGB provided a crucial service of surveillance and suppression; it was a state within a state. Now, however, it has become the state itself"* (The Economist, 2007, §4, §6). It might also be added that the edition concerned is even entitled "Putin's people. The spies who run Russia." In the same way, some researchers went so far as to warn against "a peaceful military takeover" (Petrov, 2002) happening in Russia as soon as "the institution of the envoys is one of the major elements within the new Putin model of replacing state institutions with substitutes" (Petrov, 2005, p. 56): *"A year and a half may be too short a period for definite conclusions, but one thing that is already sufficiently clear is that, whatever the Kremlin's initial plans and words, what is really happening is the insertion of police-state mechanisms into a delegative and declarative democratic state (...) Putin's aim is to create a strong state under his leadership; everything else — including de-democratization and de-federalization — is mere side-effect"* (Petrov, 2002, p. 82).

Thus, the characteristics of the military people would influence their way of ruling the administrations and, therefore, the whole state. The values and attitudes that they acquired within the security forces determine their actions whilst in power. This matches with the work of Mills (1956), who wrote in this respect, in *The Power Elite*, that military people did not lose the effects of both the education and training that modeled their personality and their vision of the world. Meanwhile, this perspective could also be reversed. Indeed, instead of considering only a militarization of politics, couldn't we think of a civilization — in the sense of a "politization" — of the military area? It would result in us taking into account the politization of military people and security forces as well as law enforcement organizations. We think here of Jean Joana's reflexion about the position of military personnel and their relation to power mentioning among other Alfred Stepan's writings about Brazil and the example of the *Escuela superior de Guerra* (1971, 1973). Actually, the military might become so bogged down in politics that it would neutralize their ability to be a problem for the government. For instance, the sociology of comparative politics has been reluctant to consider "military regimes" as a category of regime in itself. Indeed, Linz (1985) has already suggested, the nature of these regimes cannot be reduced to the military origin of those who rule, since their influence tends to fade while the regime is stabilizing (Joana, 2006, pp. 7–9).

The quantitative dimension of the "militocratic paradigm" has been demonstrated. The calculations have certainly been well overestimated at the very beginning and have favored a catastrophic outlook (see Rivera & Rivera, 2008 revising data of Kryshtanovskaïa & White, 2003). Still, it seems that this dimension is globally attested. According to the data of Rivera and Rivera (2008) one in eight members of the Russian administrations has served in the power ministries. And this number has increased by 25% since Vladimir Putin came to power. As a consequence, the aim of our paper is not to contradict the data but to question the qualitative dimension of it. In other words, to what extent has Russia become a militocratic regime?

... But a Distorting Prism to Look at Russian Elites

Beyond a normative and pathological look, a closer look at plenipotentiary envoys' career paths shows variety and diversity. Our empirical research consisted of a prosopography of all the polpredy (24) who have been in office since the creation of the function in 2000 until May 2012. The study of the biographical characteristics of these individuals is a good way of analyzing the role of the cultural factor in the process of distinction of Russian elites since Vladimir Putin came to power. In fact, they are both the personification of the "new centralism" and the "vertical of power" and an example of the reshuffling of Russian elites since the end of the Soviet era. Thus, the empirical work consisted of compiling information and data from various sources to compose, as far as possible, the most detailed biography for every individual that has been in office within this administration between 2000 and 2012. The year 2000 refers to the first election of Vladimir Putin and the creation of the function of the *polpredy* in May. May 2012 refers to the third election of Vladimir Putin after Dmitri Medvedev's term. The election took place in March, he then entered into office on May 7th. This period includes a total of 24 people.

We started using the biographical information we could find form the two main sources edited in Russian (Chchegolev, 2008; Muhin et al., 2004). Then, we updated and cross-checked these informations with both institutional and non-governmental websites − such as the official websites of the federal districts administration and independent journalists' websites − such as *kompromat.ru*, for instance. Concerning the nature of the two principal sources, we would like to assert that they are different from the main Anglo-Saxon reference which is the biographical dictionary entitled *The Who's Who*. Actually, if they both highlight identity-building strategies of the politicians, our sources are more based on a bureaucratic than "worldly" model (Collovald, 1988). They include all the high-level officials and bureaucrats and detail their careers in a chronological and very official way.

The analysis of our empirical materials allows us to contrast sharply with the caricatural and homogeneous vision of Russian elites given by the militocratic theory. To begin with, it is important to underline that not only the career paths but even the mandate trajectories of the *polpredy* have been very diversified since these representatives were nominated and dismissed on the decision of the only President of the Federation. Firstly, some of the *polpredy* have been nominated in two different districts over the 12-year period of time we are considering. Secondly, the duration of the 24 *polpredy*'s term of office has varied between 6 months and more than 11 years. The average duration of the term of office has been three and a half years.

We paid attention to the recruitment and departure conditions. Indeed, the function of the *polpred* is unequally linked to governmental positions. Seven of them occupied a position within the government when they were nominated as a *polpred*. Nevertheless, they didn't have similar positions. For instance, Oleg Safonov (*polpred* in the Far-eastern district from 2007 to 2009), deputy Minister of the Interior (MVD) before his nomination, was far lower in governmental hierarchy than Valentina Matvyenko (*polpred* in the North-Western district in 2003), since she was herself deputy Prime Minister. The future of the *polpredy* after their mandate is also very different. In fact, only four of them have been directly nominated in the government while some started running state-controlled agencies and companies or were nominated in the regions, for instance as governors.

Center–region or region–center pathways are also hard to unify. In fact, three of the 24 *polpredy* used to be governors of some subjects of the Federation, that is, part of the regional administration before being nominated in the Presidential administration. V. Ishaev has served as Governor of the Kraï of Khabarovsk from 1991 to 2009 before becoming *polpred* of the Far-Eastern federal district. A. Khloponin was in office in Krasnoyarsk for 8 years when he was nominated in 2010 to rule the North Caucasian federal district. Finally, V. Tolokonsky was the head of the oblast of Novosibirsk for 11 years before his nomination as the new *polpred* of the Siberian federal district in 2010. On the contrary, two *polpredy* were transferred from the presidential – central – administration to the regional administration. Thus, V. Matvyenko, the only woman who has occupied the post of *polpred*, became Governor of St-Petersburg after her very short term in office as the *polpred* of the North-Western federal district in 2003. G. Poltavchenko occupied the same function as Matvienko after he was dismissed from the post of *polpred* of the Central Federal District. As a consequence, it is hardly possible to think in terms of "political spoils" (Bailey, 1969), and establish a hierarchy of national and regional functions in which we could replace with precision the *polpredy*.

The most important aspect highlighted by the large diversity of the *polpredy*'s career pathways is certainly their professional background. Indeed, it results from a detailed analysis of the various professional positions occupied by the *polpredy* before their coming in office that three major groups could be distinguished. This strongly undermines the militocratic theory, not just because only eight of the twenty four *polpredy* have been working within the power ministries but also because even these eight individuals are far from having such a common professional identity.

Therefore, the first group of individuals that can be identified is composed of eight individuals who have worked in the so-called power ministries. Thus, they are considered as being part of the so-called *siloviki*. Among these eight individuals that have worked in the power ministries, four have served in the KGB and/or for its successor the FSB. V. Tcherkesov is a former colonel general of the KGB and was the Deputy Director of the FSB. G. Poltavchenko is a former officer of the KGB and was the head of the Direction of the Federal tax police in Saint-Petersburg. G. Rapota worked in the First General Direction of the FSB (foreign intelligence) and was involved in long-term missions in western countries. Finally, O. Safonov, a former KGB agent, has been decorated with the Order of the Red Flag of the KGB Institute of the Soviet Union. Then, three individuals are former professional soldiers. Indeed, V. Kazantsev, K. Pulikovskiï, and A. Kvashnin are respectively General in Chief, Lieutenant-General, and Colonel General of the Russian army and have served in various conflicts such as the war in Afghanistan or the two Chechen conflicts. Lastly, we can add P. Latyshev, who is a former Colonel General of the Ministry of Interior of the Russian Federation (MVD).

Sixteen of the *polpredy* (2/3) thus have a different professional origin. Indeed, nine of the plenipotentiary representatives occupied an intellectual profession or were former senior managers in the Civil service. Among them were four former magistrates, three former University Professors, and two former senior civil servants. They consist of the second identifiable group. The third and last group is composed of five plenipotentiary representatives who came from the business sector. They were all leading banks and/or industries – such as Noris Oïl or Noris Nickel – during the 1990s. Finally, we could notice here that two trajectories do not match with our categorization: V. Matvienko and K. Ishakov had particular career paths that we will analyze further.

The close look we just had at the plenipotentiary representatives career path allows us to have a more nuanced picture of these individuals than the one depicted after V. Putin's coming into office and that we described before. It also invites us to consider *siloviki* as a polysemic notion that should be debated. Therefore, if five out of the seven first *polpredy* were former members of the power ministries, there were "only" eight out of 24 twelve years after the introduction of their function. Nevertheless, it still corresponds to a third of the total. Consequently, it would still be possible to consider that this new level of administration is a testimony of the "military takeover" (Petrov, op. cit.) that has occurred since V. Putin came to power in 2000, without any further examination. This is the reason why we currently need to develop our analysis on the nine key individuals known as former power ministries members, that is, *siloviki*.

Firstly, the notion of *siloviki* itself – as well as the one of power ministries – should be debated (Bacon, Cooper, & Renz, 2007). The concept of *siloviki* products a homogeneous reality. It thus tends to lead to the conclusion that, for instance in the case we are interested in, the eight individuals who have worked in the power ministries are broadly similar to each other. Nevertheless, it is now time to assess this problematic notions of "silovik" and "power minister." To summarize on this issue, a relatively consensual and operational definition has already been established as follows: *"The power ministries in Russia are those state agencies in which the personnel generally wear uniforms and in which some people carry guns. More precisely, those bodies are military, security or law enforcement bodies that possess armed units of formations. People with power ministry backgrounds are referred to as siloviki"* (Taylor, 2007, p. vii). However, as Edwin Bacon, Julian Cooper and Bettina Renz noted: *"The concept of a silovik, though an attractive shorthand term, masks wide-ranging differences between those who are labelled with this epithet. A silovik could have served in a diverse group of force structure (for examples, the military, the police, the intelligence services), in a diverse range of roles, at different level of seniority, in different periods, and for differing lengths of time. There are democratic siloviki, and authoritarian non-siloviki"* (Bacon et al., 2007, pp. 42-43). We could not agree more to the three authors' statement in this case. The notion of silovik actually functions as a stereotype that smoothes out asperities and erases the differences between trajectories that can be particularly various, providing a distorted vision of the reality. As a consequence, there might be more differences than similarities between some or the totality of the individuals categorized as *siloviki*.

Secondly, a careful look at the recent political history of the Russian Federation might also help us to put this particular recruitment back into its context. Indeed, when Vladimir Putin was chosen as his successor by Boris Yeltsin and the so-called Family – as the Yeltsin entourage has been nicknamed – he only had a few months experience on the national political stage (Daucé, 2008, pp. 60–62). Besides, he was not affiliated to any of the political parties existing in Russia. Therefore, he could not recruit in a political party's reserve of individuals and had no other choice but to rely on the individuals he already knew through other ways (Solovev quot. in Renz, 2006). That is why he decided to rely on people he used to know by working with them either in the security forces or in the St-Petersburg City council where he started his political career, after the fall of the Berlin wall. We can add that when Boris Yeltsin came to power, he proceeded the same way, nominating people from his hometown, Sverdlovsk, to assume various strategic positions (Kryshtanovskaïa & White, 2003). Actually, we can use the comparison of Alekseï Salmin, Director of the Russian Centre of

Public Policies: *"Of course Putin relies on those he understands and knows. This is absolutely natural. If a professor happened to become president, he, too would invite some people from his environment"* (quot. in Renz, 2006).

According to this point of view, the professional socialization of Vladimir Putin would explain the nature of his recruitment. That might be a reasonable explanation. Nevertheless, this cannot be the only valuable explanation for the large amount of people from the power ministries coming to power on both national and local scales. Consequently, the introduction of the cultural factor has to go further than an insight into Vladimir Putin's professional background.

CONSIDERING RUSSIAN ELITES BEYOND THE MILITARIZATION

The Cultural Factor as an Alternative Clue

The cultural factor will be studied in two steps in order to put forward an alternative explanation to the militarization theory — which makes the incursion of the military in Russian politics a concerted plan. On the one hand, the elite culture of liberal democracy — especially in western countries but also among Russian intellectual elites — explains the development of the militarization theory. On the other hand, the Soviet cultural legacy in Russia might be a clue to understand the reshuffle of Russian elites about the law around the beginning of the XXIst century.

The culture of liberal democracy has been playing a major role in the construction of the militarization theory. Thus, before discussing the findings of the prosopography concerning the cultural factor, we have to consider the cultural aspect of the knowledge on democracy and more specifically on transitions to democracy. In fact, the topic of elite political culture — understood as the circulation of cultural knowledge concerning transitions to democracy — helps to have a better understanding of both the construction of Russia's attitude toward democracy and the future collective political behavior in Putin's Russia. Thus, considering the cultural dimension of politics allows to complete the deconstruction of the militocratic paradigm. That is the reason why we need to identify deeply both its theoretical and contextual origins, that are closely related to the production of democratic knowledge. The militocratic paradigm is, by and large, a construct of analysts' pathological look at the Russian political regime and, therefore, at the Russian elites. Although transitology as well as all theories of democratization have been widely discarded, the fact remains that they still have effects on the field of comparative politics and political regimes analysis. The main objections that have been raised against transitology and its grip on comparative analysis of political regime change might apply to the militocratic paradigm. Indeed, transitology suggests that liberal democracy is the end of the transition process which, by the way, is placed at the very core of the analysis. Its normativity, that comprises sometimes a very prescriptive dimension, has had a strong influence on the production of knowledge on the new-born Russian political regime since the end of the 1980s. Yet, if liberal democracy is considered an ideal in terms of political regime, the Russian political regime is to be regarded, at least, as an incomplete or imperfect one (1990s), or even as an antithesis or a concurrent model (2000s). As a consequence, Putin's Russia has been gradually observed from a pathological standpoint. According to it, Russia got lost on its way toward democracy. This has become particularly obvious since Vladimir Putin came to power because he departed from the liberal and pro-western policy of his predecessor.

It seems that some of the main objections made to transitological approaches (see for instance Carothers, 2002; Dobry, 2000a; Zalewski, 2009) should be reinvested to discuss the pathological look at both Russia's political regime and the elites. For instance, the tree structure used by Przeworski (1979) in *The Games of Transition* to describe the sequence of choice-situations on the path to democracy represents the finalist aspect of transitology. It has been demonstrated that one should rather question the process of social and political reproduction explaining the original forms of the State in postcommunist societies (Dobry, 2000b). It is a matter of restoring the importance of political structures while transitology is only centered on political actors and their strategies. Transitology also emphasizes the gap between the historical path of postcommunist societies toward democracy and the ideal democratic path by conceptualizing it. This gap approaches the gap that Bailey (1971) put in evidence between normative and pragmatic rules. On the one hand there are general political guidelines. On the other, there are goal-oriented leverages and tactics.

Last but not least concerning the issue of democratic knowledge, a careful look should be given to the study Guénard (2007) made on the debates held in the field of democratization studies in the United States and more particularly within the *Journal of Democracy*. The author first notes that the Journal was created on R. Reagan's initiative at the beginning of the 1980s and was intended to be the fundamental guide during the war of ideas with the Soviet Union. Thus it aimed at supporting the export of the "democratic model." Indeed, its founders M. J. Plattner and L. J. Diamond, both close to the American neo-cons, wanted to challenge the ideologies of authoritarian and totalitarian States with a militant support of democracy. The journal was supposed to favor the expression of a "science of democracy." Yet, this ideological end encouraged theoretical reshuffles such as the creation of the concept of *consolidation* that renewed and consolidated the transitologic paradigm. Nevertheless, the theoretical inputs that came with the notion of consolidation did not modify the objections we already expressed. For instance, the confirmation of the existence of "hybrid regimes" (Diamond, 2002) does not change the fact that the analysis is relying on a *one best way*. Political elites are still regarded as pluralistic and stratified elites remain the norm of democratization as, for instance, in the analysis of the relations between elites and political regimes (see, e.g., Carothers, 2002, p. 301; Genieys, 2011, p. 266 where Russia is associated with China, Cuba, North Korea, and Iran as a country where the "political elite is (until then) ideologically unified," p. 300). Elites are indeed, in this conception, made to compete with a large variety of capitals. It might sound quite normative to consider that Russian elites are supposed to *become* pluralistic. It results in two main effects. It first suggest that they are perfectly ideologically unified at the moment, which deeply underestimates the complexity of relations and interactions not only between the various configurations of elites but also within each of them. It secondly implies that Russia is lagging behind comparing to the West which is supposed to embody political modernity.

Nonetheless, it must be acknowledged that, after a period of hesitation about the way Russia should follow to make its transition, the new team that came to power in the end of 1999 quickly ensured the shutdown of the political game. Following on from Juan J. Linz about authoritarian regimes (1985), academics such as William Genieys (op. cit.) tend to attach authoritarian regimes to a limited elite pluralism. This reinforces the pathological look at Russian elites as a consequence of the analysis of Russia's political regime. We in fact assume that Russian political elites are commonly evaluated in reference to the incompleteness of its democracy. Furthermore, all these developments fit in perfectly with the militarization theory which is essentially based on the idea that Russian elites have become strikingly homogenized — since Vladimir Putin came to power in 1999 — around a common military ethos. It has been finally corroborated in the course of both journalistic and scientific narratives focused on the victory of the former KGB members over the liberal democrats and the reformers. As a consequence, the analysis of elites in post-Soviet Russia, where the competition is restricted and favors the reproduction of an oligarchic elite linked by stable collusions, makes Russia a black sheep among modern western democracies that are legitimated by a knowledge they developed across the world's political, diplomatic, and scientific fields (Wagner, 2007).

Reconsidering the Reshuffle of Russian Elites

Considering the issue of the cultural factor to think about both political elites and political regime changes in Post-Soviet Russia is to establish the preliminary basis of a more nuanced reading of their evolution since the fall of the USSR. The cultural factor is not only a way to identify how the militocratic paradigm is an obstacle to the analysis of Russian elites. It is also a clue to identify a more relevant binding agent between them. As we saw, one of the interests of the analysis of the career paths of the 24 *polpredy* who have been in function from 2000 to 2012 is to underline the heterogeneity of a particular body of the presidential administration behind a homogeneous representation. Besides, it allows us to go beyond the identification of the militocratic paradigm. In fact, asserting that answering Robert Dahl's famous interrogation — "*Who governs?*" (1961) — is a harder that it looks concerning contemporary Russia, does not mean that we cannot find some clue.

Back to our corpus, some career paths make it clear that a continuity exists among Russian political elites between the Yeltsin era and the Putin era. This is in line with some major theoretical contributions provided on central and eastern Europe (Mink & Szurek, 1999) and Russia (Szelenyi, Wnuk-Lipinski, & Treiman, 1995) which analyses former high-ranking communist cadres' career paths after the fall of the Berlin wall and more specifically their retraining in politics and economy. For instance, trajectories such as the one of S. Kiriyenko confirm the continuity between the Yeltsin and the Putin years. A former high-ranking official of the CPSU during the 1980s and then close to the late B. Nemtsov — former liberal politician who was one of Yeltsin's lieutenants — in Nizhny-Novgorod, he became Prime Minister in 1998 when Yeltsin was President of the Russian Federation. He was one of the founders of the Union of Right Forces (SPS) which was the main political movement of the right-wing liberals created in 1999. He then became the first *polpred* of the Siberian Federal District after V. Putin came to power. We can consider his term was a success since V. Putin then named him to become the head of the Federal Atomic Energy Agency (Rosatom) when it was created in 2005. He is now 52 years old and is still in office.

This example of a liberal politician of the early 1990s recruited by V. Putin fights against the idea that military people erased the past, shunting Yeltsin years' liberals into early retirement. We might also give the example of G. Poltavchenko who was the first *polpred* in office in the Central Federal District. He had been chosen, before, to act on behalf of Yeltsin in the Leningrad oblast under the previous administration.

Highlighting these trajectories, we cannot help trying to understand how V. Putin gathered such different people in this state administration body and globally in his political entourage. What kind of vector of "the unity in diversity" (Highley & Pakulski, 2000, p. 658) – did V. Putin find to make everyone pull together? It seems to us that law is part of the answer even beyond the concepts of dictatorship of law and power vertical (see below). Keeping in mind the importance of both historical and geographical context in the study of transitions and regime change (Bunce, 2000) a look should be taken at the political, economic and social developments of the late 1990s in Russia. In the generalized crisis context corresponding to Putin's coming to office, the power elites have been developing a legal discourse to insure their own legitimation. This part of the work has been especially symbolized by Vladislav Surkov's ideological work within the Kremlin and the two main concepts we already talked about – the vertical of power and the dictatorship of law – aimed at building a "sovereign" or "managed" democracy (Laruelle, 2010).

The concept of "sovereign democracy" set up by Vladislav Surkov is indeed helpful to portray not only what is assumed to be the practical gap between Russian regime and the ones in western countries but also the theoretical conceptualization of differences between democracy in Western understanding and the Russian regime. The epithet concentrates on the Surkov ideological construction intended to justify Russia's choice to take a different path, leading away from the Western conception of the liberal democracy – as claimed in particular by the US and the European Union State members. The sovereign democracy should firstly be seen as a reaction – not to say reflex – from the Russian head of state to the colored revolutions that happened in Georgia, Ukraine and Kyrgyzstan between 2003 and 2005. This revolutionary wave in several former Soviet Union countries was indeed interpreted by the Russian power as the result of various external interferences from the West. It is then supposed to show everyone – and especially the United States – that no foreign interference will ever be tolerated. Then, Surkov's concept has to be understood as a subtle blend of Russia's political past and historical conquests. It actually insists on the nationalist dimension and is based on a positive vision of the country's past, highlighting for instance the successes and achievements of the Soviet era. As M. Laruelle details it (op. cit., p. 228): the Soviet Union was sovereign but not democratic, Russia during the 1990s was democratic but lost its sovereignty, Vladimir Putin's Russia is supposed to reconcile these two main orientations. Finally, this ideological construction aims at embodying political modernity and the future of the Russian society in a globalized and evolving world which requires every country to be open to develop. To conclude on this point, we can contend that Vladislav Surkov's concept of sovereign democracy serves two main goals: on the domestic side, it is used to justify and defend its own path to democracy; at an international level, it can be considered a competing offer, especially intended to Russia's partners that might be willing to escape the US or EU influence such as India, China or even some countries in eastern Europe, as Polish political events of the beginning of 2016 suggest.

Accordingly, recruiting people who have competencies in both law and law enforcement would have made sense for the team in power in addition to the questions of prestige and sociability networks (Raviot, 2006, pp. 48–52). Then, the recruitment of people from law enforcement bodies would not be due to their military background but to the fact that the power in place actually believes that they master knowledge and know-how related to law. This hypothesis actually corresponds to some classic theories of the State's construction in Political science and refers to the classic notion of the rational-legal authority (Weber, 1971). Law is thus valued and the power in place needs personnel that are familiar with it, not to say specialists. Accordingly, specific knowledge and know-how connected with legal training and sociability networks as well as a particular position within judicial field would make some individuals particularly valuable resource persons. In this respect, judicial and legal fields are considered as "positional" spaces or areas (Boltanski, 1973; Passeron, 1990) and the construction of a monopoly on a complex knowledge – legal, in this case – must be regarded as a key factor to ensure social power (Konrad & Szelenyi, 1979). Considering our corpus, we can mention that not only is law at the core of the education and training in law enforcement bodies, but also four of the *polpredy* are former magistrates. N. Vinnichenko, V. Ustinov, D. Kozak, and A. Konovalov all worked in the General Prosecution both in Moscow and the regions. This hypothesis might be further investigated on the basis of the model provided by some research conducted on the EU staff members (see for instance Cohen & Vauchez, 2005).

In fact, not only do we consider knowledge stricto sensu but also know-how and skills as well as interpersonal relationships, cultural background etc. that generate a "entre-soi." It results from this that individuals and groups of individuals revolving around law in Russia could not be limited to lawyers or other legal experts. Those knowledge lato sensu then logically comprise everything referring to the notion of habitus (Bourdieu, 1980) of theses elites. Such resources provide cultural capital/asset, that comes in three "forms": "incorporé"/"embedded," "objective"/"objectified," and "institutionnalisé"/"institutionalized" (Bourdieu, 1979, pp. 3–5). Elites are arising, in this regard, from this shared bedrock of cultural asset: "Belonging to an Elite implies mastering its behavior codes, its language, its relationships that shape modes of sociability (...) It also implies having a specific field of competence and being endowed with a particular know-how"... (Leferme-Falguières & Van Renterghem, 2000, p. 63).

Furthermore, the power's ideological and political discourse emphasizing the importance of law and legality seems to be in line with political modernity and must be endorsed by international political elites. A sample of the international reactions to D. Medvedev's coming to power in 2008 — which was actually a highly fictional succession — is indicative of this wide-ranged acceptance. Lawyer by training and former University teacher of roman and civil law, he was supposed to be a very good match for the globalized intellectual elite since they were assuming that he was a part of it. Nevertheless, Dmitri Medvedev's policy as a President of the Federation showed the relativity of his modernity discourse. This is especially true knowing that V. Putin introduces himself as a modernizer since his very first term in office.

Furthermore, we might postulate the relevance of the connection with Charles' Tilly's work (1992) on coercion — associated with capital — in state development in Europe and the leading role of war or, at least, its preparation — whether from a practical point of view or at a symbolic and discursive level. According to C. Tilly, the establishment of an army generated a stable state structure and the preparation of war has been the source of internal structures of the European states. However, he highlighted a militarization—civilization process after which the civilian bureaucracies and assemblies regain control over military people and structures. Yet, this process is not supposed to consist of a compulsory step of the states' development. In this perspective, Tilly's work emphasizes the parallel existence of states where militaries remain on the top of power, especially when institutions led by civilian people have failed. In the case of Russia, the 1990s can be considered as the failure and disrepute of civilian and democratic institutions. Russia's contemporary regime is then, again, considered in pathological perspective since the civilization is regarded as missing or failed. The constant references to the rule of law might be seen as a countervailing measure to ensure the existence of a civil State.

LAW AS A RELEVANT ELEMENT OF POLITICAL ELITES CULTURE TO BUILD A "SOVEREIGN DEMOCRACY"

According to N. Elias' fundamentally relational conception of the society (1981), the social equilibrium of forces results in the interdependent relationships that occur among elites and are related to the law. We are prone to think that although the existence of a common habitus of silovikis making them a homogeneous category is hardly relevant, the power in place may have developed a common belief in the existence of a common ethos relying on law and legality among political and administrative elites. In other words, whether or not these common characteristics and shared values are an illusion of the team in power, it seems that they bet on building their authority and power on it. This belief might be scrutinized in the light of M. Dobry's concept of "confidence in the *habitus*" (1992). It means that people in power and V. Putin in particular are betting on what they assume to be the habitus of the individuals they recruit. According to the representation that they have of them, they are "the men for the job," the ones that should be trusted in a context of crisis – that is, a context of overturning of the institutional references.

It is hard to identify a coherent ideological construction in today's Russia except for a common denominator based on a massive and multifaceted nationalist reinvestment (Laruelle, 2010). It is worth noting in this regard that scholar books are currently being rewritten, as demonstrated by V. Putin's recent project to edit a common textbook for all Russian students of classes nine and eleven (that students usually attend when they are 15 and 17). This emerging enterprise already aims at presenting an idealized and pacified vision of the Soviet era (Konkka, 2014). According to the same logic, Law might play a role as the "lowest common denominator" and a symbolic resource for the elites in Putin's Russia. Putin came to power while Russia was in the middle of a political, economic and social crisis that followed the collapse of the USSR. Both the discourse and action increasingly valued law and legality, partly through revaluation of the Soviet cultural heritage. For instance, Vladislav Surkov, who was for a long time the personal spin doctor of V. Putin and is considered to be "the man behind" the Presidential party *United Russia* as well as the concept of the sovereign democracy, has made clear that the power wants to repeat not the warrior rhetoric but the discourse of modernization of the Soviet Union (Surkov, 2007). Since 2000, the social and political consensus around V. Putin resulted in both the comeback of economic growth — mostly due to the huge increase of oil prices — and the promise of a return of State authority. The team in power has been gradually looking for an ideological contribution to replace the economic aspect of the pact. Indeed, the economic crisis of 2008 and the first massive demonstrations of winter 2011 revealed the need of such a bind, not only among elites, but also between elites and the rest of society (Le Huérou, 2012).

Considering this ideological construction and the bet of the team in power on a common commitment to law and legality, the Soviet legacy must be taken into account. Actually, this may particularly be seen as a generational effect among elites. Almost all of the 24 *polpredy* come not only from the secondary and higher education system but also from the training bodies of the USSR's and CPSU's cadres. Two of them even made all of the "Soviet part" of their career within the CPSU organs. In fact, V. Mativienko started in the komsomols and gradually rose to the top of the Party from 1972 to 1986 when she became Deputy President of a Soviet District Executive Committee in Leningrad. Khamil Ishakov also made a name for himself within the Party by becoming the Head of the City of Kazan. He even stayed in office after the fall of the Soviet Union since he was the mayor of Kazan until 2005.

The 24 *polpredy* were on an average 35 years old when the USSR collapsed. They were then at the middle of their professional careers and already deeply involved in their personal paths. A majority of them have been awarded by Soviet honorary prices and medals that made them "Heroes of the Soviet Union" for instance. Their personal and individual socializations have been deeply influenced by their experience of the communist regime and the main role assigned to legality and the law. The Socialist legality is a legacy of Lenin's "revolutionary legality" and was renamed as soon as Stalin came to power. Its concept was to give to an undemocratic political system a formal democratic frame (Ginsburgs, 1957; Lavigne, 1980). As far as we are concerned, the continual reference to law in today's Russia can be seen as a legacy of this design. Indeed, the Soviet concept of socialist legality helps us to understand both how political culture is significant in unifying political and administrative elites and how it may be identified as a common denominator beyond the opposition of democratic and autocratic.

The militarization theory we highlighted might distract from a more complex — and classical, assuming it follows Max Weber's conception of legal-rational authority — process of legitimation of power in post-Soviet Russia: using law as an instrumental resource. As French sociologist B. Pudal, drawing on various works of historians, wrote about the concept of totalitarianism in the specific case of Soviet Union, we consider the militarization theory to be a "smokescreen-concept" (Pudal, 2009, p. 164). The establishment of the plenipotentiary envoys in 2000 has clearly been regarded as a personification of the movement of "recentralization" of power. The prosopographical review though strongly shades the militarization thesis and allows to escape the "militocratic paradigm" as we understand it. In order to legitimate its policy, the power in place instrumentalizes both the law and the relation to legality in the political and administrative fields. By historicizing the process of reshuffling of the elites in post-Soviet Russia since the end of the 1980s and the Gorbatchevian perestroïka, we can bring up the idea of a reinvestment of the socialist legality by the power in place. According to this concept, we could assume that the group in power bets on sort of an elite ethos grounded on a common commitment to law and considers this bet an efficient political strategy.

REFERENCES

Bacon, E., Cooper, J., & Renz, B. (2007). *Securitising Russia: The domestic politics of Vladimir Putin*. Manchester, NY: Manchester University Press.
Bailey, F.-G. (1969). *Stratagems and spoils: A social anthropology of politics*. Oxford: Basil Blackwell.
Bailey, F. G. (1971). *Les règles du jeu politique: étude anthropologique*. Paris: Presses universitaires de France.
Boltanski, L. (1973). L'espace positionnel: Multiplicité des positions institutionnelles et habitus de classe. *Revue française de sociologie, 14-1*, 3–26.
Bourdieu, P. (1979). Les trois états du capital culturel. *Actes de la recherche en sciences sociales, 30*(novembre) 3–6 (L'institution scolaire).
Bourdieu, P. (1980). *Le sens pratique*. Paris: Éditions de Minuit.
Bunce, V. (2000). Comparative democratization. Big and bounded generalizations. *Comparative Political Studies, 33*(6–7), 703–734.
Carother, T. (2002). The end of the transition paradigm. *Journal of Democracy, 13*(1), 5–21.
Chchegolev, K. A. (2008). *Kto est' kto v Rossii. Ispolnitel'naïa vlast'*. Moscow: Izdatel'stvo Astrel'.
Cohen, A., & Vauchez, A. (2005). Les juristes et l'ordre politique européen. *Critique Internationale, 26*, 97–158.
Collier, D., & Levitsky, S. (1997). Democracy with adjectives: Conceptual innovation in comparative research. *World Politics, 49*(3), 430–451.

Collovald, A. (1988). Identités stratégiques. *Actes de la recherche en sciences sociales, 73*(juin), 29–40 (Penser la politique – 2).

Dahl, R. (1961). *Who governs? Democracy and power in an American city*. New Haven: Yale University Press.

Daucé, F. (2008). *La Russie post-soviétique*. Paris: La Documentation française, coll. Répères.

Diamond, L. J. (2002). Thinking about hybrid regimes. *Journal of Democracy, 13*(2), 21–35.

Dobry, M. (Ed.). (1992 ed. 2009). *Sociologie des crises politiques. La dynamique des mobilisations multisectorielles*. 3e édition revue et augmentée, Paris: Presses de Sciences Po.

Dobry, M. (2000a). Les transitions démocratiques regards sur l'état de la transitologie. Introduction. *Revue Française de Science Politique, 50*(4–5), 579–584.

Dobry, M. (2000b). Les voies incertaines de la transitologie. *Revue Française de Science Politique, 50*(4–5), 585–614.

Elias, N. (1981). *Qu'est-ce que la sociologie*. Paris: Presses Universitaires de France.

Favarel-Garrigues, G., Sapir, J., Rousselet, K., … et al. (2004). *La dictature de la loi*. Paris: Alternatives économiques, coll. L'économie politique.

Gazier, A. (2002). Le bouleversement des institutions et de la vie politique. In D. Colas (Ed.), *L'Europe post-communiste*. Paris: PUF.

Gazier, A. (2008). Le Président de la Fédération de Russie et l'instauration d'une "verticale executive". *Revue d'études comparatives Est-Ouest, 39*(2), 73–92.

Genieys, W. (2011). *Sociologie politique des élites*. Paris: Armand Colin, Collection U Sociologie.

Ginsburgs, G. (1957). Socialist legality' in the USSR. since the XXth party congress. *The American Journal of Comparative Law, 6*(4), 546–559.

Gel'man, V. (2006). Возвращение Левиафана? Политика рецентрализации в современной России. *Полис*, 2006, N2, С.90-109.

Guénard, F. (2007). La promotion de la démocratie: une impasse théorique? *La vie des idées*, 28 novembre.

Highley, J., & Pakulski, J. (2000). Jeux de pouvoir des élites et consolidation de la démocratie en Europe centrale et orientale. *Revue française de science politique, 50*(4), 657–678.

Joana, J. (2006). Le pouvoir des militaires, entre pluralisme limité et démocratie Communication au Congrès de l'AFSP. Retrieved from http://www.afsp.msh-paris.fr/activite/2006/colllinz06/txtlinz/joana1.pdf.

Konkka, O. (2014). La recherche d'un modèle de présentation de l'histoire soviétique dans les années 1990-2000: l'exemple du manuel scolaire Histoire de la Russie XXème – début XXIème siècles d'A. Danilov, L. Kosulina, M. Brand. *La Revue Russe*, (42), 97–106.

Konrad, G., & Szelenyi, I. (1979). *The Intellectuals on the road to class power* (1st ed.). Paris, Seuil: Harcourt Brace Jovanovich.

Kossolov, V. (2007). Vertical administrative: Fondements et obstacles. *Outre-Terre, 2007/2*(19), 149–162.

Kryshtanovskaïa, O., & White, S. (2003). Putin's militocracy. *Post-Soviet Affairs, 19*(4), 289–306.

Lallemand, J.-C. (2010). La mise au pas des pouvoirs régionaux. In K. Rousselet & G. Favarel-Garruigues (Eds.), *La Russie contemporaine* (pp. 129–143). Paris: Fayard.

Laruelle, M. (2010). *Le nouveau nationalisme russe*. Paris: Editions de l'Œuvre.

Lavigne, P. (1980). La légalité socialiste et le développement de la préoccupation juridique en Union Soviétique. *Revue d'études comparatives Est-Ouest, 11*(3), 5–20.

Le Huérou, A. (2010). Un Etat en guerre. La Russie et le conflit russo-tchétchène. In *La Russie contemporaine* (pp. 145–156). Paris: Fayard.
Le Huérou, A. (2012). *Les mouvements de protestation: une nouvelle génération dans la rue. Février*. Online working paper. Retrieved from http://www.ceri-sciences-po.org
Leferme-Falguières, F., & Van Renterghem, V. (2000). Le concept d'élites. Approches historiographiques et méthodologiques. *Hypothèses*, *4*(1), 55–67.
Levitsky, S., & Way, L. (2002). The rise of competitive authoritarianism. *Journal of Democracy*, *13*(2), 51–65.
Linz, J. J. (1985). *Totalitarian and authoritarian regimes*. Boulder, Colorado: Lynne Rienner Publishers.
Linz, J. J., & Stepan, A. (1996). Toward consolidated democracies. *Journal of Democracy*, *7*(2), 14–33.
Mendras, M. (2007). *Russie. L'envers du pouvoir*. Paris: Odile Jacob.
Merlin, A. (2007). Le Nord-Caucase au miroir du fédéralisme russe. In A. Merlin (Ed.), *Où va la Russie*. Bruxelles: Éditions de l'Université de Bruxelles.
Mills, C. (1956). *The power elite*. Oxford: Oxford University Press.
Mink, G., & Szurek, J.-C. (1999). *La grande reconversion. Le destin des communistes en Europe de l'Est*. Paris: Seuil.
Muhin, A. A. (2004). *Federal'naïa i reguional'naïa elita Rossii – Kto est' kto v politike i ekonomike*. Moscow: Izdate'stvo GNOM i D.
Passeron, J.-C. (1990). Biographies, flux, itinéraires, trajectoires. *Revue française de sociologie*, *31*(1), 3–22.
Petrov, N. (2002). Seven faces of Putin's Russia: Federal districts as the new level of state territorial composition. *Security Dialogue*, *33*(1), 73–91.
Petrov, N. (2005). How have the presidential envoys changed the Administrative-political balance of Putin's regime? In P. Reddaway & W. Orttung (Eds.), *The dynamics of Russian politics. Putin's reform of federal-regional relations* (Vol. 2), Lanham, Maryland: Rowman & Littlefield.
Przeworski, A. (1979). *Some problems in the study of the transition to democracy*. Latin American Program, The Wilson Center.
Pudal, B. (2009). Le soviétisme. In A. Cohen, B., Lacroix, & P. Riutort (Eds.), *Nouveau manuel de science politique* (pp. 162–172). Paris: La découverte.
Raviot, J.-R. (2006). Comprendre le nouveau régime russe. *Strates*, *12*.
Raviot, J.-R. (2008). *Démocratie à la russe, pouvoirs et contre-pouvoirs en Russie*. Paris: Ellipses.
Renz, B. (2006). Putin's militocracy? An alternative interpretation of siloviki in contemporary Russian politics. *Europe-Asia studies*, *58*(6), 903–924.
Rivera, D., & Rivera, S. W. (2008). The Militarization of the Russian Elite Under Putin: How wide and how deep? Department Of Government, Hamilton College. Paper presented at the annual meeting of the MPSA Annual National Conference, Palma House Hotel, Hilton, Chicago, Illinois, April 2008.
Sakwa, R. (2008). *Russian politics and society* (4th ed.). London, New York: Routledge.
Schedler, A. (2002). The menu of manipulation. *Journal of Democracy*, *13*(2), 36–50.
Stepan, A. (1971). *The military in politics: Changing patterns in Brazil*. Princeton, NJ: Princeton University Press.
Stepan, A. (1973). *Authoritarian Brazil: Origins, policies, and future*. New Haven, CT: Yale University Press.

Surkov, V. (2007). *Soverennaïa demokratïa. Ot idei k doctrine*. Moscow: Evropa.
Szelenyi, I., Wnuk-Lipinski, E., & Treiman, D. (1995). Circulation or reproduction of elites during post-communist transformation in Russia and Eastern Europe. *Theory and Society*, 24(5), 625–668.
Taylor, B. (2007). *Russia's power ministries: Coercion and commerce*. Monograph of the Institute for National Security and Counterterrorism, Syracuse University.
The Economist. print edition, (2007). Briefing: Russia under Putin, The making of a neo-KGB state. *The Economist*, August 25.
Tilly, C. (1992). *Coercion, capital and European States, A.D. 990 – 1992* (Rev. ed.). Wiley-Blackwell.
Wagner, A.-C. (2007). *Les, classes sociales dans la mondialisation*. La découverte, Collection "repères sociologiques".
Weber, M. (1971). *Économie et Société*. Paris: Plon.
Zalewski, F. (2009). Les transitions démocratiques en Europe centrale et orientale. In A. Cohen, B. Lacroix, & P. Riutort (Eds.), *Nouveau manuel de science politique* (pp. 210–217). Paris: La découverte.

CHANGING POLITICAL FORTUNES: RACE, CLASS, AND "BLACK POWER" IN THE RISE AND FALL OF A BLACK URBAN REGIME IN OAKLAND

Eric S. Brown

ABSTRACT

This paper analyzes the connection between black political protest and mobilization, and the rise and fall of a black urban regime. The case of Oakland is instructive because by the mid-1960s the ideology of "black power" was important in mobilizing two significant elements of the historically disparaged black community: (1) supporters of the Black Panthers and, (2) neighborhood organizations concentrated in West Oakland. Additionally, Oakland like the city of Atlanta also developed a substantial black middle class that was able to mobilize along the lines of its own "racialized" class interests. Collectively, these factors were important elements in molding class-stratified "black power" and coalitional activism into the institutional politics of a black urban regime in Oakland. Ultimately, reversal factors would undermine the black urban regime in Oakland. These included changes in the race and class composition of the local population: black out-migration, the "new immigration," increasing (predominantly white) gentrification, and the continued lack of opportunity for poor and working-class blacks, who served as the unrequited base of the black urban regime. These factors would change the fortunes of black political life in Oakland during the turbulent neoliberal era.

Keywords: Race and class; black power; Black Panthers; political mobilization; urban regime; neighborhood organizations

INTRODUCTION

Most research on African American protests for equality and opportunity has focused on the civil rights movement in the South. However, there has also been (and remains) a conflict for racial equality in the North as well. There has been a slowly growing literature on this under-researched regional topic. The predominant research literature on the subject comprises what might be termed *the Northern black protest tradition* (NBPT) and focuses on both the national and local aspects of the black struggle against racism in the Northern United States. Most of this work has been done by historians, and focuses on an interconnected tradition of black protest that echoes from the South but has a distinct basis in the ghettoes of Northern cities.

The NBPT approach emphasizes the substantial role that black protest has played in the history of the United States, but also sees that protestation as part of the construction of African American collective identity itself. The late Manning Marable has characterized the overlapping streams of Southern and NBPTs in the context of the failure of both the First and Second Reconstructions (Marable, 2007). Other work in the Northern protest tradition focuses on widespread racial discrimination in the institutions of the North such as employment, housing, and public accommodations (Sugrue, 2008, 2014). Other recent research has focused on the tradition of "black power" as such (and its predecessor forms) as a cohesive ideology that shaped postwar black protest (Joseph, 2007, 2009).

The NBPT scholarship has been indispensable in pushing forward evidence and analysis about African American protest against racial inequality in the North. While readily acknowledging the contributions of the

NBPT approach, the argument of this paper seeks to recalibrate the analysis of African American protest in Northern cities. This paper seeks to extend a model of race (and class) analysis that I've termed *racialized class formation* elsewhere (Brown, 2014, pp. 11–17). That is, race like class is an important feature of inequality in the United States. While class is arguably the more "basic" feature of stratification, race (like gender) is intertwined, as in intersectionality theory. Furthermore, the relationship of race to class is not merely ideological or "superstructural." Rather race, like class, also has a *material* effect on institutional patterns of inequality in the stratification system. That is, race is not reducible to class. In this regard, my argument has affinity with that of racial formation theory.

Similarly, as with other structural processes in society, class formation is itself a racialized process. African American class groupings such as the black professional middle class or the black working class (in contrast to their white social class counterparts for example) typically find their life chances delimited by the effects of institutional racism. This includes, for example, employment discrimination (loss of opportunities in hiring and promotion), residential segregation (poorer schools, lower property values, and wealth accumulation), and discriminatory policing (greater likelihood of incarceration for minor transgressions and subjection to police violence).

It should be noted, of course, that patterns of race and class inequality are not static under the dynamic economic and political conditions of the United States. The role of the state is key in its relationship to the institutions of capitalism and private markets that drive the economic life of the United States. Notably, social movements (e.g., labor, women, civil rights) have themselves been key to challenging the institutional patterns of the political economy itself. The earlier conditions of laissez-faire capitalism (and classical liberalism as a corresponding ideology) were challenged and altered by labor movement struggles that pushed changes in social policy during the Great Depression.

During the New Deal (and briefly the Great Society) era (1933–1968) capitalism was "tamed" to some degree by Keynesian policies and the creation of a basic welfare state in the United States. It was in that period in which social movements were strong in terms of pushing the state toward the reforms of the era and benefiting the subaltern groups in whose name the movements were formed (e.g., labor, civil rights, women, etc.). By the early 1970s a "counterrevolution" had solidified and could be associated under the broad rubric of *neoliberalism*. The neoliberal era and its neoclassical ideology is linked to policy developments such as: deregulated markets, declining unionization rates, "free trade," curtailing of civil rights reforms, the devolution of the welfare state, and the rise of increased incarceration, anti-immigrant hostility, and domestic repression directed at poor and minority communities (Harvey, 2005).

This is the backdrop under which the rise and fall of black power can be seen. Blacks moved to Northern cities during the 20th century as the sharecropping economy collapsed in the South and employment demand in Northern industry increased. The Great Migration reshaped black regional demography as well as the hopes and expectations of newly urbanized black communities in Northern cities. Black power as a movement arguably started in the South, but it would be strongest in the North. Southern cities would maintain relatively low rates of industrialization, but Northern cities had already begun deindustrialization after World War II. By the mid-1960s, young blacks were already becoming a "surplus population." The Southern-based civil rights movement didn't speak of their most basic concerns. The forceful nationalistic declarations of Malcolm X, the Black Panthers, and others would draw their political attention instead.

Few scholars have taken black power seriously as a social movement with goals and objectives. The black power era is seen largely in terms of cultural symbols like afros, raised fist salutes, black berets, and the like. However, there were ideologies and praxis — however, ultimately flawed — that were discernible in the black power movement. Much of the research on Northern black protest and black power postulates on that phase of the black liberation struggle at a national or regional level. Alternatively, my paper focuses on developing a detailed case study at the local level. I frame the rise and fall of black power, and on a related but separate track the black urban regime, against the backdrop of changing economic and political conditions in the city of Oakland from the post-World War II era into the early 21st century.

Oakland is, arguably, the best city in which to examine the phenomena of black power protest and politics. Oakland is the birthplace of the Black Panther Party, which produced the most coherent ideology and praxis based on black power. In addition community organizations in West Oakland formed their own version of black power protest and politics. As McAdam notes, social movements represent a "political process" and undergo transformations that, ultimately, can only be understood through a historical lens (McAdam, 1997). The revolutionary ideas of the Panthers, and the practical concerns of black neighborhood protest organizations would ultimately find their way into Oakland electoral politics as repression increased against the radical variants of black power in the emerging neoliberal era. Regarding the concept of racialized class formation, I note that the "base" of the black power movement – the black community – was itself divided by class. This "contradiction" would play a role in the decline of black power, particularly in the conflict over protest versus electoral strategies. The electoral incarnation of "black power" represented by the inchoate black urban regime in Oakland would become the altar on which the flawed struggle for black power would ultimately be laid.

PROBLEM AND METHOD

This paper analyzes the historical connections among black protest, political mobilization, and the rise and fall of a black urban regime in Oakland. The case of Oakland is instructive for several reasons. First, relatively little research on black urban institutional politics has focused on West Coast cities. Second, Oakland is the only large city on the West Coast to nearly achieve a black majority population (between 1970 and 1980). See Table 1. Third, Oakland was the birthplace of the Black Panther Party which laid claim to politically represent working class and "lumpen" segments of the black community, and exemplified the zenith of the black power movement

Table 1. Population by Race in Oakland, 1940–2010.

Race	1940	1950	1960	1970	1980	1990	2000	2010
White	287,936	328,797	270,523	213,512	129,692	120,849	124,921	134,925
Black	8,462	47,562	83,618	124,710	159,281	163,355	141,294	109,471
Latino[a]	NA	NA	19,309	NA	32,492	51,711	87,443	99,068
Asian[b]	NA	NA	NA	NA	26,341	54,931	60,110	65,811
Total[c]	302,165	384,575	367,548	361,561	339,337	372,242	399,477	390,724

Source: U.S. Bureau of the Census. Census of Population. 1940–2010. Characteristics of Population. California. Washington, DC: U.S. Government Printing Office, 1940–2010.
[a]Data for Hispanic or Latino was not collected by the census before 1960. Based on the census category, "white, Spanish surname" for 1960. Data is not available for 1970 census. For 1980 and 1990, Latino can be of "any race."
[b]Data for Asian Americans was generally lumped into the categories of "nonwhite" or "other race" before the 1980 census.
[c]Total Population numbers do not equal the total of the distinct "racial" categories because Latinos are not officially defined by the Census Bureau as a racial group. They may be members of any of the other "racial" groups. Also, the category of "other" race is included in the total population. Additionally, the 2000 and 2010 Censuses allow the public to choose "two or more races" which is also included in the total population.

of the 1960s and 1970s. Fourth, Oakland like the city of Atlanta also developed a relatively large and prominent black middle class (Hazard, 1980) that was able to wrest local electoral power. Collectively, these key factors were important elements in molding neighborhood activism, protest, and mobilization into the institutional politics of an entrenched black urban regime in Oakland in the late 20th century.

The black urban regime provides a research problem that lends itself to *historical* analysis. This involves analyzing connections among race *and* class inequalities, black protest movements, political mobilization, electoral politics, coalitions, and governance at the local level. Doing research on the city of Oakland represents such an opportunity. Accordingly, this paper poses several interrelated questions for consideration. How did the black professional middle class begin to organize as a politically conscious leadership group in the postwar period in Oakland and the East Bay? What were the factors that led to political mobilization of the "black community" in Oakland in the 1960s and 1970s? How did the mobilization of the black community lead to successful African American participation in local electoral politics? What brought about the rise of a black urban regime in Oakland? Why did the black urban regime in Oakland fall?

The main evidence for this paper comes from a combination of primary and secondary sources. Historical-archival research was conducted concerning the development of the black community and politics in postwar Oakland. This historical data provides a window on the changing class dynamics and institutional patterns of black neighborhoods in Oakland since the 1960s, and the relationship to the growth of increasingly effective black local political organizing. The archival research was conducted at multiple institutions affiliated with the University of California at Berkeley and the Oakland Public Library system.[1]

ALL POLITICS ARE LOCAL?: PROBLEMATIZING BLACK COMMUNITIES, LOCAL POLITICS, AND URBAN REGIMES

The "black community" contains residents living in neighborhoods in many localities across the United States. In the post-civil rights era, African Americans still live primarily in residentially segregated neighborhoods (Massey, Rothwell, & Domina, 2009, pp. 74–90). However, these contemporary neighborhoods are increasingly dispersed throughout the metropolis, in contrast to the more centralized ghettoes of the earlier industrial era. Life in varied black neighborhoods is shaped, to one degree or another, by shared grievances regarding *racialized urban problems* such as poverty, unemployment, job discrimination, housing affordability, neighborhood crime, police brutality, hyperincarceration, low-performing schools, inadequate local services, and the like.

"Racialized urban problems" become popularly cast as problems specific to the black community when they are in fact problems shared by, and responsible for by all citizens (although experienced disproportionately by African Americans). This racialized attribution serves to falsely characterize these problems as being "created" in the black community and needing to be "solved" in the black community rather than through public policy. Such problems are concentrated disproportionately among blacks because of historic and contemporary patterns of institutionalized racial inequalities and entrenched residential segregation (Massey & Denton, 1993, pp. 130–162). Middle-class blacks generally tend to live in neighborhoods that are less affluent than those of equivalent middle-class white peers, and that are also likely to be near poor and working-class African American neighborhoods (Pattillo, 2005, pp. 305–329).

Black political activity at both the local and national level is generally focused on efforts to solve racialized urban problems. Local black politics is shaped by the connection between *concrete* (local and neighborhood based) and *symbolic* black communities. Symbolic black communities are socially constructed at a national or diasporic level. African Americans generally conclude – even across class lines – that they have problems that are shaped by common experiences based on race and that these require some degree of black political unity (Dawson, 1994, pp. 45–68). Indeed, the theme of "nationalism" has a long history in African American political discourse. The "black community" (concretely and symbolically) also corresponds well to the concept of an "imagined community" (Anderson, 2006). These frames provide a foundation for the development and maintenance of *black politics*. It is an effort to use political means (protest or electoral) to give voice to common grievances perceived by African Americans.

Racialized urban problems experienced by blacks filter across class, gender, age, sexuality, ethnicity, regional, ideological, and other intersectional lines (Collins, 2005). One issue is that not all African Americans are equally represented by the discourse and activity of black politics (e.g., black women, gays, and the poor), either at the local or national level. However, given the traditional limits of the expression of black political concerns through "mainstream" (and even progressive) organizations and movements, "black politics" remains an effective organizing principle for politically mobilizing African Americans in the United States (Tate, 1994, pp. 1—19).

In turn, "black power" is a historically specific expression of black cultural and political ideology that formed in the 1960s and 1970s. Black power as political praxis is less well understood. As a unilateral approach to political strategy and action, black power has always had significant limitations. *Internally* among African Americans, black power assumes a unity within the "black community" that is difficult, if not impossible to attain. As discussed, blacks in the United States are divided by differences such as: social class, gender, age, sexuality, ethnicity, ideology, place, and other intersectionalities. *Externally* (in relation the larger society), black power is trumped by "white power." White privilege and power is overdetermined and institutionally ubiquitous, and seemingly invisible to whites themselves. Despite the periodic elevation of individually prominent African Americans into key positions of power, influence, or notoriety, white dominance of society is thorough and ongoing. This is the case with the periodic election of black mayors, not to mention the unprecedented election of Barack Obama as U.S. president.

MEN OF TOMORROW: RACIALIZED CLASS CONSCIOUSNESS AND THE BLACK PROFESSIONAL MIDDLE CLASS IN POSTWAR OAKLAND

By the postwar period, and in the shadow of the Great Migration, a "traditional" black professional middle class had entrenched itself within the expanding and increasingly segregated black neighborhoods of Oakland. The *traditional black middle class* provided professional services to a segregated black clientele. This included black teachers in segregated schools, black clergy, attorneys, physicians, and other professionals primarily serving the black community. Many of these traditional professionals would have opportunities to become part of the *mainstream* segment of the black professional middle class when opportunity structures were opened by the efforts of the civil rights movement and subsequent civil rights legislation (Brown, 2014, pp. 54—66). In Oakland and the East Bay, black professionals were able to effectively organize and network among themselves through civic, professional, and political associations in the postwar period.

The blending of personal, professional, and political concerns within the black middle class was a common feature of black-middle-class life even before the Great Migration era (Sugrue, 2014, pp. 181−207; Taylor, 1991, pp. 587−600). Informal organizing by middle-class black professionals both in their own *racialized class interests*[2] and those of *the black community as a whole* has been a prevalent strategy in the postwar period. An important example of this was the Oakland-based *Men of Tomorrow*. It was an organization that first emerged in embryonic form in 1954. As the traditional black professional middle class grew and the prospects of local black political influence also grew, so did the Men of Tomorrow. Arguably, the organization − including many southern migrants − illustrated DuBois's progressively elitist concept of black community leadership by the "better class."[3]

The decidedly patriarchal Men of Tomorrow limited its membership to "adult male persons of good character and of good community and/or professional, business or occupational repute" (Men of Tomorrow, 1959, p. 1). This meant that the organization was made up of a small local black male-middle-class social network of professionals and small-business owners who were "civic-minded." The objectives of the Men of Tomorrow were rather broad involving the betterment of the community:

> This organization shall have as its objectives the development, by precept and example, of a more intelligent, aggressive and serviceable citizenry; to encourage and foster the recognition of the worthiness of all useful occupations and the dignifying by each member of his occupation as an opportunity to serve society through fellowship (Idem).

The Men of Tomorrow was a nonpartisan civic organization that officially took no stand on political matters or candidates as such (*ibid*: 2). However, the organization was an important unofficial base for the rising black politicians and other would-be brokers of black political power of the day. Several members found on the 1961 Directory of Members would come to play significant roles in the political life of the local black neighborhoods, the city of Oakland, the East Bay, and in the state of California. These include important political players such as: Lionel Wilson (future Oakland mayor), Joshua Rose (future Oakland city council member), and Berkeley City Council member Wilmont Sweeney (Men of Tomorrow, 1961, pp. 1−5). Allen Broussard had a distinguished legal career and eventually served on the California Supreme Court (Broussard, 1997, pp. 96−97). Men of Tomorrow and the social and political networks that the organization provided, were helpful in generating the notable accomplishments of these local black "firsts."

Another important black-middle-class political actor in Oakland was Evilio Grillo. He was born in Florida, of black Cuban descent. Grillo was a professional social worker; he was more directly involved in community activism than Gibson but also an important behind-the-scenes political actor in the East Bay. He was central to the complex linking of segments of black political and institutional actors with community organizations, the NAACP, Democratic Party regulars, private foundations, coalition with Latino activists, and local, state and federal government bureaucrats (Grillo, 2000, pp. 131–133). Norvel Smith was another key member Men of Tomorrow. He was involved in bridging black access to local public institutions (i.e., Oakland public schools, Merritt College, and the University of California) and behind-the-scenes political work (Smith, 2004, pp. 38–44).

Whereas the Men of Tomorrow can be considered a key civic and nonpartisan organization for the black professional middle class in the postwar period, the East Bay Democratic Club was its political and partisan counterpart. It was an important venue for liberal mainstream-oriented *political mobilization* of the emergent black electorate in the postwar period in Oakland and other Northern California cities (Browning, Marshall, & Tabb, 1984, pp. 75–120). These organizations would help to provide blacks in Oakland with opportunities to elect local black officials beginning in the postwar period. Most of the early key actors in the emergence of black political expression were elected and appointed executives, legislators, and judges and behind-the-scenes operators who networked through these two key black middle class organizations in the East Bay.

D. G. Gibson was a profoundly important black political power broker in the East Bay. He was the man behind Byron Rumford's successful 1948 election to the California State Assembly. The election of Rumford (a pharmacist) to the California State Assembly represented the first notable infringement of mainstream political institutions by the black professional middle class in Oakland. Gibson was also a key founder of the East Bay Democratic Club, which launched many prominent local black political careers and would have noticeable influence within the mainstream Democratic Party organization in California (Rumford, 1978, pp. 8–15).

The challenges for these early black politicos were formidable. In the postwar era, political power in Oakland was consolidated around the conservative statewide California "Knowland machine." Joseph Knowland, a Republican, was the wealthy and powerful owner of the *Oakland Tribune* and booster for downtown financial and commercial business interests. Knowland's influence came to be widely felt in the state of California and in Alameda County, even before he consolidated his influence in Oakland proper. By the 1930s the Knowland machine had used its influence to initiate city charter reform and change Oakland's governing system from the graft-ridden commission system to a late Progressive Era style council-manager system. The Knowland machine, with its white nativist middle-class base, was in conflict with emergent postwar liberal and progressive political forces (e.g., organized labor, civil rights activists, and student protesters) in the state and in the city of Oakland over several decades (Montgomery, Johnson, & Manolis, 1998, pp. 96−172).

POLITICAL MOBILIZATION I: WAR ON POVERTY AND "CLASS CONFLICT" IN THE BLACK COMMUNITY

In the South, blacks mobilized under the rubric of the civil rights movement (Morris, 1986). In northern cities, blacks also organized against segregation, discrimination, and racial inequality. In the North, charismatic leaders like Malcolm X, and groups like the Black Panthers had goals of creating a larger and more cohesive movement based on "black power"[4] but this did not come to full fruition. Without an overarching shared condition such as Jim Crow, it was difficult to mobilize blacks along singular lines of collective racial interest. Northern black protest was largely splintered along local, neighborhood, class, and sectarian lines (Allen, 1970, pp. 246−273). Although black-power ideology and praxis had national and even international (i.e., pan-African) dimensions, most organized efforts based on black protest in northern cities became centered at the local and neighborhood levels. By the late 1960s the civil rights movement proper had dissipated and given way to the more salient, but fleeting, expressions of "black power" and "community activism" throughout the United States (Joseph, 2009, pp. 751−776; Marable, 2007, pp. 84−145; Sugrue, 2008, pp. 356−448).

This was the dynamic of consistently rearticulated "black power" that shaped political activism in Oakland during the 1960s and 1970s. West Oakland formed the traditional heart of the black community and the center of efforts of poor and working-class blacks to collectively mobilize on their own behalf in the city. These organizing efforts varied in form and substance, but one key struggle centered on the local execution of federal Great Society programs during the 1960s. Activists organizing on behalf of poor and working-class blacks in West Oakland came into conflict with various social forces, including federal policymakers, white political leadership in Oakland, downtown business interests, and in some contexts the black professional middle class. These different groups sought to capture and administer the federal programs for their own varied political purposes (Pressman, 1975, pp. 58–83).

In the late 1960s and 1970s, the *Oakland Project*, carried out by political scientists at the University of California at Berkeley, produced a series of scholarly publications that considered the structuration, actors, and efficacies of the Great Society programs that were implemented in Oakland. These included Ford Foundation grants, Office of Economic Opportunity (OEO) policies, and Model Cities programs. The research of the Oakland Project also raised critical insights into the kinds of local political participation that were encouraged by those federal policies (Levy, Meltsner, & Wildavsky, 1974; Pressman, 1975; Pressman & Wildavsky, 1973). On the other hand, many other analysts of the period were highly critical of the participatory aspects of the Great Society and raised tropes about the "culture" of the poor, suggesting that too much power was being given to the poor through the antipoverty programs.

Nevertheless, community action was a significant dimension of the OEO programs that expanded the possibilities for increasing black participation and representation in the political life of Oakland. This was the "maximum feasible participation" called for by the Johnson administration, and it was in effect in Oakland's flatland neighborhoods – particularly West Oakland. The Oakland Economic Development Council (OEDC) was the local organization created and sanctioned by Mayor John Houlihan to operate as the city's official Community Action Agency (CAA) 1965.

The emergence of black community activism in West Oakland during the 1960s sprouted independently of federal policies in Washington, but was also subsequently abetted by them. As Judith May points out, much of the political contention over Great Society policies in Oakland concerned how they would be implemented. Would they be glossed in conventional Keynesian form to promote economic "growth" (i.e., boost demand in ways that generally benefited dominant business interests)? Or rather, could the programs actually be implemented in the community to promote genuine economic "redistribution," to the black urban poor in particular (May, 1970, pp. 5–7). That is, would Model Cities funds be primarily used to expand the capacities of the Port of Oakland, Bay Area Rapid Transit (BART), the Oakland Airport, and the City Center project, or would such resources be used primarily to help produce jobs, affordable housing, and neighborhood development for poor and working-class residents within the flatland neighborhoods? This was the fundamental political question for black activists and struggling residents in black neighborhoods in West Oakland, and other parts of the city.

For the most part, downtown and black neighborhood interests seemed fundamentally incompatible. In this political conflict, prominent professional middle-class blacks were collectively well positioned to play a significant role on the OEDC board. The board would oversee the implementation of the OEO and Model Cities programs in Oakland. Many members of the black professional middle class were situated within key institutions and sites such as professional practices that served the black community, civic organizations (e.g., the NAACP), black churches, and city government positions. These politically networked middle-class black leaders were able to designate themselves as responsible mediators between the black community (i.e., working-class and poor African Americans in the flatlands) and the forces of white public and private power that ruled the city (May, 1973, pp. 311–318).

The black professional middle class in Oakland was relatively small and marginal to mainstream institutions. Thus any effort at creating an independent political base involved their being linked to the numerical strength of the larger black community. From the point of view of powerful white business and political interests, dealing with middle-class black leadership was decidedly preferable. This was far less politically threatening to white elites than accommodating representatives of the black working class and poor, who wanted their fair share of power in the city. Mayor Houlihan appointed several black professional middle-class members to the OEDC from the circles of the East Bay Democratic Club, the Men of Tomorrow, and the local NAACP branch. Appointees included future mayor Lionel Wilson as OEDC chairman, Norvel Smith, Clinton White, and Oakland NAACP President Don McCullum (Idem).

Mayor Houlihan resigned suddenly in April of 1966.[5] Lionel Wilson was able to wrest real control of the OEDC from John Reading, Houlihan's replacement as mayor (Wilson, 1992, pp. 46–49). By this point Wilson was professionally successful and moving into mainstream social and political circles traditionally closed to blacks. He was the first black Alameda County Superior Court judge, and the first black on the Oakland Museum Board. Wilson was, however, challenged by some black representatives from the Neighborhood Advisory Committees (NAC). The NACs were designed to provide political input from the people in the West Oakland neighborhoods. NAC activists highlighted class distinctions with Wilson and other middle-class blacks that were to represent them concerning problems of unemployment, poverty, and community development in West Oakland. Wilson made the point to the activists of his own poor working-class origins in West Oakland. The OEDC did eventually accede to the demands of community organizers to allow a 51 percent representation on the council from the neighborhood committees (Self, 2003, p. 235). These events helped to produce a volatile "intraracial" cross-class alliance between middle-class black representatives on the OEDC and black-working-class representatives of the West Oakland neighborhoods. It was an expedient black political alliance that would soon find itself ideologically torn, but in mutual conflict with the white establishment.

One key battleground over the political direction of Great Society programs in Oakland was the Model Cities program. Model Cities was specifically concerned with promoting community control over local economic and neighborhood development projects. Many African Americans complained that downtown interests preferred "urban renewal" projects that were more likely to displace neighborhood residents than to genuinely serve their interests. Model Cities was funded through the recently created (1965) Department of Housing and Urban Development. Grants were focused at the neighborhood level for the promotion of local jobs, small-business programs, and local social services designed to benefit poorer residents. The organization formed to provide representation for the residents of West Oakland was the West Oakland Planning Committee (WOPC). Model Cities was supposed to exemplify the concept of "maximum feasible participation" by promoting the idea of local redevelopment with local control.[6]

Mayor Reading and the business interests he represented voiced strong opposition to the idea of black neighborhood control of OEDC. Reading and his political fellow travelers were also hostile to OEDC efforts to redefine the objectives of promoting more job opportunities for the poor through conventional growth objectives. The irresolvable conflict between the goals of the black community, as defined by the OEDC, and the political status quo as represented by the mayor and key business interests led the OEDC to declare itself an independent nonprofit organization renamed the Oakland Economic Development Council Incorporated (OEDCI) in 1967. This at least gave them nominal independence from the power of the mayor and the city council. The new executive director of the OECDI was Percy Moore, a native of West Oakland and a key mover in the effort to actualize true community control of the Model Cities program by sidestepping the mayor and city council. Moore would become a polarizing figure who was ultimately at odds with mayor Reading, the Office of Economic Opportunity in Washington, and liberal middle-class blacks on the OEDCI board, including Lionel Wilson, the chairman who had appointed him (Hayes, 1972, pp. 151–161; Pressman & Wildavsky, 1973, pp. 51–53).

Moore's tenure as executive director of OEDCI highlighted the ideological split between a black-middle-class liberal agenda (represented by people like Lionel Wilson and former OEDC executive director Norvel Smith) and that of younger, neighborhood-based activists like Moore and those in the WOPC. Moore attempted to put the idea of black power into actual practice through both community-based activism *and* electoral politics. In doing so, he sought to completely sidestep the city administration of mayor Reading and the city council. Moore realized both entities were hostile to efforts to promote the redistribution of resources to black neighborhoods in Oakland. Moore and his allies had an audacious employment redistribution plan. They sought to take away public and private sector jobs in the city of Oakland from white suburbanites (who held most of the jobs in the city of Oakland) and literally reallocate those jobs to unemployed Oakland residents. This was to be accomplished by means of locally controlled "central labor committees" (Self, 2003, pp. 238–239).

After the Nixon administration took office in 1969, the War on Poverty was scaled back in Washington. Indeed, Republicans held the executive offices of the U.S. president, governor of California, and mayor of Oakland. All three of these government leaders were hostile to "black power" (especially but not exclusively in the form of the Black Panthers) and the disruptions caused by the community action programs. The withering rhetorical and fiscal attack on the OEDCI reached its culmination in 1971. Moore announced that he planned to use OEDCI funds to directly support a campaign for city council seat by political ally Stephen Brooks, the OEDCI community services director. This move was an explicit violation of federal campaign spending laws. OEDCI refused to reconsider its decision. That was all that was needed for Governor Ronald Reagan and the OEO in Washington to finally pull the plug on federal grant funding of OEDCI, which subsequently ceased to exist as Oakland's community action agency (Pressman, 1975, pp. 77–83; Rhomberg, 2004, pp. 166–167).

These events effectively ended the role of the community action programs in black protest politics in Oakland. The feat of linking preexisting black community protest politics in Oakland to the federal community action programs gave these activist efforts unexpected resources. On the other hand, it tightly bound black community activists to the federal programs, which were clearly not designed in Washington to be the vehicles of radical change desired by activists in Oakland. Regardless, the termination of OEDCI was a significant setback for black power activists in West Oakland and elsewhere in the city.

This further highlighted the difficult balancing act between *protest* politics and "legitimate" *electoral* politics. Another area of tension for this version of black power politics was the search for putative black unity, which was stymied by class, ideological, and sectarian differences in the black community. Much of the political vanguard of the black professional middle class, which was making headway into mainstream politics, was at odds with the kind of community action-based black power politics in the service of working-class and poorer blacks. Nevertheless, there was another, even more radical track of black power politics that was also driving efforts at social change in Oakland in the 1960s and 1970s: the Black Panthers.

POLITICAL MOBILIZATION II: THE BLACK PANTHER PARTY FOR SELF-DEFENSE AND THE RISE OF BLACK ELECTORAL POLITICS IN OAKLAND

The Black Panther Party for Self Defense was born in West Oakland in 1966. It was cofounded by Huey P. Newton and Bobby Seale. The two of them personally epitomized what might be termed the "expressive black political anger" of that era. Black Panther Party (BPP) efforts to mobilize blacks in Oakland were highly contentious. Black Panther politics combined an ideology of black nationalism (derived from the Student Nonviolent Coordinating Committee and Malcolm X), Maoist ideas of revolutionary socialism, and claims to the legitimacy of armed black community self-defense (championed by those like Robert F. Williams). This combination of ideas created an incendiary framework of praxis that would alarm the local and national political establishments, and most whites in general (Seale, 1968, pp. 59–112). The Black Panthers would be sensationalized in the media for several ignominious reasons. These included: the misogyny of men in the party, criminality, the cult of personality surrounding Newton, and the legacy of Panther violence visited upon the police, political foes, and amongst the Panthers themselves (Brown, 1994; Hilliard & Cole, 1993; Pearson, 1994).

The Black Panthers famously issued their ten-point program, which enumerated a political agenda for the black liberation struggle

(Newton, 1972, pp. 3–6). More generally, the Panthers sought to mobilize and speak for the working class and "lumpen" elements of the black community.[7] They were known for providing a breakfast program for children, community health clinics, day-care services, school lunches, shoes, and clothes for the poor. They were also known for standing up to police violence and abuse by patrolling the police presence in black neighborhoods – an idea that strongly resonated with young black males in Oakland's flatland neighborhoods. Working-class and lumpen blacks have generally been seen in everyday (and political) terms as "threatening" by white business and political elites, and the white public at large. Alternatively, working-class blacks were seen as the key base of political support for the professional middle-class leaders of the black community. This would become one of the key problems of the emergent middle class led black urban regimes: having to mobilize electoral support from poor and working-class blacks without ceding too much of the policy agenda to their interests.

Of course the federal government responded to the Black Panthers with its counterintelligence program (COINTELPRO) in order to combat the organization as a designated "threat to national security." As has been documented, COINTELPRO involved espionage, planting evidence, utilizing informants and agents provocateurs, false convictions, targeting subjects for assassination, and other extralegal methods to destabilize the BPP and other radical organizations in the 1960s and 1970s. These efforts were frequently coordinated with state and local officials and police agencies (Austin, 2006, pp. 189–248). The Black Panthers also had numerous run-ins with the Oakland Police Department (OPD), including the infamous shootout in which seventeen-year-old Bobby Hutton was killed (Oakland Tribune Staff, 1968).

One important result of COINTELPRO and local police confrontations was that it fostered internecine sectarian conflict within the Black Panther Party. It also led to conflict between the Panthers and other black organizations, such as US, led by Ron Karenga. For example, as the Oakland-based Black Panthers organized chapters in other cities, conflicts between Panther branches in different cities – particularly Oakland and Los Angeles – became prevalent. These "party splits" were promoted and readily exploited by the FBI to undermine the political viability of the Panthers (Brown, 1994, pp. 208–225; Hilliard & Cole, 1993, pp. 295–332). As the "revolution" unraveled, it helped to push the Black Panthers and other black power activists in cities around the United States toward a path of less resistance – that is, toward electoral politics (Tate, 1994, pp. 151–163).

Given the internal political turmoil in which the Panthers were embroiled and Newton's increasing problems with drug usage, violent behavior, and criminal indictments, by 1972 much of the day-to-day leadership of the Panthers had passed to Seale as party chairman and the information minister Elaine Brown (Pearson, 1994, pp. 251–292). However, Newton remained the dominant figure and unquestioned de facto leader of the BPP as minister of defense. The Panthers decided to wage campaigns for elected office in Oakland in 1973. The party decided to capitalize on the personal notoriety of Seale and Brown. They became candidates for Oakland mayor and city council, respectively. The BPP would put extensive party funds into these two campaigns (Brown, 1994, pp. 320–327).

These populist campaigns for office garnered significant support in the black community and among other progressives in the East Bay. They endorsed a "people's plan" that emphasized the needs of the neighborhoods over the interests of "downtown" and the growing economic importance of the Port of Oakland. They called for increased taxes on businesses to facilitate the redevelopment of poorer neighborhoods and expand needed public services. Seale, Brown, and the Panther rank and file produced an impressive neighborhood-level organizing effort in the poor black flatland neighborhoods of East, West, and North Oakland to register voters. In fact, these registration efforts would greatly exceed the efforts of the Wilson campaign four years later. Seale managed to get into a runoff with Reading. However, Reading prevailed and won another term as mayor. Seale received 36 percent of the vote, which was far more than most expected for a candidate from the Black Panther Party. Elaine Brown (who would replace the expelled Seale as BPP chairman in 1974) came close to beating black incumbent council member Joshua Rose of West Oakland for a seat on the city council (Brown, 1994, pp. 324–327; Montgomery, 1973).

The Panthers were able to claim a degree of symbolic success when they veered down the path of electoral "reformism." The 1973 campaign of Bobby Seale for mayor of Oakland fell well short in terms of electoral tally but proved a challenge to the political establishment in Oakland. White business and political elites were made nervous at the prospect of looming black electoral dominance in the city. On the other hand, the Black Panther's lumpen and working class-oriented effort to capture Oakland's city hall was also a further challenge to the claims of black professional middle class leadership of the local black community.

Important questions prevailed in the 1970s for black power as praxis. How would it be expressed both in social movement form and in electoral politics? How would black power relate to predominantly white mainstream economic and political institutions? Would it be possible to actually unite the black community and its various social intersections? This included uniting divisions between a more established black professional middle class with proper credentials, social capital and networks, and increasing access to mainstream institutions with the interests and unmet needs of the larger and less privileged African American populace.

The ominous fate of the OEDCI demonstrated the limits of independent black power operating within the regular political institutions – in this case, the city of Oakland's community action agency. Moore and his WOPC activist allies were able to "capture" a mainstream political institution and sought to mobilize it – with public funding – primarily for the benefit of traditionally neglected black neighborhood residents of Oakland. This was an audacious political effort at *reformist black power*, which quickly roused the virulent opposition of elite power brokers. Ultimately, institutions of executive authority at the federal, state, and local levels worked together to expel this expression of independent black power from the formal institutions of the body politic. Furthermore, the COINTELPRO inspired decimation of the Black Panther Party would illustrate the far harsher and violent rejection by the state of *revolutionary black power*. These two intermingled black power struggles both sought to promote the interests of poor and working-class blacks in particular. They met with qualitatively different, but substantively similar fates: thorough political defeat and admonishment by the political establishment.

These events presented timely lessons for the relatively well-placed members of the black professional middle class about how "black power" could be appropriately constituted, and how far it could push the boundaries of acceptable political discourse and practice. A more watered down and less politically threatening version of black power that would be considered acceptable from the perspective of the establishment, would come in the form of the black urban regime. That is, as long as the regime accepted the hegemony of private capital, did not seriously challenge the prerogatives of the "mainstream politics," or the fetishism of the "two party" system. Thus, the "legitimate" expression of black power would work within mainstream institutions without attempting to significantly challenge or reform them. Finally, it was the black professional middle class that would exercise leadership in this reconstructed political venture in "black power."

LIONEL WILSON AND THE RISE OF THE BLACK URBAN REGIME IN OAKLAND

Lionel Wilson was typical of many black Oakland citizens of his generation in that he was a product of the Great Migration, having come to Oakland from New Orleans as a child. He was raised in the black community in West Oakland and graduated from McClymonds High School. He was atypical because he became a very successful black attorney in the pre-civil rights era. He earned his law degree from the Hastings School of Law at the University of California campus in San Francisco. His appointment to the Alameda County Municipal Court in 1960, and later the county Superior Court in 1965, groomed him for future electoral office (Wilson, 1992, pp. 20–40). Wilson's work with the OECD was both frustrating and instructive. His agenda did not prevail, but it provided him with more extensive connections in the black community, including links with both neighborhood activists and the Black Panthers.

The failed 1973 Bobby Seale campaign functioned to organize the Oakland black electoral base in a rehearsal for Wilson's 1977 mayoral campaign. As in other cities, a black mayoral campaign was compelled to reach out to the broader urban citizenry, conventional party politics, and always to the interests of business. Varied and conflicting constituencies backed Wilson's successful initial run for mayor of Oakland. These included the Black Panthers, other black community activists, organized labor, white progressives, and the regular Democratic Party organization. All of these groups were united in forming a winning Democratic coalition to defeat the remnants of Republican Party power in Oakland. Wilson's successful campaign was designed to be "mainstream," and to pull together a broader coalition than that found in Bobby Seale's 1973 campaign.

On May 17, 1977, Lionel Wilson defeated Dave Tucker, the Republican candidate, and became the first black mayor of Oakland. Despite his groundbreaking victory, Wilson's staid mainstream-oriented campaign was less inspiring to those flatlanders seeking a more progressive candidate. Voter turnout for the 1977 mayoral election was down significantly compared to 1973, as the stakes were far different. Both the more progressive and more conservative voters appear to have stayed away in significant numbers from the polls for Wilson's triumph. His campaign was not particularly inspired and he was the epitome of the politically pragmatic black moderate. As Rod Bush puts it:

> However, neither was Wilson a particularly exciting candidate, nor one who could mobilize the black community. Thus turnout in the primary was only 46%, and in the runoff only 52%. Wilson drew 42,640 votes to Tucker's 36,925; both candidates received fewer votes in actual numbers than Bobby Seale in the 1973 runoff. Wilson of course drew upon Seale's strength, doing best in North Oakland, West Oakland, and East Oakland, the areas where the Panther campaign had been strongest. There was further consolidation of the working-class vote behind Wilson: in some working class precincts he pulled 97% of the votes cast. At the same time, there was an astounding drop in the conservative vote, from 77,000 votes for Reading to 33,000 for Tucker. (Bush, 1984, p. 326)

Despite low turnout, Wilson still had political coattails. White flight and growth of a postwar progressive left helped to push politics in Oakland and the East Bay further away from the past heyday of Republican rule. In 1979 a small progressive grouping emerged from East Bay elections. Wilson Riles Jr. from East Oakland became another black member of the Oakland City Council under the progressive banner. Tom Bates, a white progressive, was elected to the State Assembly from Berkeley. John George was elected as the first African American member of the Alameda County Board of Supervisors. In addition, Ron Dellums was re-elected to Congress. This small coterie of progressives would sometimes support, and sometimes oppose Wilson's agenda from the left (McGrath, 1987).

The large black electoral plurality in Oakland was paying political dividends for Wilson and the emergent black urban regime. Wilson made dramatic changes in terms of minority appointments to key offices in his administration. He appointed Henry Gardner as the first black Oakland city manager, and his old friend Norvel Smith as the second black member of the Oakland Port Commission (Wilson's legal mentor Tom Berkeley was appointed by Mayor Reading). Smith would eventually serve as president of the commission. Wilson appointed far more minorities and women to leadership positions in city departments and on commissions in the city than any of his predecessors. Outside of city hall during Wilson's administration, Oakland also saw the arrival of other accomplished black professional and administrative "firsts." In 1979 Robert Maynard became the first black editor of the *Oakland Tribune* and Calvin E. Simmons was hired as the first black conductor of the Oakland Symphony (Browning et al., 1984, pp. 66–67; Hazard, 1980).

Aside from his black political appointees, Wilson was able to incorporate several key elements of the black professional middle class into his regime. These included other black politicians, black pastors (and their vote laden congregations), black-middle-class political organizations (e.g., the East Bay Democratic Club), middle-class blacks seeking employment by the city or in the private sector, and black business interests looking for access to government contracts. Efforts were also made to expand black representation among prized blue-collar jobs in the police and fire departments. These objectives were pursued in part through "minority equity," which was adopted as the theme of the Wilson Administration's affirmative action policy (Slater, 1998a, 1998b, 1998c, p. 16). However, for most job-seeking working class Oakland citizens (blacks and others), Wilson pushed private sector investment and business development as an employment strategy. The days of mayors and their "political machines" providing a slew of working-class government jobs with the city for ethnic constituents were long gone.

Voters re-elected Wilson in 1981, as he solidified his local power base. In 1980, the city of Oakland, with Wilson's support, adopted district elections for the city council to replace "at large" elections (City of Oakland Code of Ordinances, 2008). This introduced a more representative basis for council membership and increased the likelihood of electing blacks to the city council. Indeed, by 1983 there was a black majority on the Oakland City Council. Wilson had already formed effective working majorities on the council to pursue his agenda before the black majority was reached. Rather, some black council members helped to raise cumbersome "neighborhood" issues that took a decided back seat in Wilson's agenda. This allowed some political activists to give voice to concerns about neighborhood neglect by the Wilson administration.

In fact, Wilson was fully on board with the priority of wooing business interests and melding the agendas of the public and private sectors through the urban regime. On the day after his first election, Wilson had stated as much to the *Oakland Tribune*:

> My administration is not and will not be anti-business and I don't interpret my election as a repudiation of business. I never at any time during my campaign took that kind of position. I've said all along that I felt that I have a history of being able to work with those people. I expect to have strong support and cooperation from the business community. (Martin, 1977)

Whereas some traditional Republican business elements were initially cool toward him, in his pursuit of the mayor's office Wilson did have financial campaign support from key corporate interests, including Pacific Gas and Electric (PG&E) and Oakland-headquartered Clorox Corporation (Bush, 1984, p. 35). Such major corporate support demonstrated that Wilson was sufficiently probusiness, and certainly not captured by his black-working-class electoral base. Wilson also relied on campaign funds from developers and realtors, who provide the traditional campaign war chests for local politicians (McGrath, 1987, pp. 10–11).

Despite whatever hopes neighborhood activists and other left-leaning Wilson supporters may have held about a more daring and progressive political agenda, Wilson gave priority to the interests of business for the same reason that previous mayoral regimes did: the vast majority of economic resources are in the private sector (Stone, 1989). Thus Lionel Wilson's ability to solidify his black electoral base – even with relatively low election turnout – and to keep important business interests happy was key to the viability of the black urban regime in Oakland. He was able to craft winning majorities in council votes, often without the full support of black council members. His agenda was generally acceptable to Republican council holdovers Dick Spees and Frank Ogawa – particularly when issues of downtown development were at stake (McGrath, 1987, pp. 11–12).

The issue of conflicting interests between "downtown" and "the neighborhoods" remained prevalent throughout Wilson's three terms in office. Many Wilson supporters felt that a black mayor should be properly (if not primarily) focused on the problems of poor and working-class black neighborhoods in the West Oakland and East Oakland flatlands. By the time Wilson decided to seek his third term as mayor in 1985, he faced a challenge by former protégé Wilson Riles Jr. from the left. Riles was a progressive maverick on the Oakland city council with loose ties to the left-leaning Dellums-Bates-George "machine" in the East Bay. Riles failed to gain support from Dellums (who stayed formally neutral) or the Oakland electorate as a whole as he lost the election. Riles had tried to organize his own base of black flatlanders and white progressives through the Oakland Progressive Political Alliance (OPPA), but he was up against an entrenched and well-funded incumbent mayor who had a fourfold advantage in campaign funding (Smith, 1985). Wilson had become the "establishment" mayor, backed by business and competing against the progressive, neighborhood-oriented Riles. In the 1987 council elections, Riles and OPPA backed three progressive candidates, and all three lost. They were unable to compete with the financial resources and long political reach of the entrenched Wilson regime (Herron, 1987).

Wilson's third mayoral victory indicated that his regime had intensified the process of black political *incorporation* (Browning, Marshall, & Tabb, 2003, pp. 17–48) that was established in his second term. The black urban regime in Oakland was solidified around its select black professional middle-class inner circle, black working class electoral base, multiethnic liberal voters, and hegemonic business interests. By the mid-1980s the question of development became *the* agenda for the city. Developers, banks, realtors, investors, major corporations, and smaller commercial businesses were all behind the downtown redevelopment agenda. Middle-class black professionals were in search of access to mainstream mobility opportunities on either side of the regime's bridged public and private sectors. Working-class blacks were in search of jobs in general. This was the typical private sector-led urban development approach based on the assumption that cities are primarily designed to be "growth machines" (Logan & Molotch, 2007, pp. 50–98).

Oakland — like many cities in the United States — was attempting to make the transition from a declining manufacturing center to a viable postindustrial city. Oakland was once considered the "Detroit of the West," with railroads, steel foundries, auto plants, shipyards, warehouses, and other industrial activities at the center of its economic life (Bagwell, 1982, pp. 196–197). Deindustrialization had taken its toll on Oakland and left many of its citizens, particularly the black poor, in search of jobs (Lemke-Santangelo, n.d., pp. 1–36). The ability of the postindustrial economy to meet the employment needs of large, economically dispossessed populations was problematic. On the one hand, the rise of the postindustrial economy has generally produced many well-paying professional, technical, and managerial jobs (Noyelle, 1987). On the other, it also produces working class jobs in retail and other consumer services that tend to generate minimum or low-wage incomes (Appelbaum, Bernhardt, & Murnane, 2006; Kalleberg, 2013). Nevertheless, postindustrialism has become the uneven centerpiece of contemporary economic activity. In Oakland, these effects were quite visible in the dynamics of downtown (re)development.

These redevelopment goals originated and evolved through a series of city plans that went back to the 1950s and cemented cooperation among important business interests, city planners, and outside academic advisors. In rejecting a 1949 report focused on West Oakland by the Oakland City Planning Department, top executives from major firms in the Bay Area formed an organization called Oakland Citizen's Committee for Urban Renewal (OCCUR) in 1954. This informal group played a key role in planning for a series of urban renewal projects in the city of Oakland (Hayes, 1972, pp. 110–115; Oakland Redevelopment Agency, 1966).

The bulk of redevelopment planning focused on either downtown or West Oakland. Preceding much of the early redevelopment was the "creative destruction" of old buildings and neighborhoods. Initial redevelopment attention in the 1950s and early 1960s went into federally sponsored "urban renewal" of West Oakland. Congress passed the housing acts of 1949 and 1954, which underwrote urban renewal projects designed to remedy "blight" in cities across the country (Gelfand, 1975). Generally speaking, the poor black neighborhoods of West Oakland were seen as logical starting points for the infrastructural, commercial, and residential redevelopment of the city as a whole (Hayes, 1972, pp. 75–127; Rhomberg, 2004, pp. 124–137).

A major downtown development project that was seen as anathema by local progressives was the City Center project. Neighborhood activists involved in the OECDI board and the WOPC were highly critical of the City Center project, and other redevelopment projects in downtown and West Oakland deemed to benefit business interests over those of neighborhood residents. Bobby Seale and Elaine Brown were also critical of the project in their electoral campaigns in 1973. The City Center project existed in different incarnations since 1967, when the city council provided a transfer of $3 million in federal funds from another redevelopment plan; the West Oakland-Downtown "Corridor" project. The Corridor project – also pushed by downtown business interests – was originally a large and ambitious urban renewal plan that dated back to the 1950s to raze and redevelop a large swath of "blighted" residential blocks where West Oakland bordered downtown (Rhomberg, 2004, p. 156).

In 1969 an early version of the City Center project envisioned the transformation of 25 blocks of downtown space. Initial development of the City Center plan included a first low-rise office building in 1973. The modernist Clorox Building office tower was later opened in 1976 as the company's corporate headquarters. After that, other aspects of the development plan were stalled for several years, including a planned commercial mall area. Setbacks in development and withdrawal of potential tenants at the City Center site occurred despite the infusion of more than $300 million from a combination of federal funds, municipal bonds, and private investment (Bush, 1984, p. 327).

By the time Wilson was in his third term as mayor, the City Center project was still in development. There was essentially a hole in the middle of downtown where space had been cleared for the new construction of office and retail space. Financially strapped commercial real estate developers Grubb and Ellis sold 80 percent of their share of the redevelopment project to Bromalea Limited, a Toronto-based company. San Francisco-based international engineering and construction firm Bechtel opted out of the project as well. On the retail side of the City Center project, plans for a major mall were dropped and downscaled to a smaller plan for retail, including eateries and other stores. The existing office space was underutilized while developers still waited for the construction of the two main towers that would eventually anchor the City Center. Nevertheless, as of 1986 Mayor Wilson remained optimistic about the major downtown development plan, stating "City Center has been on the boards for many, many years. But in the past six months, we've seen a lot of action. Things are starting to come together now" (Maita, 1986).

Lionel Wilson spent much of his dwindling political capital trying to redevelop downtown Oakland. The City Center project was central to this, seeking to expand office space and corporate settlement in the confines of downtown. There were also efforts to expand commercial investment – keeping and expanding an anchor department store in the downtown near the central nexus of Telegraph Avenue and Broadway. Oakland's major downtown department store, Emporium Capwell, was heavily damaged in the 1989 Loma Prieta earthquake and boarded up; it ultimately disappeared from the Oakland landscape. In formulating his redevelopment strategies, Wilson relied heavily on economic advice from select faculty from the University of California in neighboring Berkeley.

Mayor Wilson's emphasis on downtown development – whatever the merits or demerits – were in conflict with solving problems faced by poorer residents in the "neighborhoods" (e.g., jobs, crime, poor schools, affordable housing, etc.). Growing discontent in the flatlands with Wilson's inability to put a dent in those problems became more apparent. After three terms, many Oakland citizens had concluded that it was probably time for the seventy-four-year-old public servant to retire gracefully.

STILL RISING?: ELIHU HARRIS INHERITS THE BLACK URBAN REGIME IN OAKLAND

Lionel Wilson stubbornly decided to run for a fourth term as mayor of Oakland. Apparently voters were ready for someone else to have the job. Wilson lost badly in the 1990 mayoral primary, coming in third in a multi-candidate race. The field was narrowed in the runoff election to perennial mayoral candidate and local progressive stalwart Wilson Riles Jr. and his opponent state assemblyman Elihu Harris (Johns & Staats, 1990). The election of either would assure the continuity of the black urban regime in Oakland. However, Harris, the better-funded "establishment" candidate who had been endorsed by the *Oakland Tribune* finally won the election.

Harris was born in Los Angeles but raised in Berkeley from early childhood. He graduated from Berkeley High School in 1965. His father was a mortician, known for providing services to the East Bay's black middle class. Both Harris and Riles (son of Wilson Riles, Sr., the first black California state superintendent of schools) were from middle-class backgrounds. Harris received his bachelor's degree in political science from California State University at Hayward. He later obtained a master's degree in public administration from Berkeley. Finally, he earned his law degree from the University of California at Davis in 1972 (Raber, 1990). Both mayoral candidates had also belonged to the progressive Niagara Democratic Club in the 1960s (Johns, 1990). However, Harris was the more conventionally moderate and probusiness politician.

In his earlier days, Harris was a student at Merritt College and met Huey Newton. He was asked about his opinion of Newton after the former Panther leader was shot to death in West Oakland by a drug dealer in 1989. Newton was both revered and reviled in his hometown of Oakland, so Harris' sentiment about Newton was not an uncommon one. However, it did demonstrate the political distance put by some second-generation black elected officials (who indirectly benefited from past black political mobilization) between themselves and the controversial legacy of 1960s era black power activists. By contrast, Lionel Wilson (whose worldview certainly differed from Newton's) always acknowledged the role that the Panthers had played in his own election as mayor in 1977.[8] As Harris dryly put it:

> I remember him saying that he liked Cuba because everybody had a gun. That's when I decided I didn't want to be part of that group. Newton was a larger than life figure, romanticized by some. Some people would argue that Huey's been dead a long time, and his body just caught up with the situation. (Pearson, 1994, p. 319)

By the time he considered running for mayor, Harris had lived in Oakland for many years. Yet he had not done his "political apprenticeship" in city politics or been directly linked to the black urban regime. Rather, he served in the California State Assembly from 1978 to 1990 representing Oakland and other parts of the East Bay comprised by the 13th district. He was tied to the John Burton–Willie Brown machine in San Francisco, which was a dominant force in Democratic Party politics in the Bay Area and in California state politics. Perhaps because he was an "outsider" to Oakland city politics, Harris had been considered Wilson's preferred successor (over African American Oakland council member Leo Bazile) at one point (Raber, 1990).

Nevertheless, it was Harris who inherited the black urban regime founded by Wilson. As Wilson did before him, Harris would have to navigate the hostile political terrain between the expectations of his base in the black community on the one hand, and those of the larger public and powerful business interests on the other. This political tension had been part of the undoing of Wilson and represented a looming challenge for Harris when he took office in January of 1991. With fewer tools than the old political machines of past eras, contemporary local governments hemmed in by the interests of private capital are greatly challenged to develop policies that can benefit a working class electorate.

During the mayoral campaign in 1990, Harris released an "Issues for 1990" document that described his policy positions on key issues for Oakland. The first four of the nine issues in the document are, in order: education, economic development, the Port of Oakland, and neighborhood reinvestment. At the center of all of these "position papers" was an underlying emphasis on economic growth and investment. The section on economic development seemed to question the major "pie in the sky" downtown commercial and office plans that the Wilson administration had negotiated with developer James Rouse. While pursuit of downtown development to revitalize Oakland was also important for Harris, less emphasis was put on conventional anchor department store commerce. Large retailers were not interested in settling in disproportionately poor and minority Oakland when shiny new suburban malls beckoned. In another section on economic development, the plan emphasizes the confines of Oakland's place in the *regional* development of the Bay Area. In addition to downtown development, the document also emphasizes reorganizing the Port of Oakland (Elihu Harris Campaign for Oakland, 1990).

In his first year in office, Harris faced the devastating Oakland "firestorm." This event was partly a result of the unique terrain, flora, and demographic settlement patterns of many California cities that feature hills and flatlands. A small brush fire near Grizzly Peak Boulevard grew into a massive conflagration that spread from the edge of Berkeley well into the neighborhoods of the North Oakland hills during the fall of 1991. These neighborhoods contained mostly white, affluent residents who lived in the urban wooded hills that are spatially separated from the homes of less prosperous residents of the flatland neighborhoods of North Oakland below. Twenty-five people died, nearly 3,000 homes were destroyed, and total damages were estimated at $1.5 billion (Reinhold, 1991). On top of this, the city was still attempting to deal with the need for reconstruction after the disaster of the 1989 earthquake. That massive disaster had caused the collapse of much of the 880 overpass in West Oakland and heavily damaged the vitally important Bay Bridge.

Harris was accepted as a politically moderate, and probusiness politician by important business actors on the Oakland scene. This included the retired Admiral Robert Toney (an African American), who served as president of the Oakland Chamber of Commerce. Harris was able to ingratiate himself with important members of the Bay Area's New Ways Leadership Forum, a network of 100 or so important business leaders who would contribute $500 each to political fundraising and in turn were in a position to offer policy advice to the mayor. "The forum's steering committee meets once a month to give the mayor advice on topics ranging from the port to press relations and housing" (Quinn, 1992).

As Harris began to forge his own economic strategies for the city, he, like Wilson, entertained advice from urban development-oriented faculty at the University of California at Berkeley. A group of urban planning and policy advocates on the Berkeley campus was constituted as the University-Oakland Metropolitan Forum. The Forum issued a report recommending urban development policies for the Wilson administration to consider in 1991. But of course Harris was elected instead. The report neatly summarized Oakland's positional problem in the larger regional Bay Area economy. Not surprisingly, it identified San Francisco as the "traditional center" of the region. The report also pointed out that San Francisco had a notably diversified urban service center "possessing a strong corporate headquarters and office base, especially for the financial, insurance, and real estate sectors" (University-Oakland Metropolitan Forum, 1990, p. 69). These financialized sectors are central to the core of the postindustrial economy and were lacking as a base across the bay in Oakland. Instead, Oakland had traditionally been a manufacturing, transportation, and warehouse center. The forum's recommendations for Oakland were suggestive of the policies that Harris would pursue:

> [Oakland] cannot compete with San Francisco for corporate headquarter locations because it lacks the required sophisticated and diversified business service base. Recent shifts in back office location have also passed over Oakland. Nonetheless, within the East Bay economy, Oakland remains a major node of economic activity, a function that will be strengthened with the revitalization of the downtown core. The build-out of the redevelopment area will greatly increase Oakland's attraction for offices, retail, and

other commercial development which, will in turn, strengthen its economic base. The key to Oakland's future lies in strengthening its position as the East Bay's regional, governmental, and distributive center. (*ibid.*, pp. 69–70)

Even with the ongoing City Center project, Oakland had difficulty attracting major corporations to settle into its underutilized downtown office space. In terms of major retail, the city had difficulty attracting significant investment into the retail space set aside at the City Center and elsewhere downtown. Even Sears closed its monolithic Art Deco uptown store at 26th and Telegraph in 1993. It had originally opened in 1929. Combined with the previous closure of Emporium Capwell, this left Oakland without a major department store. However, Sears would return to downtown in 1996, taking over the old Emporium Capwell location and targeting a market of "medium scale" and bargain-hunting minority shoppers that could easily be found in Oakland (Tanaka, 1996).

Harris recalibrated Oakland's efforts at downtown development by luring government services and focusing on making Oakland a central location for government offices. What would eventually become the Ronald V. Dellums Federal Building housing offices of the General Services Administration would begin during Harris's first term as mayor. Congressman Ron Dellums worked behind the scenes to see that the project was located in Oakland rather than San Francisco. This twin tower provided 4,000 jobs, and the office building would help to fill in the "holes in the ground" that existed at 13th and Clay Street, as the City Center Project had long struggled to find corporate interest in locating in downtown Oakland. The California State Transportation Agency (Caltrans) and the East Bay Municipal Utilities District (EBMUD) would also find new office space in Oakland. Additionally, planning began in 1992 for a new state office building, which would be set alongside the Dellums buildings at 15th and Clay. The state office building would eventually be named the Elihu M. Harris State Office Building (City of Oakland, 1994; Quinn, 1992).

Another major effort at economic development in Oakland during the Harris administration was the effort to reinvigorate the shipping capacity of the Port of Oakland. Oakland's port faced traditional competitors on the West Coast – namely Long Beach, Los Angeles, and Seattle – and needed improvements to prevent the further decline of Oakland's traditional status as a key port city. Ground transport was the centerpiece of Oakland's economy as "end of the line" since the golden age of the Southern and Pacific Railroad in the 19th century. Shipping transport was also important with the development of the Port of Oakland, which originally opened in 1927. By the early 1990s the Oakland port's depth of 35 feet was too shallow to compete with other West Coast ports for the business of the large container ships that were arriving from other ports throughout the Pacific Rim. Harris made some bluster about having the city take over the port, but that idea had little support (Halstuk, 1992). Despite criticism and protest by environmental activists, Harris — working with the independent Port of Oakland — pushed through a project to dredge the port so that larger container vessels could dock there. American President Lines, Oakland's most important port tenant, demanded as much. As a result, the Army Corps of Engineers was contracted to dredge the port to a depth of 38 feet in 1992, and later to 42 feet in 1994 (City of Oakland, 1995; Slater, 1998a, 1998b, 1998c; Wastler, 1992).

Harris' tenure as mayor oversaw other economic developments. This included the controversial deal that brought the once-beloved Raiders football franchise back to Oakland from Los Angeles. The deal negotiated with volatile Raiders owner Al Davis by the Harris administration and Alameda County officials was very expensive. It included luxury boxes, "seat licenses," and expensive renovations to the Oakland Coliseum. Other developments included the beginning of a new Amtrak station at Jack London Square, renovations of City Hall aimed at repairing damage from the 1989 earthquake, and the beginning of the Cypress (880) Freeway replacement in West Oakland. The freeway reconstruction was supposed to generate as many as 30,000 jobs, although little "trickled down" to the hopeful residents of West Oakland. Other low- to medium-end retail jobs arrived in Oakland by way of new store openings by Kmart, Pak N Save, and Costco (City of Oakland, 1994, 1995). All in all, economic development efforts in Oakland improved the appearance of downtown and produced some new white-collar jobs. However, as in the Wilson administration, most of that new development — or redevelopment — did not have much of an impact on the most needy residents of the city. These economic developments did not really provide much for the base of the black urban regime — the poor and working-class blacks in the flatland neighborhoods of Oakland.

Most of the projects initiated by the Harris administration specifically for the neighborhoods were small in scale and had little apparent impact. Of course, gone were the days of the Great Society, when far greater resources were mobilized at the federal level to benefit local citizens in Oakland and elsewhere. The city did fund the construction of several hundred affordable housing units, emergency housing, and a multiservice center for the homeless was initiated, abandoned and "blighted" homes were torn down, midnight basketball and other small youth programs to deter crime were implemented. Head Start programs for hundreds of children in the city were provided, and funds for community art (murals, exhibits, community dance performance) were also dispensed (*ibid.*). However, like other cash-strapped city governments in the age of neoliberalism, Oakland did not provide much to its most economically deprived residents.

By the time Harris faced re-election in 1994, the cracks in the black urban regime were showing. The rapidly changing demographics of the state were being expressed in Oakland. The proportion of black residents and voters in the city was declining, while the proportion of Latino and Asian American residents was rapidly growing. For example, the 1992 election of Ignacio De La Fuente to represent the increasingly Latino Fruitvale District on the Oakland city council (replacing the retired black progressive stalwart Wilson Riles Jr.) was illustrative of the changes in the political landscape (O'Brien, 1993). The basic foundation of black electoral power in Oakland was diminishing.

A politically unknown Chinese American businessman named Ted Dang was able to force Harris into a runoff election by seeking to unite the "non-black" vote, including disaffected Asian American, Latino, and affluent white voters in the Oakland hills neighborhoods. Harris prevailed, but the election foretold the weakening grip of the black urban regime on Oakland. As Berkeley political scientist Bruce Cain observed, "The African American community is faced with losing the control and power they gained in the '60s and '70s. ... Many feel they are losing the power when they were never able to realize the policy benefits" (cited in Muto, 1994).

FALL OF THE BLACK URBAN REGIME: JERRY BROWN TAKES A POLITICAL DETOUR THROUGH OAKLAND

As Elihu Harris's second and final term as mayor of Oakland wound down, he contemplated the next move in his political career. He decided to run for his old seat in the California State Assembly, now reconstituted as the 16th District. Harris, in a shocking turn of events, lost that "safe seat" by 327 votes to Audie Bock, an unknown white Green Party candidate. Harris's loss was apparently attributable to low black voter turnout and lackluster campaigning (Rodriguez, 1999). Nonetheless, it was an unexpected and ignominious end to Harris' political career.

The black urban regime in Oakland was also facing its end. In late 1993, former California Governor Jerry Brown moved to a specially designed $2 million dollar "live-work space" in Oakland's gentrifying Jack London Square. Despite being criticized by some as a carpetbagger, by 1998 Brown had been elected mayor of Oakland (Nieves, 2000). He had made a successful transition from being a liberal radio talk personality across the bay in San Francisco, to his latest elected office in Oakland. He defeated an innocuous assortment of ten candidates, most of whom were black. This was suggestive of fractious divisions among the black middle class political leadership in the city. Brown's election did not require the usual runoff, as he won 59 percent of the vote in the general election. On the same ballot was Measure X, a proposition pushed by Brown, which also passed and would give him "strong mayor" powers on his first day in office at Oakland City Hall (Slater, 1998a, 1998b, 1998c). Brown had wandered in the political wilderness without public office for several years. The *Wall Street Journal* reported that Brown, in order to accomplish this, was promising to "dismantle the African American-dominated political machine that presided over much of the city's decline since the 1970s (Waldman)." Those sentiments did not go over well with black political activists and supporters of the fallen regime.

Brown ran a campaign geared to the mix of mostly liberal and progressive voters in the Oakland electorate, with rhetoric culled from his radio days. In power he pursued a fairly conservative political agenda, which amounted to a very effective "bait and switch" strategy. He had City Manager Robert Bobb craft a four-point administrative program dedicated to: (1) fighting crime, (2) reforming the schools, (3) increasing community development, and (4) promoting the arts (Waldman, 1999). Of these, at least the first three led to some significant degree of political conflict with segments of the black community.

In 2000, Brown sought to gain control of the school board (an important source of black neighborhood-based political power) through his support of Measure D. However, he was unable to get a majority of supporters on the school board. The financially strapped and poorly performing Oakland School District was later put in receivership by the state of California in 2003 (May, 2003; Thompson, 2001). Mayor Brown was a champion of charter schools in Oakland. Education privatization through charter schools has been a key parallel policy linked with contemporary neoliberal urban redevelopment and gentrification policies (Lipman, 2011, pp. 22–73). Jerry Brown personally promoted two of Oakland's charter schools. One was the Oakland School for the Arts. The other was the

Oakland Military Institute, an academy that emphasizes military style discipline. Brown helped to raise more than $11 million dollars from private donors for his two highly favored charter schools since 2007 although "their test scores remain less than stellar despite the fact that the two schools spend far more money educating students than other Oakland public schools" (Gammon, 2010).

Brown also fired Joseph Samuels, the police chief previously appointed by Elihu Harris. Samuels was the first African American chief of police in Oakland and advocated minority recruitment and community policing tactics. Black pastors and others publicly attacked Brown, who was forced to hire another African American to replace Samuels as chief. However, the new chief Richard Word implemented Brown's preferred Guilianiesque "broken windows" policing strategy. This approach emphasized aggressive tactics that concentrated police officers in low-income neighborhoods and emphasized making mass arrests for minor crimes like loitering – with the rationale of deterring more serious crimes. This led to increasing hostility toward the police among the young blacks and Latinos in the flatland neighborhoods who were targeted by de facto racial profiling. There were resulting increases in both police brutality complaints and protest from black and Latino communities (Walsh, 1999).

However, Brown's parrying with black community activists was a political sideshow to the ongoing main agenda of downtown development. Jerry Brown once championed "creative development," which included: mixed-use planning, affordable housing, environmentalism, and promoting ethnic and income diversity. This was called for in Brown's own commissioned study, entitled *Oakland Ecopolis* (Waldman, 1999). After his election as mayor, Brown took a more conventional approach to development. Unlike previous black-middle-class mayors, whose redevelopment plans might be somewhat constrained by political obligations to their base – that is, poorer and working-class black residents – Brown had no such constraint. In actuality, Brown's development policies could be described as "value free" and revanchist (Smith, 1996), rather than creative or sustainable.

Indeed, Jerry Brown's publicly stated goal was to bring 10,000 new residents to (gentrify) downtown Oakland during his tenure. This goal was exceeded. Under Mayor Brown, the appropriation of progressive ideas about promoting the proliferation of the "creative class" (Florida, 2002) in cities seeking redevelopment became mixed with the conventional neoliberal pro-growth agenda of local developers, realtors, and financiers. The Brown administration saw a quadrupling of new housing units in the city, from 211 per year between 1990 and 1998 to 880 per year by the end of

Brown's first term (Kurapka, 2002). Brown was working with important financial benefactors such as Bank of America CEO Hank McColl and developer and fundraiser Douglas Shorenstein (son of Walter), who bought Oakland's City Center Project for pennies on the dollar when it fell into foreclosure in 1996 (Walker, 1996). Shorenstein subsequently benefited as Oakland's rents rose by 50 percent two years after the purchase (Waldman, 1999). This was symbolic of the rapid transformation of Oakland's commercial center under "Downtown Jerry Brown."

By the end of his second mayoral term, Brown was planning his return to statewide office in Sacramento as California Attorney General in 2007. He was nostalgically re-elected as Governor of California in 2011. Before he departed Oakland, he received both praise and scorn from varied political writers, critics, allies, and activists. The local paper *East Bay Express* even tried to "grade" Brown's administration and to distinguish "truth from fiction" in assessing his accomplishments (Thompson, 2007a, 2007b). His administration noticeably remade the landscape of downtown through gentrification by courting and giving freer rein to investors, financiers, developers, and realtors via neoliberal ideas of "value free" development. Rents and property values rose. Brown left Oakland before the Great Recession dropped property values and increased economic insecurity in the city and throughout the state. Oakland was left with the usual problems of joblessness, poverty, crime, and underperforming schools.

After the departure of "Downtown" Jerry Brown, Oakland did elect another black mayor in 2006. The city chose retired Congressman Ron Dellums, the celebrated "lion" of progressive causes. He was a professional social worker by training, and also the nephew of the dean of black labor activism in Oakland, C. L. Dellums (Dellums and Halterman, 2000). Ron Dellums, like his prominent uncle, represents the long history of black progressive politics in the East Bay. He was effectively drafted for the mayoral race by the black professional middle-class core supporters of the former black urban regime — the informal collectivity of politically engaged black clergy in the city.

The comments of Pastor J. Alfred Smith crystallized the political tension that existed between the black clergy, congregations, and others who supported the departed black urban regime, and the administration of Jerry Brown. Smith suggested that hard fought black political power had been "disrespected" and "called out" by Brown, rather than cooperated with during his mayoral reign. Many of these black ministers initially supported progressive Latino council member Ignacio De La Fuente for mayor, but belatedly decided that they would try to draw Dellums into the race to once again project a black political agenda into the political life of the city (Smith, 2007).

Dellums, who was a very formidable and savvy legislative player in Congress, was unexpectedly disengaged and ineffective in the executive role as mayor of Oakland. The paradox of rising crime rates and increased concerns about police brutality (including the infamous BART Police killing of black resident Oscar Grant), budget problems, poor public relations, his own personal and political distractions, and the continuous problems of poverty, joblessness, and failing schools undermined Dellums' single, highly criticized and unpopular term as mayor (Thompson, 2007a, 2007b).

The election of Ron Dellums as mayor was supposed to signal the return of consequential black political power to Oakland, but it was not to be. At the end of Dellums' term of office in 2011, political conditions in the city had qualitatively changed, and the foundation of the black urban regime had been fully dislodged. Whereas blacks had a majority on the city council for much of the 1980s and 1990s, black representation on the city council had been reduced to two seats. These last two seats represented districts six and seven, which are centered in the flatland neighborhoods of East Oakland. This is where most of the current black population was once again both politically segregated and delimited. This has been the disconcerting full circle of "black power" in Oakland.

CONCLUSION

Several factors undermined the local dream of "black power" and the once entrenched black urban regime. First, Oakland's local economy was buffeted by the harsh effects of deindustrialization and high rates of joblessness among its most disadvantaged residents. Second, population changes in Oakland have included: the demographic and electoral effects of the "new immigration" from Latin America and Asia, an exodus of African American residents (including "reverse migration" to the South), and gentrification (which has brought more middle-class whites into the city and driven out poorer and working-class blacks). Finally, new postindustrial economic and political influences from investors and business owners (e.g., developers, realtors, charter schools, and new commerce catering to upscale residents, etc.) have reset the dynamics of local politics in Oakland.

The fall of the black urban regime has corresponded with a volatile neoliberal era that has exacerbated race and class inequalities in Oakland and elsewhere. Indeed, in Oakland (as elsewhere) the urban regime — of whatever ideological or ethnic cast — has been charged with the task of pacifying racial inequalities and conflict (Cazenave, 2011), while maintaining the prerogatives of private capital and advantaged residents of the metropolis.

NOTES

1. The libraries and archives utilized at the university of California, Berkeley include: the Bancroft Library, the Institute of Governmental Studies Library, the Regional Oral History Office at the Bancroft Library, and the Newspapers and Microforms Room at Doe Library. Libraries and archives referenced at the Oakland public library include: the African American Museum and Library, and the Oakland History Room at the Oakland Main Public Library.

2. By racialized class interests of the black professional middle class, I refer to a "consciousness" (political, social status, or otherwise) that shapes the interests of members of the black professional middle class. These interests are shaped by membership in a disadvantaged racial group, but also by a sense of class advantage or privilege relative to other blacks in the larger intersectional "black community." This also includes a sensibility among many that they should play a "leadership" role amongst less privileged blacks in the political and civic spheres of society.

3. DuBois prefigures his arguments about the "talented tenth" in his classic study of the problems of life in the pre-Migration black urban community. He argues for the importance of the leadership of the "better class of Negroes" in Philadelphia, by which he primarily meant the small class of black professionals. See DuBois (1996 [1899], pp. 392–397).

4. The late Kwame Toure (Stokely Carmichael) is generally given credit for the first public utterance of the term "black power." He and his coauthor sought to develop this political slogan into both theory and practice for the analysis and promotion of black political activism as the civil rights movement faded. See Carmichael and Hamilton (1967).

5. Houlihan was charged with, and convicted of, embezzlement in a case concerning the management of a client's estate in which he had been involved as a private attorney.

6. For a general overview of Model Cities programs see Frieden and Kaplan (1975). For a discussion of Model Cities in Oakland see May (1971, pp. 57–88).

7. Marx considered the *lumpenproletariat* to be the "refuse of all classes" and a group that would not play a role in the progress of the working-class struggle. The Black Panthers noted the significant unemployment facing African Americans and argued alternatively that the "lumpen" segment of the larger society would grow in size as capitalism developed and they would have to be organized along with the working class. See Newton (1972, pp. 26–30).

8. Lionel Wilson acknowledged a dual perspective on the Black Panthers. "One, in terms that I never have condoned violence and confrontation as solutions to social problems. And the other one was that I saw the Panthers as a catalyst to bring about meaningful change." He also acknowledged the role that they played in

his election as mayor. "The Panthers were active in my campaign in 1977. Now I had been told that Huey Newton had said that if I had been willing to run in 1973 that Bobby Seale would not have been a candidate then. I don't know whether that's true or not." Wilson (1992, p. 55).

REFERENCES

Allen, R. L. (1970). *Black awakening in capitalist America: An analytic history*. New York, NY: Anchor Books.
Anderson, B. (2006). *Imagined communities: Reflections on the origin and spread of nationalism* (rev. ed.). London: Verso.
Appelbaum, E., Bernhardt, A. D., & Murnane, R. J. (Eds.) (2006). *Low-wage America: How employers are reshaping opportunity in the workplace*. New York, NY: Russell Sage Foundation.
Austin, C. J. (2006). *Up against the wall: Violence in the making and unmaking of the Black Panther party*. Fayetteville, AR: University of Arkansas Press.
Bagwell, B. (1982). *Oakland, the story of a city*. Novato, CA: Presidio Press.
Broussard, A. E. (1997). *A California supreme court justice looks at law and society, 1964–1996*. An Oral History conducted in 1991, 1992, 1995, and 1996 by Gabrielle Morris, Regional Oral History Office, the Bancroft Library, University of California, Berkeley, 1994. Berkeley, CA: Regents of the University of California.
Brown, E. (1994). *A taste of power: A Black woman's story*. New York, NY: Anchor Books.
Brown, E. (2014). *The black professional middle class: Race, class, and community in the post-civil rights era*. New York, NY: Routledge.
Browning, R. P., Marshall, D. R., & Tabb, D. H. (1984). *Protest is not enough: The struggle of Blacks and Hispanics for equality in urban politics*. Berkeley, CA: University of California Press.
Browning, R. P., Marshall, D. R., & Tabb, D. H. (2003). *Racial politics in American cities* (3rd ed.). New York, NY: Longman Publishers.
Bush, R. (1984). Oakland: Grassroots organizing against Reagan. In R. Bush (Ed.), *The new Black vote: Politics and power in four American cities*. San Francisco, CA: Synthesis Publications.
Carmichael, S., & Hamilton, C. V. (1967). *Black power: The politics of Liberation in America*. New York, NY: Vintage.
Cazenave, N. (2011). *The urban racial state: Managing race relations in American cities*. Lanham, MD: Rowman and Littlefield.
City of Oakland. (1994). *Restoring the dream: 1993 Annual report to the people of Oakland*. Oakland, CA: City of Oakland.
City of Oakland. (1995). *The best of Oakland: 1994 city of Oakland 1994 annual report*. Oakland, CA: City of Oakland.
City of Oakland. (2008, November). *Code of ordinances, The charter of the city of Oakland*. Article III: The Council, Section 203. Oakland, CA
Collins, P. H. (2005). *Black sexual politics: African Americans, gender, and the new racism*. New York, NY: Routledge.
Dawson, M. C. (1994). *Behind the mule: Race and class in African American politics*. Princeton, NJ: Princeton University Press.

Dellums, R. V., & Halterman, H. L. (2000). *Lying down with lions*. Boston, MA: Beacon Press.
DuBois, W. E. B. (1996 [1899]). *The Philadelphia Negro: A social study*. Philadelphia, PA: University of Pennsylvania Press.
Elihu Harris Campaign for Oakland. (1990). *Issues for 1990*. Oakland, CA: Elihu Harris Campaign for Oakland.
Florida, R. (2002). *The rise of the creative class*. New York, NY: Basic Books.
Frieden, B. J., & Kaplan, M. (1975). *The politics of neglect: Urban aid from model cities to revenue sharing*. New York, NY: Cambridge University Press.
Gammon, R. (2010). Jerry brown raised $12 Million for his two Oakland schools. *East Bay Express*, April 28.
Gelfand, M. (1975). *A nation of cities: The Federal government and urban America, 1933–1965*. New York, NY: Oxford University Press.
Grillo, E. (2000). *Black Cuban, Black American: A memoir*. Houston, TX: Arte Publico Press.
Halstuk, M. (1992). Mixed reviews for Oakland's mayor. *San Francisco Chronicle*, April 4.
Harvey, D. (2005). *A brief history of neoliberalism*. New York, NY: Oxford University Press.
Hayes, E. C. (1972). *Power structure and urban policy: Who rules in Oakland*. New York, NY: McGraw-Hill.
Hazard, B. (1980). Oakland: That other great city by the bay. *Ebony*, October.
Herron, J. (1987). Voter apathy may doom progressive Oakland City Council challengers. *San Francisco Bay Guardian*, April 8.
Hilliard, D., & Cole, L. (1993). *This side of glory: The autobiography of David Hilliard and the story of the Black Panther party*. Boston, MA: Little, Brown and Company.
Johns, B. (1990). Miley, Harris first new council faces since 1983. *Oakland Tribune*, November 8.
Johns, B., & C. Staats (1990). Wilson graceful in defeat. *Oakland Tribune*, June 7, 1990.
Joseph, P. E. (2007). *Waiting 'Til the midnight hour: A narrative history of black power in America*. New York, NY: Henry Holt and Company.
Joseph, P. E. (2009). The Black power movement: A state of the field. *Journal of American History*, December.
Kalleberg, A. L. (2013). *Good jobs, bad jobs: The rise of polarized and precarious employment systems in the United States 1970s to 2000s*. New York, NY: Russell Sage.
Kurapka, D. (2002). Mayors in the middle. *Blueprint*, 15, 43–45.
Lemke-Santangelo, G. (n.d.). Deindustrialization, urban poverty, and African American community mobilization in Oakland, 1945–1995. Unpublished manuscript.
Levy, F. S., Meltsner, A. J., & Wildavsky, A. (1974). *Urban outcomes: Schools, streets, and libraries*. Berkeley, CA: University of California Press.
Lipman, P. (2011). *The new political economy of urban education: Neoliberalism, race, and the right to the city*. New York, NY: Routledge.
Logan, J. R., & Molotch, H. L. (2007). *Urban fortunes: The Political economy of place* (2nd ed.). Berkeley, CA: University of California Press.
Maita, S. (1986). Oakland pushes city center. *San Francisco Chronicle*, December 1.
Marable, M. (2007). *Race, reform, and rebellion: The second reconstruction and beyond in Black America, 1945–2006* (3rd ed.). Jackson, MS: University Press of Mississippi.
Martin, B. (1977). Wilson tells plans. *Oakland Tribune*, May 19.
Massey, D., Rothwell, J., & Domina, T. (2009). The changing bases of segregation in the United States. *The Annals of the American Academy of Political and Social Science*, 626(1), 74–90.

Massey, D. S., & Denton, N. A. (1993). *American apartheid: Segregation and the making of the underclass*. Cambridge, MA: Harvard University Press.
May, J. (1973). *Struggle for authority: A comparison of four social change programs in Oakland, California*. Ph.D. Dissertation, University of California, Berkeley.
May, J. V. (1970). The politics of growth versus the politics of redistribution: Negotiations over the model cities program in Oakland. Paper presented at the meeting of the American Orthopsychiatric Association, San Francisco, March 24.
May, J. V. (1971). Two model cities: Negotiations in Oakland. *Politics and Society*, 2(1), 57–88.
May, M. (2003). State's take charge Guy Walks and talks in Oakland. *San Francisco Chronicle*, June 3.
McAdam, D. (1997). *Political process and the development of black insurgency, 1930–1970* (2nd ed.). Chicago, IL: University of Chicago Press.
McGrath, M. (1987). The assault on Pax Wilsonia. *East Bay Express*, January 23.
Men of Tomorrow. (1959). *Constitution and Bylaws*. Oakland, CA: The Men of Tomorrow, Incorporated.
Men of Tomorrow. (1961). *Directory of members – 1961*. Oakland, CA: Men of Tomorrow, Inc.
Montgomery, G. (1973). Reading beats Seale decisively in runoff. *Oakland Tribune*, May 16.
Montgomery, G. B., Johnson, J. W., & Manolis, P. G. (1998). *One step from the white house: The rise and fall of senator Knowland* (pp. 213–271). Berkeley, CA: University of California Press.
Morris, A. (1986). *The origins of the civil rights movement: Black communities organizing for change*. New York, NY: Free Press.
Muto, S. (1994). The Oakland mayoral contest: The ghost of politics future. *California Journal Weekly*, October 3.
Newton, H. P. (1972). *To die for the people: The writings of Huey P. Newton*. New York, NY: Random House.
Nieves, E. (2000). As Mayor, Jerry Brown is down to earth. *New York Times*, January 11.
Noyelle, T. J. (1987). *Beyond industrial dualism: Market and job in the new economy*. Boulder, CO: Westview Press.
O'Brien, B. (1993). Oakland's new city council takes office. *East Bay Express*, January 8.
Oakland Redevelopment Agency. (1966). *Oakland: A demonstration city report*. Oakland, CA: Oakland Redevelopment Agency.
Oakland Tribune Staff. (1968). One killed, 4 shot in gun battle here. *Oakland Tribune*, April 7.
Pattillo, M. (2005). Black middle class neighborhoods. *Annual Review of Sociology*, 31, 305–329.
Pearson, H. (1994). *The shadow of the panther: Huey Newton and the price of black power in America*. Reading, MA: Addison-Wesley.
Pressman, J. (1975). *Federal programs and city politics: The dynamics of the aid process in Oakland*. Berkeley, CA: University of California Press.
Pressman, J. L., & Wildavsky, A. (1973). *Implementation: How great expectations in Washington are dashed in Oakland*. Berkeley, CA: University of California Press.
Quinn, M. (1992). The sound and the fury. *San Francisco Examiner Magazine*, Vol. 6, No. 13.
Raber, P. (1990). The Undertaker's Son vs. the Lonely Warrior. *East Bay Express*, November 2.

Reed, A., Jr. (1999). *Stirrings in the Jug: Black politics in the post-segregation era.* Minneapolis, MN: University of Minnesota Press.
Reinhold, R. (1991). Fire in Oakland ranks as worst in state history. *New York Times*, October 22.
Rhomberg, C. (2004). *No there there: Race, class, and political community in Oakland.* Berkeley, CA: University of California Press.
Rodriguez, E. C. L. (1999). Deconstructing Harris. *California Journal*, 30(5), 20–21.
Rumford, W. B. (1978). D. G. Gibson as I knew him. In H. Nathan & S. Scott (Eds.), *Experiment and change in Berkeley: Essays on city politics, 1950–1975.* Berkeley, CA: Institute of Governmental Studies, University of California at Berkeley.
Seale, B. (1968). *Seize the time.* New York, NY: Vintage.
Self, R. O. (2003). *American Babylon: Race and the struggle for postwar Oakland.* Princeton, NJ: Princeton University Press.
Slater, D. (1998a). Oakland's once and future port. *East Bay Express*, Vol. 21, No. 1.
Slater, D. (1998b). The life and times of Mayor Wilson. *East Bay Express*, October 9.
Slater, D. (1998c). The race for second place. *East Bay Express*, Vol. 20, No. 34.
Smith, J. A. (2007). Author Interview, Oakland, CA, June 7.
Smith, J. L. (1985). Wilson's funds pour in; Riles' donations trickle. *Oakland Tribune*, April 5.
Smith, N. (1996). *The new urban frontier: Gentrification and the revanchist city.* New York, NY: Routledge.
Smith, N. (2004). *A life in education and community service.* An Oral History conducted in 2002 and 2003 by Nadine Wilmot. Regional Oral History Office, the Bancroft Library. University of California, Berkeley, 2004. Berkeley, CA: Regents of the University of California.
Stone, C. M. (1989). *Regime politics: Governing Atlanta, 1946–1988.* Lawrence, KS: University of Kansas Press.
Sugrue, T. J. (2008). *Sweet land of liberty: The forgotten struggle for civil rights in the North.* New York, NY: Random House.
Sugrue, T. J. (2014). *The origins of the urban crisis: Race and inequality in postwar Detroit* (rev. ed.). Princeton, NJ: Princeton University Press.
Tanaka, W. (1996). Sears and Robust. *San Francisco Examiner*, October 26.
Tate, K. (1994). *From protest to politics: The New Black voters in American elections.* Cambridge, MA: Harvard University Press.
Taylor, H. L. J. (1991). Social transformation theory, African Americans, and the rise of Buffalo's Postindustrial city. *Buffalo Law Review*, (39).
Thompson, C. (2001). Brown versus board of education. *East Bay Express*, Vol. 24, No. 6.
Thompson, C. (2007a). Anybody seen Hizzoner? *East Bay Express*, Vol. 29, No. 35.
Thompson, C. (2007b). Grading Jerry. *East Bay Express*, Vol. 29, No. 13.
University-Oakland Metropolitan Forum. (1990). *Oakland's Economy in the 1990s: A sourcebook of planning and community development issues facing the city, its neighborhoods, and the region.* Berkeley, CA: University of California.
Waldman, P. (1999). As mayor of Oakland, Jerry Brown woos business and trumpets order. *Wall Street Journal*, August 10.
Walker, T. (1996). Developer lands deal in Oakland/ S.F. Firm to take over city center buildings. *San Francisco Chronicle*, December 18.
Walsh, J. (1999). Brown's town. *The New Republic*, August 30.

Wastler, A. R. (1992). Feelings run deep over Oakland port dredging – environment, jobs at odds in battle over shipping center. *Seattle Times*, May 28.

Wilson, L. (1992). *Attorney, judge, and Oakland mayor*. An oral history conducted in 1985 and 1990 by Gabrielle Morris, Regional Oral History Office, the Bancroft Library, University of California. Berkeley, CA: Regents of the University of California.

THE STRENGTH OF CIVIL SOCIETY TIES: EXPLAINING PARTY CHANGE IN AMERICA'S BLUEST STATE

Johnnie Lotesta

ABSTRACT

This paper develops a new theory arguing that party change results from ruptures in political parties' ties to civil society organizations. I demonstrate the utility of this approach by using it to explain why the Rhode Island Democratic Party (RIDP) changed from a hierarchical machine to a porous political field occupied by multiple interlegislator cliques and brokered by extra-party political organizations and professionals. While others attribute party change to bureaucratization, electoral demand, or system-level changes, I analyze historical, observational, and interview data to find that a severance in the RIDP's relationship with organized labor prompted party change by causing power to diffuse outward as leadership lost control over nominations and the careers of elected office holders. In the spaces that remained, interest groups and political professionals came to occupy central positions within the party field, serving as brokers of the information and relationships necessary to coordinate legislative activity. This analysis refines existing theories of party change and provides a historically-grounded explanation for the institutionalization of interest groups and political professionals in American party politics.

Keywords: Political parties; party change; Rhode Island; Rhode Island Democratic Party (RIDP); organized interest groups

INTRODUCTION

Why do party organizations change? Dominant theories of party change in the United States contend that it is a response to voter demand and poor electoral performance. However, these approaches fail to explain party change in cases of consistent electoral performance, such as the Rhode Island Democratic Party (RIDP). In spite of decades-long electoral success from the 1940s to the present, the RIDP transformed from what was a hierarchical party machine to a porous political field that is occupied by mutual interlegislator cliques and brokered by extra-party political organizations and professionals.[1] If electoral performance has remained consistent for over 60 years, how do we explain this transformation?

In this paper, I argue that a severance in the RIDP's relationship with organized labor prompted the party's organizational change by causing power to diffuse outwards as leadership lost control over nominations and the careers of elected office holders. In the spaces that remained, interest groups and professional lobbyists came to occupy central positions within the party field, serving as brokers of the information and relationships necessary to coordinate legislative activity. Parties may change, then, due to ruptures in their relationships with civil society organizations, which may sever parties' access to key resources and create spaces for new actors to join the party apparatus.

This paper makes several contributions to the sociology of political parties. First, it refines existing theory to emphasize how transformations in parties' ties to civil society organizations may prompt organizational change, a factor overlooked by the extant literature. Second, it provides a historically grounded explanation for the rise of interest groups and political professionals as institutionalized actors within political parties, a phenomenon observed in states across the country (Aldrich, 2011; Bawn et al., 2012; Masket, 2009; Schwartz, 2006). In these ways, to sharpens our understanding not only of party change, but also of the structural transformations that have allowed private interest groups and political professionals to move to the center of American politics.

Three Contending Explanations of Party Change in Rhode Island

Existing literature presents three contending explanations for the RIDP's organizational change. The first of these is provided by what sociologist Cedric de Leon (2014) calls the "oligarchical party tradition," most famously represented in the work of Max Weber and his protégé Roberto Michels. The central argument of this approach is that parties become increasingly centralized and bureaucratized over time as they mobilize mass bases to gain power in the state. Due to their large numbers, mass-based parties must form bureaucratic organizations to unite and direct their political activity (Michels, 1911/1962). This bureaucratization separates parties from their base by delegating decision-making and management authority to party leaders and their staff, bringing about a hierarchical and centralized command structure in which a class of professionals leads and party members follow (Michels, 1911/1962, p. 365; Weber, 1922/1968, pp. 285, 1128). Similarly, Martin (2009) has conceptualized political parties as centralized command structures who extend patronage networks downward and horizontal alliances outward to secure control over power and resources in the state. In all three accounts, parties emerge as organizations that evolve toward centralized and hierarchical command structures from which professional leaders direct party activities.

The oligarchical tradition fails to provide an adequate explanation for the RIDP's organizational change for two reasons. The first is that professionalization of the RIDP has occurred alongside a flattening of party organization, not greater hierarchy and centralization. Additionally, the oligarchical tradition misrepresents the locus of power within party politics. For each of these scholars, but for Martin especially, party power resides in a central locus from which leaders direct activity outwards. But as this analysis will show, power in the contemporary RIDP is not concentrated within a centralized command post. Rather, it is mobile, diffuse, and available for use by multiple actors. For these reasons, the oligarchical party tradition does not provide an adequate description of or explanation for the RIDP's organizational change.

A second explanation for the transformation of the RIDP may be found in demand-side approaches, the reigning account of party change in the

United States. These approaches argue that party organizations change in response to shifting electoral coalitions - as in the party realignment tradition (Moakley, Abramson, Aldrich, & Rohde, 2010; Beck, 1974; Burnham, 1970; Carmines & Stimson 1989; Key, 1959; Knoke, 1976; Manza & Brooks, 1999; Moakley, 1992; Nie, Verba, & Petrocik, 1976/1979; Sundquist, 1983) — or in response to poor electoral performance — as posited in performance theory (Janda, 1990; Panebianco, 1988).[2] Indeed, a number of political scientists and sociologists have noted profound shifts, or "realignments," in American voters' party affiliations. For instance, Knoke (1976, p. 58) found that Southern whites' support for the Democratic Party fell drastically in the postwar period while independent affiliations doubled. Manza and Brooks (1999, p. 5) found that between the 1950s and mid-1990s professionals shifted from the most Republican to the most Democratic class while self employed workers became more Republican and non-skilled workers moved to the center. In the aggregate, these studies pointed towards a dealignment of American workers from the Democratic Party, a realignment of professionals towards it, and the end of the New Deal coalition of labor unions, ethnic, racial, and religious minorities, the poor, Southern whites, and liberal intellectuals (Lawrence, 1997; Ladd, 1980; see also Moakley, 1992). Given this, some might argue that the RIDP organization changed in response to shifting electoral support or demand.

However, this argument does not hold against the historical record. While authors have documented a shift toward a more highly educated, professionalized electorate in Rhode Island since the 1980s (West, 1992, p. 247) this shift has not amounted to a realignment of the RIDP's base of support. As explained by political scientist Darrel West, Democratic party identification remained steady at 30 percent of the electorate from 1978—1990, well above Republican identification, which reached no more than 19 percent during this period (West, 1992, p. 254). Furthermore, the RIDP has demonstrated outstanding electoral performance, holding the majority of executive and legislative seats for almost all years since 1941.[3] Even in 1980 and 1984, when the country was swept by Republican votes under the Reagan ticket, the RIDP maintained majority control of both legislative houses, as well as the lieutenant governorship and state treasury. In other words, voter realignment and poor electoral performance — the prime movers of party change in the literature — are not in evidence for the case of Rhode Island. We must therefore look for other factors to explain the party's organizational transformation.[4]

A third explanation lies in the system-level approach presented by Kirchheimer (1966) and Katz and Mair (1995, 2009). This approach contends that the decreased saliency of class distinctions and the rise of post-war mass-media campaigns in Western democracies during the mid-to-late twentieth century forced parties to appeal to broader constituencies while, at the same time, increasing the technical and financial costs of campaigns (Kirchheimer, 1966, pp. 184, 186). In response to these pressures, parties became more ideologically uniform and reliant on the state for financial resources and legal protections (Katz & Mair, 2009, p. 755). The end result, according to Katz and Mair (1995, p. 2009) is a political system in which parties become "self-referential, professional, and technocratic," appealing to the public through "image and theatre" and "function[ing] like cartels, employing the resources of the state to limit political competition and ensure their own electoral success" (2009, pp. 755, 753).

This account makes several improvements to those provided by the oligarchical and demand-side traditions. First, it allows us to see how parties may professionalize and detach from their bases while simultaneously diffusing power and decision-making authority to new types of actors. Indeed, this resonates with findings from an emerging body of literature documenting the incorporation of public relations specialists, new media consultants, policy "wonks" and professional strategists into party networks (Aldrich, 2011; Johnson, 2010; Kreiss, 2012; Medvetz, 2012). Second, it recognizes party change as a contingent and strategic process, not a natural response to shifting electoral demands coalitions, as demand-sided approaches tend to suggest.

Yet the systems-level approach still fails to provide an adequate explanation for party change in Rhode Island or the United States more broadly. This is because the key factor leading to party change in this account — namely, dependence on public financial subventions — is not replicated in the Rhode Island or American cases. While Rhode Island allows candidates for statewide offices to apply for public campaign funds, these amounts are capped; they do not apply to the majority of party candidates, and they provide far fewer resources than the regular, direct state subsidies considered by Katz and Mair (1995, 2009).[5] As such, the systems-level approach still falls short of a sufficient explanation for the RIDP's organizational change.

The Strength of Civil Society Ties: An Alternative Framework

As detailed in the section above, neither the oligarchical party, demand-side, nor the systems-level approaches provide adequate explanations for the organizational transformation of the RIDP. To address the foregoing gaps, I develop a new theory of political party change which emphasizes the role of nonparty, civil society organizations. Specifically, I draw insights from Schwartz's (1990) concept of the networked political party and Seth Masket's (1990) informal party organization (see also Bawn et al., 2012) to emphasize how ruptures in parties' ties to civil society organizations prompt party change by disrupting parties' access to key resources and creating space for new actors to enter party fields.

This theoretical framework proceeds in three steps. First, I argue that American political parties, and the RIDP in particular, most closely resemble what Aldrich (2011) calls the legislative party – an endogenous organization created by elected office holders to solve three collective action problems (5, 17, 19). These collective action problems are: (a) building legislative coalitions that will work together to enact policy (32–35), (b) building policy majorities from otherwise disparate viewpoints (35–43), and (c) mobilizing collective action in the electorate (45–47). In this model, the party is a beast of the legislative politician. It is created by and for the politician to facilitate the winning of office and to coordinate activity in the legislature.[6]

Unlike Aldrich, however, I argue that these collective action problems are often solved by extra-party civil society organizations and actors, not party politicians themselves. This insight comes from the "network perspective" of political parties, which argues that parties are diffuse networks of diverse actors who work together to achieve shared goals through the state (Bawn et al., 2012; Cohen, Karol, Noel, & Zaller, 2008; Karol, 2009; Masket, 2009; Schwartz, 1990, 2006). From this perspective, civil society organizations normally considered separate from political parties – unions, business associations, and interest groups – are part and parcel of the political party organization, providing the resources and ties necessary to party operation (Schwartz, 1990). For instance, they may fund political campaigns (Masket, 2009, p. 14; Schwartz, 1990, pp. 154; 247), supply skilled staff and expert advice (Schwartz, 1990, p. 154), or provide job opportunities and access to political networks for aspiring candidates (Masket, 2009, p. 35). Indeed, much attention has been given to interest groups' and other civil society organizations' ability to solve collective action problem (a) by vetting candidates for their commitment to particular ideologies (Bawn et al., 2012, p. 571; Masket, 2009, pp. 117, 123–124; Schwartz, 1990, pp. 183–184). In the case of California, for example, Seth Masket (2009, pp. 117–118) shows how the Orange County Lincoln Club helped to elect a new conservative majority within the California Republican Party by controlling the material resources and political capital necessary for primary election.

Given the resources and tie-building capacities extra-party civil society organizations provide political parties, I hypothesize that changes in parties' relations to civil society organizations will prompt a change in political party organization. I argue that this organizational change occurs through two mechanisms: disrupting party organization's access to key resources and creating space for new types of political actors. For instance, a fall-out with a major community group may result in a shortage of campaign volunteers or party votes. As a result, the party may lose control over the nominating process and, subsequently, its elected office holders. This may then shape the distribution of power within the party-in-government, bringing about a reorganization of party relationships and, perhaps, a new practice of party governance. Ruptures in party ties to civil society organizations may also prompt party change by creating space for new actors. In the example above, the weakening of party control over the nomination process allows for the election of new types of office holders and, subsequently, a new party membership. Alternatively, the loss of tie-building capacities from one civil society organization may create an opportunity for other organizational actors to insert themselves within the party apparatus, changing its membership and composition.

This framework of party change makes several improvements upon the foregoing theoretical perspectives. First, it modifies the legislative party model to account for the material and human resources extra-party civil society organizations provide. In this way, it offers a more accurate depiction of the political party field and the actors who determine what parties do. In plain terms, parties may be created by and for elected officials, but this does not mean elected officials are captains of party ships. Second, my analytic framework improves upon the network theory of political parties by explicitly theorizing the process of party change. Indeed, for an approach so sensitive to parties' dependence on other actors, the network perspective has surprisingly failed to problematize the historical process by which specific groups have moved from the periphery to the center of party fields, and *vice versa*. Thus, I expand upon the network approach by connecting it explicitly to party change and empirically investigating how specific civil society organizations – namely, private interest groups and the political professionals they employ – came to occupy the privileged position of brokers within the RIDP.

RESEARCH METHOD

Under what conditions do party structures change? The case of the RIDP offers an intriguing empirical puzzle. As explained above, the party's transformation from a hierarchical party machine to a porous political field cannot be explained by the factors identified in the existing literature. It thus encourages us to ask what else, besides these factors, may lead to party-organizational change.

To answer this puzzle, I collected data from four sources. The first was analysis of contributions and expenditures from Democratic House Speakers' and Senate Presidents' campaign finance records from 1974[7] to 2010, which were sampled as a proxy measure for the RIDP's organizational ties.[8] These campaign contributions are an ideal measure of party-organizational ties, because they are a key medium through which party actors establish relationships with each other (Schwartz, 1990, p. 245). Furthermore, the records of legislative leaders are most likely to reveal the party's strongest allies, as established insiders tend to focus their contributions on protecting incumbents (Schwartz, 1990, p. 243). Records were sampled for the first electoral year after each House Speaker and Senate Majority Leader or President acquired their leadership position. This provided seven observations in the House (2010; 2004; 1994; 1988; 1980; 1978; 1974) and nine in the Senate (2010, 2004, 2002, 1994, 1990, 1984, 1980, 1978, 1974).[9] Total contributions and expenditures were collected from each record, including the following for every itemized contribution: contribution/expenditure type, amount, date, and purpose; name and city of contributor/payee; contributor employer and employer city. These data were used to identify major sources of individual and collective campaign support, map patterns of intercandidate relations, and analyze changes in the RIDP's organizational structure over time.

The second research method was eight months of participant observation in the Rhode Island General Assembly from January to August 2013. During this time, I attended committee meetings, public hearings, press conferences, and floor sessions. I selected events for attendance based on their relevance to the Democratic leaderships' legislative initiatives for the 2013 session — economic development reform, marriage equality, the state budget, and the 38 Studios loan default.[10] From June 2013 to August 2013 I also interned with a legislative policy office, for whom I drafted policy reports, tracked bill status, and attended committee hearings. These experiences allowed me to examine the RIDP's legislative practices first-hand, providing fruitful insight into the structure and operation of the RIDP today.

The third method was 34 interviews with Rhode Island legislators, party leaders, policy professionals, and political experts from January 2013 to August 2014. Interviews were unstructured but focused around four broad topics. The first topic was candidates' entry into the General Assembly, where respondents discussed their path into politics, any financial or in-kind support they received, and how they came to acquire leadership positions (if relevant). The second topic was the relationship between party leaders and legislative members, focusing on the methods party leaders use to coordinate legislative activity. A third set of questions asked respondents to describe the legislative process from beginning to end, and a final series asked respondents to describe how key events shaped party organization and operation. Respondents were selected based on their leadership position within the General Assembly and the Republican and Democratic parties or for their expert knowledge of Rhode Island party politics. Following the "saturation" sampling logic (Small, 2009), I first interviewed those closest to the center of the party network (Democratic party leaders and their staff) and continued sampling throughout the network until I no longer found new patterns. All interviews were recorded, transcribed, and uploaded into NVivo for coding and analysis.[11] Together, they allowed me to assess the RIDP's level of centralization, the organization of party actors in relation to one another, the methods party leaders use to establish ties with their members, and the influence key events had on the party's trajectory.

The fourth and final research method was historical research using secondary accounts. Three histories of Rhode Island state politics were especially informative to this analysis: Lockard's (1959) *New England State Politics*, Goodman's (1967) *The Democrats and Labor in Rhode Island 1952–1962*, and Moakley and Cornwell's (2001) *Rhode Island Politics and Government*. Milburn and Doyle's (1983) edited volume *New England Political Parties*, and Moakley's (1992) *Party Realignments and State Politics* also provided useful chapters with electoral and party identification data. These sources allowed me to identify key events in the party's history and provided narratives against which to evaluate my own observations and hypotheses.

EMPIRICAL ANALYSIS: PARTY CHANGE IN AMERICA'S BLUEST STATE

Argument Primer

In this section I advance an alternative account of the RIDP's organizational change based on transformations in its ties to nonparty civil society organizations. I begin this analysis by outlining the key organizational characteristics of the mid-20th-century RIDP Machine and the RIDP today, in order to demonstrate the change I seek to explain. Next, I analyze the series of events that lead to this change. Specifically, I show how a severance in the relationship between the RIDP and organized labor set the party down a path toward organizational change by breaking its electoral and material bases of support. Following the severance of this relationship, legislative reforms and a statewide banking crisis further weakened the leadership's ties to elected office holders, causing the party to splinter as power diffused outwards. As I will show, these changes made room for reform-minded and pro-business interest groups and professionals to occupy a new, functional role within the party, serving as brokers of the information and relationships necessary to coordinate party activity.

From Party Machine to Porous Political Field

From the 1930s to the 1980s, the RIDP constituted one of the nation's most notorious urban machines. As a party machine, the RIDP was tightly organized around a clear hierarchy of command, like that displayed in Fig. 1. At the top of the organization sat the governor (most famously Governor Dennis Roberts), state chairman, and the legislative leadership. These leaders directed party operations down to the precinct level, leveraging the party's control over Rhode Island's urban areas to garner patronage resources that were used to secure political loyalty (Lockard, 1959, pp. 203–204). In the words of Richard A. Gabriel, Rhode Island politics in this era were "Democratic, disciplined, and patronage oriented" (1970, p. 3).

The hierarchical nature of the RIDP is demonstrated through its near-complete control over the electoral process, from individual voter to elected official. Until the 1970s, Democratic leaders handpicked legislative

G = Governor
C = Chairman
L = Legislative leadership
● = Elected official

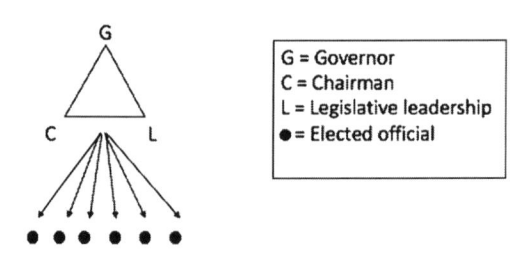

Fig. 1. RIDP Party Machine.

candidates (Profughi, 1983, p. 75), using their vast and unparalleled patronage networks to guarantee the success of their preferred candidates. As one former party worker recounted, "They would literally get in there and they would say, 'Hey, Steve, we got you a job in the highway department ... You better get your family out to vote.'" Indeed, the RIDP's grip over the electoral process was so tight that not a single party-endorsed candidate for statewide office lost a primary election between 1948 and 1956 (Lockard, 1959, p. 188). It simply was not possible to advance one's political career save through the party. As one respondent stated, "The Party would essentially decide who was gonna run. They would have the resources. They would control the Party, the mechanism, the get out the vote effort."

Once in state government, the Machine leveraged centralized leadership and closed-door legislative tactics to ensure adherence to the party line. With committee hearings closed to the public until 1976 and no legal requirements to publish committee agendas, the legislative leadership was able to restrict knowledge of a bill's status to a small group of preferred leaders, leaving the majority of members in the dark (Moakley & Cornwell, 2001). In essence, rank-and-file Democrats were excluded from the gut of the legislative process, expected only to follow the leadership's direction. For example, one Democratic legislator recalled the following:

> I mean, this place in the 70s. You hear the stories. There would be a bill. A bill would go for hearing. And they'd say, 'hey, they're meeting on your bill right now!'. The committee room would be guys ... sitting around the table with the door locked. There was no public participation. There was no hearing. They'd review it, talk about it, maybe ask a few questions but that was it. There was no public debate.

Another likewise remembered, "You didn't lobby ... You had a meeting ... You figured out what you were gonna get for the year. And that was it!."

Today the RIDP appears in strikingly different form. Rather than a tightly-organized hierarchy, the party appears as a porous political field of multiple interlegislator cliques (see Fig. 2). These cliques are defined by alliances which may be built on social, economic, or ideological ties as in Schwartz's (1990) model of the party network, but they are no longer strictly defined by formal command structures. In sum, this new party organization has three features.

First, the party no longer controls nominations, and membership is open to most any candidate bearing the Democratic label who mobilizes sufficient financial and electoral support to garner their own election. As one Senator recounted, he had never involved himself in politics or even

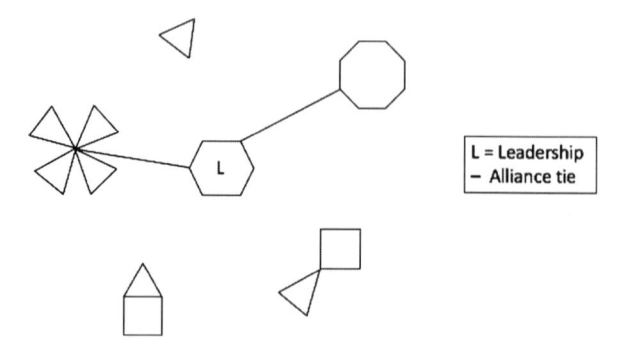

Fig. 2. The Contemporary RIDP.

registered as a Democrat until the day he filed papers to become a candidate in 1991. With no endorsement and no campaign support from the party organization, he defeated three other candidates, including two candidates supported by sitting House Democrats, to secure the Democratic nomination. The same is true of a female representative, elected in 1992, who ran unendorsed against two other Democratic candidates. As the representative explained, "I had no direction, no support, no understanding of what do you do next." Still, she went to secure an overwhelming victory, winning the Democratic nomination by 124 votes to 1.[12]

Second, rather than a clear hierarchy of command, the party is composed of multiple interlegislator cliques which compete to acquire leadership power and enact particular policies. This fractured nature of the RIDP is demonstrated by legislative leaders' use of campaign contributions to build ties with legislators who are not in the leadership. Beginning in 1980 with Senate Majority Leader Rocco A. Quatrrocchi, campaign finance records demonstrate legislative leaders contributing to rank-and-file Democrats' campaigns, building vast networks of relations to carry over into the legislative session. For instance, Quatrocchi's campaign committee, known as the Fourth Ward Political Club, contributed $6,465 to support 32 separate campaigns.[13] In 1988 House Speaker Joseph DeAngelis contributed $8,125 to 48 campaigns,[14] and Senate President Paiva Weed contributed $8,500 to 33 campaigns in 2010.[15] As one senior Senator explained, these contributions help build ties of "goodwill," which legislators need to form alliances within the General Assembly and move votes. In his words:

> You know, you're also building goodwill, because sometimes it is the house of ambition. Everybody wants to run up and move up the ladder and, you know, if you help

the people that are below you all the time, sometimes ... you're running for Speaker and ... it's easier for them to say "yes hey, you've got my vote."

In short, legislative leaders can no longer rely on a clear hierarchy of command. Instead, they must use "media of exchange" (Schwartz, 1990, p. 120), like campaign contributions, to court legislative members for their loyalty and cooperation.[16] Rather than stable structures, the party is composed of flexible and contingent ties.

Third, political interest groups have moved to the center of the RIDP field, serving as brokers of the information and relationships necessary to coordinate legislative activity.[17] In an environment where overt exercise of hierarchical power is no longer respected, partnership with outside interest groups becomes an effective strategy for furthering one's legislative agenda and directing votes. As explained by a member of the Senate staff, the leadership often needs "someone who is passionate about [an] issue who can champion it on the floor and who can protect it." They need actors who can go out and be "advocates." Describing reform legislation she passed in the early 1990s, a former Democratic Senator explained how a large government reform interest group was critical to the success of her efforts, working alongside her to cumulate legislative support for the bill. As she states, "They were building coalitions, legislation coalitions, on behalf of those bills."

Put simply, the RIDP is no longer a centralized command center. It is a porous political field in which party leaders contend with multiple interlegislator cliques. Though the leadership may enjoy formal alliance with one or a few cliques, coordinating legislative activity now involves the active courting of votes. According to the experiences of Democratic legislators, this courting of votes is often achieved by leveraging the relationship-building capacities of extra-party lobbyists and interest groups, granting these actors the institutional position of party brokers, as displayed in Fig. 3.

Explaining Party Change: The Strength of Civil Society Ties

As described by Rhode Island Scholars (Moakley & Cornwell, 2001; Gabriel, 1970; Lockard, 1959), the mid-20th-century RIDP Machine established its base from Rhode Island's long-disenfranchised and economically marginalized immigrant working class, relying on grassroots mobilization and neighborhood-based patronage networks to secure its electoral success. However, the solidification of this machine would not have been possible

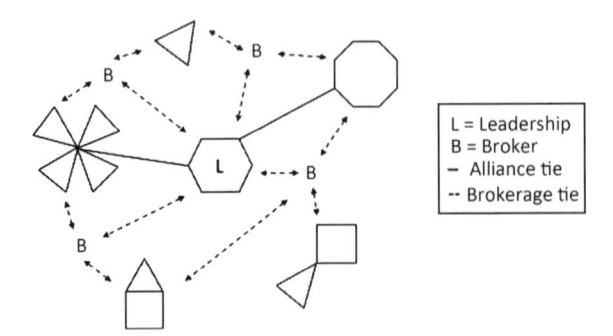

Fig. 3. The Contemporary RIDP, with Brokerage Ties.

without ties to organized labor. Indeed, it was organized labor — chiefly the Congress of International Organizations (CIO) and the American Federation of Labor (AFL) — who provided the workers and the votes necessary to maintain the RIDP Machine's electoral success. They made endorsements, mobilized volunteers, and donated financial and in-kind contributions to the Democratic Party and its candidates, offering privileged access to the state's largest voting population (Goodman, 1967, pp. 22; 26; Lockard, 1959, p. 224). They hosted rallies and fundraisers, invited candidates to their annual Labor Day picnics, and urged union members to vote the Democratic slate (Goodman, 1967, pp. 22; 26). For instance, in October 1954 the AFL and CIO cosponsored a television program in which they endorsed Democratic governor Dennis J. Roberts for his re-election bid and called upon the public to reclaim a Democratic majority in the Senate (Goodman, 1967, p. 22). Indeed, labor's support of the Democratic slate was so great that between 1952 and 1962, roughly 50 percent of all Democratic legislators reported receiving support from organized labor (Goodman, 1967, p. 59).

This Liberal–Labor (Luebbert, 1991) alliance was further solidified by labor officials' appointment to executive posts and their election to legislative offices. For instance, Democratic Governor Dennis J. Roberts appointed AFL President Arthur Devine to serve as Director of Labor (Goodman, 1967, p. 21). In 1954, In 1954, Roberts also appointed the AFL's Edwin C. Brown to the State Board of Education and the CIO's John Bellow to the Workmen's Compensation Commission (22).[18] In return, labor provided great aid to Democratic campaigns and, indeed, was able to elect many of its own to the state legislature. From 1952–1962 fifty percent of all Democratic legislators reported receiving support from organized labor (Goodman, 1967, p. 59), and in 1956 13 percent of Democratic House Representatives were either leaders or members of labor organizations (54). Furthermore, after Democrats won the lieutenant governorship and Senate majority in 1954, AFL organizer Frank Sgambato acquired the coveted Senate Labor Committee chairmanship (23).

The result of these ties was a solidified, well-oiled, Democratic machine. With the labor vote, Democratic leaders could ensure the success of their endorsed candidates, protect the party from outsiders, and be sure that all Democratic candidates sought the blessing of the party itself. In the words of a former party chairman, "Without an endorsement there is no way you could win. No way you could win." Ties with organized labor also helped to solidify the Party's centralization of power around the Governor, Party Chairman, and legislative leaders. With labor at the table, there were few with the political clout to pose a reasonable challenge to the Party's closed-door legislative tactics. And as long as organized labor had the ear of the Governor and the legislative leadership, the centralized command structure worked in labor's favor. In short, organized labor helped build and maintain the Machine, and, as a result, Rhode Island saw the passage of some of America's most progressive, labor-friendly policies. As political scientist Victor L. Profughi writes:

> Between the thirties and the sixties an effective partnership was achieved between organized labor and the majority Democratic Party, a partnership which has resulted in some of the nation's most labor-oriented legislation. For more than thirty years the constituencies of the two were virtually identical, as were their policy goals. (Profughi, 1983, p. 91)

The Liberal–Labor Break-up

This alliance was not to last forever and, indeed, by the 1960s it was fast unraveling. This disintegration was initiated by the 1959 legislative session, a session marked by interparty conflict and legislative gridlock. In the preceding 1958 legislative election, the newly-merged AFL–CIO endorsed all Democrats running for state office, contributing to the election of Democratic majorities in both the House and Senate. It was in 1959, however, that labor leaders began to feel the sting of Democratic leader's centralized command. During this session, Democratic legislators adopted a defensive strategy against the Republican Party, focusing more on blocking legislation supported by the newly elected Republican Governor than passing new Democratic legislation.[19] By April 1959, the Democrats had passed only two of the 32 bills proposed by the AFL-CIO for that year (Goodman, 1967, pp. 28–29).

Coupled with frustration over Rhode Island's stagnating industrial economy, this event sparked within labor leaders a disdain for the Democratic leadership's use of closed-door legislative tactics and a growing sense that the liberal–labor alliance was no longer working for labor (Goodman, 1967, pp. 28–30.) In April 1959, the AFL–CIO held a special meeting with 200 local union officials, at which they proclaimed labor independent of all political parties (29). To the unions who had long maintained mutually supportive relationships with the RIDP, the 1959 session signaled, "that the Democrats had forgotten they were the party of the workers" (29). The only way to guarantee the continued representation of workers' interests, so the AFL–CIO presidents reasoned, was to support candidates only on an individual basis. In a November 1960 speech, AFL President Edwin C. Brown proclaimed, "Organized labor in Rhode Island is not tied up with the Democratic Party, but supports those who's voting record and activities are favorable to it" (qtd. in Goodman, 1967, p. 31). While the AFL-CIO coalesced around the Democratic ticket for the 1960 election, tensions continued to grow in 1961 as Democratic Governor John A. Notte appointed nonunion professionals to administrative posts and Democratic legislators moved slowly on labor's agenda (31–34). Accordingly, no politicians, from either party, were invited to the AFL-CIO's 1961 or 1962 Labor Day picnics (34; 37), and in a April 1962 board meeting the AFL–CIO decided to stop endorsing the Democratic Party on a wholesale basis (37).[20]

Splintering of the Democratic Party Machine

Following labor's break-up with the RIDP, the party itself began to splinter and lose its organizational, electoral, and procedural bases of power.

Loss of Primary Control
Shortly after the AFL-CIO severed its relationship with the RIDP, the Party began losing control over primary elections and, subsequently, party membership. As noted above, a key feature of the Rhode Island Democratic Machine was its near-complete control over primary elections. To repeat, the Party's hold over the primary process was so complete that no party-endorsed candidate for statewide office failed to win a primary election from 1948 to 1956 (Lockard, 1959, p. 188). But by the 1970s "the

days when the organization dictated who its candidates were was becoming a thing of the past" (Profughi, 1983, p. 75). Between 1948 and 1970, 14 percent of Democratic primary challengers in Providence districts were successful. By 1974, the success rate of primary challengers in these districts more than doubled (Profughi, 1983, p. 76). As Profughi explains, these changes in primary control were due not to changes in election regulations. (Parties could still endorse candidates prior to the primaries, and endorsed candidates still had preferential positions in the first column of the ballot.) What had changed was the Party's ability to control the nominating process and to guarantee the election of its endorsed candidates (Profughi, 1983, p. 75).

One of the reasons for the Party's inability to control the succession of candidates through primary elections was due to its break-up with organized labor. In the words of one respondent, with union support the party endorsement "really meant something." They had the people, the numbers, to turn out the vote. With the disintegration of the Liberal–Labor relationship, the Party lost the organizational ties that guaranteed volunteers, materials, financial contributions, and, ultimately, the ability to turn out the vote for the entire Democratic slate. To be sure, labor leaders and their members still supported Democratic candidates, but gone were the days where a party-endorsed Democrat could rely on the labor vote to assure her or his seat.

Additionally, profound demographic changes contributed to the loosening of the patronage networks on which Democratic leader's voter mobilization strategies were based. Most notably, by the 1980s the majority of the Party's voters were no longer poor, first-generation immigrants. As political scientist West (1992) observed, Rhode Island moved from 26th to 14th in per-capita income in the nation from 1980 to 1988. Literacy increased, and the state experienced an influx of highly educated professionals seeking financial opportunities in the Northeast (West, 1992, p. 247). With these developments, the patronage networks that the party had once used to deliver votes for its endorsed candidates started falling apart and the value of the party vis-à-vis Democratic candidates declined. As a former party chairman recounted:

> Prior to the 1970s it had always been possible for the endorsed candidate to win. There was a lot more party loyalty then, and the endorsement meant something in those days. Then the effect of the endorsement from the late 70s on began to erode. And the party organization began to lose more and more influence among Democratic voters ... Today, I'm not even sure what the value of the endorsement is.

As a result of these changes, campaigns became increasingly candidate-centered and removed from the purview of the party. Party endorsement would come to mean little to Rhode Island Democratic candidates, and campaign strategy would evolve to focus on individual candidate's abilities to cultivate financial and electoral support. As one Rhode Island political insider explained,

> Over time, and particularly now ... I don't think anyone even thinks ... I mean, if they endorse you, fine. If they don't, it doesn't matter. If you have a capacity to either fund your own campaign or to seek and get funds from outside sources ... you're viable.

In fact, pollster and political consultant Victor Profughi has gone so far as to advise his clients not to rely on party support:

> I always told candidates I worked with to never count on the party to do anything for them ... Bottom line is that today the party endorsement is probably not worth much in helping with resources, and is virtually meaningless in most campaigns when it comes to delivering vote numbers for the endorsed candidate. (qtd. in Nagle, 2014, n.p.)

As these statements demonstrate, Democratic endorsement and financial or in-kind support is of little concern for Democratic candidates and their political advisors. This is an important development, because it suggests that the key vehicles through which the RIDP bread loyalty amongst its members — party endorsement and the delivery of votes — have collapsed. As a result, the RIDP is increasingly faced with a legislative membership lacking strong ties to the party organization. This presents the party with a key challenge — how to coordinate Democratic office holders once they have reached the legislature.

Legislative Reforms

Just as the Party's control over the electoral process was waning, the election of Edward P. Manning to the Speakership in 1977 ushered in a series of reforms that would loosen the RIDP's control over its legislative members. The backdrop for these reforms was years of centralized leadership under Speaker Harry F. Curvin, a key figure in the RIDP Machine. Holding office from 1941 to 1964, Curvin was "the all-powerful leader of the house"; the epitome of closed-door, centralized legislative leadership (Moakley & Cornwell, 2001, pp. 73, 74—75). Following a brief interim under John Wrenn, Joseph Bevilacqua, commonly known as "Joe B," would acquire the speakership in 1969, continuing the Curvin ways (75). Committees were closed, no records were shared, and quorums were not required for a vote. As one political journalist recounted,

> When I first covered the Senate in 1972, all of the meetings were closed and the only exception was sometimes, when they were taking testimony, if the Chairman was in a

good mood, he'd let you in. But that was an exception. And for the most part they couldn't give you – they were not allowed to tell you – not only the roll call, they wouldn't tell you the tally.

However, recall that the 1970s marked a sea change in the RIDP's control over party nominations. Increasingly, leaders were contending with legislative membership not socialized through the machine and who garnered their election without serious assistance from the party organization. As these new members entered the legislature, distaste for the practices of centralized leadership grew. This distaste turned even more sour when, in January 1976, Speaker Bevilacqua ran for and was elected to the state Supreme Court. As the Rhode Island political journalist further recounted:

> The thing had a sort of bad taste, because he had been a criminal lawyer and he was thought to have mob friends. And just the process; there weren't any hearings of anybody's qualifications. And it was just real old-time backstage politics. As a matter of fact, I don't think there was an open vote. So, although he was elected overwhelmingly, it ... not everybody felt good about it. The public thought it was pretty heavy-handed.

It was in this context that the internal reform movement spearheaded by Edward Manning emerged. When Bevilacqua vacated the Speakership for a supreme court seat in January 1976, those who had been on the outs under Bevilacqua – many of them proponents of ethics reforms – coalesced around Edward Manning and secured the speakership (see also Moakley & Cornwell, 2001, p. 75). Upon acquiring his post as Speaker, Manning immediately established a rules committee. This led to the passage of numerous legislative reforms, including: quorum requirement for committees, the opening committees to the public, the formal recording of committee actions and votes, requirements to post committee agendas a week in advance and to supply each legislator with a copy of all bills, deadlines for bill introduction and consideration, electronic voting for public bills and procedural questions, and a rule guaranteeing principal sponsors the right to request consideration of their bills (Moakley & Cornwell, 2001, pp. 75–76).

These legislative reforms had profound implications for the centralization of power within the party in the legislature. In simple terms, they diffused power outwards. By setting in place quorum, open meetings, and recording requirements, the reforms increased the power of individual legislators vis-à-vis the leadership, such that leaders had to contend with the demands of legislative members and work with them in order to keep their leadership positions secure. Of course, these reforms did not eliminate power discrepancies between legislative leaders and member. As others have observed, Rhode Island's legislative leaders have been quite apt at minimizing the effects of reform (Moakley & Cornwell, 2001, p. 79; West, 2014). However, they did inaugurate in a qualitative change in the practice of legislative leadership. In the words of Moakley and Cornwell (2001, p. 77):

> The key difference in leadership position and style was a subtle but important one. The new leadership could not assume that, come hell or high water, their position was secure and they could do virtually anything they pleased (the assumption during the Curvin-Bevilacqua years). The new team felt it should, and politically must, work actively to keep the troops happy through consultation and conciliation.

RISDIC

It was a statewide banking crisis — initiated by the mismanagement and collapse of the Rhode Island Share and Deposit Indemnity Corporation (RISDIC) in 1991 — that struck the final blow to the disintegrating Party machine. The crisis began in November 1990 when state auditors reported that a Providence bank owned by Joseph Mollicone Jr. — The Heritage Loan and Investment Company — lacked documentation for millions in loans.[21] Seven days after investigators contacted Secretary of State James O'Neil with news of the scandal, Joseph Mollicone Jr. had disappeared. Heritage clients began emptying their accounts, and, as the state-chartered credit insurer, RISDIC provided $6.6 million to back the withdrawals. On November 18, Governor Edward D. DiPrete ordered the bank to be closed (West, 2014, p. 38). It quickly became clear, however, that RISDIC did not have the funds to cover its commitment. On January 1st, newly-inaugurated Governor Bruce Sundlun signed an executive order declaring RISDIC insolvent and closing every financial institution it insured, including 45 credit unions, three banks, and seven loan-investment companies. The result was the most severe financial crisis in Rhode Island since the Great Depression (West, 2014, p. 41).

As investigations unfolded, stories surfaced revealing a long trail of misconduct. For instance, in January 1991 the *Providence Journal* released a confidential report from 1985 detailing severe mismanagement at RISDIC. Later known as the "Stitt Report," it warned that institutions backed by RISDIC were engaging in "reckless management practices," including improper documentation of loans, dangerously small reserves and even intimidation of state examiners (qtd. in West, 2014, p. 42). It was also revealed that the Vice-Chair of the House Finance Committee was not only president of the Rhode Island Credit Union League — RISDIC's trade association — but also wined-and-dined committee members alongside RISDIC president Peter A. Nevola to defeat legislation that would have required credit unions to secure federal deposit insurance and thus undercut RISDIC's business (44).[22] And in March more reports surfaced revealing that Governor DiPrete had accepted contributions from RISDIC and that RISDIC-endorsed bills had been favored in the legislature (West, 2014, pp. 50–51).

The release of this information fostered noticeable disdain for elected officials and, in particular, the Democratic legislative leadership. In face of the scandal, many incumbent legislators decided not to run for re-election, and a new class of rookie, reform-minded legislators flooded the General Assembly. As one Senator recounted from his campaign, "I just ran to bring to light and say 'hey you know these people weren't looking out for us' … I was going to go down there and do work on behalf of everyone else and not take care of my own number one." By 1992, nearly 70 percent of legislative seats had been replaced with legislators elected after 1990 (Moakley & Cornwell, 2001, p. 77). This not only removed many of old party holdouts from the General Assembly, but also introduced large cohorts of freshman legislators with little respect for the hierarchies of the past and who would not necessarily fall in line with leadership's demands. Another Senator expressed this maverick mentality, stating, "I don't care one way or the other about the issue; if the leadership wants it, I vote against it" (qtd. in Moakley & Cornwell, 2001, p. 79).

Thus, from 1992 onwards, the party in the legislature would take a decidedly different form. First and foremost, it would comprise a new cohort of Democratic politicians not tied to the Machine and uninhibited by the Party's old style of politics. Second, this new cohort would do their best to increase their power within the Assembly and eliminate what remained of the centrally-controlled legislative practices that once characterized the Machine. Under the leadership of Democratic House Speaker John B. Harwood, reformer wings of the Democratic party further diffused power outwards through new reforms like the requirement that all bills be reported on the floor or that bill sponsors be able to appeal committee recommendations (Moakley & Cornwell, 2001, p. 79). In conjunction with the Liberal-Labor break-up, the disintegration of Democratic patronage networks and legislative reforms, this crisis slashed the joists of the old party apparatus, making room for ties to a new set of actors and, with these ties, a new style of party organization.

Interest Groups: Building the New Ties that Bind

The foregoing events left the RIDP in a fractured position, facing a legislative membership not necessarily tied to the party organization and without its former mechanisms of coordination. In short, the party faced a crisis of governance. With the loss of its labor alliance, the party could no longer control the nomination process or deliver the votes necessary to ensure the loyalty of its elected officials. As one Rhode Island political journalist described, the party would come to be characterized by "tides" of legislators who flow in and out of the General Assembly. In his words, "It is very hard to control them. [It] is like if you are a lion-tamer in the circus. If you have 10 lions that's one thing. If you have 50 lions that's something else." Amongst these contending tides, one's leadership position is highly precarious, and one cannot be a "tuff, mean, inside dealer" without facing the threat of removal. In this environment, a new challenge emerges, a challenge not faced by the Party Machine – how to coordinate all these contending tides around a coherent policy program. In the words of one lobbyist, "A leadership position is not going to guarantee that you will get what you want. You still have to get the votes and that can be very difficult to do."

It is in regard to this collective action problem – the problem of coordinating legislators around bills – that interest groups and political professionals have become the new brokers of party relationships in Rhode Island. Where during the Machine days they entered the legislative process only at the behest of the leadership, today they provide the knowledge and relationship-building capacities necessary to coordinate votes. One of the most notable of these new policy actors has been organized business, whose influence Rhode Island political experts Maureen Moakley and Elmer Cornwell (2001, p. 153) have described as "formidable." Beyond bringing new ideas to state government, these groups bring knowledge and relationship-building capacities, augmenting the leadership's ability to enact particular policy programs.

One way private interest groups and political professionals help coordinate legislative activity is through the provision of information and knowledge to which legislative leaders and members might otherwise not have access. As explained in multiple interviews, this service is especially important in Rhode Island, where legislators are constrained by a part-time schedule and a small staff. As one Senator explained:

> Do I rely on a lot of it [information from interest groups]? Absolutely. Especially in Rhode Island. We're a part time legislature. We're not full time. And the policy staff who is available to me is also available to eight or nine other senators so resources aren't all there. And to be honest with you, there are issues where I have no idea what they are talking about. I've never had to deal with it. Never came across it. So, I was like 'OK' ... You rely on the information coming in.

This information can be an important leadership and coordination device. For instance, it can help party leaders identify problems and potential solutions (O'Connor, 2001). As one legislator stated, "Lobbyists have a bad name but they are critically important to providing education to the legislature ... At least they can tell you what the issues are. You know, what do you know about the dental legislation?" Interest-group provided information can also give leaders the tools to evaluate policy proposals, support proposed interventions, and orient legislative actions (Hirschman & Berman, 2014). As one senior Senator explained, to move votes on a bill often what a legislator must do is "answer the questions that people have ... and get them [the] information that they need to digest to help make their decision." Private interest groups not only readily provide this information; they also help legislators find the arguments that are most effective. In working with legislators, interest groups can also narrow the field of viable policy options, pointing legislators toward specific of interventions. In the words of one freshman legislator:

> The problem as an elected official is that you've got 50 different perspectives thrown at you and you don't have time to figure out what to do. You need something to focus plans and put them together into one. You need orientation and direction.

It is exactly this orientation and direction that partnership with private interest groups and political professionals provides.

Another way private interest groups help broker legislative activity is by establishing and extending policy alliances. With the reform waves of the 1970s and 1990s, it is no longer acceptable (at least formally) for legislative leaders to direct action through threat of sanction or exclusionary practices. Instead, legislators must be enrolled into policy alliances. In many cases, this is a task which moves beyond the capacity of the leadership's own policy staff, who has the authority to collect requested information, but who may not legally advocate for specific positions. This, however, is not true of outside interest groups and policy professionals who may lobby, advocate, or and use their ties to mobilize activity in favor of particular legislative outcomes.

For instance, one House committee chairwoman gave the example of a lobbyist who, after proposing a bill to the chairwoman, conducted the necessary legal research and worked with other groups to develop with an ultimately satisfying bill that passed the floor. As she recalled, "He [did] all of the legal research. He came up with some language that satisfied the truckers, that satisfied Division of Transportation (DOT) and satisfied Department of Business Regulation (DBR)." In other words, the lobbyist enrolled all the actors necessary for the bill to pass.

Respondents explained that private interest groups and their staff build these policy alliances through a number of methods. They may use their pre-existing relationships to find bill sponsors, arm sponsors with arguments to defend their bills, bring experts or constituents to testify before committee, or help legislators arbitrate between competing demands. They may also pressure individual their by organizing constituents in legislators' home districts or even by sponsoring primary challengers. Through these practices, they orient, direct, and place pressure on individual legislators, extending the network of political actors organized around a particular issue.

CONTRIBUTIONS

This paper set out to develop a new theory of political party change through a case analysis of the RIDP. After reviewing the three predominant theories of party change, it found that none could explain the RIDP's evolution from a hierarchical machine to a porous political field congealed by the brokerage capacities of private interest groups and political professionals. In contrast to previous accounts, this historical and interview-based analysis found that the RIDP's puzzling organizational change can be accounted for by transformations in the party's ties to civil society organizations. Specifically, this paper found that the RIDP's transformation was set-in-motion by a severance in its relationship to organized labor, which ruptured the RIDP's material and electoral bases of support. Without the guaranteed support of organized labor, the party lost control over the electoral process and, subsequently, its elected officials. Following the break-up with organized labor, demographic changes, legislative reforms and a statewide banking crisis further disintegrated the RIDP's ties to its elected officials, causing the party to fracture and diffuse power outwards. In the spaces that remained, extra-party interest groups and political professionals emerged as the brokers of party ties, providing the knowledge and relationship-building capacities necessary to coordinate legislative activities.

This analysis makes two important contributions to political sociology. First, it develops a new theory of party change that provides an explanation for organizational transformation where other accounts fall short. Specifically, this new theory argues that party change may be prompted by ruptures in parties' ties to civil society organizations, as such ruptures may sever parties' access to key resources and make space for new actors to enter party fields. This theory is not specific to the Democratic Party, but may be used to understand changes in the Republican Party as well. Specifically, I expect this theory to hold in other states where parties are or were closely tied to civil society organizations, as was the case of the Michigan Democratic Party and the United Auto Workers, the Indiana Republican Party and the Indiana Chamber of Commerce, and the New York Democratic Party and the Tammany Society of New York City. Indeed, as the case of the RIDP suggests, close ties to a civil society organization is an important condition for the theory I pose, as the severance of ties should only matter when parties are, in fact, dependent on such ties. In this regard, I also expect the theory to hold more for state and local parties than for the national Democratic and Republican parties, as state and local entities tend to be more dependent on localized communities and the civil society organizations who operate in those communities.

Second, the foregoing analysis provides a historically grounded explanation for the rise of organized interest groups and political professionals within party organizations. Indeed, Hershey (2014), Aldrich (2011), and others have described the evolution of U.S. state and local parties from hierarchical command structures to candidate service centers where contending groups compete for legislative influence. In this new field, power is no longer confined to formal, institutionally-defined party leaders. Rather, it is brokered by interest groups and activists who intervene in party politics to achieve specific policy goals (cf. Bawn et al., 2012; Masket, 2009; Schwartz, 2006). While other scholars have identified private interest groups and political professionals as important actors in American parties (Bawn et al., 2012; Kreiss, 2012; Masket, 2009; Medvetz, 2012), this paper attempts to systematically account for their historical emergence. In these ways, this paper not only deepens our knowledge of the factors that prompt party change, but also takes initial steps toward understanding how a specific set of actors has moved to the center of American politics.[23]

Lastly, the findings presented here pose implications for political sociologists interested in policy and programmatic change. Indeed, the organizational change described here occurred alongside a notable policy reorientation, by which the RIDP shifted from passing some of the United State's most progressive welfare and labor policies (Lockard, 1959; Profughi, 1983) to neoliberal interventions aimed at growth through decreased regulation, education and business friendliness, as demonstrated by the "business friendliness" reform packages of 2013 passed by the Democratic-controlled House and Senate (Legislative Press & Information Bureau, 2013a, 2013b). By severing ties with the Democratic Party, organized labor opened up space for new actors to move to the center of Democratic Party politics, most notably those representing the interests of business (Moakley & Cornwell, 2001, pp. 153, 161–162). The question remains, then, whether similar changes have occurred in other settings and, furthermore, how the acquisition of these privileged positions by specific actors shapes the policies parties will consider and pursue.

NOTES

1. As explained in the analytic framework section, this paper is concerned with party in government, or the branch of party activities concerned with building government majorities and organizing elected officials around policy objectives. For more on the structure and various functions of political parties, see Key (1964).

2. For a more thorough review of the realignment literature, see de Leon (2014).

3. The RIDP has held consecutive majority control of the state House since 1941 and the state Senate since 1959. The Democrat's control of the House afforded it the largest number of legislative seats even before taking the Senate, with the exception of legislative sessions 1947–1948, when Republicans and Democrats split legislative seats equally 72/72. Control of executive seats has been more volatile. Following 1941, Republicans held majority control of state executive seats from 1967 to 1968, 1985 to 1986, and 1993 to 1998. All dates inclusive.

4. Note that Rhode Island's electoral success is not unique. Indeed, beyond the RIDP there are numerous state and local parties who have demonstrated long-standing electoral dominance. To name a few, these parties include the Chicago Democratic Party, the Virginia Democratic Party, and the Pennsylvania Republican Party.

5. Title 17, Chapter 25 of the Rhode Island State Statutes allows candidates for general offices to apply for public funds at a match of $2 for every $1 received in private contributions which do not exceed an aggregate of $500 from a single source and $1 for every $1 received in private contributions over $500 from a single source. The total amount of matching funds received by gubernatorial candidates may not exceed $750,000 for a total of $1,500,000 in public and private contributions. The total amount of matching funds received by any other candidate for general office may not exceed $187,500 for a total of $375,000 in public and private contributions. For more information, see Rhode Island General Law 17-25-19 (2011).

6. Note that voters are not members of the political party under the legislative party model. They are targets of party activity used to facilitate politicians' election to office (Aldrich, 2011, pp. 18–19). In this sense, it is chiefly a theory of party in government, or the branch of party activity concerned with building government majorities and organizing elected officials around policy objectives (Key, 1964).

7. Candidates were first required to file campaign finance records in 1974 (Rhode Island General Law 17-25-11, 1974). Under the 1974 law, candidates were only required to file reports if they received contributions in excess of $200.00 from a single source, or if their total expenditures exceeded $5,000. In 1992 the law was revised to require that candidates report all contributions in excess of $100 and to file a schedule of campaign expenditures if total expenditures exceeded $1,000 (Rhode Island General Law 17-25-7, 1992). The law was again revised in 2012 and 2014. These revisions did not affect the data collected as campaign records were only sampled up to 2010.

8. All samples prior to 2002 were collected from each individual candidate's campaign finance records housed in the Rhode Island State Archives. The documents sampled were Rhode Island forms CCER-1 and CCER-2. CCER-1 lists the total amount of campaign contributions and expenditures broken down by type (individual, political party, political action committee (PAC), loan proceeds, payroll check-off, and other). CCER-2 lists details about each individual campaign contribution and expenditure, including information such as the donor's name, address, and place of employment. All 2002 and post-2002 samples were collected from the Public Information page of the Campaign Finance section of the Rhode Island Board of Elections website. Records may be searched by candidate, PAC party committee, and narrowed by specific date ranges. The search engine used for this study is located at http://www.ricampaignfinance.com/RIPublic/Filings.aspx

9. Due to missing files, I was unable to collect a 1974 sample for House Speaker John J. Skiffington Jr. or a 1992 sample for Senate Majority Leader John J. Bevilacqua.

10. In May 2012, the Rhode Island-based IP development company 38 Studios declared bankruptcy after receiving a $75 million loan guarantee from the state's Economic Development Corporation. The bankruptcy prompted multiple investigations and a legislative debate about Rhode Island's obligation to repay the company's debt.

11. All respondents were assigned a pseudonym to ensure confidentiality, and they are referred to by these pseudonyms in text. Respondents are referred to by their organizational position only where they gave written consent to do so.

12. Numbers are self-reported.

13. See "Financial Statement for United Fourth Ward Political Club" (10/9/80) and (12/12/80). Rhode Island State Archives, Location 159B, Box 6, Democratic Senatorial District 4.

14. See DeAngelis CCER-2 (10/12/88) (11/1/88) and (12/6/88). Rhode Island State Archives, Location 159F, Box 21, Democratic Representative District 57.

15. This excludes $6,000 in contributions Paiva Weed made to the Democratic Party in 2010. Paiva Weed campaign finance reports were collected from the Public Information page of the Campaign Finance section of the State of Rhode Island

Board of Elections website. The search engine used for this study is located at http://www.ricampaignfinance.com/RIPublic/Filings.aspx

16. The concept "media of exchange" comes from Mildred Schwartz's network model of the political party. Money in the form of campaign contributions is one of the tools party members use to build and manage ties. For more on how campaign contributions help build ties, see Schwartz (1990, pp. 245–216).

17. Note that I am talking about interest groups as brokers of *policy alliances* — the alliances of legislators necessary to pass particular pieces of legislation. As described in the paragraph above, legislators still rely on other means, such as financial contributions, interpersonal relationships, and the trading of political favors, to secure leadership positions.

18. Note that there was still significant in-fighting between the AFL and the CIO at this time. These disagreements revolved largely around the two organizations' attempts to maintain influence over Rhode Island's policy process, as well as disagreements over labor's partisan strategy. While the CIO felt labor should remove itself from party politics, the AFL had a closer relationship with Governor Roberts and "saw no conflict between serving labor and serving the Democratic party" (Goodman, 1967, p. 25). In the end each coalesced around the Democratic slate until 1962, when both AFL and the CIO became convinced that a candidate-centered strategy would better serve the interests of Rhode Island's working women and men.

19. See "Hopeful Prospects at the R.I. State House" *Providence Journal Sunday* January 3, 1960: N27.

20. For a more thorough description of the Rhode Island Democratic Party's relationship with organized labor, see Goodman (1967) *The Democrats and Labor in Rhode Island: 1952–1962: Changes in the Old Alliance.*

21. Joseph Mollicone Jr.'s father also owned and operated a bank in Providence that had notoriously been the money purse for New England mobster Raymond L. S. Patriarca. For more on RISDIC and organized crime in Providence see West (2014).

22. Bianchini was later tried for violating the state's conflict of interest law, but was found not guilty when only four of the five votes needed to convict were placed. One of the not-guilty votes was cast by Michael A. Morry, the president of a RISDIC-backed credit union (West, 2014, p. 45).

23. This is where my argument differs markedly from Dahl's (1974/2005) *Who Governs*. Dahl interprets New Haven's transformation from a machine-style oligarchy to a polyarchy as inherently democratic. With the incorporation of consultants, policy practitioners, and white-collard professionals into American party fields, however, I contend that modern American parties are no less elite and detached than the party systems described by Michels (1911/1962) and Martin (2009). Where I differ from Michels and Martin is in my account of party organization. Where the oligarchical party tradition sees centralization and hierarchy, I see diffuse and flexible coalitions. Put differently, my alternative focus on party-civil society organization splits the difference between Dahl and Michels: the party may be less centralized, as Dahl claims, but with Michels and Martin I caution that this diffuse network is not necessarily democratic.

ACKNOWLEDGMENTS

I am deeply grateful to Jennifer Bouek, Anthony Chen, Nitsan Chorev, Cedric de Leon, José Itzigsohn, Stephanie Lee Mudge, Apollonya Porcelli, and two anonymous reviewers for their constructive feedback. This paper also benefited from comments received at the 2014 Chicago Ethnography Conference and the 2014 ASA Political Sociology Roundtables. Special thanks are due to Gianpaolo Baiocchi and Josh Pacewicz for overseeing various stages of this project. Errors and omissions are my own.

REFERENCES

Abramson, P. R., Aldrich, J. H., & Rohde, D. W. (2010). *Continuity and change in the 2008 elections*. Washington, DC: Congressional Quarterly Press.

Aldrich, J. H. (2011). *Why parties? A second look*. Chicago, IL: University of Chicago Press.

Bawn, K., Cohen, C., Karol, D., Masket, S., Noel, H., & Zaller, J. (2012). A theory of political parties: Groups, policy demands and nominations in American politics. *Perspectives on Politics*, *10*(3), 571–597.

Beck, P. A. (1974). A socialization theory of partisan realignment. In R. G. Niemi (Ed.), *The politics of future citizens: New dimensions in the political socialization of children* (pp. 199–219). San Francisco, CA: Jossey-Bass.

Burnham, W. D. (1970). *Critical elections and the mainsprings of American politics*. New York, NY: Norton.

Carmines, E. G., & Stimson, J. A. (1989). *Issue evolution: Race and the transformation of American politics*. Princeton, NJ: Princeton UP.

Cohen, M., Karol, D., Noel, H., & Zaller, J. (2008). *The party decides: Presidential nominations before and after reform*. Chicago, IL: University of Chicago Press.

Dahl, R. (1974/2005). *Who governs? Democracy and Power in an American city* (2nd ed.). New Haven, CT: Yale University Press.

de Leon, C. (2014). *Party & society: Reconstructing a sociology of democratic party politics*. Malden, MA: Polity Press.

Gabriel, R. A. (1970). *The political machine in Rhode Island*. Providence, RI: Bureau of Government Research, University of Rhode Island.

Goodman, J. S. (1967). *The Democrats and labor in Rhode Island, 1952–1962: Changes in the old alliance*. Providence, RI: Brown University Press.

Hershey, M. R. (2014). *Guide to U.S. political parties*. Los Angeles, CA: Sage/CQ Press.

Hirschman, D., & Berman, E. P. (2014). Do economists make policies? On the political effects of economics. *Socio-Economic Review*, *12*(4), 779–811.

Janda, K. (1990). *Toward a performance theory of change in political parties*. Paper prepared for the 12th World Congress of the International Sociological Association, Madrid, Spain, 9–13 July. Retrieved from http://www.janda.org/bio/parties/papers/Janda%20(1990).pdf. Accessed on January 1, 2015.

Johnson, J. (2010). *Political consultants and political campaigns: One day to sell*. Boulder, CO: Westview Press.

Karol, D. (2009). *Party position change in American politics: Coalition management.* New York, NY: Cambridge University Press.

Katz, R. S., & Mair, P. (1995). Changing models of party organization and party democracy: The emergence of the cartel party. *Party Politics, 1,* 5–28.

Katz, R. S., & Mair, P. (2009). The cartel party thesis: A restatement. *Perspectives on Politics, 7*(4), 753–766.

Key, V. O., Jr. (1959). Secular realignment and the party system. *Journal of Politics, 21,* 198–210.

Key, V. O. (1964). *Politics, parties, and pressure groups* (5th ed.). New York, NY: T. Y. Crowell.

Kirchheimer, O. (1966). The transformation of the western European party systems. In J. LaPalombara & M. Weiner (Eds.), *Political parties and political development.* Princeton, NJ: Princeton University Press.

Knoke, D. (1976). *Change and continuity in American politics.* Baltimore, MD: Johns Hopkins University Press.

Kreiss, D. (2012). *Taking out country back: The crafting of networked politics from Howard Dean to Barack Obama.* New York, NY: Oxford University Press.

Ladd, E. C. (1980). Liberalism upside down: The inversion of the new deal order. In W. Crotty (Ed.), *The party symbol: Readings on political parties* (pp. 274–287). San Francisco, CA: H. Freeman and Company.

Lawrence, D. G. (1997). *The collapse of the democratic presidential majority: Realignment, dealignment, and electoral change from Franklin Roosevelt to Bill Clinton.* Boulder, CO: Westview Press.

Legislative Press & Information Bureau. (2013a). *33 house bills addressing economic development enacted into law in 2013 session.* Press Release of the Rhode Island General Assembly. July 31, 2013. Retrieved from http://webserver.rilin.state.ri.us/News/pr1.asp?prid=9653. Accessed on December 5, 2013.

Legislative Press & Information Bureau. (2013b). *28 Moving the Needle initiatives passed.* Press Release of the Rhode Island General Assembly. July 24, 2013. Retrieved from http://webserver.rilin.state.ri.us/News/pr1.asp?prid=9640. Accessed on December 5, 2013.

Lockard, D. (1959). *New England State politics.* Princeton, NJ: Princeton University Press.

Luebbert, G. M. (1991). *Liberalism, fascism, or social democracy: Social classes and the political origins of regimes in interwar Europe.* New York, NY: Oxford UP.

Manza, J., & Brooks, C. (1999). *Social cleavages and political change: Voter alignments and U.S. party coalitions.* Oxford: Oxford University Press.

Martin, J. L. (2009). *Social structures.* Princeton, NJ: Princeton University Press.

Masket, S. E. (2009). *No middle ground: How informal party organizations control nominations and polarize legislatures.* Ann Arbor, MI: University of Michigan Press.

Medvetz, T. (2012). *Think tanks in America.* Chicago, IL: University of Chicago Press.

Michels, R. (1911/1962). *Political parties: A sociological study of the oligarchical tendencies of modern democracy.* New York, NY: Free Press.

Milburn, J. F., & Doyle, W. (Eds.). (1983). *New England political parties.* Cambridge, MA: Schenkman Publishing, Inc.

Moakley, M., & Cornwell, C. (2001). *Rhode Island politics and government.* Lincoln, NB: University of Nebraska Press.

Moakley, M. (Ed.). (1992). *Party realignment and state politics.* Columbus, OH: Ohio State University Press.

Nagle, K. (2014). Are Rhode Island's political parties dead? *GoLocal Providence News*. Retrieved from http://www.golocalprov.com/news/are-rhode-islands-political-parties-dead. Accessed on May 06, 2016.

Nie, N. H., Verba, S., & Petrocik, J. R. (1976/1979). *The changing American voter*. Cambridge, MA: Harvard University Press.

O'Connor, A. (2001). *Poverty knowledge: Social science, social policy, and the poor in twentieth-century U.S. history*. Princeton, NJ: Princeton University Press.

Panebianco, A. (1988). *Political parties: Organization and power*. New York, NY: Cambridge University Press.

Profughi, V. L. (1983). The party is sick but it isn't dead – yet. In J. F. Milburn & W. Doyle (Eds.), *New England political parties* (pp. 73–95). Cambridge, MA: Schenkman Publishing, Inc.

Rhode Island General Law 17-25-7. (1992). Rhode Island Campaign Contributions and Expenditures Reporting Act (1974, amended). January Session, 1992, Chapter 21, Section 1 of the Rhode Island General Laws.

Rhode Island General Law 17-25-11. (1974). Rhode Island Campaign Contributions and Expenditures Reporting Act (1974). January Session, 1974, Chapter 298, Section 1 of the Rhode Island General Laws.

Rhode Island General Law 17-25-19. (2011). Rhode Island Campaign Contributions and Expenditures Reporting Act (1988, amended). January Session, 2011, Chapter 230, Section 1 of the Rhode Island General Laws.

Schwartz, M. A. (1990). *The party network: The robust organization of Illinois republicans*. Madison, WI: University of Wisconsin Press.

Schwartz, M. A. (2006). *Party movements in the United States and Canada: Strategies of persistence*. Oxford, UK: Rowman and Littlefield Publishers, Inc.

Small, M. L. (2009). How many cases do I need?: On science and the logic of case selection in field-based research. *Ethnography*, *10*(1), 5–38.

Sundquist, J. L. (1983). *Dynamics of the party system: Alignment and realignment of political parties in the United States*. Washington, DC: The Brookings Institution.

Weber, M. (1922/1968). G. Roth & C. Wittich (Eds.), *Economy and society: An outline of interpretive sociology*. New York, NY: Bedminster Press.

West, D. M. (1992). Stalled realignment: Party change in Rhode Island. In M. Moakley (Ed.), *Party realignment and state politics* (pp. 245–258). Columbus, OH: Ohio University Press.

West, H. P. (2014). *Secrets and scandals: Reforming Rhode Island, 1986–2006*. Providence, RI: RIPS.